Helping Children Learn Mathematics

A Competency-Based
Laboratory Approach

Helping Children Learn Mathematics

A Competency-Based Laboratory Approach

Second Edition

Gregory R. Baur
Indiana University, South Bend

Linda Olsen George
Indiana University, Bloomington

Kendall/Hunt Publishing Company

To Our "Better Halves"
Darleen and Bob

C   403462   01

Preface

This text was written for people who need to learn about the instruction of elementary school mathematics. Although several texts on the subject are available, a careful examination of the contents of this book will reveal some unique features and some fundamental differences as compared with most materials on the market.

Plan of the Book

The text consists of four parts: "Developing a Philosophy," "Developing Strategies," "Facilitating the Learning of Mathematics," and "Evaluating Mathematical Outcomes." Each part relates to the other parts and, in total, to the overall complex problem of helping children learn mathematics.

The first part of the book is concerned with *development of a philosophy* of teaching elementary school mathematics. The effective classroom teacher must have a sound theoretical base for the design and implementation of an instructional program in mathematics. Chapter 1 discusses contemporary viewpoints of the components of mathematics, while Chapter 2 discusses the composition of mathematics education. Because varying viewpoints are discussed, the reader will have an opportunity to form his own philosophy about the teaching of elementary school mathematics.

Part II (Chapters 3, 4, and 5) emphasizes the *formulation of strategies* for helping children learn elementary school mathematics. Alternatives are explored which will aid the reader in determining goals and objectives and in planning to meet those goals and objectives. Discussions of such areas as questioning, choosing instructional materials, implementing the mathematics laboratory, the atypical learner and classroom management also receive particular attention.

The discussion in Part III turns to *teaching techniques* related to the specific content of elementary school mathematics programs. The content is separated into arbitrary strands simply to facilitate discussion. Emphasis is upon the movement of the child from the concrete to the abstract stages of learning for given mathematical concepts and skills. Of particular interest are the chapters on computer and calculator literacy, applications, and problem solving.

Part IV centers around a discussion of *evaluation,* an area many times either neglected or treated haphazardly. Since the accurate identification of pupil difficulties and subsequent remediation of these difficulties is so important to educational success in mathematics, emphasis is upon techniques which should enable more accurate performance of these tasks. Finally, the role of evaluation and its relationship to the entire school situation are discussed.

Special Features and Textbook Use

Among the special features of *Helping Children Learn Mathematics* is that it stresses for the classroom teacher a role quite different from that of the traditional authoritarian figure. As ascribers to the belief that to *learn* mathematics one must *do* mathematics, the authors have emphasized throughout the book total involvement of the child in his learning of mathematics. It follows, then, that an effective teacher of mathematics must assume the role of facilitator, or catalyst, in helping children learn mathematics; or, stated more concisely, teaching mathematics resolves itself to helping children learn mathematics. This task is not an easy one for the teacher. Not only must he create the proper classroom environment but he must also be able to make decisions relative to such matters as when to tell students something, when to ask questions, what kinds of questions to ask, when to act as a silent partner, and when to withdraw completely from the learning situation. Although no simple, overt statements as to how to accomplish the aforementioned tasks have been made, or indeed could be made, it is hoped that the reader will be able to make more thoughtful, considered decisions relative to the above after studying the text.

Second, the book is not a "cookbook." It is neither possible nor desirable to tell a person the exact steps to be taken in helping children learn mathematics because teacher competencies, student abilities, and classroom settings vary to such a great degree. Given a specific classroom situation, it is the teacher who must ultimately make curriculum and instructional decisions; therefore, it seems more appropriate to discuss possible alternatives which may be implemented to meet the needs of the students.

Third, it is assumed that the reader has a basic knowledge and understanding of the content of elementary school mathematics, child growth and development, and learning theory. Such content will be used, but only as a vehicle to develop different methodological strategies. Instead, the reader will be helped to apply basic foundational learnings in the above areas specifically to a child's learning of mathematics.

Fourth, the book serves as a resource for both pre-service and in-service teachers. The text includes many ideas and suggestions which may be used in the classroom, and references are provided which may be of interest and benefit to classroom teachers.

The final feature of the book is the statement of *teacher competencies* at the beginning of each part and the beginning of each chapter. Chapter competencies are keyed to part competencies. All of these competencies should be attained so that the reader may become a more effective teacher of elementary school mathematics. To help with this goal, *laboratory exercises* have been included to supplement and extend each chapter of the text. Just as it is important for children to be actively involved when they are learning mathematics, so also should the reader become actively involved in the study of these materials. By studying the text and then by performing the laboratory exercises, the competencies as stated may be attained.

Generally, the laboratory exercises have been designed to simulate actual teacher tasks which might be performed in the classroom. They also feature active student involvement in the study of methodologies designed to help children learn mathematics.

Each set of laboratory exercises has been divided into three parts: (1) objectives, (2) materials needed, and (3) procedure. Even though provision for evaluation is also a necessary part of every laboratory situation, the authors believe that the desires of individual instructors, coupled with the specific needs exhibited by different students, necessitate the leaving of this culminating portion of laboratory activity completely to the discretion of the instructor.

In examining the various parts of each laboratory, it may be noted that not always do the objectives as stated for individual laboratory exercises read exactly the same as the competencies. This is because the various competencies can be demonstrated in different ways. Every stated laboratory objective does relate to at least one specific teacher competency, however, as indicated within the parentheses following each objective.

The materials for all laboratory exercises are easily obtainable. However, if these specific materials are not available in a given situation, substitutions can be made.

All procedures have been designed to relate to specific teacher competencies, and the instructor may wish to add to or delete from this list of exercises according to his desires and the needs of his students. The laboratories have been designed to allow a variety of experiences, both within the classroom and in the field. The students will find that the exercises in Part I are designed to help them develop a more refined philosophical base for the study of mathematics and mathematics education. As they complete laboratories associated with Parts II and IV, they will find themselves involved in simulated teaching activities and, if their instructor wishes, in actual field activities working with small groups of children. As they complete laboratories related to Part III, they will find that they are gaining experience in working with a variety of learning aids and activities.

As mentioned earlier, even though the evaluation section is left to the discretion of the instructor, suggested types of evaluation which might be used include the following: some of the laboratory exercises themselves, field experiences, written examinations, practical examinations, and peer group evaluations and discussions. Whichever techniques are used, the final evaluation of student performance should be in terms of the stated objectives as related to the corresponding teacher competencies.

G. R. B.
L. O. G.

Contents

Helping Children Learn Mathematics

A Competency-Based Laboratory Approach

PART I
Developing a Philosophy

Teacher Competencies

After studying Part I and completing the laboratories in Part I, you should be able to achieve each of the following:

A. Describe the nature of mathematics.

B. Describe the nature of mathematics education.

1
What Is Mathematics?

Teacher Competencies

After studying Chapter 1 and completing Laboratory 1, you should be able to achieve each of the following:

A. Describe different viewpoints of what constitutes mathematics. (Part Competency I-A)

B. Describe different dimensions of mathematics and give examples of each. (Part Competency I-A)

C. Briefly describe mathematics from your own point of view. (Part Competency I-A)

To help children learn mathematics a teacher must first have a thorough understanding of what mathematics is. Certainly, any teacher's reflections upon the subject will determine to a great extent his or her approach to the subject with children.

How do you, as an elementary teacher, envision mathematics? If you limit your mathematical thinking to computation with numbers, then your pupils' learning will be similarly limited. If you view mathematics as a structured body of knowledge, then you will teach it as such. If you view mathematics as a way of thinking and doing, then you will help children learn it as such. If you view mathematics as a search for patterns, then this will influence your approach. Your pupils will benefit or be hindered according to the limits of your understanding of the scope of the subject. It is for this reason that before you consider how to help children learn mathematics, you should investigate the varied facets of the subject and begin to develop your own philosophy of what constitutes mathematics. Once you have done this, you may begin to select those aspects of mathematics which you consider most important to include in your elementary school mathematics program.

DESCRIPTIONS OF MATHEMATICS

While descriptions of mathematics abound, no single statement about the term seems quite sufficient. Even so, comments reflecting the philosophies of others should help capsulize, and yet extend, your thinking about mathematics. Descriptions range from brief statements to almost poetic, book-length dissertations. Note the divergence and the similarities of the following statements about mathematics:

> Mathematics may be briefly described as that field of knowledge which devotes itself to exploration in number, form, abstract structures, and order relationships.[1] [H. T. Freitag and A. H. Freitag]

> [Mathematics is] the logical study of shape, arrangement, and quantity.[2] [Mathematics Dictionary]

> Mathematics is the alphabet with which God has written the Universe.[3] [Galileo]

> Let us grant that the pursuit of mathematics is a diverse madness of the human spirit, a refuge from the goading urgency of contingent happenings.[4] [Alfred North Whitehead]

> Nature's great book is written in mathematical symbols.[5] [Galileo]

> Mathematics is the rock upon which the arts and sciences of the world rest.[6] [D. E. Smith]

> Mathematics is the queen of the sciences and arithmetic is the queen of mathematics.[7] [Gauss]

The first two descriptions represent the more definitive of the group insofar as they attempt to inform about the scope of mathematics. Notice that neither description limits mathematics to the study of arithmetic. Instead, both extend mathematics to include logical explorations in the realm of shape and arrangement as well as of quantity. The remaining descriptions, while not as definitive as the first perhaps, remain important insofar as they reflect the value attributed to mathematics by historical figures and by contemporaries. The comments of Galileo and Whitehead reflect an esthetic, almost religious connotation, while the statements of Gauss and Smith indicate the value of mathematics as it applies to other fields of study.

In addition to these statements, Bertrand Russell presented the world with what initially appears to be an irreverent statement about mathematics when he said: "Thus mathematics may be defined as the subject in which we never know what we are talking about, nor whether what we are saying is true."[8] The noted philosopher and mathematician has sparked the attention of

---

1. Herta Taussig Freitag and Arthur H. Freitag, *The Number Story,* p. 76.
2. Glenn James and Robert James, *Mathematics Dictionary,* p. 244.
3. Galileo, cited in the film *Donald in Mathmagicland* (Walt Disney Productions, 1960).
4. Alfred North Whitehead in *Science and the Modern World,* cited by Edward Kasner and James Newman, *Mathematics and the Imagination,* p. 1.
5. Galileo, cited by H. T. and A. H. Freitag, op. cit., cover.
6. D. E. Smith, cited by H. T. and A. H. Freitag, op. cit., cover.
7. Karl Gauss, cited by H. T. and A. H. Freitag, op. cit., cover.
8. Bertrand Russell, cited by James Newman, *The World of Mathematics,* p. 4.

many students through this statement, and careful study of its meaning reveals a great deal of insight into mathematics.

It is apparent that the term "mathematics" has different connotations for different people. Mathematicians and laymen alike harbor differing viewpoints, not only relative to the subject as a whole, but also relative to various facets of the subject, as may be seen from the following discussion.

DIMENSIONS OF MATHEMATICS

In commenting about various answers offered to the question "what is mathematics?", Kasner and Newman stated that ". . . the opinions which range from those of Pythagoras to the theories of the most recent schools of mathematical philosophy reveal the sad fact that it is easier to be clever than clear."[9] It is true that, no matter how well stated, no description of mathematics can be totally revealing. However, clarity remains our goal at this point, so we begin by discussing several dimensions of mathematics in order to extend understanding of the subject.

The Historical Dimension

Mathematics, like all fields of knowledge, had a beginning at some point in the past, and so it has a history. As a matter of fact, mathematics began in the days of prerecorded history when man needed some way to quantitate his surroundings. Historians suggest that man initiated his mathematical study with a matching one-to-one relationship of pebbles and sheep or tally marks and days in order to introduce some regularity into his life. Later, finding his fingers a handy set of counters, he developed a base ten counting system. While names associated with numbers have varied with the people and the times, the quantifying idea has remained constant and number has developed as needed.

Other branches of mathematics also emerged centuries ago. The Egyptians developed a practical kind of geometry when they found need for such activities as surveying land and building huge edifices for their pharoahs. People in the Middle East developed money systems to simplify trading, and they also developed such mathematics as was needed for navigation.

In time, people began to study mathematics for its own sake rather than for a specific real world application. The Greeks, for example, began to transform geometry from its practical applications to a field of study which included proofs using the rules of logic and constructions using a straight edge and compass. The Orientals were also carrying out theoretical, speculative study of mathematics, and they were not confining themselves to the development of practical mathematics. Their work in such areas as magic squares, permutations, and combinations was confined to their part of the world, however, because of their geographic isolation.

Basically, two facets of mathematical study were emerging: applied mathematics and pure mathematics. On the one hand, man needed a tool by which to quantify his world, and he invented such mathematics to fulfill this need. When he applied this mathematics to the world around him,

9. Edward Kasner and James Newman, *Mathematics and the Imagination,* p. 357.

Early man used tally marks for a counting system.

applied mathematics developed. On the other hand, man was also beginning to study mathematics as an organized body of knowledge, giving little heed to any practical uses. He arbitrarily decided upon certain terms, made some basic assumptions, and deduced theorems from them; through logic he carried these studies to their conclusions with little regard to any immediate real world need. In short, man was developing pure mathematics.

Actually, throughout the centuries applied and pure mathematics have complemented each other. Not only is applied mathematics fundamental to the functioning of our civilization, but it also provides a springboard for further explorations in the realm of pure mathematics. Pure mathematics in turn has often in its theoretical pursuits developed mathematics which later found common use in applied work. Reminders of times when the mathematics being developed was thought of as pure abstractions but which later found valuable applications remain with us today in such unlikely terms as "irrational numbers" and "imaginary numbers."

The history of mathematics is still being written because mathematics is still being developed, some of it having foreseeable applications and some of it not. At any rate, that dimension of mathematics called its *history* has been a lifelong pursuit of some people, and it deserves consideration by those of us attempting to clarify what mathematics is.

The Scientific Dimension

Mathematics is a science insofar as many of its methods are the same as those incorporated by science and insofar as the use of these methods has resulted in the development of a unified body of knowledge. Let us examine the methods of mathematics as they relate to science.

Briefly, both deductive and inductive formal reasoning methods are used in mathematics. While these and other more or less rigid techniques whereby "only one correct answer" or "one valid conclusion" may be arrived at are more commonly associated with mathematics, there are other methods which allow for predicting, making guesses, and following hunches. We will consider these latter methods first because they form a fundamental basis for the scientific dimension of mathematics.

Both the scientist and the mathematician must *brainstorm*. There are times when each needs to stretch his mind, to reach out, to hypothesize, to guess at "what might happen if. . . ." Both need freedom for thought and freedom to make conjectures. Why? Polya describes this need:

> Yet mathematics in the making resembles any other human knowledge in the making. You have to guess a mathematical theorem before you prove it; you have to guess the idea of the proof before you carry through the details. You have to combine observations and follow analogies; you have to try and try again. The result of the mathematician's creative work is demonstrative reasoning, a proof; but the proof is discovered by plausible reasoning, by guessing.[10]

In other words, *plausible reasoning,* or educated guessing, provides the basis for later, more formal proofs. The importance of the plausible reasoning and brainstorming aspect of the science of mathematics has often been ignored in the past. Although it has always been a method of the mathematician and the scientist, it has only recently been recognized as an important part of everyone's mathematical thinking.

On a more formal level than brainstorming and plausible reasoning is a method of procedure which has been so closely related to science that it has been called the *scientific method*. The scientific method involves observing, making hypotheses, collecting and analyzing data, drawing conclusions, and applying and generalizing findings. Such a scientific method is also an integral part of mathematical procedure and thought, however, and so it reaffirms the importance of the scientific dimension of mathematics.

Although these methods described are important to the scientific dimension of mathematics, mathematical method does extend beyond them. Mathematics in its purest sense is an abstraction—a product of the mind—in that various facets of it may or may not be related to the real world as we see it. Therefore, methods used in its study are not limited by physical situations as are methods used in most sciences. There are times, then, when more formal reasoning techniques are important. Because a complete description of these techniques is beyond the scope of this discussion, suffice it to say that these methods may be either deductive or inductive in nature and that they are always governed by the rules of logic.

The Language Dimension

If indeed language consists of written and spoken forms of communication, then mathematics does have a language dimension. Mathematical language is naturally limited to certain kinds of ideas, which are related to form, size, and quantity.

10. George Polya, *Induction and Analogy in Mathematics,* p. vi.

The functions of mathematical language are twofold: (1) mathematical language enables the individual to record his ideas and to communicate them to others, and (2) it aids the individual in his efforts to organize and clarify his own thoughts. Such functions are possible because of several special characteristics of mathematical language. First, the language of mathematics is

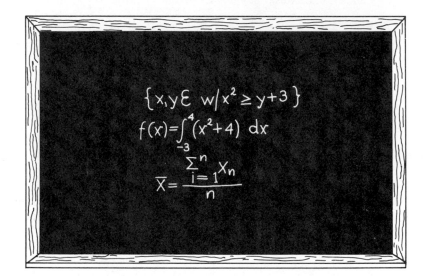

The language of mathematics is often expressed symbolically.

exact; no ambiguous meanings and no multiple interpretations are allowed. Recall the concern over the use of undefined terms and defined terms in the construction of a mathematical system. Second, mathematical language is *concise;* much is stated in very little space. Recall your own experiences with mathematics when certain symbols and forms represented many words in English translation or stood for pages of note-taking in proofs. Finally, mathematical language is *universal.* Mathematical translations can be made both from and to all languages.

Like other languages, mathematical language consists of more than symbols and terms. It has parallels to nouns, pronouns, and verbs; it has phrases; and it has sentences. Consider $2 + 3 = 5$. The translation of this mathematical sentence is "two plus three equals five," a sentence complete with nouns and verbs. Mathematical sentences may be true, false, or they may not have a truth value, just as in other languages. For example, the mathematical sentence $2 + 3 = 5$ is true of course, while $2 + 3 = 6$ is false, and $2 + 3 = \square$ has no truth value at all until a numeral is substituted for $\square$.

The Artistic Dimension

Because we can derive esthetic satisfaction from art or, in other words, because art is that produced which is beautiful, many individuals would certainly signify art as a bona fide dimension of mathematics. Such was attested to by W. F. White when he said:

The beautiful has its place in mathematics for here are triumphs of the creative imagination, beautiful theorems, proofs, and processes whose perfection of form has made them classic. He must be a "practical" man who can see no poetry in mathematics.[11]

Poincaré intimated much the same philosophy in this statement:

A scientist worthy of the name, above all a mathematician, experiences in his work the same impressions as an artist; his pleasure is as great and of the same nature.[12]

Unfortunately, the artistic dimension of mathematics would be considered least valuable by most individuals. This condition could be attributed to a lack of exposure of many to mathematics beyond the rules of arithmetic. Kasner and Newman summarized this plane of thought when they wrote:

Mathematics is an activity governed by the same rules imposed upon the symphonies of Beethoven, the paintings of Da Vinci, and the poetry of Homer. Just as scales, as the laws of perspective, as the rules of metre seem to lack fire, the formal rules of mathematics may appear to be without lustre. Yet ultimately, mathematics reaches pinnacles as high as those attained by the imagination in its most daring reconnoiters.[13]

Although mathematics does have an artistic dimension as just described, it differs from art insofar as one must "do" the mathematics to appreciate it. One cannot be a "listener" as with music, an "observer" as with paintings, or a "reader" as with poetry. Instead, one must be a performer of mathematics; he must produce mathematics to fully appreciate it. This does not mean that the mathematics must be entirely new, never before invented, but that it must be done by the individual himself.

Today it is more important than ever before that mathematics become as pleasurable as possible—that we find beauty in the study of mathematics—because mathematics is becoming integral to all walks of life.

The Recreational Dimension

Another dimension of mathematics which usually has been attributed too little value when characterizing mathematics is that of recreation. What in mathematics can be called relaxing, enjoyable, and interesting? Puzzles, optical illusions, and mathematical tricks just begin the list. Here are some classical examples which most people enjoy trying to solve.[14]

1. Three Indians and three missionaries need to cross a river in a boat which is only large enough for two. The Indians are peaceful if they are left alone or if they are with the same number or with a larger number of missionaries. They are dangerous if they are left alone

11. W. F. White, cited by B. M. Stewart, *Theory of Numbers*, p. 162.
12. Henri Poincaré, cited by B. M. Stewart, op. cit., p. 187.
13. Edward Kasner and James Newman, op. cit., p. 362.
14. Bruce E. Meserve and Max A. Sobel, *Introduction to Mathematics*, pp. 13–17.

in a situation where they outnumber the missionaries. How do they all get across the river without harm?

2. A man goes to a well with 3 cans whose capacities are 3 gallons, 5 gallons, and 8 gallons. Explain how he can obtain exactly 4 gallons of water from the well.

3. Three men enter a hotel and rent a suite of rooms for $30. After they are taken to their rooms the manager discovers he overcharged them; the suite only rents for $25. He thereupon sends a bellhop upstairs with the $5 change. The dishonest bellhop decides to keep $2 and only returns $3 to the men. Now the room originally cost $30, but the men had $3 returned to them. This means that they only paid $27 for the room. The bellhop kept $2. $27 + $2 = $29. What happened to the extra dollar?

4. Write the numbers from 1 through 10 using four 4's for each. The first three are completed for you.

$$\frac{44}{44} = 1; \qquad \frac{4}{4} + \frac{4}{4} = 2; \qquad \frac{4 + 4 + 4}{4} = 3.$$

5. Think of a number. Add 3 to this number. Multiply your answer by 2. Subtract 4 from your answer. Divide by 2. Subtract the number with which you started. Your answer is 1. Why will the answer always be 1?

6. Which of the segments, AB or CD, appears to be the longer in each of the four sections of the following figure? Check your estimates with a ruler.

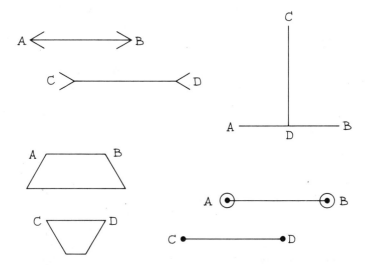

The Activity Dimension

Implied in each prior discussion of mathematical dimensions is an activity dimension of mathematics. This dimension relates to both physical and mental activity.

Although traditionally mathematics has been considered a product of the mind, still there has existed the possibility of relating most elementary aspects of mathematics to corresponding physical situations. Such activities might include setting out enough glasses so that there is one for each child; counting how many cookies are left after giving one to each person; or measuring the length of a table. In this respect, doing mathematics is physical.

There is also activity associated with performing mathematical operations and working mathematical problems. Here also one must "do" the mathematics. In this sense the following statement by Sophocles gains relevance: "One must learn by doing the thing; for though he thinks he knows it, he has no certainty until he tries." In fact, the doing dimension of mathematics has gained such prominence recently that it has been suggested that the term "mathematics" be a verb.

The Tool Dimension

Not only can mathematics be classified as having historical, scientific, artistic, and other dimensions as just described, but it can also be considered a tool, or aid, to help people work within each of these areas. The following list shows only a few of the areas which use mathematics as a tool.

Architecture	Mechanics
Astronomy	Meteorology
Biology	Music
Chemistry	Physics
Economics	Political science
Education	Psychology
Geology	Statistics
Journalism	

Indeed, where is mathematics not present? We find it in everyday life, in games, in nature, in professional areas, and so forth. Whether the emphasis is on applied or pure mathematics, the subject always must be allowed a logical structure and it must be correct and precise.

MATHEMATICS AND CHILDREN

Having considered several ways in which people view mathematics and having examined various dimensions of mathematics, your own concept of mathematics should now be in an expanded state. The point is, though, which viewpoint(s) of mathematics, which mathematical dimension(s), will you relate to your students? What relative importance will you give to the historical dimension of mathematics? the scientific dimension? the language dimension? the activity dimension? the recreational dimension? the artistic dimension? the tool dimension? To a great extent these are your choices to make. External influences will partially determine your mathematics program, but your philosophy and your approach in striking an appropriate balance will be the primary determinant of this program.

Lewis Carroll, a famous mathematician as well as writer, recorded the following conversation between Alice and the Cat in his classic *Alice's Adventures in Wonderland:*

"Cheshire-Puss," she began, rather timidly. . . . "Would you tell me, please, which way I ought to walk from here?"

"That depends a good deal on where you want to get to," said the Cat.

"I don't care much where—" said Alice.

"Then it doesn't much matter which way you walk," said the Cat.[15]

It may not have mattered which way Alice traveled, but it matters a great deal which way a teacher proceeds with his or her students in mathematical pursuits. Responsibility for the mathematical development of a classroom of children provides a challenge for every teacher of elementary school mathematics.

CHAPTER KEY POINTS

1. Mathematics has been described in many ways; many descriptions note that it is a logical study of such areas as shape, quantity, and arrangement.

2. Mathematics is multidimensional. Its dimensions include the historical, the scientific, the language, the artistic, the recreational, the activity, and the tool dimensions.

3. The teacher is a primary factor in determining which dimensions of mathematics will be emphasized in the classroom.

15. Lewis Carroll, *Alice's Adventures in Wonderland*, p. 85.

Laboratory 1

What Is Mathematics?

The question "what is mathematics?" is not easy to answer. Yet, without an understanding of the nature of mathematics, you will not be able to do justice to the subject in your instructional program.

  I. *Objectives:* Upon completion of this laboratory exercise, you should be able to do the following:

    A. Using the thoughts of other people and the dimensions of mathematics, write a brief response to the question, "what is mathematics?" (Chapter Competencies 1–A, 1–B, and 1–C)

 II. *Materials:* None

III. *Procedure:*

    A. Read Chapter 1 of *Helping Children Learn Mathematics.* Consult your instructor if you have any questions.

    B. What is your first impression when someone says the word "mathematics"? Discuss your thoughts with some classmates.

With some classmates, write a brief answer to the question "what is mathematics?" Compare your work with that of other groups of classmates. How are your answers similar or different?

After your discussions, write a brief response to the question "what is mathematics?" which best represents your ideas.

2
What Is Mathematics Education?

Teacher Competencies

After studying Chapter 2 and completing Laboratory 2, you should be able to achieve each of the following:

   A. Identify and describe the three factors which influence mathematics education. (Part Competency I-B)

   B. State how the thinking of Piaget, Gagné, and Bruner each has affected mathematics education. (Part Competency I-B)

   C. Describe different viewpoints of current thought in mathematics education in the elementary school. (Part Competency I-B)

Mathematics education consists of a comprehensive effort by teachers, administrators, authors, and others to help each child know, experience, and understand those dimensions of mathematics considered important at the time. Just as there have always been variations in the way people view mathematics, so also have the aims of mathematics in the schools been continuously changing.

In the past, as now, numerous factors exerted varying degrees of influence upon the choice of mathematical dimensions to be emphasized. The needs of the subject itself, the needs of society as a whole, and the needs of the learner are all factors which have influenced the direction of mathematics education. Let us first examine the shifts of emphasis which have occurred in mathematics education in America and then relate these shifts to mathematics education today.

HISTORICAL PERSPECTIVE

In the colonial period the common people knew only the arithmetic which was directly involved in their livelihood. Initially, children learned primarily through home, church-oriented education, or through apprenticeships. Later, as schools were established, arithmetic assumed its position as one of the "three R's." This part of a child's education enabled him to do such activities as read a calendar and participate in trade and commerce effectively.

At first few classrooms had more than the teacher's copy of an arithmetic textbook. Instead, instruction followed this basic pattern: Each child was given a ciphering book and usually chalk and a slate. The schoolmaster then gave the pupil a "sum" and the rule by which to solve it. The child tried to work the problem given him on his slate. When his solution agreed with the one in the master's book, the child was allowed to record the problem and solution in his ciphering book along with the rule for solving it. If his solution did not agree with the master's, he was directed to try again. Explanations by the master were either minimal or nonexistent. The child was required to memorize the rules he encountered. Understanding was not necessary, and practice was not customary. Essentially, work was done in the abstract with no attention being given to the concrete.

Actually the master's procedures were largely determined by his own textbook; that is, because his text dealt extensively with rules and problems, so also did the master. Because his text dealt primarily with such topics as notation, numeration, and the four fundamental operations, so also did the master. Thus, inclusion of fractions, decimals, denominate numbers, puzzles, or any other such topics in the master's text also encouraged their introduction into the instruction.

Basically, then, in colonial days the subject of mathematics was in an embryonic state. Although some attention was given to such topics as permutations, duodecimals, and mensuration, little was known beyond the rudiments of arithmetic. Therefore, the influence of the subject itself was not great. Societal influence also was not as extensive as it is today, for example.The only mathematical learning necessary for the colonial society to exist was of a fundamental, arithmetic type. Certainly, too, how children learn mathematics exerted little positive influence upon the teaching of the subject, as can be noted from the topical presentations, the abstract emphasis, and the basic lack of explanation for learners.

Beginning about 1821 the pendulum shifts of educational emphasis upon mathematics began approximately thirty- to forty-year cycles. Although this time sequencing is something of an oversimplification, the generalization should help to focus upon the fundamental movements rather than upon fragments of the historical perspective.

In 1821, Warren Colburn published a book which was to exert a powerful influence upon arithmetic schooling for several decades. His book was based upon the teachings of Johann Heinrich Pestalozzi, a Swiss educator, who believed that concrete beginnings with objects and activities involving sense perceptions were vital to a child's learning. He felt that the child should understand clearly what numbers represented and what relationships existed among the numbers, and he believed that initial work should be done orally. These beliefs centered around Pestalozzi's basic theory that arithmetic learning was important in training the mind to form clear ideas. Colburn utilized these ideas in his works. He encouraged the use of practical problems simple enough to be solved mentally; he used objects extensively; he used induction rather than restricting himself to deduction; he made the schoolmaster's role more actively a teaching one. Other texts followed this pattern, and so arithmetic education proceeded as such for about thirty years.

SOLUTIONS OF PROBLEMS.

Ex. 8.
25968286
3734441
5159839
141223
242844
Ans.

Ex. 9.
36843291
6632549
6679943
Ans.

Ex. 10.
5744006
807157
2204
107703
18873
Ans.

Ex. 11.
3526
4733
5944
5128
3457
5467
7518
3633
7214
2795
2942
2385
3863
Ans.

Ex. 12.
10684
14902
11943
6039
10642
18154
16651
19033
16679
10379
8468
9189
7011
20727
35614
381
80
Ans.

Page 38.

Ex. 13.
89444
3065761
159547
17893
560453
Ans.

Ex. 14.
8746921
228047
1631
568941
97007
10474
255778
Ans.

Long computations characterized mathematics textbooks about a century ago. (*Key to Standard Elementary Arithmetic,* by Standard School Book Company, 1887.)

In the late 1850s the education pendulum began its swing back to deductive presentations, to drill, and to extrinsic motivation. Influencing this swing was the then popular faculty psychology in which the mind was viewed as a muscle which could be strengthened by exercise.

A number of factors converged upon mathematics education at the turn of the century and continued to exert influence until a peak in the 1920s. Johann Friedrich Herbart, a German psychologist, set forth the principle of *apperception,* which states that new ideas are learned in terms of the old. Because the content of the subject is the important factor, the child must continuously store new ideas in his mind so that he can build upon them later. Each topic must be explained and the "whys" presented, induction being the method stressed. Herbart's influence, coupled with the influence of the works of another psychologist William James, produced a decrease in both the amount of time allotted to arithmetic in the schools and in the emphasis on memorization. Not only did psychologists influence the direction of mathematics as a subject at this time, but other professional people exerted influence. A prominent educator named John Dewey, an example of such an influence, was also voicing concern about educational practices. He believed that the child should experience and learn arithmetic as it relates to quantitative aspects of real life situations.

The net result of these influences led to a period in education commonly called the *social-utility* period. During this period those aspects of mathematics which were not directly applicable to everyday living were dropped from the curriculum. The tool dimension of mathematics was brought to a peak as children measured to bake cookies and played "grocery store" at school. The "how" of the operations became more important than the "why." Obtaining the correct answer was of utmost importance. Once again, children were taught the sequence of steps to a procedure and then they were drilled on their learning. This approach to teaching corresponded to the theories of learning being set forth by Edward Thorndike and other connectionist psychologists of the period.

By the 1920s the movement had advanced to a point wherein the type of mathematics which was taught was determined by the need for it; that is, it was taught incidentally or as it was needed in the teaching of other subjects. During this period, influences upon mathematics education, as reflected by societal needs, mathematical needs, and learner needs, were in a relative state of imbalance. In terms of societal needs, even though social uses solely determined that mathematics which was taught, there was not maximal benefit because of problems with the learner influence and the subject influence. In terms of learner needs, motivation was high but understanding was low. Because the subject was dealt with entirely as a tool, no effort was made to allow it to be approached as a structured area of learning. Gaps were found in the children's mathematical understanding because mathematics is too sequential in nature to allow a totally sporadic treatment.

By 1935 new ideas on how people learn were being applied in education. These new field theories of learning were more popularly characterized by *Gestalt* psychology, which emphasizes the importance of the learner seeing the whole of an idea as well as its components. Insight is important and learning occurs when the person sees the total configuration, or pattern, or Gestalt. Application of this theory of learning to education led to teaching for meaning rather than teaching by step-by-step memorization of procedures. General understandings and relationships were stressed. Now children were taught not only the "how" of arithmetic but also the "why." The social-utility period was declining, and the *meaning theory* period was gaining impetus.

In the 1950s and 1960s society began to exert perhaps greater influence than ever before upon mathematics education. The Russians launched Sputnik; the job market assumed an ever-increasing technological emphasis based upon various kinds of mathematical knowledge; and society in general recognized a need for its citizens to know more than the rudiments of arithmetic.

38   EVERYDAY PROBLEMS

CAN YOU READ YOUR ELECTRIC METER?

If you use electricity, there is in your house an electric meter which measures the number of kilowatt hours of electricity

that are used.

In reading the electric meter at the left, read it like a four-figure number in which dial

A B C D

A represents thousands, dial B represents hundreds, dial C represents tens, and dial D represents units.

When the pointer on a dial is between two numbers, read the smaller number for that dial.

Thus, the dials of the above meter are read as follows:

On A the pointer is between 2 and 3.   The reading is 2.
On B the pointer is between 1 and 2.   The reading is 1.
On C the pointer is between 9 and 10.   The reading is 9.
On D the pointer is between 1 and 2.   The reading is 1.

Hence the reading of the above meter is 2191 K.W.H.

Note that the 0 on the dials stands for 10 when the pointer is between 9 and 0, as shown above on dial C.

Reading the Electric Meter

1. On the above meter, does the pointer move to the right or to the left on dial A? on dial C? on dial B? on dial D?

2. The first set of dials at the right shows the electric meter of a store on Oct. 31, while the second set of dials shows the same meter on Nov. 30. Read each set of dials. How many

K.W.H. of electricity has the store used since Oct. 31?

Social-utilitarian aspects of mathematics were emphasized during the first half of the twentieth century. (*Strayer-Upton Arithmetics, Higher Grades* by George Strayer and Clifford Upton, © 1928. Reprinted by permission of D. C. Heath and Company.)

The federal government and private agencies generously funded projects in research and development in mathematics education. Although each project had its own set of goals, some general results and prescriptions for change arose from the movement as a whole and came to be called "modern mathematics." Among the characteristics of the period were the emphasis on discovery; the introduction into the elementary curriculum of topics formerly reserved for later use; the teaching of mathematics for understanding as a total structure; the making of the learning of mathematics as pleasant as possible; and the introduction of teaching-learning aids in addition to the traditional basal textbook.

In conclusion, various factors have influenced mathematics education. In the subject, in society as a whole, and in the learner himself different needs were recognized at different times in the history of this country. As each need was recognized, it interacted with other needs of the period, and so mathematics education evolved to its current phase. Still, mathematical needs, societal needs, and learner needs are being recognized and dealt with. To help us better understand what mathematics education is today, let us examine it according to these needs.

THE MATHEMATICAL NEEDS FACTOR

Discussion in Chapter 1 of the many dimensions of mathematics implies that mathematics should no longer be considered narrowly, but instead should be approached in education as the multifaceted study into which it has developed over the centuries. Surely, teacher biases and other influences of a given period are reflected in the relative emphasis being given to each mathematical dimension; the tool dimension and the scientific dimension, for example, have separately shared the educational spotlight as important aspects to be studied. Unfortunately, equilibrium has not always been achieved, and in stressing one dimension of mathematics, other dimensions were often eliminated or abused. For example, during the social-utility period the tool dimension was emphasized, while the artistic, scientific, and language dimensions were virtually ignored. The end result was necessarily that the learner of mathematics, and society in turn, developed distorted views of what mathematics is.

Mathematics educators today recognize that different people will always emphasize different dimensions of mathematics. These educators have taken a step forward, though, by trying to include in their mathematics programs basic components of each dimension while at the same time trying not to abuse basic tenets of any dimension, thereby producing a balance. Numerous examples may be cited to confirm this point; for example, the tool dimension is not developed to the extent that only "the answer" is important and that mathematically correct techniques are subservient to shortcuts and tricks. Similarly, the scientific dimension is not emphasized to the extent that the learner is unable to relate abstract mathematics to real world uses. The recreational dimension is included, but it is not allowed to reduce mathematics to a totality of "fun and games." The activity dimension is not emphasized to the extent that the child can engage in mathematical activities but cannot produce a correct result. Mathematics education today is seeking an appropriate blending of these dimensions, while attending to the needs of the subject of mathematics itself to be correct, a total structure, interesting, useful, and even esthetically pleasing.

THE SOCIETAL NEEDS FACTOR

Society itself has consistently played a role in the kind of mathematics taught in school. Initially, colonial society required that the individual know only the rudiments of arithmetic. The society in which we live today, however, has become increasingly complex—more scientifically and technologically oriented. To function within society the individual must be able to perform a multitude of complex tasks, many of which are mathematically oriented.

Not only are many occupations mathematically oriented, but they also require various *kinds* of mathematical knowledge; that is, a person employed in the insurance business will require a different kind of mathematical knowledge and understanding than a person employed as a laboratory technician. A person educated in the mathematics necessary for one job will often find that, due to job mobility or job attrition, he or she must look for a position in another area requiring different mathematical knowledge. Such circumstances require that society educate people with broad, fundamental mathematical understandings who can, with minimal retraining, adapt to different kinds of livelihoods.

Similar basic mathematical learning also serves the individual who does not function in a mathematically oriented occupation. Balancing a checkbook, driving a vehicle, shopping for groceries, telling time, and buying a carpet to fit a specific room size are only a few of the activities involved with daily living which require basic mathematical understandings.

Also important, but in a broader sense, is that society pass on a certain cultural-intellectual heritage from one generation to another. Mathematics is a fundamental part of this heritage. It has been a branch of learning passed down through our culture from Plato to Newton to Einstein.

Societal needs of today, therefore, require that mathematics be learned by everyone; that it be viewed in its widest perspective; that its fundamentals be understood; and that it be approached with as positive an attitude as possible.

THE LEARNER NEEDS FACTOR

Possibly the most important factor in determining the course of mathematics education is the learner himself and his needs. Indeed, the type of mathematics considered important by society is of no real consequence if it is not learned by the child. Learner needs are of even more immediate importance to you, a prospective teacher, because how well you understand the needs of learners bears a direct relationship to how well you will help children learn mathematics in your own classroom.

As with societal needs and with needs of mathematics itself, there has been an evolutionary movement associated with understanding the needs of learners. We have marked much progress from the times when phrenologists studied bumps on a person's head to determine his strengths and weaknesses! Today, to better understand the nature of learner needs, the areas of child growth and development and of how children learn mathematics should be considered. You might wish to review the general area of child growth and development briefly before proceeding with this discussion.

Classifications of the Needs Factor

Learner needs may be classified into three categories: cognitive, affective, and psychomotor. Each category is important to the child in the development of mathematical maturity. No instructional program in mathematics can deal with these categories separately for they are very much interrelated.

The *cognitive* needs of the child (learner) are embodied in the content and process of elementary school mathematics. Content refers to the facts, concepts, and principles which make up the body of mathematics; $2 + 2 = 4$, number, and the addition algorithm are examples of mathematical content. The process of mathematics refers to such areas as problem solving and development of computational skills. Any instructional program in elementary school mathematics will be based on the content and process of mathematics, and it should be designed to meet cognitive needs of the students.

The *affective* needs of the child refer to his self-concept and attitude. The instructional program should help every child develop a positive self-concept by providing activities for him in which he is successful and in which he experiences a sense of accomplishment. Attitude has not been conclusively correlated highly with achievement in the content area of mathematics, but most mathematics educators agree that if a child has a positive self-concept and a positive attitude toward mathematics and learning, then his opportunity for good mathematical achievement will be greatly enhanced.

The *psychomotor* needs of the child relate to the physical aspects of learning, such as developing certain muscular or motor skills. Such skills as hand-eye coordination and physical coordination can be developed through the instructional program in mathematics. Mathematical activities which physically involve the learner, such as connecting two points with a pencil and straight edge or "putting a round peg in a round hole," will aid in meeting his psychomotor needs and should form an integral part of mathematics instruction.

THEORIES OF LEARNING THAT INFLUENCE MATHEMATICS EDUCATION

As noted briefly in the discussion of historical perspectives of mathematics education, various theories of learning have gained prominence in educational theory and practice at different times in the past. The effects of some of these theories are still harbored in mathematics education today. The best-known theories may be included under two general classifications: association theories and field theories.

Before describing how adherents to each position believe that their respective theories describe the learning process, it is important to note that in actuality the two schools of thought are not mutually exclusive. It is not necessary for a teacher to subscribe to just one point of view and repudiate all others, for example. Since certain learning theories seem to conform to certain circumstances better than others, an eclectic approach is permissible if, indeed, not advisable. G. T. Buswell agreed with this basic contention when he wrote:

Much harm has been done to the organization and teaching of arithmetic by trying to force all learning situations to fit any one theory of learning. . . . The very reason that there are conflicting theories of learning is that some theories seem to afford a better explanation of certain aspects or types of learning, while other theories stress the application of pertinent evidence and accepted principles to other aspects and types of learning. . . . Theories grow and are popularized because of their particular value in explaining the facts, but they are not always applied with equal emphasis to the whole range of facts.[1]

Association theories, which have a common underlying emphasis on reaction to the environment, have been more specifically known by such terms as connectionism and behaviorism. Connectionists explain behavior in terms of bonds, or connections, between stimuli (S) and responses (R); or if you prefer, they explain behavior in terms of reactions (R) associated with given situations (S). Thorndike, perhaps the best-known connectionist, went on to develop from his experiments various laws of learning; his laws of exercise, readiness, and effect perhaps have had the most direct bearing on educational practices. According to connectionists, the learning of number facts and computational processes with emphasis on speed and accuracy lends itself to repetition, to drill, and to the idea of rewarding correct responses and punishing incorrect ones. Behaviorists extend connectionism to include only physical situations and responses. They point out that mental processes are covert in nature and so cannot be observed directly; they conclude that it is therefore only possible to study observable physical responses or overt behavior. This viewpoint has regained prominence recently in the development of competency-based learning and instruction.

On the other hand, *field* theories emphasize the organized nature of experience. Gestalt psychologists or proponents of the field theory contend that each situation is experienced as a totality—that it is structured into a definite pattern and is more than the isolated parts which comprise it. In fact, an often-coined description of the Gestalt position is that, in essence, the whole is greater than the sum of its parts. The elements of any situation are only important insofar as they are related to each other and to the whole. Insight is important; trial-and-error learning is not. The Gestalt idea as applied to learning mathematics lends itself well to accomplishing such goals as those related to understanding the number system and to developing problem-solving abilities. Adherents to the Gestalt position would insist upon stressing structure, relationships, and meaning, and they would de-emphasize the importance of drilling on facts as isolated bits of learning.

Using such bases, educators and psychologists have proceeded to attempt determinations of how young children might be helped to learn mathematics. The more influential of these people and their respective points of view relative to the needs of young learners will be discussed in the following section.

THE LEARNING OF MATHEMATICS BY CHILDREN

Literature in mathematics education spanning the past two decades seems to have attributed great significance to the term "discovery." "Discovery is the new panacea . . . and every child . . . must

---

1. G. T. Buswell, "The Psychology of Learning in Relation to the Teaching of Arithmetic," in *The Teaching of Arithmetic,* ed. Nelson B. Henry, p. 144.

engage in nothing but the process of discovery,"[2] is Schulman's summary of the literature. In many writings discovery has been contrasted with such terms as "rote learning" and "mastery learning." Such a contrast may be considered an oversimplification of the problem of determining how children learn mathematics; perhaps other comparisons and contrasts would be more appropriate. As Schulman points out:

> It should be noted at this point that the learning by discovery controversy is a complex issue which can easily be oversimplified. . . . The controversy seems to center essentially about the question of how much and what kind of guidance ought to be provided to students in the learning situation. Those favoring learning by discovery advocate minimal teacher guidance and maximum opportunity for exploration and trial-and-error on the part of the student. Those preferring guided learning emphasize the importance of careful sequencing of instructional experiences through maximal guidance.[3]

Discussion contrasting learning by discovery as pioneered by Bruner and undergirded by Piaget, with guided learning as espoused by Gagné, might be most appropriate then. Learning by discovery may be viewed as process-oriented learning while guided learning may be viewed as product-oriented learning. As such, the two areas are typically identified with different types of learning.

Process-Oriented Learning

The process-oriented view of learning states that the process which a child uses to reach a desired product or capability is the most important result of his learning; the product or capability is not neglected, but its importance is considered secondary to the process. Piaget and Bruner are considered proponents of the process-oriented viewpoint.

Jean Piaget, Swiss psychologist, mathematician, and biologist, has studied the conceptual development of children for several decades. The results of his studies suggest that the child passes through a developmental pattern of stages which are clearly defined in the maturation of basic mathematical concepts and principles. The stages of development are briefly described in the following paragraphs.

1. *Sensori-motor stage:* This stage occurs from birth to about two years of age. It is primarily characterized by a lack of language facility and by behavior which has not yet been internalized.

2. *Preoperational stage:* This stage lasts from two until approximately six or seven years of age, although for some children and for certain mathematical concepts it may extend to as late as nine or ten years of age. It is at this stage that language develops, signs are understood, imagery is used, and symbolic games like "let's pretend" are played. However, the child is not yet able to

---

2. Lee S. Schulman, "Perspectives on the Psychology of Learning and the Teaching of Mathematics," in *Improving Mathematics Education for Elementary School Teachers, A Conference Report, 1967,* ed. W. Robert Houston, pp. 23–37.

3. Ibid., p. 81.

conserve continuous or discontinuous objects, does not perceive part-whole relationships, and is not capable of reversing his thinking or of seriating. Because of being unable to do these activities, the child is also unable to understand concepts associated with number, spatial relationships, and quantity.

3. *Concrete operations stage:* Following the preoperational stage and continuing until the child is eleven or twelve years of age is the concrete operations stage. This stage is of particular importance to the elementary teacher because it is during these years that the child is in elementary school. A child who is not at the concrete operations stage may experience numerous difficulties in his mathematical progress which otherwise might not occur.

The concrete operations stage may be characterized by such abilities as *classifying* objects according to similarities and differences; *seriating* objects according to a given characteristic (e.g., ordering rods of varying lengths from shortest to longest); *reversibility* (e.g., knowing that subtracting a given quantity "undoes" what adding it did originally); and *conservation* (e.g., realizing that certain characteristics or relations remain invariant regardless of possible changes in what they are perceived to be).

Some of Piaget's most famous experiments have occurred in the area of conservation. One classic example, often replicated, involves a child being shown two jars with exactly the same number of marbles in each and being asked to compare them.

The marbles in one jar are then poured into a taller, thinner jar, and the child is asked again to compare the number of marbles in the two jars.

A child not yet in the concrete operations stage will focus upon one aspect or another. He might note the height of the second jar and say that there are now more marbles, but he might also note the thinness of the same jar and say that there are fewer. When he understands that the number of marbles in the two jars is still the same, he has achieved conservation. In realizing that there are the same number of marbles in each jar he has had to reject what his perceptions have told him.

As Copeland points out, the concrete operations stage is important mathematically as well as psychologically. Many of the operations Piaget describes are mathematical in nature; classification, ordering, number, spatial operations, elementary relations, and many others.[4]

4. *Formal operations stage:* This stage generally begins around the age of eleven or twelve years. During this stage, the child begins to use hypotheses and deductive reasoning to arrive at conclusions and generalizations. He is now creating new operations and structures so that he no longer needs to manipulate objects in the physical world.

As one studies the developmental stages, it seems natural to ask whether a child's rate of progress through them can be accelerated. Piaget answers the question as follows:

> This question (of accelerating learning) never fails to amuse students and faculty in Geneva, for they regard it as typically American. Tell an American that a child develops certain ways of thinking at seven, and he immediately sets about to try to develop those same ways of thinking at six or even five years of age. Investigators in countries other than America have tried to accelerate the development of logical thinking, and we have available today a considerable body of research on what works and what doesn't work. Most of the research has not worked. It hasn't worked because experimenters have not paid attention to equilibrium theory. The researchers have tried to teach an answer, a particular response, rather than to develop operations. They have tried to teach the child that of course the hot dog (shaped piece of clay) will weigh as much as the clay ball; just put both on a "two-pan balance" and you'll see. But the child is completely unconvinced unless he shuffles the data around in his mind, using one or more of the operations I've described. Learning a fact by reinforcement does not in and of itself result in mental adaptation.[5]

Expanding on the preceding points, Jensen summarizes Piaget's views succinctly when she says:

> Piaget rejects the notion that adults can "teach" children these processes of creating, inventing, discovering, verifying, and criticizing rationally. According to Piaget, the child himself develops these processes through his interaction with his environment.[6]

Paul Rosenbloom adds his own perspective to the acceleration question when he makes the following observation about Piaget's work:

> In considering the acceleration of stages of development, the question of cultural milieu is significant. Certainly, a wide variety of cultures exists even in our own country. Many of Piaget's experiments were conducted during the 1930s in Switzerland. Toys available today in many American homes may influence the outcomes of some of his experiments. For example, there are wooden shoes and mailboxes with different shaped holes in them. The child fits the appropriately shaped blocks into holes that are triangles, squares, and circles. Some have worked with Montessori materials in which the child fits different shaped pieces into different kinds of cav-

---

4. Richard W. Copeland, *How Children Learn Mathematics,* p. 16.
5. Ibid., pp. 20–21.
6. Rosalie Jensen, *Exploring Mathematical Concepts and Skills in the Elementary School,* p. 27.

ities. Experiences such as these seem to aid children in distinguishing between a circle and a triangle at very early ages. And so I have a hunch that to a certain extent, Piaget's results are culturally determined; and by giving the child different experiences, by changing his environment, one might change his course of development. The implications of this notion for Head Start programs and nursery schools are important as they develop formal educational programs.[7]

There are differences of opinion among mathematics educators about the implications of Piaget's findings. Certainly, work still needs to be done, not only in research in this country, but in implementing valid findings into teacher education and curricular materials. Few educators would disagree, though, with Piaget's comments about the processes of education as they relate to process-oriented learning.

> The principal goal of education is to create men who are capable of doing things, not simply of repeating what other generations have done—men who are creative, inventive, and discover. The second goal of education is to form minds which can be critical, can verify, and not accept anything they are offered.[8]

Let us turn now to the views of another proponent of process-oriented learning, Jerome S. Bruner, an American psychologist. Bruner was a student of Piaget, and many of his views are similar to those of his teacher. Basically, he hypothesizes that children should engage in the processes of discovery and problem solving in order to effectively learn. The learning of facts is necessary only if the facts are essential to the solution of some problem confronted by the child. Bruner believes that manipulation of physical objects is essential to learning and feels, like Piaget, that the child moves through developmental stages as he matures as a learner.

The first level of learning is the *enactive* level where the child manipulates concrete materials. He moves next to the *iconic* level where he works with mental images of the physical objects. He then moves to the *symbolic* level and manipulates symbols rather than mental images. Careful inspection of these levels reveals that they are adaptations of Piaget's developmental stages.

Bruner is well known for his statement, "Any subject can be taught effectively in some intellectually honest form to any child at any stage of development."[9] This statement has been controversial among educators. Piaget has said that he cannot understand why Bruner made such a statement. Bruner attempts to clarify his words when he says:

> . . . The basic ideas that lie at the heart of all science and mathematics and the basic theories that give form to life and literature are as simple as they are powerful. . . . It is only when such basic ideas are put in formalized terms as equations or elaborated verbal concepts that they are out of reach of the young child, if he has not first understood them intuitively and had a chance to try them out on his own.[10]

7. Paul Rosenbloom, "Implications of Piaget for Mathematics Curriculum," in *Improving Mathematics Education for Elementary School Teachers, A Conference Report, 1967,* ed. W. Robert Houston, p. 49.

8. Eleanor Duckworth, "Piaget Rediscovered," in *Piaget Rediscovered,* eds. Richard Riple and Vern Rockcastle, p. 5.

9. Jerome S. Bruner, *The Process of Education,* p. 33.

10. Ibid., pp. 12–13.

Schulman reflects on Bruner's statement in this manner;

> I believe that what Bruner is saying, and it is neither trivial nor absurd, is that our older conceptions of readiness have tended to apply Piagetian theory as some have for generations applied Rousseau's. Their thesis was "There is the child—he is a developing organism, with invariant order, invariant schedule. Here, too, is the subject matter, equally hallowed by time and unchanging. We take the subject matter as our starting point, watch the child develop and feed it in at appropriate times as he reaches readiness." Let's face it, that has been our general conception of readiness. We gave reading readiness tests and waited to teach the pupil reading until he was ready. The notion is quite new that the reading readiness test tells not when to begin teaching the child, but what has to be done to get him more ready. We used to just wait until he got ready. What Bruner is suggesting is that we must modify our conception of readiness so that it includes not only the child but the subject matter. Subject matter, too, goes through stages of readiness. The same subject matter can be presented at a manipulative or enactive level, at an iconic or representational level, and finally at a symbolic or formal level.[11]

Bruner's theory of how children learn can be summarized as being developmental and Socratic in nature and related to the Gestalt premise. Bruner has probably contributed more than any other person to advance the notion of learning by discovery. One example of process-oriented learning or learning by discovery is adapted from his book, *Toward a Theory of Instruction.*[12] The project by Bruner was done in collaboration with Z. P. Dienes with a group of ten nine-year-olds. The purpose of the lesson was to teach the children the basic elements of group theory.

The children were first led to the idea of a mathematical four-group through the use of a book with an arrow drawn down the middle of its front cover.

Four maneuvers of the book were used: a quarter turn to the right, a quarter turn to the left, a half turn (in either direction), and leaving the book in the same position. The children were able to quickly grasp the idea that any series of maneuvers could be repeated using only a single maneuver from the starting point; this is an important property of groups. (Bruner noted that this is not the usual way that the property is considered mathematically but it worked well for the children.) Examples of sets of movements which did not constitute groups were then considered so that the property could be formally studied and stated. The children were able to generate these latter examples themselves, an indication that they understood the property. The children were next asked to make up games with four, six, and eight maneuvers which had the closure property. To aid the children in their imagery, a matrix of the following form was devised to help record the work with the different sets of maneuvers.

11. Schulman, op. cit., p. 90.
12. Jerome S. Bruner, *Toward a Theory of Instruction,* pp. 66–68.

	s a b c
s	s a b c
a	a c s b
b	b s c a
c	c b a s

s = stay
a = quarter turn to left
b = quarter turn to right
c = half turn

(Bruner noted that the use of the matrix was merely an aid and contributed nothing to the abstraction of the group concept.)

During their work, the children were asked such questions as: Are there any four-groups with a different structure? What about a game using a cube with the following maneuvers: leave it where it is, rotate it 180 degrees on the vertical axis, rotate it 180 degrees on the horizontal axis, and rotate it 180 degrees on each of the cubic diagonals. Is it a group? Can it be simplified to a smaller number of maneuvers? Does it contain the group we described earlier? Bruner summarized his work as follows:

> We should suggest that learning mathematics reflects a good deal about intellectual development. It begins with instrumental activity, a kind of definition of things by doing them. Such operations become represented and summarized in the symbolic notation that remains invariant across transformations in imagery; the learner comes to grasp the formal or abstract properties of the things he is dealing with. But while, once abstraction is achieved, the learner becomes free in a certain measure of the surface appearance of things, he nonetheless continues to rely upon the stock of imagery that permits him to work at the level of heuristic, through convenient and nonrigorous means of exploring problems and relating them to problems already mastered.[13]

Product-Oriented Learning

The product-oriented view of learning states that the end product, or what has been learned, is the most important factor. A child may use any process, including discovery, to achieve the desired product or capability, but it doesn't really matter which one(s) he uses. So that nothing is left to chance, the teacher must carefully guide the child through his learning experiences to insure that the desired result will be reached. This is the approach to learning subscribed to by Robert Gagné.

The work of Gagné has produced a very different approach to learning from that of the process-oriented approach. Gagné feels that the final result of learning is of the most importance. This end result may be referred to as a *capability*. A capability is that which the child can do as a result of his learning. Some people would call this capability a terminal behavior. At any rate, we shall refer to the capability as a task which the child is to perform under a specified set of conditions.

When a capability has been determined for a child to learn, a task analysis must be performed. The result of this analysis may be the formation of a complex pyramid of prerequisites which must be learned by the child before he can be expected to achieve the desired capability. Such a pyramid might look like this:

13. Ibid., p. 68.

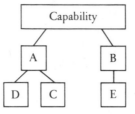

In this task analysis, it has been determined that A and B are necessary prerequisites to the achievement of the capability. In addition, C and D are prerequisites to A, and E is a prerequisite to B. Thus, a sequence of tasks[14] can be set up to achieve the necessary prerequisites and finally the desired capability. To aid in the setting up of the sequence, a pretest should be given. This will determine which, if any, of the prerequisites have already been achieved. The sequence can then be started at the point at which the child needs to begin. In the preceding example, suppose that the child can perform tasks C and E but not D. His sequence would then start with task D and proceed to the learning of tasks A and B and hence to the capability.

If the capability to be learned is problem solving in nature, then the child must learn certain principles which may be used to solve the problem. Before he can learn these principles, he must first learn certain concepts or generalizations which are learned from particular facts or knowledge. Thus, the child must proceed through certain levels of learning which build from the simple to the complex. Diagrammatically, the procedure looks like this:

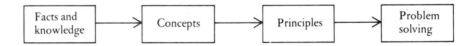

These levels of learning will be discussed in Chapter 17 when they are related to evaluation of mathematical outcomes.

There are many different sequences of tasks which may lead a child to the acquisition of the desired capability. Children will approach the learning of the capability with different backgrounds and will be able to work with different processes; some children will be able to learn by discovery while others will need much structure in the sequence of their learning tasks. Whichever process is appropriate is not the key issue as long as the child achieves the desired capability. The teacher, then, must carefully guide the child into the proper sequence and be sure that he achieves the capability, leaving nothing to chance. This last statement is in direct contrast to the process-oriented approach to learning.

In pausing to reflect on product-oriented learning, the notion of programmed instruction may come to mind. Gagné's approach, having evolved from the connectionist theory of learning, is indeed the basis for programmed instruction.

14. In some cases, the sequence may be set up in a number of different ways.

Readiness to Learn

Reflecting on both the process- and product-oriented approaches to learning, it is not difficult to ascertain the positions of the approaches with respect to an often-discussed and usually contended topic in mathematics education: the readiness of the child to learn.

The process-oriented approach views readiness as being a function of a child's developmental stage. If the cognitive structure of the notion to be learned fits into the structure of the child's present developmental stage, then the child is "ready" to learn the notion. If the cognitive structure of the notion does not fit the present stage of development, then the notion must wait to be "learned" until there is a match between the cognitive structure and the developmental stage.

The product-oriented approach, on the other hand, maintains that the child is "ready" to learn a capability as soon as it can be divided into subcapabilities which the child is capable of learning. As soon as this point can be found, the child is ready to enter the learning sequence leading toward the desired capability. This viewpoint rejects the notion that developmental stages can be considered in the readiness question.

It seems then that the way to approach the question of readiness is not to ask "is the child ready?" but to ask "for what is the child ready?" By addressing himself or herself to the latter question, the teacher will be better able to provide learning experiences that will facilitate the child's growth. An important consideration will be the position of the child on the concrete-to-abstract continuum, which is discussed next.

The Concrete-to-Abstract Continuum

While there is no general consensus among mathematics educators about how children learn mathematics, the concept of the concrete-to-abstract continuum, which has its basis in Bruner's premises, seems to be an important one. Simply stated, a child, given any mathematical idea to be learned, proceeds along a continuum of levels toward the learning of that idea. Let's look at the continuum more closely and consider some implications for its use in mathematics education. Diagrammatically, the continuum looks like this:

The *concrete* level involves the use of manipulative devices and materials that the child can handle and use to gain understanding of the desired idea. For example, as a child attempts to master the concept of "three," he may engage in activities such as counting out three bottle caps or taking three books from the shelf.

The *semiconcrete* level is the next higher level of learning and involves the use of pictures and diagrams. In the preceding example, the child may demonstrate his understanding of "three" at the semiconcrete level by drawing a picture of three trees or drawing a line around a set of three objects chosen from sets containing other numbers of objects.

The highest level of learning is the *abstract* level, in which the child works with the mathematical symbols involved in the idea under consideration. Referring back to the concept of "three," the child may write the appropriate numeral beside each pictured set or he may use the numeral to solve a mathematical sentence.

Obviously, it would be desirable for all children to be able to pass through the first two levels uneventfully and be able to work at the abstract level with every mathematical concept, but it is unrealistic to expect this to happen regularly with every child. It is true that some children, given a particular concept to learn, will enter at the semiconcrete or abstract level and proceed rapidly to mastery of that concept. Others, though, will have to enter at the concrete level and proceed sometimes slowly and perhaps frustratedly toward the abstract level. Movement through the levels often has become overwhelming for children because some teachers have tended to push the children into abstract-level activity before they were ready. In mathematics education today it is recognized that learning experiences children receive should always be appropriate to the level at which they are able to work successfully.

Different Types of Learning and Meeting the Child's Needs

Discussion thus far about how children learn mathematics has been rather generalized in terms of the population being described; in other words, it has not related to individual learning patterns of different children. Let us turn now to meeting the needs of learners with special characteristics.

The Role of Diagnosis.   Before an effective instructional program in mathematics education can be provided for the individual child his specific needs must be determined. Questions such as "which learning approach is appropriate for him?" and "at what level is he capable of working?" must be answered as clearly as possible by a variety of techniques as discussed more completely in Chapters 16 and 17. The process of diagnosis is used throughout the planning and implementing of every instructional program in mathematics. The teacher who knows specific needs of a child can better plan for his or her mathematical progress.

Meeting the Needs of the Exceptional Child.   Learners who are classified as exceptional have special needs to be met. This discussion will be concerned with special needs of the higher achiever, of the low achiever, of the disadvantaged, and of the mentally retarded in mathematics education today.

Because of his needs, the *high achiever* can experience many problems in a classroom in which provision has not been made for him. Characteristically, the high achiever is a highly motivated child with a high degree of intelligence. Lock-stepping him into the same regimen as the rest of the class may produce boredom and frustration in him, thereby creating problems for him, the teacher, and possibly the rest of the class. Among the techniques which the teacher might use to meet the higher achiever's needs for a more challenging curriculum are acceleration, vertical enrichment, and horizontal enrichment.

Acceleration is a procedure by which a child is advanced in his grade level to a higher grade. This practice is not an especially popular one among educators because of potential sociological and psychological problems.

Vertical enrichment is another technique which a teacher might use to meet the needs of the high achiever. It almost always involves a situation in which the child works independently in the same set of instructional materials (usually the textbook) as the rest of the class but at a faster pace and with only occasional assistance from the teacher. Upon completion of these materials, he may proceed to the next level text and begin working there. Sometimes there may be several members of the class working in this manner and they might work together.

Under the use of *horizontal enrichment,* the child is kept with classmates for part of the time and then allowed to pursue the various topics in depth and breadth. For example, the child who has quickly grasped the notion of addition of whole numbers with regrouping may turn to the operation and its use with nondecimal numbers or to modular addition. To provide effective horizontal enrichment, the teacher must have access to a wide variety of instructional materials which can be used by the child. The basis for such materials may be obtained from professional trade books and journals which are ready sources for ideas. Consultation with other teachers will also be helpful.

The *low achiever* presents a different set of needs from those of the high achiever. Basically, there are two factors which may cause low achievement: ability and motivation. The child who has low ability often displays such characteristics as poor reading achievement, low intelligence quotients, and a record of failure in mathematics. Many of these children do not have low motivation; they simply do not achieve. The low achiever takes much longer to grasp the idea under study and is not able to make many meaningful generalizations. Letting the child work with physical objects will be helpful, as will giving him extra time to work on problems. Every attempt should be made to provide as many successful learning experiences for this child as possible.

The child who has good ability but is a low achiever because of low motivation is perhaps the most difficult and frustrating for the teacher to handle. He is often a behavior problem and enjoys seeking attention by disrupting the class. Initial steps in alleviating such problems involve finding areas of interest to the child and relating them to the mathematical topic being studied.

The child who has both low ability and low motivation provides another type of need. Low motivation is probably caused by constant failure which is, in turn, complicated by low ability. It seems reasonable to attempt to raise the child's motivation level first and then attack his low ability by providing learning experiences designed to maximize opportunity for success.

A technique which may prove useful with a low achiever is to let another student work with him. This technique enables the low achiever to receive more individual attention, and at the same time it takes advantage of peer interactions that sometimes accomplish more than the teacher could. The student "helper" should be chosen carefully, and the teacher should keep informed so as to insure maximum possible learning from the situation.

The *disadvantaged* child presents a set of special needs not totally dissimiliar from those of the low achiever just discussed. He has learned to distrust adults, to expect failure in school, and to settle most of his problems in a hostile manner. This child often has low motivation, low reading and listening levels, and lives in a deprived area which is culturally and economically poor. Not every disadvantaged child has low achievement in mathematics, and not all low achievers in mathematics live in deprived areas. There does seem to be a special set of needs which a disadvantaged child has, however.

First, the disadvantaged child usually has a poor self-concept, generally precipitated by the environment in which he lives. He has very few, if any, of his own possessions, which causes him to be very possessive of his textbook, paper, and pencils. He has no particular need or desire to attend school and to study mathematics. This is caused in part by the fact that he is asked to work with situations which are unfamiliar to him. His continued failure has compounded to the point where his motivation is negligible.

Working successfully with the disadvantaged child is obviously a challenge. The building of the child's self-concept is perhaps most important; *what* is taught is probably not as important as *how* it is taught. It is also important to have the child work frequently with concrete materials and with mathematical situations with which he is familiar, thereby increasing motivation, chances for success, and realization of a need for mathematics.

The pace of the learning situation must be slow enough for the child to be able to grasp new ideas before proceeding forward. Teacher expectations of what the disadvantaged child can do should be high enough to give the child a sense of accomplishment but not so high that learning will become frustrating; above all, the disadvantaged child should never be underestimated.

The child who is *mentally retarded* has many of the same needs as the child with low ability, basically that he needs much individual attention. The educable mentally retarded child may learn to be proficient in one type of arithmetic but be deficient in another. For example, he may be able to do computation with speed and accuracy but be unable to read well enough to understand the principle underlying the operation. It is important for the instructional program in mathematics to help each child develop each arithmetic ability. Developing competence in one process will help the child develop competence in other processes and will assist the teacher in helping the child make generalizations.

The teacher can take several steps to help the mentally retarded child in the classroom.

1. Develop a readiness program for the child.
2. Make certain that units of instruction are experience-oriented and contain work with concrete materials.
3. Keep reading to a minimum in the child's arithmetic instruction.
4. Introduce new material and learned skills with careful planning and over a long period of time.
5. Keep standards of evaluation at a reasonable level, and make frequent use of diagnostic and evaluative techniques.[15]

This brief discussion of the needs and problems of the exceptional child in mathematics education has been, of necessity, superficial. The commentary is intended only to give you, the prospective teacher, some familiarity with these children and to help you understand how they might be helped to progress in the area of mathematics education.

In conclusion, influencing mathematics education in a forceful way has been the factor of learner needs. Recently, much has been discovered and is still being discovered about how children learn mathematics. For example, it has been found that in mathematics education attention should be paid not only to a child's cognitive development, but also to his affective and psychomotor development. Both product- and process-oriented learning concepts offer positive suggestions on how children learn mathematics. There is still controversy about certain aspects of children's

---

15. Janet Thomas, *Teaching Arithmetic to Mentally Retarded Children*, pp. 10–11.

learning; readiness, for example, is a matter still to be dealt with conclusively. And lastly, even after all of these generalized areas are resolved, mathematics educators will still find that children are individuals who often have special needs.

CHAPTER KEY POINTS

1. The direction of mathematics education has been influenced by (1) the needs of the subject itself, (2) the needs of society as a whole, and (3) the needs of the learner.

2. Mathematics educators today include in their mathematics programs basic components of each dimension while at the same time trying not to abuse basic tenants of any dimension, thereby producing a balance.

3. Societal needs of today require that mathematics (1) be learned by everyone; (2) be viewed in its widest perspective; (3) be fundamentally understood; and (4) be approached with as positive an attitude as possible.

4. Learner needs are the most important factor. There are three categories of learner needs:
   a. Cognitive—the content and process of elementary school mathematics.
   b. Affective—the child's self-concept and attitude.
   c. Psychomotor—the physical aspects of learning.

5. Theories of learning in the past that influence mathematics education may be classified as association theories and field theories.

6. Learning by discovery may be viewed as process-oriented learning while guided learning may be viewed as product-oriented learning.

7. The process-oriented view of learning states that the process which a child uses to reach a desired product or capability is the most important part of his learning, the product or capability is secondary; Piaget and Bruner are considered its proponents.

8. Jean Piaget's studies suggest a developmental pattern of four stages which are clearly defined: (1) the sensory-motor stage (birth–2 years); (2) the pre-operational stage (2 years–6 or 7 years); (3) the concrete operations stage (6 or 7 years–11 or 12 years); and (4) the formal operations stage (beginning at 11 or 12 years).

9. Jerome S. Bruner hypothesizes that children should engage in the process of discovery and problem solving in order to effectively learn. He believes that manipulation of physical objects is essential to learning. He describes three levels of learning: enactive, iconic, and symbolic.

10. The product-oriented view of learning states that the end product, or what has been learned, is the most important factor and the teacher must carefully guide the child to insure the desired capabilities reached. This is the view of Robert Gagné.

11. Readiness to learn should be approached by asking "for what is the child ready?"

12. The concrete-to-abstract continuum has its basis in Bruner's premises and states that a child proceeds along a continuum of levels toward the learning of a mathematical idea.

13. The process of diagnosis when used throughout the planning and implementing of an instructional program in mathematics allows the teacher to provide for the specific needs of the child.

Laboratory 2

What Is Mathematics Education?

Anyone who plans and implements an instructional program in mathematics is a mathematics educator. As such, he or she must be aware of the development of mathematics education, its current thought, and possible future trends in order to provide the most effective instructional program possible for the child.

I. *Objectives:* Upon completion of these laboratory exercises, you should be able to do the following:
   A. Identify factors which have led to changing influences in mathematics education. (Chapter Competency 2–A
   B. State how different thinking about learning has affected mathematics education. (Chapter Competency 2–B)
   C. Describe differing viewpoints of current thought in mathematics education. (Chapter Competency 2–C)

II. *Materials:* None

III. *Procedure:*
   A. Read Chapter 2 of *Helping Children Learn Mathematics.* Consult your instructor if you have any questions.
   B. Three factors were identified in the chapter as influencing mathematics education. Do you think that any of these factors could be eliminated as an influence without jeopardizing the positive effects of the others? Discuss your position with a classmate and then state your thoughts, justifying your position.
   C. Having read about the shifts in emphasis in mathematics education in the past and about the status of mathematics education today, describe the direction(s) *you* would like mathematics education to take in the schools during the next few decades.
   D. Both Bruner and Gagné have influenced mathematics education during the last decade. Identified below are positions taken by each of the two men. Match the position with the appropriate person by placing a G (Gagné) or a B (Bruner) in the blank at the left.

   _____ Guided learning
   _____ Objectives of instruction are capabilities, or behavioral products, specified in operational terms.
   _____ Learning *by discovery*
   _____ Sequence curriculum from the simple to the complex
   _____ Objectives emphasize process, not product.
   _____ Massive transfer from one learning situation to another
   _____ Knowledge is additive.
   _____ Based on associationist-connectionist background

With some classmates, discuss the advantages and disadvantages of both the process- and product-oriented approaches to the learning of mathematics. What do you consider to be the major similarities and differences between the two approaches? Discuss your thoughts with other groups of classmates.

E. Recall that the concrete-to-abstract continuum is a generally accepted sequence to follow in helping children learn mathematics. Knowledge of that continuum can also prove helpful in solving some commonly encountered difficulties in teaching mathematics. Suppose, even at this early stage, that you are confronted with the following situation.

> Johnny consistently works some problems associated with the language dimension of mathematics correctly. For example, he always is able to solve the following types of problems correctly.

$$2 + 6 = \square \qquad 7 + 3 = \bigcirc$$
$$7 - 4 = \triangle \qquad 2 \times 4 = \triangle$$

However, he nearly always misses problems like:

$$2 + \triangle = 8 \qquad 12 - \square = 5$$
$$\square + 7 = 9 \qquad 3 \times \square = 9$$

With a classmate, first try to determine what types of errors are being made and then how you might help the child by using the concrete-to-abstract continuum. Chapter 16 of this text might be helpful.

PART II
Developing Strategies

Teacher Competencies

After studying Part II and completing the laboratories in Part II, you should be able to achieve each of the following:

A. Choose and prepare appropriate goals and objectives for your instructional program in mathematics.

B. Plan instructional strategies to meet determined goals and objectives of your instructional program in mathematics.

C. Design techniques for the use of questions, instructional materials, and the mathematics laboratory to provide individualization in your instructional program in mathematics.

D. Describe the factors that affect classroom management and how these factors can be controlled to provide an effective classroom environment.

E. Describe techniques for selecting various types of instructional materials such as textbooks and games.

3
Goals and Objectives

Teacher Competencies

After studying Chapter 3 and completing Laboratory 3, you should be able to achieve each of the following:

A. Given a selected mathematical concept or skill, write at least one informational objective and at least two instructional objectives for that concept or skill. (Part Competency II-A)

B. Given a verb, state whether or not it denotes an observable behavior. (Part Competency II-A)

C. Given a selected objective, classify it as informational, instructional, or neither. (Part Competency II-A)

One recent trend in education which has had considerable impact on the teaching of elementary school mathematics has been that educators must justify the outcomes of their instructional programs. A first step in justifying these results is to state desired goals and objectives in clear, concise terms.

Distinction should be made between the terms "goals" and "objectives." Goals refer to "the broad aims or outcomes that justify the inclusion of mathematics as a body of knowledge worthy of serious study."[1] These goals may be separated into several different levels, some very specific and others very general in nature. Objectives refer to task goals,[2] tasks that are to be performed by those attempting to reach a goal. We will first discuss goals and then concentrate on objectives.

1. Otto C. Bassler and John R. Kolb, *Learning to Teach Secondary School Mathematics*, p. 61.
2. Ibid.

GOALS

As you think about appropriate goals for your mathematics program, it may be helpful to consider some of the general goals of mathematics instruction. Your philosophy of teaching elementary school mathematics will determine which of the general goals you will choose. It will also be your choice as to how you will implement your chosen goals in your mathematics program.

For purposes of discussion, several authors, including Heathers and Buffie, Welch, and Paige, have classified the goals of mathematics instruction into three general categories: content goals, process goals, and personal-social goals.[3]

Content goals deal basically with the knowledge of the content of elementary school mathematics. This knowledge includes the facts, terminology, classifications, and applications of mathematics: it can be succinctly referred to by the single descriptive word, "information." For many years, these information-centered goals were considered the most important in the mathematics classroom, but a gradual recognition by educators that education is concerned with more than only gaining information has broadened this view and increased the importance of the other goal categories.

Process goals refer to what the student is able to *do* with the information he or she has gained. A popular phrase is that "to learn mathematics, a person must do mathematics"—a statement in which there is much truth, for information gained is of little value until it can be used. The first process goal that probably comes to mind is the development of computational skill. Tool skills traditionally were all that mathematics students practiced with their knowledge. But other processes, such as acquiring, interpreting, evaluating, and communicating mathematical knowledge, are equally important as calculating.

Of all the *personal-social* goals in education, the development of a positive self-concept by the child is perhaps most important. It is the teacher's responsibility to help the child gain a realistic understanding of his strengths and weaknesses and to assist him in the development of positive means for overcoming those weaknesses. The effective mathematics program implements these personal-social goals to help develop the entire individual.

The three classes of goals just described are not distinct from each other. For example, let us examine some statements of goals of elementary school mathematics to learn how they might be classified. Buffie, Welch, and Paige express the goals of elementary school mathematics in the following way:

1. Development of computational facility;
2. Development of mathematical understanding;
3. Development of rational power (including divergent, logical, and creative thinking); and
4. Development of a positive attitude toward mathematics.[4]

These four goals can be classified further. Computational facility and mathematical understanding might be viewed as both content and process goals, while rational power and positive attitude might be viewed as having more emphasis in the process and personal-social goals.

---

3. Edward G. Buffie, Ronald C. Welch, and Donald D. Paige, *Mathematics: Strategies of Teaching,* p. 6.
4. Ibid., pp. 8–12.

In the past, only the development of computational facility was considered important by the teacher of elementary school mathematics. Students devoted almost all of their mathematics instruction time to pursuit of this goal. Gradually, however, the importance of the other three goals has increased.

We have now stated some goals of mathematics instruction. They are necessarily very broad and general statements that reflect the biases of the authors. It is not important that your goals may be somewhat different. What is important is that you carefully examine, state, and continually reassess those goals which you have chosen.

OBJECTIVES

Earlier in this chapter, objectives were defined as task goals. Goals represent broad, general aims of instruction and may be divided into many levels or *subgoals*. These subgoals are statements of tasks that may be performed by those who are attempting to reach a goal; they are referred to as *objectives*.

Objectives are very important to the teacher because they form the basis for the planning of instruction and so, in turn, are the means for achieving desired goals of mathematics instruction. Consequently, it is important to state objectives in clear and concise terms so that the teacher, students, administrators, and lay people will know precisely what is planned. Unstated or poorly stated objectives often lead to confusion and inefficiency in planning and carrying out instructional programs. The result is an undesirable learning situation.

How, then, should objectives be stated? First, there must be *clarity of language*. Suppose you had written the following objectives:

The student should know how to add two whole numbers.

The student should understand the difference between a prime number and a composite number.

Are these objectives stated so that there is no ambiguity in meaning? If your answer is affirmative then it must be assumed that you can define the words *know* and *understand*. Perhaps you can. But will the teacher in the next room or your principal have the same meaning for these words? They probably will not have the same definitions. You may feel that as long as you can define these words, there is no problem. If that is true, then inform all people concerned what your meaning is in the statement of the objective so that there will be no question of meaning. A possible rephrasing of the preceding objectives might be:

The student should be able to compute the sum of any two whole numbers.

Given a whole number greater than one, the student should be able to state whether it is a prime number or a composite number.

Second, objectives should be stated in terms of *observable student behavior*. It is difficult, if not impossible, to determine whether an objective has been achieved if the expected outcomes cannot be observed and hence measured. The sample objectives cited earlier serve also to illustrate this point. For example, the terms *know* and *understand,* in addition to being vague and ambiguous, do not define observable student behavior, while *computing* and *stating* as used in the rephrased objectives are definitive. Observable behavior may occur in different forms: paper-and-pencil work, student action, or oral exchanges. Words such as *know, understand, think,* and *appreciate* do not in themselves describe observable behavior. If, however, an observable behavior is stated as a definition of these terms, then the objective has meaning. For example, if *knowing* means *stating,* then its use would be acceptable.

An additional benefit associated with stating objectives in terms of observable behavior is that the achievement of the objectives may be readily evaluated. Evaluation of pupil performance has too often been less than successful because the evaluation methods used did not reflect the objectives of instruction. This problem was most likely caused because neither the teacher nor the student had a clear knowledge of the desired objective. (The topic of evaluation will be discussed in Chapter 17.)

Finally, objectives should be stated in terms of *what the students are to do* and not what the teacher is to do. Suppose you had written the following objective:

The teacher will explain the addition algorithm for whole numbers.

It is evident what the teacher is to do, but it is not at all clear what the students are to do. The teacher could explain the addition algorithm for whole numbers to an empty classroom; no students need be present. Since it is the students for whom the instruction is designed, the desired outcomes should be stated in terms of their behavior. For example, the preceding objective might be restated in this way:

The child will be able to add two whole numbers with regrouping.

Objectives may be classified into two basic categories: *informational* and *instructional.* An informational objective is one that communicates to other people what is to be accomplished as a result of instruction. This type of objective is characterized by those factors just mentioned: clarity of language, statement in terms of observable behavior, and statement in terms of what the student is to do.

Each informational objective may have associated with it one or more instructional objectives. An instructional objective is an informational objective with two additional features: a statement of conditions under which the observed behavior will occur and the minimum acceptable level of performance.

Consider the following examples of informational and instructional objectives.

Example 1

Informational objective: The student will be able to order a set of whole numbers.

Instructional objectives:
a. Given a sequence of fifteen whole numbers with six of them missing, the student will be able to correctly name at least five of the missing numbers.
b. Given any whole number greater than zero, the student will be able to correctly name the predecessor and successor of that whole number.

Example 2

Informational objective: The student will be able to compute the sum of whole numbers.

Instructional objectives:
a. Given ten pairs of two-digit whole numbers, the student will compute the sum to at least eight of them.
b. Given ten columns of whole numbers with at least three numbers in each column, the student will be able to compute the sum to at least seven of the columns.

Although *stating* the minimum level of acceptable performance is a simple process, *determining* the minimum level or standard is not. On what basis do you decide that a student should be able to solve eight out of ten addition problems correctly? Why shouldn't he have to solve six correctly or all of them? There is little evidence to support particular standards of achievement in mathematics at different grade levels. Hence, you must depend on your own arbitrary judgment in determining the standards as based upon the difficulty of the material, the nature of your student group, and the learning conditions that exist. Although the setting of such standards gives you a rough guideline as to the extent that the objective is being achieved, remember that the standards are arbitrarily set and thus are tentative.

The conditions under which the behavior is to be observed are also arbitrary. They will depend on the nature of the instructional situation; on the instructional materials that are available and appropriate; and on the students themselves. As with the minimum performance levels just discussed, the conditions are also arbitrarily set and tentative in nature.

RELATIONSHIP BETWEEN INFORMATIONAL OBJECTIVES, INSTRUCTIONAL OBJECTIVES, AND GOALS

The diagram which follows clearly shows the relationship between informational and instructional objectives and determined goals. By way of explanation, any chosen goal of mathematics instruction must lead into at least one informational objective. In addition, each informational objective leads into at least one instructional objective. Thus, there is a sequencing for any stated goal of mathematics instruction in terms of informational and instructional objectives associated with the goal.

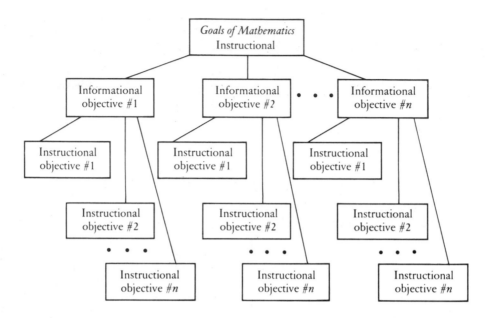

SELECTING APPROPRIATE GOALS AND OBJECTIVES

Now that you have studied the mechanics of writing objectives and have examined how objectives are related to goals, you must be aware of the matter of *teacher expectations*. Because these expectations are of considerable importance to your students, they should be formulated carefully. A student from whom little is expected probably will not disappoint you; he or she will accomplish very little. On the other hand, your expectations may be so high that a student will see no possible way to achieve them and therefore will not try to meet them. Teacher expectations need to be sufficiently high to be appropriate but not so high as to be unattainable. Since a chosen objective may be appropriate for one student but not for another, there may be different objectives for different students in a class. The utilization of varied objectives when appropriate recognizes that students are individuals and that they learn at different rates.

How do you determine the appropriate goals and objectives for *your* teaching situation? This question was alluded to earlier in the chapter when we noted that the nature of your philosophy of mathematics education, of your teaching situation, and of your students would help determine your goals and objectives.

In developing a list of goals and objectives, each teacher must consider three main problems: (1) what goals to select for the mathematics instruction; (2) how to state the objectives in terms that clearly express the outcomes of the program of instruction; and (3) how to select objectives that are pertinent for a particular unit. To this point, we have concentrated on the second problem; in this section, we discuss the other two problems.

Each teacher has his or her own value system which provides guidance in the selection of learning outcomes that are considered most important. Some teachers, for example, may feel that stressing computation is most important while others may feel that stressing critical and logical thinking is most important. Similarly, one teacher may stress form and neatness in written work while another may feel that such stress stifles creativity. Such preferences, or biases, will always to some extent be reflected in the choice of goals and objectives. Thus, we can only suggest procedures that may lead to a list of goals and objectives which are relevant and representative.

Acquiring Ideas for Goals and Objectives

There are many possible sources of goals and objectives of elementary mathematics education. Some of the most useful sources are described in the following paragraphs.

1. *Bloom's Taxonomy of Educational Objectives.*[5] This source describes the taxonomy of educational objectives and describes each category. While it does not specifically cite goals and objectives for elementary school mathematics, it provides an overall view of the wide range of possible learning outcomes. The taxonomy is especially helpful to those teachers who have a tendency to place a major emphasis on memorization of specific facts.

2. *Teacher's guides to text materials:* These sources often contain many ideas for goals and objectives which may be appropriate for those materials.

3. *Scope and sequence charts:* Every teacher of elementary school mathematics should have a thorough knowledge of the scope and sequence of the elementary mathematics curriculum. Such familiarity will suggest the appropriateness of certain goals and objectives at particular grade levels.

4. *Professional materials:* Many professional materials in mathematics education also contain ideas for goals and objectives. Methods books, journals such as *The Arithmetic Teacher,* and *Evaluation in Mathematics,* the Twenty-Sixth Yearbook of the National Council of Teachers of Mathematics, all contain thoughts and ideas on appropriate goals and objectives. A list of possible goals was also expressed earlier in this chapter.

5. *State and local curriculum guides:* Many states and local school systems publish curriculum guides to aid teachers. These guides usually contain suggested goals and objectives which a teacher may use in the design of an instructional program. Some school systems hold their teachers responsible for the goals and objectives in their curriculum guide so the teacher may have more guidance than usual.

6. *Your own philosophy of teaching mathematics:* There is, of course, your own viewpoint as to what goals and objectives are appropriate for your students. This viewpoint and the individual needs of the children will probably undergird the decision as to the final list of goals and objectives of your particular mathematics instructional program.

5. Benjamin S. Bloom, et al., eds., *Taxonomy of Educational Objectives: Cognitive Domain.*

Considerations in Selecting Goals and Objectives

It is usually possible to identify more goals and objectives than can be achieved in a particular period of instruction. The following questions will serve as criteria to determine the adequacy of the goals and objectives to be included.

1. Do the goals and objectives indicate learning outcomes that are appropriate to current philosophy in mathematics education?

To answer this rather difficult question, you must turn to the recommendations of the experts in mathematics education. This review will help indicate which of your goals and objectives receive the greatest support. It will also enable you to avoid any serious omissions and preserve consistency with current thinking in mathematics education.

2. Are the goals and objectives attainable by your students?

To answer this question, you must consider the ability and cultural background of the children for whom the goals and objectives are being developed. Is the group gifted, average, or low ability? Is it a heterogeneous group which will require different objectives for different children? Is the cultural background of the children a relevant factor? Are special facilities needed? It may be necessary to modify some of the goals and objectives to meet the needs of the children.

3. Are the goals and objectives consistent with the philosophy of the school and desires of the community?

Since the child cannot exist in isolation from the rest of the school and the community in which he lives, it is unwise and unfair to place him in a possible conflict situation. This may occur if the goals and objectives of your instructional program differ significantly from those of the school and the community.

4. Are the goals and objectives consistent with basic principles of learning?

Since goals and objectives are stated as learning outcomes, it seems logical to check their consistency with known learning principles. To do this, you must have current knowledge of learning principles in the area of mathematics and consider what is known about such factors as readiness, motivation, transfer of training, and retention.

These questions provide a basis for helping to determine appropriate goals and objectives for your instructional program in mathematics. Such determination of appropriate goals and objectives is the necessary initial step to a successful program of mathematics instruction.

CHAPTER KEY POINTS

1. The success of the instructional program depends to a great degree upon the choice of appropriate goals and objectives. Affecting this choice are considerations such as current thought in mathematics education, the nature of the students involved, the philosophy of the school, and current knowledge of learning principles.

2. Goals are the broad aims of the curriculum while objectives can be defined as "task goals."

3. Goals and objectives of elementary math education can be gleaned from various sources: Teacher's guides, scope and sequence charts, professional materials, state and local curriculum guides, and your own philosophy of teaching mathematics.

4. Objectives must be stated clearly and in terms of observable behavior on the part of the student.

5. Informational objectives are characterized by the statement of some observable student behavior. Instructional objectives are informational objectives which also state the conditions under which the behavior is to be observed and the minimal level of acceptable performance by the student.

Laboratory 3

Goals and Objectives

Every teacher of mathematics must know exactly what he or she wants pupils to be able to do as a result of their learning, from both a long range and a short range point of view. Without purpose or direction, learning is inefficient. The following laboratory exercises have been designed to help you develop appropriate, clearly defined goals and objectives for your mathematics program.

I. *Objectives:* Upon completion of these laboratory exercises, you should be able to do the following:

  A. Given a selected mathematical concept or skill, write at least one informational objective and at least two instructional objectives for that concept or skill. (Chapter Competency 3–A)

  B. Given a verb, state whether or not it denotes an observable behavior. (Chapter Competency 3–B)

  C. Given an objective, classify it as informational, instructional, or neither. (Chapter Competency 3–C)

II. *Materials:* All necessary materials for these exercises are provided for you.

III. *Procedure:*

  A. Read Chapter 3 of *Helping Children Learn Mathematics*. Consult your instructor if you have any questions.

  B. Classify the following objectives as informational (Inf.), instructional (Ins.), or neither (N).

  _____ **1.** The child should be able to count by twos to ten.

  _____ **2.** The child should know basic facts of addition.

  _____ **3.** Given scissors and paper, the child should be able to cut out a triangle, a quadrilateral, and a pentagon and name each correctly.

  _____ **4.** Given ten subtraction problems of two-digit numbers, the child should be able to compute the difference to at least eight of them.

  _____ **5.** The child should appreciate mathematics.

  _____ **6.** The child should be able to give different mathematical names for the number "four."

The correct numbers are:

1. Inf.	**3.** Ins.	**5.** N
2. N	**4.** Ins.	**6.** Inf.

How did you do? If you identified all six objectives correctly, proceed to the next task. If you did not do so, consult your instructor.

C. Rewrite the objectives in the preceding exercise which were classified as neither informational nor instructional so that they are informational objectives. Compare your work with a classmate's. Do you agree?

D. Make a list of at least ten verbs which describe observable mathematical behavior. Show your list to a classmate. Do all of your verbs describe observable behavior? Do you have some verbs that are different from your classmate's list?

E. Write one informational objective and one instructional objective for each of the following concepts or skills.
  1. Area of a circle
  2. Multiplication of two fractions
Have a classmate check your objectives to see if they are stated correctly. If there is disagreement, consult your instructor. If there is no problem, proceed to the next task.

F. Consult the teacher's edition of an elementary text series. Does it state objectives for individual lessons or pages? If so, are the objectives stated as informational objectives? Give examples. If they are not, choose five objectives and rewrite them in the form of an informational objective. Cite the bibliographical information and page numbers for the objectives you have written.

4
Planning to Meet Determined Goals and Objectives

Teacher Competencies

After studying Chapter 4 and completing Laboratory 4, you should be able to achieve each of the following:

A. Given a selected objective, list at least two instructional strategies which might be used to achieve that objective. (Part Competency II-B)

B. Given a selected mathematical concept or skill, prepare a written lesson plan which might be used to achieve a stated objective. (Part Competency II-B)

C. Given a selected objective and an accompanying instructional strategy, state whether that strategy is appropriate to the achievement of the objective and be able to justify your response. (Part Competency II-B)

D. Analyze strengths and weaknesses of a selected lesson plan. (Part Competency II-B)

Once goals and objectives have been decided upon, it is necessary to begin planning strategies to meet them. Yearlong, unit, and daily phases of planning need to be considered.

PLANNING FOR THE YEAR

There are several factors to consider as you begin to plan your mathematics program for the year ahead. Some of these factors are:

1. General goals of mathematics instruction;
2. Local curriculum;
3. Available instructional resources;
4. Pacing of instruction; and
5. Evaluation.

First, consider your own general goals of mathematics education; these may consist of development of a positive attitude, development of computational ability, development of problem-solving skills, development of understanding of mathematical concepts and ideas, and development of logical and creative thinking. Then consider how these goals may be included in your program of instruction. The proper blending of your goals will be different for each of your students because of the children's individuality and different needs.

Also note that an instructional program in mathematics cannot be planned in isolation. Your students will have come to you from other teachers and will go on next year to other teachers. Consequently, there must be some vertical articulation in your program. One possible source of aid is the local curriculum guide. In addition, discussing with your colleagues what your students have already accomplished and what will be expected of them as they progress to the next level of instruction will be very helpful.

Consider, too, available instructional resources. Most schools use at least one basal textbook series; study it carefully because it will contain many useful ideas. However, the text should be used to supplement your program, not to determine it; there is no such rule as "you must cover two pages per day" in mathematics education. Properly used, the text can be of invaluable assistance. Most teacher's manuals which accompany the text offer a variety of ideas for teaching mathematics concepts; take advantage of suggestions appropriate for your situation. In some schools the text is used as the course of study, but an effective teacher of elementary school mathematics will work within this structure to let the text supplement his or her instructional program and, hence, make it more appropriate for the needs of the students.

The text is not the only source of instructional materials. Your school may have many visual and manipulative aids, examples of which will be mentioned throughout Part III. However, if it has none, materials can be developed for classroom use with a little creativity, time, and planning on your part.

Once you have a general idea of the content in your mathematics program and of the facilities available, you can begin to pace your instructional program for the year by first separating it into *units of instruction.* By identifying those units which seem most vital and beginning the year with them, you can avoid the problem of "eight weeks worth of work to do in the last three weeks" which afflicts many teachers. A little preplanning may avoid the difficulty. However, individual student understanding and mastery of content should not be overlooked in the attempt to "cover the material."

Finally, consider the types of evaluation procedures that will be used throughout the year. Evaluation will cover three basic areas: pupil achievement, the effectiveness of your mathematics program, and your effectiveness as a teacher of elementary school mathematics. You will need to examine alternative procedures to evaluate each area. Such alternative means of evaluation will be discussed in Part IV.

As an example of the preceding discussion, let's look at a sample yearlong plan made by Mary Wilson, who is beginning her first year at Burnley School. Her outline is necessarily general, but it should help you follow the points made previously.

Tentative Year Plan

Grade 3—Mary Wilson, Burnley School

1. *Major goals* (not in order of importance)
   a. Develop computational ability.
   b. Develop understanding.
   c. Develop positive attitude.
   d. Develop thinking and problem-solving skills (small group work, lab approach, etc.).

2. *Major topics to be covered* (school curriculum guide)
   a. Place value
   b. Addition and subtraction
   c. Geometry
   d. Multiplication
   e. Division
   f. Measurement
   g. Number theory
   h. Multiples
   i. Fractions

3. *Instructional resources available*
   a. Textbook
   b. Other text materials
   c. Films and filmstrips from school system; check A-V center—must get catalog
   d. Manipulative materials—there aren't many, I need to make more
   e. Resource teacher—Mrs. Adams at the curriculum center
   f. Other third-grade teachers at Burnley School

4. *Tentative yearlong program and approximate time allocated (180 days)*
   a. Assessment of students' present skills and knowledge—3 days
   b. Place value—15 days
   c. Addition and subtraction—30 days
   d. Geometry—20 days
   e. Multiplication—27 days
   f. Measurement—20 days
   g. Annual schoolwide achievement test—5 days
   h. Division—20 days
   i. Fractions—15 days
   j. Number theory—15 days
   k. Multiples—10 days

The topics will basically be in this order although I may split up some of the areas. I also need to get a school calendar and see how I can block these day allocations into it. I may have to revise some of my planning.

5. *Evaluation procedures*
   a. State and assess informational and instructional objectives
   b. Unit performance tests
   c. Pretests for each unit
   d. Daily work
   e. Observation
   f. Oral responses
   g. Daily evaluation of the children, myself, and the classroom activities

Now that the yearlong plan has been discussed and illustrated, let's turn our attention to the unit plan.

UNIT PLANNING

After different units of instruction to be included in your mathematics program have been decided upon, you are ready to begin to plan for each unit. First, decide on your objectives. Stating them in the informational form, discussed in Chapter 3, may be most helpful. For each objective, decide whether your students have the necessary prerequisite skills and knowledge to attain the objective. If the necessary prerequisites have not been fulfilled, either (1) modify your objective or (2) maintain the same objective and help your students achieve the skills or knowledge needed.

Once you have tentatively written your objectives for the unit of instruction and have determined that they are indeed appropriate for your students, construct a pretest covering these objectives. The purpose of this pretest is to determine the extent to which each student can already perform the specified objective, as it would be wasteful to devote instructional time to an objective which the students can already perform. A pretest does not necessarily have to be a timed, paper-and-pencil examination.

Results on the pretest may indicate a need to modify or to delete some of your original objectives. The needs of the student who can achieve most of your objectives will be considerably different from needs of the student who can achieve some or none of the objectives; this difference must affect your planning.

Observation of student work and oral examination may also provide required information. Also, as you become better acquainted with your students and their backgrounds, you can make a tentative, but perhaps adequate, assessment about their levels of competence.

After modifying your unit objectives, sequence them into a meaningful order. This sequencing gives an approximate order of the topics to be covered in the unit and may form a strand of an instructional strategy to be used later. The chosen sequence of topics may differ from the sequence in the text, but this should not be of major concern to you as a teacher. Select only appropriate text materials to supplement your unit.

Now select instructional materials and special activities that may be used in your unit of instruction. Many sources of instructional materials and special activities are available to teachers of elementary school mathematics. Periodicals (such as *Arithmetic Teacher, Grade Teacher,* and *Instructor*), trade books, other teachers, and other textbooks are a few of the multitude of sources available. The National Council of Teachers of Mathematics and various publishers, organizations, and governmental agencies offer free and inexpensive materials to the classroom teacher that may be very beneficial. Also, gather enrichment materials for your unit so that those students who are capable may pursue one or more topics in depth to enhance their knowledge and understanding of the content in the unit.

Finally, consider how you will evaluate the extent to which your students have achieved the unit objectives. Remember that observation and oral examination may reveal as much information as a written test. For many of your objectives, however, you may decide upon written test items. Following rules of good test-item construction and selecting items appropriate to your objectives will help insure that your testing program will be successful.

It is now time for Mary Wilson to think about planning a unit in multiplication. We will follow her through her planning procedure.

Unit on Multiplication (approximately 27 days)
Grade 3—Mary Wilson, Burnley School

A. *Unit objectives*   (with aid of school curriculum guide)
The children should be able to:
1. recognize a simple multiplication situation;
2. identify some multiplication situations;
3. find products using
    a. factors 0–9,
    b. commutative property,
    c. associative property with numbers that are multiples of 10 and 100,
    d. distributive (multiplication over addition) property with factors 0–9 and multiples of 10.

B. *Pretest for unit objectives*
1. Bob has three sets of special issue stamps. Each set has four stamps in it. Draw a diagram to show how many stamps Bob has and write a multiplication sentence which tells how many stamps Bob has. (objective 1)
2. Given $\triangle \triangle \triangle \triangle \triangle \triangle \triangle \triangle$, draw a circle around subsets of two elements. How many subsets are there? Write a multiplication sentence which tells the number of subsets of two elements. (objective 2)
3. Find the products. (objective 3a)

$$4 \times 5 = \underline{\quad} \qquad 2 \times 7 = \underline{\quad}$$
$$3 \times 6 = \underline{\quad} \qquad 8 \times 9 = \underline{\quad}$$

4. Give an example of the commutative property of multiplication. (objective 3b)
5. Use renaming and the associative property to find the product of 3×50. (objective 3c)
6. Show how the distributive property of multiplication over addition may be used to multiply 6×14. (objective 3d)

C. *Activities and materials for the unit*
1. Manipulative materials: pop-bottle caps (to make arrays), Napier's rods, Cuisenaire rods
2. Activities and games

    Enoch Dumas, *Math Activities for Child Involvement* (Boston: Allyn and Bacon, 1971), ch. 4.

    Sylvia Fishback, "We Learn to Multiply," *Instructor* 78, no. 7 (1969): 63–66.

    Leonard Kennedy and Ruth Michon, *Games for Individualizing Mathematics Instruction* (Columbus, Ohio: Charles Merrill, 1973), pp. 59–68.

    Jane Stern, "Counting: New Road to Multiplication," *The Arithmetic Teacher* 16, no. 4 (1968): 31–33.

3. Ideas that I encountered at the workshop at the teacher center last week from Mrs. Bosman, the math supervisor, and Mr. Frye, the resource teacher

D. *Evaluation procedures*
   1. Unit performance test (I may be able to use parts of the test provided in the teacher's manual, but I'll have to wait and see how the students perform.)
   2. Oral examination
   3. Observation of pupil work
   4. Daily work

Note that Ms. Wilson's unit plan is again an outline which she can use in preparation of her daily plans. It contains more detail than the yearlong plan, and as we proceed further we are ready to focus on some daily lessons. First, comments on daily planning are essential.

DAILY PLANNING

It is readily evident that daily contact with your students is the most important of your activities as a teacher of elementary school mathematics. Certainly your effectiveness as a teacher is ultimately judged on the day-by-day activities and progress of your students.

Daily lesson planning (although the lesson may extend into several days) may be accomplished in a variety of ways. Some teachers write in detail what is to be accomplished, while others write nothing but have in mind what they wish to do. Whether you adopt the formal or informal method is your decision, but suffice it to say that the successful teacher of elementary school mathematics is systematic in planning procedures. Although diligent and careful planning does not guarantee the success of a lesson, it will greatly increase its chances for success; careful planning helps to provide the best possible environment for facilitating learning.

Several areas must be considered as you begin your daily planning.

1. *Objectives:* What informational and instructional objective(s) do you want your students to achieve?
2. *Prerequisite skills and knowledge:* What prerequisite skills and knowledge must your students have before embarking on your plan so that there is good chance of success?
3. *Instructional materials:* What instructional materials do you need for your plan?
4. *Approach:* How will you start your lesson? Will it appeal to as many senses as possible? Why will it interest your students?
5. *Procedure:* What sequence of activities will you use for your students?
6. *Evaluation:* How will you determine whether your instructional objective(s) has been achieved?

The importance of identifying objectives, prerequisite skills, and knowledge and instructional materials has already been emphasized and needs no further comment. Evaluation has been discussed briefly with the enumeration of procedures to be discussed in Chapter 17.

Let us now turn our attention to the basis of the lesson plan: the approach and the procedure. The term *instructional strategy* will be used to refer to a combination of these two areas. Why is the instructional strategy so important?

The successful achievement of any instructional objective is dependent upon the success of the instructional strategy, or approach and procedure. The extension and implication of this last statement is that the success of the teacher's goals for the instructional program in mathematics depends directly on the success of the instructional strategy.

The *approach* is important because it "sets the tone" for the lesson; it is the child "motivator." The approach should appeal to as many senses of a child as possible in order to capture their undivided attention. An excellent technique to help accomplish this is to use an approach that actively involves the child. It should be a child-centered situation and not a teacher-centered one.

The *procedure* is important because it "takes off" from the approach and it provides a sequence of steps designed to lead the child to achievement of the objective(s). As such, the instructional strategy which is chosen by the teacher is crucial to the success of the lesson.

How do you choose an instructional strategy? The first step is to identify alternative strategies that could be used, even though many teachers use one instructional strategy—the one found in the textbook.

There are basically two sources for identifying alternative instructional strategies. One is to generate them yourself; the other is to investigate ideas that other people have already developed. Two examples may be helpful at this point.

Example 1

Ms. Johnson is about to introduce a unit on measurement in her first-grade class. She decides that one of the objectives of her unit will be:

> The child should be able to make simple linear measurements in inches, feet, yards, centimeters, and meters.

As she considers possible strategies, she begins to ask questions based upon her teaching experience and mathematical background. Some of these questions are:

1. Should I begin with the English measurements and let the children work until they master those before I introduce the metric measurements?
2. Should I introduce the metric measurements before I introduce the English measurements?
3. Should I introduce the two simultaneously using rulers that have both scales on them?
4. Should I talk about general differences before they use a ruler, or should I let them measure lengths before I discuss the measurement systems?

This list of questions is by no means exhaustive, but it is sufficient to illustrate the point that each question requires Ms. Johnson to make a decision about the point raised in the question. Hence, she is making decisions on the best strategy which she could use to achieve the objective.

Do you feel that you are not creative enough to generate a large number of alternatives? Classroom experience may help but in the meantime, you need some help. Let's consider what Mr. Thompson, a first-year teacher, might do.

Example 2

Mr. Thompson is planning a unit on numeration for his sixth-grade class. He is particularly concerned with the topic of other number bases and is dissatisfied with the approach taken in his textbook. His unit objective is:

The child should be able to express base ten numerals in other number bases and vice versa.

In an effort to obtain some alternative strategies, Mr. Thompson turns to other sources.

1. *Another text:* This text suggests that the students should work at the process of converting from base ten to another base and then immediately back to base ten. Sufficient practice will achieve the objective.
2. *An experienced colleague:* Mrs. Mayo suggests that the meaning of the numbers in other bases be stressed before any attempt is made to convert from one base to another.
3. *The mathematics supervisor:* She suggests that other bases should be studied from the standpoint of counting in that base and then proceed to conversion.
4. *A professional journal.* The journal suggests the use of Dienes blocks to actually manipulate the change and then proceed to the conversion from one base to another.

After examining the various alternatives, Mr. Thompson decides on the strategy suggested by the professional journal. He feels that the concrete manipulation is necessary for his students to begin successfully with other number bases.

As you can see by the preceding examples, there are many sources to the acquisition of alternative instructional strategies. A feeling of insecurity should not hinder you as you seek alternative strategies.

Once the alternative instructional strategies have been gathered, the next step is to select the one that seems most suitable for your classroom situation. Three factors will affect your choice: (1) your goals and objectives, (2) the nature of your students, and (3) you, the teacher. For example, some strategies are appropriate for one set of goals and not for others. One strategy may be best for your content goals, while another may be the best one for your process goals. Some students may need to work with concrete materials, while others may be able to work at a higher level. Recall in Example 2 that it was this later consideration that caused Mr. Thompson to choose the instructional strategy that he found in the professional journal.

Finally, you should choose a strategy that you will find comfortable to use. It should be one that you can be enthusiastic about implementing.

Of course, there is always the possibility that the instructional strategy which you have chosen may not work when you actually apply it. Having alternative strategies at your disposal in case of emergency may enable you to salvage a lesson that appeared inadequate.

Let us turn now to a discussion of different types of lesson plans. There are basically two different types. The first kind is characterized by the fact that the teacher coordinated the entire plan. Ideas for the objective(s) and instructional strategy may have been generated elsewhere, but the teacher has adapted them to a unique situation. It is written out in considerable detail, and it considers relevant factors such as those mentioned earlier in this section. Writing such plans is not easy, but the benefits of so doing will evidence themselves as the lesson is implemented.

As an example of the points just made, consider the plan which follows. Do you feel that this plan could be implemented? Why?

Geometry Lesson for Grade 3

Objective: Given the geometric shape, the child will be able to state orally at least two of the basic characteristics of the square, triangle, and rectangle. (I believe I will be able to accomplish all three since this will be a review of materials they had last year.)

Prerequisite skills and knowledge: Familiarity with the square, triangle, and rectangle.

Materials: 3–6 shoe boxes; geometric shapes including square, rectangle, and triangle which may be made of wood, cardboard, or plastic.

Approach: Give each group a shoe box containing one shape. There will be a hole cut in one end in which they can place their hands. They may not look, but may feel the object and describe it. The object in each box will be given a hypothetical name.

Procedure: After all students have had an opportunity to examine the boxes I will ask each group to tell me what is in their box. I will pretend to not understand terms such as the names of the shapes, and they must tell me how I can draw a replica of each mystery item on the board. Through their explanations I will search for such terms as line segment, point, and angle. If one group has difficulty, I will allow another group to examine their geometric object and help them out. I do not plan to go too deeply into each shape, but I will use these results to show me where the class seems to be weak.

Evaluation: Did the child use the terms correctly: line segment, point, angle, and right or square angle. Was he able to describe clearly the object in the box? Did his answers indicate knowledge of the characteristics of each object?

The second type of lesson plan is characterized by the use of a previously prepared lesson plan found in the teacher's manuals of any elementary mathematics text series. This type of plan requires that very little planning needs to be written by the teacher; everything is already basically done so that the teacher needs only to implement, or vary slightly, what is available. You should consult a teacher's manual to examine the points made earlier. In what instances might a teacher decide to use such a previously prepared plan?

But what if the teacher wants to vary instruction within his or her classroom to accommodate individual differences? The writing of the multilevel teaching plan must differ to some extent from both the original plan that was illustrated and the plan that you examined in a teacher's manual. Still, some elements of each plan might remain, with the addition of some classroom reorganization notes. To explain, as small groups are identified, they might be set to work using materials which have been designed by their teacher especially for them or which have instead been selected for them from a wide range of professionally prepared materials. In essence, the teacher is preparing "mini-lessons," each requiring an objective, a procedure, and a method for evaluation. Of course, the teacher with a variety of material and a wide experiential background will be better prepared for this task than a first-year teacher who is not familiar with the materials available in the resource center. As always, though, there must be a beginning, and each packet of materials drawn together to meet a specified objective might be one less that needs to be prepared next year.

Whether these "mini-lesson" plans are original or previously prepared, however, the overall multilevel plan should contain organizational reminders for the teacher. To illustrate, let us examine some planning notes that an experienced teacher might make relative to the following situation.

Situation: Joyce Green, an experienced teacher, is working with a group of immature nine-year-old children whose grade level achievement ranges from 2.5 to 3.5. Although her class consists of only fourteen children, the techniques which she incorporates may be used with much larger groups. Multiplication and division were introduced to the entire group simultaneously about three weeks ago. The children, having exhibited wide ranges of interests and abilities, have come to be grouped today in this manner.

Planning notes made by Ms. Green: Basically, five groups have identified themselves within my classroom. One group is progressing well with multiplication by hundreds; another group needs work on multiplication by tens (and they could use some practice on basic facts); three children still do not grasp the fundamental use and value of the distributive principle; a few children need to practice basic facts to five and to use multiplication and division in problem situations; and two of my pupils still do not understand the underlying relationship between multiplication and division. A single-level plan would only serve to bore or to frustrate at least several members of the class; therefore, I will plan activities for each group.

So that each child will know exactly what he or she is to do in mathematics for the day, I will make a short list of activities for the children in each group. As they accomplish the first activity on the list satisfactorily, they may proceed to the second, and so on. The written work they do, which is not self-checking, will be placed in the "in" basket as usual for checking, and the manipulative activities will be checked in class. (Note that the groups which Ms. Green identified were not assigned labels, nor are the groups static. She believes that a child who always belongs to a given group, identified as Group E or the Canaries, can experience more problems than necessary. This does not, however, preclude her privately coding groups for a given day to help her plan her activities.)

Classroom organizational plan made by Ms. Green: After a check of possible materials and activities to meet her pupils' needs, Ms. Green may sketch the multilevel classroom organizational plan shown in Figure 1, page 63.

Although the activities are only briefly described in the Figure 1 sketch, Ms. Green must have the actual materials and directions needed by each of her groups ready to use. She will have, in effect, five "mini-lessons" planned. By the time class begins, Ms. Green will have collected audiotapes and a recorder (Group 4) and two programmed texts (Group 1) from the resource center collection. The "Old Product" card game (Group 2) was one which she had made last year and so was already available. The number lines (Group 5) were commercially made and had been taped to each child's desk. The array charts (Group 3) had been made by the children during initial work with the distributive principle. The only new material Ms. Green had to prepare was a ditto to direct the number line activity. Remember, though, that she also had to prepare lists of activities for the groups, as described earlier. Her activity during class will be to direct the work with array cards and then to do "spot-checks" on the progress of other children.

Generally, then, although the extent of her planning was directly proportional to the number of groups, Ms. Green actually was involved in a minimum of original lesson-planning activity in this particular multiplan. Most of her work for this lesson related to the identification of group needs and the collection of appropriate materials and activities.

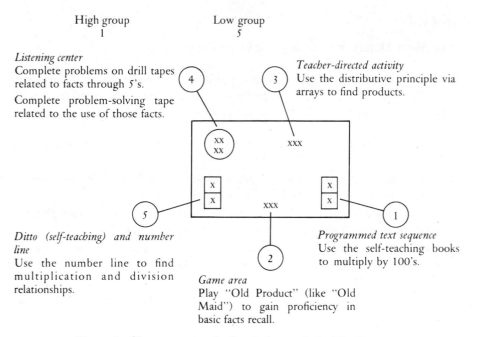

High group
1

Low group
5

Listening center
Complete problems on drill tapes related to facts through 5's.

Complete problem-solving tape related to the use of those facts.

Teacher-directed activity
Use the distributive principle via arrays to find products.

Ditto (self-teaching) and number line
Use the number line to find multiplication and division relationships.

Game area
Play "Old Product" (like "Old Maid") to gain proficiency in basic facts recall.

Programmed text sequence
Use the self-teaching books to multiply by 100's.

Figure 1. Classroom organizational plan made by Ms. Green.

CHAPTER KEY POINTS

1. Some factors to consider in planning a mathematics program for the year are:
   a. General goals of mathematics instruction;
   b. Local curriculum;
   c. Available instructional resources;
   d. Pacing of instruction; and
   e. Evaluation.

2. Unit planning involves stating your objectives and deciding if the students have the necessary prerequisite skills, constructing a pretest, sequencing unit objectives, selecting appropriate text materials, instructional aids and special activities to be used, and finally determining the evaluation procedures to be used.

3. Instructional strategy, the basis of the daily lesson plan, contains the approach and the procedure to be used. The approach should appeal to as many of the senses of the child as possible and the procedure is the sequence of steps designed to lead the child to the achievement of the objective.

4. The types of lesson plans that may be used include: original (the teacher plans the entire lesson); previously prepared (the teacher uses the basic plan in the teacher's manual); and multi-level (teacher plans several different group activities at a time).

5. Three factors affect the choice of instructional strategies: (1) goals and objectives, (2) the nature of the students, and (3) the teacher.

Laboratory 4

Planning to Meet Determined Goals and Objectives

Effective planning is a vital part of the success of any instructional program in elementary school mathematics. Without it, a program will probably fail. The following exercises should help you be more effective in planning at all three levels: yearlong, unit, and daily.

I. *Objectives:* Upon completion of these laboratory exercises, you should be able to do the following:

   A. Given a selected objective, list at least two instructional strategies which might be used to achieve the objective. (Chapter Competency 4–A)

   B. Given a selected mathematical concept or skill, prepare a written lesson plan which might be used to achieve a stated objective. (Chapter Competency 4–B)

   C. Given a selected objective and an accompanying instructional strategy, state whether that strategy is appropriate to the achievement of the objective and be able to justify your response. (Chapter Competency 4–C)

   D. Analyze strengths and weaknesses of a previously prepared lesson plan. (Chapter Competency 4–D)

II. *Materials:* none

III. *Procedure:*

   A. Read Chapter 4 of *Helping Children Learn Mathematics*. If you have any questions, consult your instructor.

   B. Are each of the following instructional strategies appropriate for the stated objectives? Why or why not? If the objective is not properly stated, rewrite it and then make a judgment about the strategy.

   Check your responses with a classmate. If you disagree, consult your instructor.

   1. Grade Level: 2

   Objective: Given a worksheet with ten curves, the student will be able to label those that are open and those that are closed with 100 percent accuracy.

   Approach and procedure: Briefly review the difference between a straight line and a curved line. Then choose seven students. Have them clasp hands and form a ring around you. Ask the others if they think you (the teacher) can get out of the ring without going over, under, or breaking through. Then have two of the students unclasp hands and ask if they think you can get out now. They will be able to see the difference between the open and closed formations.

   Have the students look around the room to see if there are any open or closed figures. For closed, they might list the clock, chalkboard, or desktop.

   Then pass out construction paper, paste, and string. Ask the students to make one open figure and one closed figure using their materials.

2. Grade Level: 3

Objectives: To develop the understanding that when more than two numbers are added, the way in which they are added does not change the sum; to develop the concept that addition is a binary operation.

Approach and procedure: Review the basic addition facts and apply the knowledge to concrete examples. Review the idea of set.

Develop the idea that when two or more numbers are combined, the sequence in which they are combined does not change the sum. Have one or more children prove the answer with concrete materials.

C. Study other student lesson plans found in the supplement to this laboratory. What are the strengths and weaknesses of each, judged in terms of what you have read in Chapters 3 and 4? Consult with several classmates. On what points do you agree or disagree? Consult your instructor if you need help.

D. For each of the following objectives, outline briefly two instructional strategies which might be used to achieve this objective. Check your strategies with a classmate. Do the strategies seem appropriate? If you have questions, consult your instructor.

    1. The child should be able to measure a given angle with a protractor.

    2. The child should be able to compute the product of any two 2–digit whole numbers.

Optional: You are now ready to try planning and teaching a lesson of your own. Ask the teacher with whom you are working in your field experience to suggest a topic or skill which you could help a small group of children (6–8) learn. Prepare a written lesson plan considering the factors discussed in Chapters 3 and 4 of *Helping Children Learn Mathematics* and using the format suggested in Chapter 4. Instead of one, however, list three instructional strategies that might be used. Indicate which one you think is best.

Type the lesson plan for duplication for other members of the class. In addition to the six areas discussed in the section on daily planning, include a brief description of your teaching situation, the grade level, and the content area of your lesson plan.

Finally, prepare a one-page, typed critique of your lesson plan after your implementation, citing strengths and weaknesses. A copy should be given to both your cooperating classroom teacher and your instructor, but it will not be duplicated for the rest of the class.

Supplement: Lesson Plan I

Addition of Fractions

Grade Level: 3

A. *Objective:* Given ten pairs of fractions with each pair containing the same denominator and the answer not greater than one, the student will compute the correct sum to at least eight of the problems.

B. *Materials:* Number line. Cuisenaire rods, chalkboard, pencil and paper

C. *Prerequisite skills:* The student must have knowledge of the basic facts in addition with one- and two-digit numbers and have worked with and shown competency with basic facts, number line, and Cuisenaire rods. The student will have had lessons explaining fractions and equivalent parts and have shown competency in this area.

D. *Approach:* Review the use of the number line and Cuisenaire rods. Explain that fractions can be added using the number line and Cuisenaire rods just as whole numbers can be added using these devices.

E. *Procedure:* Place fractions with the same denominator on the number line. Show students that the same procedure is used in adding fractions as in adding whole numbers. Add two fractions using the number line, and stress the fact that when adding fractions the bottom number or denominator always remains the same and the top numbers or numerators are to be added. Students may work with the number line on the board or at their desks. If further explanation or practice is needed, the Cuisenaire rods may be used or figures may be drawn on the board.

F. *Evaluation:* The lesson will be evaluated by class participation and interest. A worksheet will be given containing ten problems with an expected competency of at least eight of the ten problems. Since this is an introductory lesson, the students may use the number line and Cuisenaire rods to solve these problems.

Supplement: Lesson Plan II

Introduction to Sets

Grade Level: Primary

A. *Informational objective:* To explain the definition of a set and familiarize the student with symbols used in describing sets.

B. *Instructional objective:* Students should have a clear understanding of sets and symbols representing sets, and also be able to group objects into sets.

C. *Materials:* Several black and white cloth objects, a bag containing spools, cans, blocks, and silverware

D. *Approach:* Give a verbal explanation of the definition of sets, and indicate on the chalkboard the symbols that represent sets. Use the materials to provide practice in identifying sets of items.

E. *Procedure:*
   1. Definition of a set
   2. Criteria for determining which objects belong or do not belong to a set
   3. Introduction of symbols used in denoting sets: $\epsilon, \{\ \} \ . \ . \ ., \subset)$
   4. Examples of how the symbols are used
   5. Explanation of the empty set
   6. Explanation of subsets
   7. Questions and answers

F. *Evaluation:* Students should complete exercises individually on page 45 in your text, during remaining class time. You should circulate the classroom, offering help where it is needed.

Supplement: Lesson Plan III

Operations and Properties of Rational Numbers

Grade Level: 5

A. *Informational objective:* Inform the students how to construct rational numbers in classes of ordered pairs of integers.

B. *Instructional objective:* The students will represent a given positive rational number using decimals, mixed numerals, and percent.

C. *Materials:* Straight edge, ruler, pencil and paper, use of chalkboard and book

D. *Approach:* Have students read the material at the beginning of each section. Then give them an opportunity to discuss the ideas presented.

E. *Procedure:* Introduce the set of rational numbers as the set of fractional numbers and their opposite. Also introduce zero as the additive identity for the set of rational numbers.

F. *Evaluation:* Class participation and oral response. Worksheets could also be used to help evaluate the students.

Supplement: Lesson Plan IV

Sets, Numbers, and Numerals

Kindergarten Level

A. *Objective:* The child will be able to recognize the numerals 4, 5, and 6 and their values through the use of sets.

B. *Materials:* None

C. *Prerequisite skills:* The children will have already been introduced to the numerals 1, 2, and 3, and have the knowledge of what "element" is and what a set consists of.

D. *Approach:* You could start with a story in which the numerals 1–6 are "hidden" in the picture. The children should easily recognize the numerals 1, 2, and 3 from the previous lesson. Hint that there are three new numbers hidden, and let them find them.

E. *Procedure:*

   1. After the approach has been initiated, briefly review numerals 1, 2, and 3 with regard to their respective shapes and set elements.

   2. Introduce 4, 5, and 6 on the board large enough for all to see. Have the children draw 4, 5, and 6 in the air to get the feel of the numerals; then have them practice on paper. Have available some tactile reinforcements, e.g., sandpaper cards for those who have problems in making the numerals.

   3. Ask the children to name some sets that have 4, 5, and 6 elements contained in them.

   4. After 4, 5, and 6 have been introduced, let the children explore sets by themselves. Give each child paper and crayons, and tell them to illustrate two sets of 4, 5, and 6 objects. For those children who do not have a clear abstract notion of what 4, 5, and 6 are, manipulative objects will be made available for their use to serve as concrete examples.

F. *Evaluation:* You will observe each child's ability to form sets of 4, 5, and 6. The children should be able to complete the drawings. Should a child fail to complete these drawings due only to the element of time but he has demonstrated a clear understanding of the concepts involved, the latter should be weighted more heavily than the former in evaluating the child's ability. At the conclusion of this lesson each child should have experienced "four-ness," "five-ness," and "six-ness." They should be able to equate these experiences with the actual numerals.

5
Effective Classroom Environment and Management

Teacher Competencies

After studying Chapter 5 and completing Laboratory 5, you should be able to achieve each of the following:

    A. Classify questions as open-ended or closed. (Part Competency II-A)

    B. Classify questions as cognitive-memory, convergent, divergent, or evaluative. (Part Competency II-A)

    C. Given a selected mathematical concept or skill, write examples of each of the four levels of questions (cognitive-memory, convergent, divergent, and evaluative) which might be used in helping a child learn that concept or skill. (Part Competency II-A)

    D. Classify selected instructional materials as concrete, semiconcrete, or abstract in nature. (Part Competency II-A)

    E. Given a selected objective, list instructional materials that might be used to achieve that objective at each of the three levels: concrete, semiconcrete, and abstract. (Part Competency II-A)

    F. Prepare instructional materials and state how they might be used in the classroom. (Part Competency II-A)

    G. Given a selected objective, design a laboratory activity which may be used as an initial learning experience for that objective. (Part Competency II-A)

    H. Design a set of activity cards which may be used in the classroom and are appropriate for a specified level of instruction. (Part Competency II-A)

    I. Given a selected objective, determine whether or not the use of a game is appropriate as an instructional strategy and, if so, choose a game (commercial or teacher-made) which might be used. (Part Competency II-A)

    J. Design techniques for the selection of various types of instructional materials. (Part Competency II-E)

    K. Describe characteristics of various types of atypical learners and design instructional strategies and materials to meet their needs. (Part Competency II-B)

    L. Describe factors that affect classroom management and how these factors can be controlled to provide an effective classroom environment. (Part Competency II-D)

To this point in the book, we have discussed the necessary planning that must be accomplished *before* the teacher enters the classroom. However, this pre-entry planning will only have been successful *if* the implementation of the plan is successful. In this chapter, then, we will discuss implementation considerations.

    For our discussion, we will split the considerations into the major areas of instruction and management. It should be recognized, however, that these two areas are highly interactive with each other and must be considered concomitantly by the classroom teacher.

    Instructional considerations involve both teaching strategies and the use of supplementary teaching materials. In this section, we will examine both areas.

    In the area of teaching strategies, we will discuss the laboratory and expository approaches to teaching, the use of questioning techniques and the atypical learner. Another useful strategy, diagnosis and correction, is discussed in Chapter 16.

    In the area of supplementary teaching materials, we will discuss the selection and use of materials which have been classified according to the appropriate level of learning described in Chapter 2. Because of their unique nature, games will be discussed separately. The selection and use of two particularly popular teaching aids, hand-held calculators and microcomputers, are discussed in Chapter 14.

TEACHING STRATEGIES CONSIDERATIONS

The Laboratory Approach

A teaching technique which has received considerable attention among mathematics educators and elementary teachers especially during the past five years has been the laboratory approach. This technique is not really new; evidence of the use of laboratory situations in mathematics in schools has been recorded in the diaries of Johann Heinrich Pestalozzi and Frederick Froebel, educators of the mid-nineteenth century.

    We prefer to describe the mathematics laboratory as the organization of learning experiences which are designed to achieve some desired objective(s) and which feature child involvement. Labs may involve a great amount of independent discovery by the child or they may primarily involve guided discovery. Guided discovery activities are probably more effective in most classroom situations than independent discovery activities.

    The importance of child involvement cannot be overemphasized. A child who is involved in the planning of and execution of learning experiences designed for him or her finds learning meaningful and alive; exclusion from involvement may result in failure to achieve the desired objective(s). Incorporation of this technique by the elementary teacher requires much hard work and organization, but the results in terms of student progress will be worth the effort. In the following sections, we point out some of the advantages associated with a math lab, discuss some of its problems, and describe factors associated with setting up and operating a mathematics laboratory.

Advantages of the Math Lab.   There are several advantages associated with the math lab. First, it provides an opportunity for children to become involved and to find that learning mathematics is fun and not a boring and tedious chore. Second, the math lab offers an opportunity for mathematics to "come alive" and for children to see the positive relationship between mathematics and everyday life. Thirdly, it provides opportunities for encouragement of creativity and development of social skills necessary for future use.

The math lab also affords many opportunities for children to enjoy success in learning experiences. Many children become low achievers and discipline problems because they are frustrated at constant failure. Activities designed for these particular children help remove this frustration and provide an excellent way to begin individualizing instruction.

The laboratory situation also enables children to "learn by doing." The desirability of this fact seems obvious. Appropriate at this point is the old Chinese proverb, "I hear and I forget; I see and I remember; I do and I understand." It is this kind of understanding that we as mathematics educators are pursuing for our students.

As a teaching technique the math lab should not stand alone. It is most effective when used in conjunction with other teaching techniques. There is not enough time for all children to discover all facets of mathematics, nor is it necessarily desirable to discover everything. There are times when it is most effective for the teacher simply to tell the children what they are to learn. Each teacher, then, must determine how to use the laboratory approach most effectively to help his or her students learn mathematics.

Potential Problems with a Math Lab.   Critics of the laboratory approach have cited several problems associated with the technique. By itself it will most likely not meet all the needs of the children or of the classroom teacher. When utilized in conjunction with other approaches, however, it can be very effective.

Cost is often cited as a problem. It is true that any teacher could spend vast sums of money on commercial materials, but you and your children can become "scroungers." It is surprising what can be collected with just a little effort and time. There is an added benefit to collection by your students in that their participation involves them in *creating* learning experiences. A sometimes-heard complaint among children, when working with commercial materials, is that they do not feel that the materials "belong to them." Collecting materials will help them to overcome this feeling, and the actual expense will be much less.

Another problem associated with a math lab is the storage of materials. Many classrooms have storage closets which may be utilized. If such facilities do not exist, then a corner may be the only solution. In either case, small boxes such as shoe boxes can be used to store materials. These boxes should be easily accessible, carefully labeled, and stored in the same place each time.

A third possible problem may occur in the definition of the role of the teacher in the math lab situation. The teacher must assume a role not central in the learning experience. He or she must have sufficient insight to know when to act as a silent partner, when to ask questions, and when to withdraw completely from the learning situation.

It is also important to remember that not all children will be able to work effectively in the laboratory situation. Since some children need to work in a very highly structured situation, the teacher must recognize and provide for this difference.

Finally, a major problem concerns the matter of selection and management of groups. Grouping is a procedure used by the classroom teacher to help solve the problem of individual differences. Widespread discussion and disagreement occurs among mathematics educators as to what method of grouping is best, and there is probably little chance of resolving the question. Suffice it to say that every teacher ought to use grouping in the classroom to some degree, along with the traditional method of the same instruction for the entire class.

When the terms "groups" and "grouping" are mentioned to many teachers, they immediately think of ability, a criterion often determined through the use of test scores to separate children into groups for purposes of instruction. It should be noted, however, that there is little conclusive research to indicate that grouping by ability is a better method than other grouping procedures. In fact, inflexibility of movement of children from one group to another has been cited as a major problem with ability grouping.

A method of grouping which has not been as popular as ability grouping, but which can be quite helpful, is the grouping of children in terms of a common need such as the attainment of some desired objective. Use of this method implies frequent regrouping, a fact which causes some teachers to hesitate to use it. It requires a continual and careful evaluation of each child's progress in order to meet individual needs. Perhaps the logistics of such a procedure seem overwhelming; this is understandable. Experimentation accompanied by a little patience, however, may prove the key to successful implementation of this method of grouping.

A third method of grouping is by interest, either peer or academic, on the part of the child. Examples of such interest groupings might include learning to play chess or studying early man's numeration systems. Teachers are often hesitant to use this method because of its seemingly inherent problems. But, as a change of pace and with proper direction from the teacher, this method may prove quite acceptable.

The problems associated with material cost and storage, teacher-learner characteristics, and group selection and management may cause you to consider rejection of the laboratory approach. However, the advantages of the laboratory, as related to the goal of more effective instruction in mathematics, would seem sufficiently significant to warrant a serial effort on your part to incorporate this technique as one of your instructional strategies.

The Math Lab in Your Classroom.   If you have decided that you would like to use a mathematics laboratory in your classroom, you must consider several points. A successful laboratory requires careful planning and implementation of activities in order to maximize the benefits to your students.

A gradual start will probably provide the most successful results. Both you and your students need to proceed slowly since working in such a situation is likely to be new, at least to them. Begin by spending a small amount of time periodically developing the format which will be used during the laboratory sessions. As the students become more proficient in working in the laboratory setting, the time spent there can be gradually increased until it reaches the time period which you have allotted for laboratory activities.

Since there does not seem to be an optimum amount of time which should be spent by students in a laboratory situation, the time which you allot will depend on the needs of your students and your own desires. As a basic rule, however, each lab period should last approximately an hour, and the total amount of instruction time devoted to the mathematics laboratory should not exceed 60 to 70 percent of the time for your more capable students and somewhat less for the less capable students. Experimentation on your part will soon indicate the appropriate amount of time which you should use in working with laboratory activities.

Since most children will not have worked in a mathematics laboratory before, one of your first tasks will be to instruct your students in the laboratory method, or how to work meaningfully in a laboratory situation. A child will be better able to solve problems presented to him in a laboratory situation if he first has an opportunity to work on skills which may be needed. What are some of these skills?

First, the child should work on identifying the problem. He should be encouraged to think about a situation which is to be explored; he should ask questions which lead to the identification of one or more problems associated with the given situation. At first the questions will probably be vague and not yield much information. But just as you study questioning in the latter part of this chapter and its corresponding laboratory exercises, so should your students work to improve their questioning skills. As the child thinks about the situation with which he is confronted, he should ask questions such as these: How do I see the situation described here? What questions are raised by the situation? Is the situation like one which I have solved before? What kind of solution am I looking for? What kind of data will I collect? How will I know whether or not my solution makes sense? These questions and others help to develop problem-solving skills; their use should be strongly encouraged.

Second, the child should work on finding ways to attack the found problems and decide on those ways which seem most likely to bring about a solution to the problem. Unfortunately, typical exercises in textbooks do not provide encouragement of different methods. Problems in the same section are usually designed to be solved with a single method, and so the student is not encouraged to seek different methods. Therefore, you must exert extra effort in helping your children find different ways to attack a problem. "Brainstorming" is a good technique, and the laboratory provides an excellent place to encourage such activity. You can give much encouragement here, by positively reinforcing good suggestions from the students.

After one or more methods for attacking the problem have been determined, the child should proceed to implement the chosen "plan of attack." During that implementation the child may realize that the plan may need revision or a complete change. In the latter case, the procedure just described may need to be repeated in order to solve the problem.

A final step is that of evaluating results and drawing conclusions. Again, the student should be encouraged to question himself: Have the questions raised in the problem been answered? Did I find what I expected or was it totally different? Are the results going to be true for similar situations?

The mathematics laboratory offers a situation in which the child can practice the four areas just mentioned. Such practice is vital in the development of the thinking process in each child, and you, as teacher, should strongly encourage it.

Basically two physical situations exist when attempting to set up a math lab. One is to have a separate room for such activities; the other is to have only the regular classroom available. The latter situation is probably more prevalent.

If a separate room is available, all of the supplies and materials can be stored there. Many options are available for storage of materials, but whatever option you choose, keep the materials easily accessible and in the same place. It may be possible to buy or build cabinets and shelves in which to store items. If tables are not available for work space, push several desks together and place a piece of drywall or plywood on top. The floor can be used, if needed.

Depending on the needs of the children and the mathematics instructional program, the room may be used two or three times each week. A double period (or back-to-back periods) offers an opportunity for children to have ample time to explore and solve problems. When other teachers wish to use the room for math lab activities, a schedule for the room's use becomes imperative. Even though several teachers may use the lab, it is best to have one person responsible for the inventory of materials and supplies and the replacement of needed items.

A lab assistant can prove very helpful in the inventory and replacement tasks. This person could be a teacher aide, a parent, or even an older child. His or her function would be to hand out and collect materials, thereby enabling the regular teacher to assist the students in working with the laboratory activities.

If a separate room is not available, a math lab may be set up in the regular classroom. Earlier comments about storage and physical facilities also apply in this situation. Again, the use of a lab assistant would be desirable. A distinct advantage to having the math lab in the regular classroom is that the lab can be set up and used at any desired time, whereas with a separate room the lab can occur only at certain times. This additional flexibility may be very helpful because children can work on lab activities at any time during the day when finished with other assigned tasks.

A multitude of activities may be used in the mathematics laboratory. Still, however, you must gather and modify the activities in order to serve your purposes in the best possible way.

An excellent source for ideas is the children themselves. Finding and developing problems which are of interest to them may provide many stimulating and useful sessions in the laboratory; indeed, this technique should not be limited only to the laboratory situation but should be employed often in other learning experiences.

Your own creativity may also be a source. Making use of past experience with children and using your own ideas which may be "offshoots" of those of the students can provide many excellent activities. Your colleagues provide another source of ideas. Since many of their ideas have already been tried, you will benefit from their experiences.

Professional publications are a source of math lab activities, also. In recent years, periodicals such as *The Arithmetic Teacher, Instructor,* and *Grade Teacher* have contained math laboratory ideas, most of which have been tried in the classroom. Several publishing companies have also produced books of laboratory activities which may be used in the classroom. These books include *Cloudburst of Math Lab Experiments,* by Donald Buckeye, et al.; *The Laboratory Approach to Mathematics,* by Kenneth P. Kidd, et al.; and *The Mathematics Laboratory: Theory to Practice,* by Robert E. Reys and Thomas R. Post.

The out-of-doors can be considered both as a source of laboratory activities and as a setting for your laboratory. Such activities as making a sundial to tell time or examining a fallen leaf for properties of symmetry, area, and perimeter provide interesting activities for children.

In order to maximize the effectiveness of the mathematics laboratory and to avoid confusion in conducting the lab, you must engage in careful day-by-day planning, the importance of which was emphasized in Chapter 4.

There are several ways in which you can conduct the laboratory; you may wish to try different ways to see which works most successfully for your situation. Initially, while the students are learning to work with the laboratory method, you may need to use the technique of teacher demonstration with all of the students handling identical materials. Your role here, however, is not one of total dominance. You are only helping the students to formulate problems, to help them attack the problems at hand, and to ask questions about the problem that will help stimulate each student's thinking. There will be a point, however, when the children begin to exhibit independent, responsible behavior; you may then put them on their own to explore collectively, in small groups, or individually certain aspects of the problem.

You may also conduct lab sessions in which the entire class is working on the same problem with identical materials but in which your only role is to assist with problem areas. Each child is free to consult with others or to work by himself on open-ended questions which he himself has posed or which have been posed for him.

A third method is to have the students working in teams on different problems. For this purpose, you may wish to utilize *activity cards* (also called assignment, task, work, or job cards). These are simply cards on which a problem and open-ended questions about the problem are stated. The cards provide the basis for a problem-solving session by a single student or by a group of students who have decided to seek a solution.

Activity cards are always designed to have the students perform some task. The questions require them to collect data, organize it into a table or some other meaningful form, and interpret the data to answer the question(s) posed for the investigation. Activity cards may lead the child to the discovery of a pattern or generalization. They also may stimulate interest in other areas of mathematics or in the posing of new problems.

Children can make many of their own activity cards. They are capable of asking challenging questions about materials which they have examined, and one child's questions can stimulate another child's interest. Such activity also provides practice in question-asking skills.

If you have students who have limited reading ability, specially designed activity cards can be used. Some are available commercially, but you may decide to make your own. Several ideas may be helpful to you.

1. Keep the amount of writing on the card to a minimum.
2. Use a tape recorder to ask some of the questions.
3. Show pictures of the activities when possible.
4. Use open-ended questions.
5. Let the students make some of their own activity cards.

As always, once a lesson is completed there must be some assessment of student performance. How might this be done in a laboratory situation?

There are many ways to assess a child's performance in the mathematics laboratory. Techniques such as observation of the child at work, study of his written work, or a periodic check on his progress may be used in the laboratory situation; these techniques and others which also can be used in the regular classroom situation are discussed in greater detail in Chapter 17. Several points should be emphasized here, however.

First, each set of laboratory experiences should have as its basis at least one objective. Obviously, many children may exceed your expectations because of the use of open-ended questions; others will achieve only the minimum which you expect. Second, the just mentioned techniques provide opportunities for you to have either one-to-one or small group discussion about the problem at hand, both of which will personalize your instructional program.

The Expository Approach

The expository approach has been the traditional teaching strategy ever since the beginning of time. It is characterized by the teacher who is the central or dominant figure in the teaching-learning process. Activities are teacher-directed and the lecture method is also used.

Although this strategy has been disdained by many educators over the years, it can still be a useful teaching strategy. However, like any other strategy, it loses its effectiveness, especially with children, when it is used exclusively.

Advantages of the Expository Approach.   The expository approach is probably most useful when information or facts need to be given to a large group of children in a relatively short period of time. Material that is of general interest or need, such as examples to reinforce a point, is best presented in this manner.

The use of this approach also gives variety to the instructional day. This variety is good for both teacher and the children; "doing it the same old way all the time" makes the instructional program boring for all concerned. No single teaching strategy will be effective if used all the time.

Potential Problems.   Perhaps the biggest potential problem with the expository approach is that the learner can become passive and not be actively involved in the learning experience. We firmly believe that children learn best when they are actively involved in the learning experience, as is amply pointed out throughout the text. There are times, of course, when some passivity on the part of the child is desirable but these situations should be kept minimal in number.

An outgrowth of the passive learner problem is that it becomes very difficult for the teacher to assess and provide for individual child needs, both academic and social. When the teacher can only guess at a child's needs, it is more than likely that the needs will not be met. This can be an especially serious problem when dealing with the atypical learner or the child with special social needs.

Questioning

It is through the creation of an appropriate physical and psychological environment that maximum learning occurs in an activity-centered mathematics program. The establishment of a desirable physical environment is described elsewhere in the chapter. Equally important as the physical environment, however, is the *psychological* or *emotional* climate of the classroom. A nonpenalizing atmosphere of cooperative experimentation is certainly desired over a regimented atmosphere in which the children assume the role of passive absorbers of information.

The creation of an atmosphere in which the children become active seekers of knowledge depends on a number of factors, not the least of which are the kinds of questions that the classroom teacher asks the pupils and those that the pupils ask themselves and their peers. The teacher's question-asking role shifts from one in which he or she is trying solely to determine if a given pupil has the correct answer to one of guiding him or her to new levels of thought in the investigation of mathematics.

Consider the following pairs of questions:

a. Multiply 16 and 25. What is the product?
b. Solve 16×25 in as many ways as you can. Which method do you prefer? Why?
a. To find the area, multiply length and width. If $l = 4$ in. and $w = 3$ in., what is the area?
b. The fence behind our school is made of cement blocks. Approximately how many blocks are in the wall? Compare your method of solution with that of a friend. Are your approximations close? Why or why not?

The first question in each pair is *closed;* that is, there is one correct response. The student receives the question and answers either correctly or incorrectly, whereupon mathematical thinking may cease. The student then waits for the teacher to pose another question, thus perpetuating the passive learning role.

The second example in each of the preceding pairs is an *open-ended* type. Students may find numerous methods to follow, each of which provides a solution. Some students will find more solutions than others; some will find more sophisticated methods than others; but all students will hopefully experience some success, a factor very important in maintaining the desire to learn. Investigation may continue for as long as the teacher wishes or as long as the students are motivated to the task. Also, work may be carried out individually, in small groups, or with the entire class. An additional dimension to these particular examples of open-ended questions is that the student is asked to evaluate his own methods, a practice often overlooked by the use of closed situations.

The preceding discussion is not intended to imply that closed questions are not relevant in the classroom; indeed, quite the opposite is true. Too often, however, closed questions are used exclusively, thereby preventing the use of open-ended questions. The differences in student responses should make the conclusion obvious: teachers who have decided to provide an environment in which children become *seekers* of mathematical knowledge must examine their questioning techniques and begin to pose more questions which elicit different levels of thought on the part of the respondent. Actually, the selection of a particular categorization scheme is less important than the questioner's efforts to ask different kinds of questions. For purposes of discussion let us consider the classification scheme devised by Gallagher and Aschner[1] and examine its use in teaching mathematics. The four areas identified in this classification are cognitive-memory, convergent, divergent, and evaluative. The names signify the level of thought required of the respondent.

1. James Gallagher and Mary Jane Aschner, "A Preliminary Report on Analysis of Classroom Interaction," *Merrill-Palmer Quarterly of Behavior and Development,* pp. 183–194.

Cognitive-memory questions evoke immediate, almost automatic, response. They are the type most often asked in mathematics classes, and they involve such thought as recall, recognition, observation, and description of previously obtained knowledge. The following questions are examples of the cognitive-memory type:

1. What is the sum of 3 and 6?
2. Point to the divisor in this problem: $61\overline{)274}$
3. Is this a straight edge?
4. The first place to the right of the decimal point is the _____ 's place.

Convergent questions involve the synthesis of certain facts for purposes of solving problems, making comparisons and drawing contrasts, and describing relationships. Even though the questions are broader and the level of thought required is greater than that involved in the cognitive-memory realm, there is still only one correct answer that is being sought. These questions may be categorized as convergent:

1. How is this graph like the one on the board?
2. Why does the decimal point appear to move when a whole number is divided by a decimal?
3. In expressing a decimal as a percent, why does the decimal point "move" two places to the right?
4. How is this pattern different from the one on the chart?
5. Explain the distributive principle.

Divergent questions, on the other hand, allow for more than one correct answer. These questions encourage the making of predictions, hypotheses, and inferences. The child is presented with a problem situation and is encouraged to use his knowledge in his own way in problem solving. The following questions are divergent:

1. Diagram this word problem.
2. What kinds of events might have occurred in our society if zero had never been invented?
3. Solve this problem in as many different ways as possible.
4. Find as many patterns as you can in this multiplication table.

Evaluative questions involve levels of thought associated with the other three types. In addition to these, however, is the necessity to judge, choose, or defend a self-directed position which the child has taken with regard to a given situation. The following questions are evaluative in nature:

1. In your opinion, which flowchart is best?
2. Which method of solution do you prefer? Why?
3. Which arrangement of counters do you think best illustrates the problem? Why?

In addition to concern with the kinds of questions being asked in the classroom, attention should be given to the way in which the questions are being asked. If the question is negative in nature, is ambiguous, contains too many hints, or is confusing, learning will be hindered regardless of the question-type being used.

PERIMETER

Grade Level	Aim	Open-end Questions
K-2	Concept *all the way around.* Comparing Larger and Smaller Regular and Irregular shapes	How many things can you go around? In how many ways? How far is it around?
1-3	How far around?	In how many ways can we measure around? Which way is best? (easiest)
2-5	Estimating and Checking	How far do you think it is around any shapes you can measure?
	Real Measuring	See if you were right. How close were you?
	Large Perimeters	Find a way to draw a picture of your classroom floor so that others can tell its perimeter by measuring the picture.
3-6	Accuracy Symmetrical Figures	Can you find the perimeter of some shapes without measuring all the way around? Which shapes?
4-7	Scale	Make a scale drawing of your classroom or room at home.
5-8	Relationship—Perimeter Area	In what way can you arrange a fixed area to get the largest perimeter? Find the largest area (shape) you can enclose with a string one yard long.
	Relationship—Circumference Radius Area etc.	What is the relationship between area and perimeter? Can you find a relationship between the measurements of different circular objects?

Open-ended questions provide good opportunities for individualizing learning. (From Edith Biggs and James MacLean: *Freedom to Learn: An Active Learning Approach to Mathematics.* Copyright © 1969 by Addison-Wesley (Canada) Ltd. Reprinted with permission.)

In addition to the teacher's own questioning affecting student involvement, students themselves should be encouraged to question more precisely in order to arrive at solutions to problems. Although such encouragement should be abundant in all mathematics activities, there are activities designed specifically to help students improve their ability to gain information through the questions they ask. Consider, for example, a mathematical variation of the game "Twenty Questions" in which one person decides upon a number within minimal and maximal limits and then the other players try to determine which number it is in less than twenty questions. Because each question must yield as much information as possible, there is great motivation to ask the best questions possible.

The benefits derived from such activities become apparent when the student, confronted with such a problem as finding the solution to $\sqrt{27}$, but having forgotten the algorithm, neither quits nor immediately asks the teacher for help, but instead approaches the work this way: "Between what two whole numbers (minimal and maximal limits) must the square root lie? Let's see . . . between 5 and 6, of course, because 5^2 is 25 and 6^2 is 36. The answer must also be closer to 5.0 because 27 is closer to 25 than to 36; therefore, the answer is less than 5.5. By trying a number halfway between 5.0 and 5.5, I can find another minimum or maximum, thereby getting the result to the nearest tenth. 5.2^2 is 27.04—correct to the nearest tenth. I knew I could find the answer if I just thought about it a little."

Indeed, what are educators trying to achieve in the classroom but an atmosphere in which each child is willing, if not eager, to attempt a solution to a problem situation? The human aspect of classroom environment is a vital determinant to meeting this end. Surely the teacher "sets the stage" with the kinds of questions asked of pupils, with the activities provided to encourage pupils to seek information in the most beneficial way they can, and with the general positive atmosphere which is established to communicate to the pupils that the teacher is there to help them in their own personal investigations of mathematics.

The Atypical Learner

One of the major problems faced by the elementary mathematics teacher is how to work with the atypical learner. By atypical, we mean learners who are reluctant, slow, gifted, learning disabled, mainstreamed or physically handicapped. Working with these children will be challenging yet can be rewarding.

Reluctant Learners.   The reluctant learners are probably more numerous than any of the other types of atypical learners. These children have usually had a history of frustration with mathematics usually caused by a lack of success. They are now at a point where they see little use in trying to do the work. In some instances they may have built a real and severe math anxiety which will keep them from performing well.

These students need patience and understanding. The future of their mathematics education is still salvageable but it may not be for long unless the teacher can make some headway with them.

What can be done to help a reluctant learner? First, nothing will be more helpful than having some success. Second, the teacher should try to determine the child's interest(s) and use instructional activities that relate to the found interest(s). A third way, discussed in greater detail in Chapter 16, is to use diagnostic techniques so that appropriate learning experiences can be provided. Trying to make the learning of mathematics enjoyable and giving constant and immediate feedback on progress to the child are two other suggestions that we would make.

Slow Learners.   The slow learner is not able to learn mathematical concepts and skills at the same rate as other children. These children often do not have an aptitude for mathematics and find it very difficult to learn. They may also be reluctant to learn, a very understandable situation. Often, however, they do have a good attitude about learning math but are just not able to do it at the normal pace.

In addition to the ways mentioned about helping reluctant learners, there are several other things that can be done to help slow learners. Using concrete materials, breaking the instruction up into short steps, pursuing different instructional strategies and altering expectations of student performance are some of the other ways that a teacher can use to work effectively with slow learners.

Gifted and Talented Learners.   It will be quite apparent when these learners are in the classroom. A gifted child has superior ability to deal with facts, ideas and relationships. Talented children show aptitude in specific areas such as mathematics or science. There is usually a great deal of overlapping between gifted and talented children.

Once a child has been identified as being gifted or talented, the teacher should make every attempt to provide challenging supplementary instructional materials and learning experiences. It is often debated by educators whether or not the gifted and talented child should be simply given more advanced materials such as the textbook for the next grade level for independent study. The major problem in using vertical advancement is that future teachers often have difficulty dealing with a child who is far ahead of the normal curriculum.

There is some advantage in having gifted and talented children stay with their peers as much as possible. They can work on other projects and materials and the socialization process can continue to develop. Many times, gifted and talented children are found to be socially immature; a horizontal enrichment program may help reduce the probability of the immaturity problem happening. Gifted students many times are just plain neglected.

It is very easy to fall into the trap of assuming that a child in the classroom who is gifted and/or talented has all of the necessary prerequisite skills and concepts to deal with mathematical ideas in the curriculum. Don't make this assumption, check it out!

Special Learners.   There continues to be demands from society for schools to provide better quality instructional programs for children with special learning problems. Many school corporations may have special classes and teachers to work with these children. However, there is continuous effort to mainstream these children back into the regular classroom where possible so it is quite likely that most teachers will encounter such children in the mathematics classroom.

By special learners, we mean those who are learning disabled, educable mentally retarded, emotionally disturbed, or physically handicapped. Every classroom teacher should have an understanding of what these terms mean and special behavioral characteristics of each type. Reading books and/or taking classes in special education is a good way for a teacher to become familiar with the different types of special learners.

A teacher who suspects that a child in the classroom has a special learning difficulty should consult with the school nurse, principal, or a special education teacher. These sources can provide considerable help so that appropriate instructional experiences can be planned and implemented. Never, however, label a child as being a special learner without verification from a known *reliable* and knowledgeable source.

Keeping a Balance.   Throughout the last several pages we have discussed some of the different types of atypical learners and their learning characteristics. The teacher may be faced with all or some of these atypical learners in the classroom. Certainly, their needs are important. But, don't exclude the other children in the class; they also have important needs too.

Here are some guidelines to help keep a proper balance in the mathematics instruction program between the atypical learners and the other learners.

1. Don't play favorites—accept all learners.
2. Don't let a small group of learners control the classroom.
3. Present lessons by using different modalities (audio, visual, kinesthetic).
4. Make appropriate accommodations but not exceptions for atypical learners.

Remember that *all* of the learners in the classroom are important and that you cannot and should not neglect any of them. A little common sense goes a long way!

TEACHING MATERIALS CONSIDERATIONS

Traditionally, mathematics in the classroom was chalk-and-pencil oriented, with the teacher having few other options available. Along with discovering how children learn, however, has come the realization that effective mathematics learning must be accomplished by appropriate instructional aids. There has been a resultant proliferation of commercial materials, together with an ever-increasing interest in the area of teacher-made materials. This interest has resulted in yet another problem for the mathematics teacher: how to judiciously select, collect, or prepare those materials best suited to meet the goal of actively involving pupils in their learning experiences in mathematics. Selected descriptions of such materials have been included in appropriate chapters of Part III. The proceeding discussion will present general guidelines which you, as teacher, should consider when selecting materials for the class as a whole and for a given child at a specified point in his mathematical progress.

First, think back to salient points related to how children learn mathematics. Generally, it is agreed that learning proceeds best along a concrete-to-abstract continuum. It is logical, then, that materials appropriate to various points along the continuum would be desirable. For purposes of discussion, let us describe materials at the concrete level, at the abstract level, and at an interim stage called the semiconcrete level.

Materials for the Concrete Level

Basically, concrete-level materials are those physical objects which can be manipulated and through whose manipulation the child can arrive at some mathematical observations. These materials encourage the child to use as many senses as possible in learning; that is, senses of touch, sight, hearing, and even smell and taste should be included if possible. It is through concrete activities with manipulative objects that the child formulates a physical basis for and a real world relevance to mathematics. Activities at this level, then, are an integral part of mathematical progress, and instructional materials at this stage are a necessity. *Any* object which is used in the manner just described may be classified as a learning device for the concrete stage.

Concrete materials may assume a number of forms: straws and rubber bands for grouping; pocket charts for studying place value; Dienes blocks for conceptualizing number bases; objects for counting; plastic geometric shapes for figure comparison; and unit lengths for measuring. The objects themselves may be as ordinary as stones collected from a driveway or as elaborate as an abacus made of teakwood and ivory. The cost and complexity are not primary concerns; external factors usually control these two areas anyway. It is the teacher who must use initiative and creativity to bridge the gap when funds are lacking.

There are concerns over which the teacher can experience some control, however. First, he or she can collect, select, or prepare an adequate supply of concrete materials. These materials should be designed to serve as many mathematical purposes as possible. They should be durable, functional, and they should be easily available to the children. Activities associated with the materials should be made as interesting as possible. Desirable, but not always necessary, is that the materials be attractive. Regardless of other concerns, however, the primary criterion for the use of any concrete device is that a mathematical relationship must be achievable from a child's manipulation of it.

Materials Related to the Abstract Level

At the opposite end of the continuum are instructional materials that are symbolic in nature. These materials do not require any reference to manipulation of a physical object to solve a problem other than perhaps using a pencil to record a solution. Inherent in these materials is the necessity to abstract the problem and, by mentally manipulating figures, arrive at an answer. The textbook is the most widely used of these; workbooks may also be classified here, as may reference books of various types. Basically, materials at this level depend wholly upon the printed word or symbol. Used properly they are very valuable tools. But what are the proper uses for these materials? In the past, the textbook and other printed materials basically determined the curriculum in mathematics. Such practice was prompted by expediency and administrative demands that "the book must be covered." The result was that children were fit into the curriculum rather than the curriculum accommodating the children, which was an undesirable situation. Today, textbooks can and should *supplement* the instructional program in mathematics, and not direct it.

Materials Related to the Semiconcrete Level

Materials designed to bridge the gap between the concrete and the abstract levels are called semiconcrete materials. They can assume a number of forms, but basically they contain elements of the concrete together with the abstract in varying degrees. Pictures, charts, diagrams, graphs, and tables may be classified as semiconcrete. In this way, physical situations may be visualized, which helps the child to conceptualize a mathematical idea. As with materials at the other levels, semiconcrete materials are valuable tools when they illustrate graphically the exact mathematical situation being described.

A major goal has been achieved by the teacher who can provide a variety of learning experiences for his or her pupils using instructional materials appropriate to their particular advancement along the concrete-to-abstract continuum. Certainly, it is the responsibility of every teacher to identify concrete, semiconcrete, and abstract (symbolic) materials for each mathematical concept or skill and to attempt to bring into the classroom those materials most appropriate for his or her pupils.

Games

The use of games as a teaching tool in the elementary mathematics instructional program has become popular in recent years. Classroom teachers have found that games, properly chosen and used, can be very beneficial to the learning of mathematics. In this section, we will examine how games can best be used in the classroom, how games may be selected, and guidelines for managing games in the classroom.

Using Games. While games are not a panacea to solve your problems as a classroom teacher, they can be beneficial to your mathematics instructional program if properly used.

First, games may be used to reinforce mathematical concepts and skills which the children have learned. Drill and practice is often boring to children; games can help disguise the drill and practice needed to stabilize, maintain, and hopefully improve children's skill levels.

Second, games can help improve a child's attitude towards the learning of mathematics because they give an excellent opportunity for a child to experience success. We discussed the importance of success earlier in the text and in this chapter.

A third use of games is to actively involve the children in their learning experiences. Active child involvement is psychologically desirable for children and they are much more likely to learn and maintain needed mathematical concepts and skills if they are actively involved in the learning situation.

Finally, games add variety to the instructional program, help children learn to follow directions, and promote *healthy* competition. It is clear that all three of these benefits are important to the effectiveness of instruction.

Games are like any other teaching tool, however; they can be misused and so have a detrimental effect on the learning environment. Some potential problems with games include: the encouragement of meaningless "play" by children, the cost of the games, creation of discipline problems or social tension between two children because of over-emphasis on winning, and possible encouragement of cheating. Keep these problems in mind when planning the use of games and the end result will probably be the successful use of games.

Selecting Games. Once it has been decided to use games, the teacher needs to select games which are appropriate for the purpose and concept or skill needed by the children. Avoid the common mistake of using a game which does not fit into the program appropriately.

What are some criteria for selecting games? Since games may be either purchased commercially or teacher-made, criteria[2] must be considered for each type.

---

2. From *A Survival Guide for the Junior High/Middle School Mathematics Teacher,* by Gregory R. Baur, Ed.D., and Darleen Pigford, Ph.D., pp. 271–274. © 1984 by Parker Publishing Company, Inc., West Nyack, New York.

1. The game is appropriate for the instructional objective.
2. Players have the necessary prerequisite skills to play the game.
3. Little time is needed to make the game.
4. The game is inexpensive.
5. The game is easy to supervise.
6. Players will enjoy playing the game.
7. The instructions for the game are clear and easily understood by your students.
8. Players are actively involved in each play of the game.
9. The game is self-checking if played by a single player or a small group of players.
10. The game promotes good sportsmanship and does not overemphasize competition.
11. There should be an element of chance involved in the winning of the game.

The first criteria mentioned is obviously the most important. Beyond that, the weighting of the criteria will depend on the individual teaching situation.

MANAGEMENT CONSIDERATIONS

Good classroom management is essential to an effective instructional program in mathematics. There are many things to consider as plans for management strategies are considered. In this section, we will discuss some of the major points which must be considered.

Teacher Responsibilities

Good classroom management, along with an effective instructional program, is the total responsibility of the classroom teacher.

Getting off to a good start is prerequisite to good classroom management. This means that the teacher must consider things to do before the school year starts, what to do the first day, and what to do the first week or two.

Before the School Year Starts.   One of the first things a teacher must do is to decide on the rules for acceptable behavior by the children in the classroom.

Rules of classroom conduct should be communicated to the children on the first day of class. This action will enable you to be prepared for situations before they occur. Be sure that the rules you decide upon are enforceable because the children will test you. If you have any questions about the rules chosen, consult with your building principal. It would also be appropriate to check the rules against building or school corporation policies for student behavior to be sure that there are no discrepancies.

The First Day of School.   Someone has said that first impressions are lasting. The impression you make the first day of school with your children will go a long way towards successful classroom management. Remember that there must be order in the classroom before any learning can take place.

During that first day, your children must understand that you mean business—you can always loosen up later. It is almost impossible to tighten up after a loose beginning. This does not mean that you should come across as an ogre or a tyrant but it does mean that you need to clearly establish your role and the children's role in your classroom.

Here are some tasks to be completed during the first day.

1. Introduce yourself and write your name on the chalkboard.
2. Read each child's name from the class roll to check pronunciation.
3. Indicate to the children what is expected in terms of acceptable classroom behavior.

The First Week of School.   The first week of school is important because you will begin to learn a great deal about your children's current mathematical ability levels. You will also be busy developing the rapport with your children regarding their classroom behavior.

During the second day of class, establish your seating chart for the class. Check the class roll by again calling out each student's name. Go through the textbook, pointing out important features; the textbook will be discussed later in the chapter in greater detail.

Establishing Routine

Routine classroom procedures with your children are extremely important. Children want and need structure in the classroom and clearly-defined routine procedures help stabilize the classroom atmosphere. As long as the procedures you establish are reasonable and you are consistent and fair in their application, there are not likely to be discipline problems. But, remember that you will be tested early and often until the students are satisfied that you mean what you say.

We mentioned earlier in the chapter the importance of establishing ground rules for classroom behavior. Here are some examples of successful ground rules. There may be others that you want to use and some you may wish to delete.

1. Students should be in their seats when the bell rings to start class.
2. Textbook, paper, and pencil should be brought to class each day.
3. Pencils should be sharpened before class starts.
4. Students should raise their hand and be recognized by the teacher before speaking out in class.
5. Students should not talk with each other while another student or the teacher is talking.
6. Students should not leave their seats at the end of the class period until dismissed by the teacher.
7. Students should proceed in the preassigned manner during fire drill.
8. Students should not talk among themselves when the public address system is in operation.
9. Students should use the restroom during class break and not during class.

A few sensible rules will be much easier to maintain and enforce than a long list. Don't keep your students guessing what is expected of them!

Classroom Discipline

There has been much criticism in recent years about the lack of classroom discipline in our nation's schools. Unfortunately, much of this criticism is justified but it is a complex problem with no easy solution. Classroom teachers can do much to help correct the situation, however, by utilizing suggestions made in this chapter relative to the establishment of an effective classroom environment.

An effective classroom environment will do a great deal to eliminate discipline problems before they occur. There are, of course, some problems that arise without warning. The manner in which these problems are handled will go a long way towards establishing good classroom discipline. Here are some things that you, as the teacher, can do.[3]

1. *Act quickly and decisively.* Don't hesitate to deal with a problem situation. When you hesitate, it appears to students that you are unsure of what to do and this may worsen the situation.

2. *Don't over-react.* As long as you remain calm, the situation has a good chance of staying under control. Over-reaction on your part could cause a situation to magnify with potentially dangerous consequences.

3. *Never threaten action which cannot be enforced.* The other children in the class will watch your actions very carefully. If your actions are inappropriate or you threaten action which is not possible, you will lose credibility with other children. The result is usually loss of control of the situation and the classroom.

4. *Never embarrass a child in front of classmates.* When you back a child into a corner, you have created a "no win" situation. The results will usually be worse than you anticipate.

5. *Avoid sarcasm as a means of classroom control.* The use of sarcasm will cause children to lose respect for you. Loss of respect means loss of classroom control.

6. *Use good common sense.* Good common sense will get you through any problem situation. Let it prevail.

7. *Try to anticipate potential disturbance situations and determine how you will handle the situation if it occurs.* Try to plan ahead for potential problems. Many times your anticipation will keep a situation from becoming a problem. For example, moving a student to a new seat, either in front or away from another troublesome student may keep a problem from occurring. Deciding ahead of time how you will resolve a problem situation will enable you to react to the situation in a desirable manner and help eliminate the possibility of ill-advised action.

CHAPTER KEY POINTS

1. Advantages of the math lab include:
   a. provides opportunity for child involvement;
   b. provides opportunity for math to "come alive";
   c. provides opportunity to develop creativity and social skills.

2. Problems with a math lab include:
   a. cost,
   b. storage of material,
   c. teacher role definition,
   d. difficulty for some children in working in this environment, and
   e. selection and management of groups.

3. The math lab is supplementary to the normal classroom activity.

4. Much pre-planning and effort on the part of the teacher is necessary to successfully conduct a math lab situation.

3. Ibid. pp.

5. The expository approach is most useful when lots of information or facts must be given to a large group of children in a relatively short time.

6. Learners tend to become passive under the expository approach.

7. Asking good questions is a difficult skill for most teachers.

8. Questions may be classified as:
   a. cognitive-memory,
   b. convergent,
   c. divergent, and
   d. evaluative.

9. A major problem for elementary mathematics teachers is dealing with atypical learners.

10. Atypical learners include learners who are:
    a. reluctant,
    b. slow,
    c. gifted,
    d. learning disabled,
    e. mainstreamed, or
    f. physically disabled.

11. Instructional materials are available at the concrete, semiconcrete, and abstract levels.

12. Games are a useful teaching tool.

13. Games can be used to:
    a. reinforce math concepts and skills,
    b. improve child attitude,
    c. actively involve the child in the learning situation, and
    d. give variety to the instructional program.

14. Selection of games must be done systematically and carefully.

15. Good classroom management is the responsibility of the classroom teacher.

16. Rules of acceptable classroom conduct must be communicated to the children during the first day of school.

17. In handling classroom disturbances keep the following points in mind.
    a. Act quickly and decisively.
    b. Don't over-react.
    c. Never threaten action which cannot be enforced.
    d. Never embarrass a child in front of classmates.
    e. Avoid sarcasm.
    f. Use common sense.
    g. Try to anticipate potential disturbances.

Laboratory 5

The Mathematics Laboratory

The inclusion of the mathematics laboratory in the instructional program in mathematics can make a valuable contribution to a child's learning experiences. Although it is not a panacea, it can benefit most children when used properly. One key to successful experience in the mathematics laboratory is active child involvement in all phases. The following exercises should aid you in developing your own laboratory program.

I. *Objectives:* Upon completion of these laboratory exercises, you should be able to do the following:
  A. Given a selected objective, design a laboratory activity which may be used as an initial learning experience for that objective. (Chapter Competency 5–G)
  B. Design a set of activity cards which may be used in a mathematics laboratory and which are appropriate for a given level of student. (Chapter Competency 5–H)

II. *Materials:* Tagboard; scissors; ruler; marking pens of various colors; clear plastic sheets with adhesive backing (clear contact paper)

III. *Procedure:*
  A. Read the section on the mathematics laboratory in Chapter 5 of *Helping Children Learn Mathematics.* If you have questions, consult your instructor.
  B. Study the laboratory exercises in the supplement which may be found on pages 90–92. Considering them in their present form, do you think you could use them with children at the designated grade level? Why? If you feel that it is necessary, rewrite all or part of each activity so that it could be used. Share your thoughts with some of your classmates. Do they agree with you? If there are questions, consult your instructor.
  C. For each of the following objectives, outline briefly a laboratory activity which may be used as an initial (introductory) learning experience. List the materials which are needed, and write the procedure in the form of student directions.
    1. The student should be able to recognize the different American currency coins and tell how each is related to the others.
    2. The student should be able to add two 2–digit whole numbers using regrouping.

    Show your activities to a classmate. Are your discussions clearly stated? Is each activity appropriate as an initial learning activity for the stated objective? Is each evaluation appropriate? If there are any questions, consult your instructor.
  D. Design a sequence of five or more activity cards which could be used in the classroom with children. Choose any mathematical concept(s) or skill(s) that you wish. Write the objective(s) for the sequence and the grade level on the back of one of the cards. If possible, cover your cards with clear contact paper to avoid the "dog-eared" look. Cards being designed for use with young children should be brightly colored and have larger lettering. (Are any other adjustments necessary for young children?)

Optional: During your field experience, design a laboratory activity which you can use with a group of six to eight students. Consult the classroom teacher for suggestions regarding topics which might be used. After using the activity with children, correct identified weaknesses (if there are any) and type the activity for duplication for the rest of the class.

Supplement: Laboratory Activity I
Mathematical Operations

Grade Level: 3

A. *Objective:* To reinforce the two-place subtraction algorithm involving renaming by the use of an abacus. Ten problems are given in the evaluation section of this section, and it is expected that the students will do the problems correctly in at least nine of them during a period of 15 minutes.

B. *Materials:* Counting abacus

C. *Procedure:* This is a counting abacus:

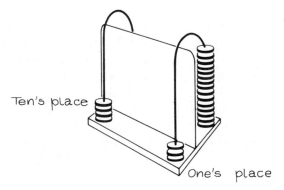

It is readily apparent that the beads show the value of 43. Let's try to subtract 25 from it. Because 5 cannot be taken away from 3 in the one's place, we must rename 1 ten to 10 ones in this way:

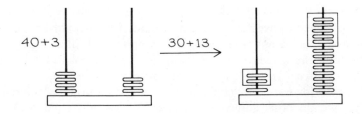

Now we are ready to take away 25 or 20 + 5. In the one's place, we take away 5 beads, leaving 8 beads. In the ten's place, we take away 2 beads, leaving 1 bead there. Therefore, the answer is 10 + 8 = 18.

Practice other two-digit subtraction problems on the abacus until you can do them in your head as if you were seeing the abacus in your mind.

D. *Evaluation:* Ask the students to solve problems 1–5 on the abacus and solve problems 6–10 using paper and pencil.

1.	2.	3.	4.	5.
54	67	34	51	48
−23	−45	−18	−26	−19

6.	7.	8.	9.	10.
63	72	64	87	60
−47	−67	−39	−45	−18

Supplement: Laboratory Activity II

The Relationship between Addition and Multiplication

Grade Level: 2 or 3

A. *Objective:* Given a geoboard with 36 pegged holes, the child should be able to:
   1. group the pegs by twos, fives, and tens through the use of rubber bands;
   2. record his findings on a data sheet as addition and multiplication problems; and
   3. state in a written form that multiplication is simply a shortened form of adding.

B. *Materials:* One of the following is needed for each student: a 36–pegged geoboard, a set of 30 rubber bands, a data sheet, and a pencil.

C. *Procedure:*
   1. Take your geoboard and group all of the pegs by twos using the rubber bands. As you group by twos, write what you find as addition and multiplication problems on the data sheet.
   2. Do the same for the fives and tens.
   3. Answer the questions at the bottom of the data sheet.

D. *Evaluation:*
   1. The teacher should watch the child as he groups by the twos, fives, and tens.
   2. The teacher should look at the data sheet answers.
      a. An example of the addition of twos is: 2 + 2 + . . . + 2 = 36.
      b. An example of the multiplication of twos is: 18 × 2 = 36.
   3. The child can now state that multiplication is a short form of adding.

Supplement: Laboratory Activity III

Number Families

Grade Level: 2

A. *Objective:* To find different addition and subtraction combinations that equal a given number.

B. *Materials:* Deck of cards for every two children; knowledge of rules of pyramid solitaire.

C. *Procedure:* Play pyramid solitaire to find the combinations which equal numbers determined by the teacher. Record the combinations.
1. Play pyramid solitaire. Find combinations that equal 7. List the combinations as you find them. (One person plays the game; the other serves as checker and recorder.) Were you able to play all the cards in your pyramid?
2. Play it again. This time find combinations that equal 9. List combinations you found this time. Did you use any related sentences? Give two of your related sentences.
3. One more time! Let your partner play pyramid solitaire, and you be the checker and recorder. Have your partner find combinations that equal 3. Could you play this and find combinations to equal a different number? Try it!

D. *Evaluation:* The learning during this lab may be evaluated by the teacher as the students are observed. If desired, the lab sheets may be collected and spot-checked.

Questioning

The asking of good questions helps students to become actively involved in their learning experiences. Also, good questions may help students to develop their rational power. Unfortunately, most mathematics questions asked by elementary school teachers require very little thinking. Often such questions may be answered by memory alone. There are times, of course, when such questions are appropriate, but used exclusively they have little effectiveness in developing the thinking process in children.

Every teacher should strive to ask varied kinds of questions. Only by acquiring knowledge of some basic principles about question-asking and then by continuous practicing can skill in this area be improved. The following exercises should be helpful in the development of this skill.

1. *Objectives:* Upon completion of these laboratory exercises, you should be able to do the following:
   A. Classify questions as open-ended or closed. (Chapter Competency 5–A)
   B. Classify questions as cognitive-memory, convergent, divergent, or evaluative. (Chapter Competency 5–B)
   C. Given a selected mathematical concept or skill, write examples of questions at each of the four levels which might be used to help the child learn that concept or skill. (Chapter Competency 5–C)

II. *Materials:* None

III. *Procedure:*

A. Read the section on questioning in Chapter 5 of *Helping Children Learn Mathematics.* Consult your instructor if you have any questions.

B. Classify the following questions as open-ended (O) or closed (C).

_____ **1.** What is 3 + 4?

_____ **2.** Of the three methods for multiplying two numbers, which one do you prefer?

_____ **3.** What is the formula for the area of a parallelogram?

_____ **4.** In what ways are the pyramid and the brick alike?

_____ **5.** What is the missing addend in $4 + \triangle = 11$?

How well did you do? Check your answers with the following key.

1. C	4. O
2. O	5. C
3. C	

If you scored at least 4 out of 5, you may proceed. If not, you may wish to reread the section on questioning in Chapter 5 of *Helping Children Learn Mathematics.*

C. Write two examples of questions that are closed and two examples of questions that are open-ended. You may choose any mathematical concept or skill to ask about. Check your questions with a classmate. Do you agree?

D. Classify the following questions as cognitive-memory (CM), convergent (C), divergent (D), or evaluative (E). Record your response at the left of each question.

_____ **1.** What is the area of a circle whose radius is 10 inches?

_____ **2.** Which method of multiplication, in your opinion, is the easiest to use?

_____ **3.** In what ways are the pyramid and the brick different?

_____ **4.** What is 5 $\times$ 4?

_____ **5.** Which puzzle do you think is most interesting?

_____ **6.** How many sides does a square have?

_____ **7.** In what ways can you bisect a circle?

_____ **8.** What is the probability that the sum of two dice will be 6?

_____ **9.** What would happen if we forgot to invert the divisor and inverted the dividend instead when dividing fractions?

Check your answers:

1. C	6. CM
2. E	7. D
3. D	8. C
4. CM	9. C
5. E	

If you missed more than two of the items, consult your instructor. If not, proceed to the next task.

E. Several mathematical topics are given below. Using any or all of these topics, write a total of eight questions representing the four questioning categories, two questions for each category.

> Use of money
> Multiplication of whole numbers
> Use of percent
> Telling of time
> Division of decimals
> Addition of fractions

Instructional Materials

Every teacher of elementary school mathematics should be able to select appropriate materials to supplement the chosen instructional strategy. The following exercises will give you an opportunity to demonstrate your skill at choosing appropriate materials.

I. *Objectives:* Upon completion of these laboratory exercises, you should be able to do the following:
   A. Classify selected instructional materials as appropriate for the concrete, semiconcrete, or abstract level. (Chapter Competency 5–D)
   B. Given a selected objective, list instructional materials which might be used to achieve that objective at each of the three levels: concrete, semiconcrete, and abstract. (Chapter Competency 5–E)
   C. Prepare instructional materials and state how they might be used in the classroom. (Chapter Competency 5–F)

II. *Materials:* The materials required for objective C will vary according to your own preferences. No other materials will be required.

III. *Procedure:*
   A. Read the section on instructional materials in Chapter 5 of *Helping Children Learn Mathematics.* Consult your instructor if you have any questions.
   B. For each of the following instructional materials, give a mathematical concept or skill and an activity which might be used to help a child learn that concept or skill and which uses the instructional material. Classify the activity as being concrete, semiconcrete, or abstract in nature.
      1. Drinking straws
      2. Wooden centimeter cubes
      3. Number line
      4. Egg carton

C. Construct two instructional aids which might be used in the classroom. Include with each aid an index card listing the objective(s) and use(s) for each aid.

Selecting Textbooks and Games

In addition to deciding how to use various types of instructional materials, it is also imperative to make the appropriate choice of material for use in the classroom. There is a proliferation of instructional materials available on the market with varying degrees of quality. An effective classroom teacher must be able to make the appropriate choice and have a basis for making the choice.

I. *Objectives:* Upon completion of these laboratory exercises, you should be able to do the following:

    A. Describe criteria for choosing a basal textbook. (Chapter Competency J)

    B. Determine criteria for choosing a game. (Chapter Competency J)

II. *Materials:* None

III. *Procedure:*

    A. Read the sections on instructionals and games in Chapter 5 of *Helping Children Learn Mathematics*. Consult your instructor if you have any questions.

    B. Below are some criteria to be considered in selecting a basal textbook. Do you feel that all of the criteria should have the same weight? Why?

    Are there criteria which should be added to or deleted from the list? What additions or deletions should be made?

    After you have decided on a final list of criteria for selecting a basal textbook, examine several basal elementary mathematics textbook series. How well do these textbook series measure up to the criteria you have selected? What are the strengths and weaknesses of each series? Assume a given classroom situation to use as a basis for your judgment. If the classroom situation were altered, how would it affect your judgment?

    1. The textbook is geared to the interests, needs, and abilities of my students.

    2. The language of the textbook is appropriate for the reading level of my students.

    3. The textbook's presentation of concepts and ideas is mathematically correct.

    4. The textbook develops concepts and skills in a spiral manner.

    5. The textbook contains sufficient and appropriate examples of the concepts and skills presented.

    6. There are an adequate number and variety of practice exercises for each concept and skill presented.

    7. The textbook is free of sexism and discrimination.

    8. The textbook emphasizes the development of problem-solving skills.

    9. The physical construction of the textbook is durable and long lasting.

    10. The textbook provides for alternative teaching strategies.

11. There is a comprehensive and useful teacher's manual for the textbook.

12. The textbook and/or teacher's manual provides suggestions and materials for the atypical learner.

13. There are adequate and appropriate supplementary materials available for the textbook.

C. Repeat the procedure from Part B above by applying it to games. Below are a set of criteria for choosing games.

1. The game is appropriate for my instructional objective.

2. My students have the necessary prerequisite skills to play the game.

3. The cost of the game is reasonable.

4. The game is easy to supervise.

5. My students will enjoy playing the game.

6. The instructions for the game are clear and will be easily understood.

7. My students are actively involved in playing the game.

8. The game enables me to maintain good classroom control.

9. The game is self-checking.

10. The game can be completed in a reasonable amount of time.

11. The game has a variety of uses or variations.

12. The game promotes good sportsmanship.

13. The game can be easily stored.

14. The game has an element of chance.

Classroom Management

No matter how well an instructional program has been planned, its implementation will not be successful without good classroom management. Good management techniques are not easily acquired but consideration of "what to do" before the fact will go a long way towards the development of good management techniques.

I. *Objectives:* Upon completion of these laboratory exercises, you will be able to do the following:

A. Describe techniques for developing good classroom management. (Chapter Competency L)

B. Describe factors which affect classroom management and how they can be controlled. (Chapter Competency L)

II. *Materials:* None

III. *Procedure:*

A. Read the section on management considerations in Chapter 5 of *Helping Children Learn Mathematics.* Consult your instructor if you have any questions.

B. Investigate whether or not there are policies and rules regarding discipline of students in a local school corporation. Are there areas which are not addressed by these policies and rules? Are the policies and rules evaluated periodically for purposes of revision?

C. Imagine that you have just been hired by a school corporation as an elementary teacher. Create a description of the community and its student population. Based upon this description, what would you do to prepare to begin your new job? Address the following time segments.

   1. Before the school year starts

   2. The first day of school

   3. The first week or two of school

In this imagined situation, how would you handle classroom disturbances?

Compare your imagined situation with that of a classmate. How would you answer the questions above in your classmate's imagined situation? What (if anything) would you do differently?

Are there procedures that you and your classmate would agree on? Disagree on? Why do you agree or disagree with your classmate?

Consult with your classmates as a group. What procedures do you agree or disagree on as a group?

PART III
Facilitating the Learning of Mathematics

Teacher Competencies

After studying Part III and completing the laboratories in Part III, you should be able to achieve each of the following:

A. Given a selected mathematical concept or skill, design foundational activities which may be used in the acquisition of that concept or skill.

B. Given a selected mathematical concept or skill, identify activities which may be used to develop proficiency in the use of that concept or skill.

C. Given a selected mathematical concept or skill, identify and/or demonstrate the use of selected instructional aids which might be used to help a child learn that concept or skill.

D. Design activities that will help a child develop necessary skills for the successful completion of problem-solving tasks.

6
From Sets to Numbers and Numerals

Teacher Competencies

After studying Chapter 6 and completing Laboratory 6, you should be able to:

    A. Given a selected concept or skill in the area of sets, numbers, and numerals, design foundational activities which may be used in the acquisition of that concept or skill. (Part Competency III-A)

    B. Given a selected concept or skill in the area of sets, numbers, and numerals, identify activities which may be used to develop proficiency in the use of that concept or skill. (Part Competency III-B)

    C. Given a selected concept or skill in the area of sets, numbers, and numerals, identify and/or demonstrate the use of selected instructional aids which might be used to help a child learn that concept or skill. (Part Competency III-C)

One of the most challenging areas of mathematics education is that of helping children learn basic number concepts. What appears on the surface to be a deceptively simple task of teaching children their "numbers" is instead a job requiring extensive knowledge, skill, and perceptive ability on the part of the teacher.

Children enter school not only with varying experiential backgrounds but also at various stages in their concept development. Most children entering kindergarten can count from one to ten and many can count to perhaps twenty or thirty. They can write a few numerals and can recognize still more. Many are also familiar with various measuring instruments and terminology associated with time, money, length, and so on. Their knowledge has been acquired incidentally in everyday situations. Concepts associated with these experiences are just beginning to form and in fact may yet be superficial, tentative, and quite possibly distorted. In school the teacher plans qualitative and quantitative experiences designed to clarify, reinforce, and expand upon these developing concepts and skills.

The question of when formal mathematics instruction should begin has been a subject of much discussion and has resulted in some extremes in practice. For several decades many schools eliminated formal math instruction completely from their primary level program on the assumption that children could not learn mathematics until they were older. Alternatively, it was not too long ago that some educators went to the other extreme teaching set symbolism to kindergarten and first-grade children and axiomatic logic to third graders. While there were some valid arguments involved in both practices, a more productive middle ground has been reached. It is generally agreed that children can learn mathematics earlier than previously thought but this mathematics must be taught within the conceptual level of the child at his or her stage of development.

So the problem for the educator has resolved itself into deciding which initial math experiences are most appropriate for children. In the selection of any such experiences certain guidelines about how children learn should be followed. At the elementary school level most children are functioning at the concrete operations stage of development as described by Piaget. (Remember, however, that some younger children may still be functioning at the preoperational stage while older children may be moving into the stage of formal operations.) These children cannot be expected to learn abstractly on a hypothetical, deductive level as do adults. They are at pre-logical stages of development and so must relate what they learn to the physical world. They are perception bound. They focus on what they see, hear and touch; they depend heavily upon their senses in all their learning. It is not enough for the teacher to "tell," "show," or "explain;" the children must "do" their mathematics. Children must have ample opportunity to manipulate objects themselves as a basis for abstracting mathematical ideas. It is through this manipulation of sets of objects that children begin to make logical sense of their perceptions, or reach a point of equilibration. The importance of providing children with ample concrete experiences cannot be overemphasized and trying to accelerate children through these initial learning phases is ill advised.

Study of Piaget's developmental theory, careful observation of children as they learn, and various research projects have revealed that certain topics and activities are important building blocks to mathematical understanding. Unfortunately, the typical traditional primary level mathematics curriculum has proven to be both inadequate in its coverage of these topics and inappropriate in its sequence of instruction. To clarify, consider counting and symbol recognition as examples. These two abilities have long been accepted as major goals of initial arithmetic instruction and were skills widely practiced. Parents and educators alike reasoned that if children can count from one to twenty and can recognize the symbol "5" as the word "five," for example, they must surely "know their numbers" and are probably ready to start learning their basic facts. This is not valid reasoning. While counting and symbol recognition are indeed a part of number learning, they are not close to the totality. Each of the tasks just described can be accomplished through memorization only, and fact and figure memorization does not guarantee number concept development. As math concepts begin to build one upon the other, children who have memorized but not understood become increasingly frustrated and negative; and the teacher, who has emphasized memorization and symbolism over foundational experiences promoting understanding and concept development, has done a great disservice to those children.

This chapter is devoted to a discussion of appropriate foundational learning experiences for children as they proceed from initial prenumber work with sets to the development of number concepts and also to the learning of numerals associated with those numbers.

PRENUMBER EXPERIENCES

Prenumber experiences encompass all those activities which preface actual number learning; they include many activities which relate to concrete operational abilities such as conservation, seriation, reversibility, and classification. These activities provide concrete referents to concepts necessary for later number work. A selection of recommended prenumber abilities and associated sample activities follows. Notice that the concept of set and the use of set language form an integral part of the discussion just as they should in all areas of mathematics learning.

Matching Objects

Pairing objects is prerequisite to enumerating objects. Counting itself is a matter of matching the set of counting numers one-to-one with the set to be counted. In initial stages, however, the child should match objects with objects. One-to-one correspondence activities abound. For example, the teacher can ask the child to do tasks such as these:

1. Take as many cookies as you have hands.
2. Get a straw for each milk carton at the table.
3. Put a button through each button hole.
4. Get a book for each child at the math table.
5. Put a cup on each saucer in the play area.
6. Set a flannel square beside each circle on the felt board.
7. Play dominoes so that equivalent dots are matched.

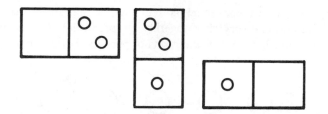

8. Make a set like a set already on the desk. (In this case the child is actually reproducing a set, but he must also match elements in order to do so.)

Because even such an apparently simple task as matching involves varying levels of comprehension, the teacher should be sure not to confuse children needlessly. For example, if a problem involves matching, the teacher should provide illustrations which do not distort the matching process through unusual or perceptively distorting arrangements. Consider the matching illustrations between circles and squares in Figure 1. Obviously, the first arrangement is more easily matched than the other two. Only after simple patterns are understood should others be used.

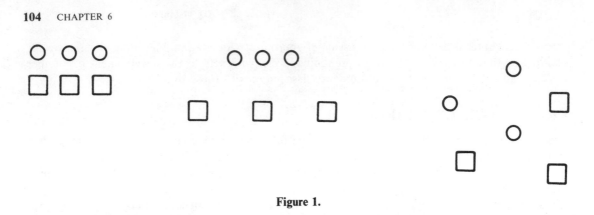

Figure 1.

Conserving Discontinuous Quantities

Discontinuous, or discrete, quantities are simply those which can be counted. (Continuous quantities must be measured.) Remember that to conserve, one must realize that the number of objects in a set remains invariant regardless of position. Therefore conserving discontinuous quantities is prerequisite to number learning.

One conservation activity involves placing ten pennies on the table. Form a line with five of the pennies before you. Ask the child to form another line of pennies beside yours matching them one-to-one.

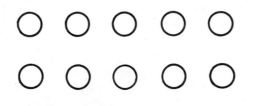

Let him or her verify that there are no more in one line than in the other. Then either stack or group the pennies in one line very close together or spread out the pennies in the other line. Ask the child, "If you could have one of these sets of pennies, is there one set you would rather have? Why?"

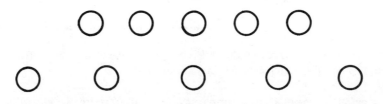

Conservers will state that there is no difference and the sets are the same regardless of position. Nonconservers will focus on only one attribute and will make a choice dependent upon that focus.

Variations on the above activities can be made in the number used, in the choice of objects (candy, rods, bottle caps, etc.), and in the patterns formed (vertical or horizontal lines, circles, random, etc.).

Reversing

Reversing is the ability to undo an operation. While reversibility is usually considered an important ability in learning the inverse operations in arithmetic (addition and subtraction; multiplication and division), it is also inherent in the more basic foundational abilities such as conserving. It is in part the child's inability mentally to restore objects to their original position which precludes his understanding that position has no effect upon numerousness.

To provide experiences involving reversing, the teacher can ask the child to do these kinds of things:

1. Repeat the initial movements of the conservation task but restore the scattered pennies to their original position.
2. Flatten out a ball of play-dough and then make it into a ball again.
3. Join and separate objects, noting each time the return to original status.

Seriating

Placing objects in order according to size or numerousness is also important in learning to count insofar as it helps establish a one-more, or progressive size, concept. Children can gain experience by doing these kinds of tasks.

1. Place rods of different lengths (Cuisenaire rods, pencils, etc.) in order from shortest to longest.

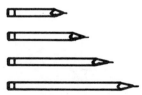

2. Arrange a set of picture cards (with from one to five pictures on each card) in order from fewest to greatest.

3. Stack discs in order of progressive size.

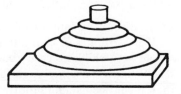

4. Build a "staircase" of unit rods with a one-unit difference between each "step."

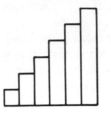

Comparing Sets Quantitatively

Comparing sets involves elements of one-to-one matching. As matching progresses, children find that some sets do not match exactly; they find that there may be more or fewer in one set than another. They are beginning to make broad quantitative comparisons. Relationships like "fewer than," "more than," and "equivalent to" are emerging as the children compare sets. Ultimately these broad quantitative relationships will develop into numerical relationships of "less than," "greater than," and "equal to."

Once again remember that the child is still bound by his or her perceptions and should not be confronted by confusing language or confounding factors. For example, a five-year-old child confronted by the two sets represented below might well be confused by the question, "Which set is larger?"

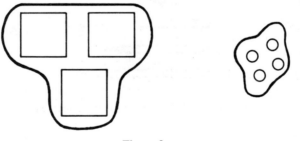

Figure 2.

Does the language of the question itself refer to the size or the numerousness of the sets? Language needs to be clear and precise on the part of the teacher. Similarly, the same child could be confused by the spatial arrangement of the objects or even by the use of different sized containers for grouping objects.

Comparing Sets Qualitatively

Set comparisons can also be of a qualitative, not quantitative, nature. Sets can be classified and grouped according to their various other attributes or characteristics, such as shape, color, size, etc. While sorting and grouping various sets, children learn about properties of sets and various relationships which exist between sets. While it is not important for the children to know the names of these properties and relations, they should be gaining intuitive understanding.

Children can make sets of any objects available in order to classify them: blocks, rocks, beads, leaves, buttons, bottle caps, toys, or any other items which have commonalities and differences. Some teachers prefer to use attribute pieces instead of random collections of objects, however. Attribute pieces are available commercially and are simply an assortment of plastic pieces which may vary in size, shape, color, and thickness. Whatever materials are available, the following activities are representative of those recommended for children.

1. *Sorting Activities.* First sorting should be with one attribute only, as in finding all the smooth rocks, RC bottle caps, blue buttons, or square shapes. After extensive work sorting one attribute, children can do two attribute sortings. For example, they might find all the red circles in a set of attribute pieces, sorting once for shape and then again for color. They might discover at this point that an object can belong to more than one set at a time as sets are related in different ways.

2. *Set-Relations Activities.* As children compare sets, they need to observe various relations which exist between different sets. Again the names of the relations are not as important as the experiences gained through working with the various set relations.

Some sets are completely contained within another set. They are subsets of the including set and the relation is called INCLUSION. The "part-whole," "all-some," "inclusion-subset" idea causes difficulty for many children at the early stages and should not be approached abstractly. At the concrete level children can work with the inclusion relation as they begin with a set of colored rods and sort all the red ones from the group. In the classroom they find that the boys make up a subset of the entire class.

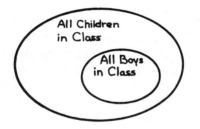

Some sets have no members in common and are called DISJOINT sets. Disjoint sets can be found in the classroom: boys and girls, softballs and basketballs, papers and pencils, and so on.

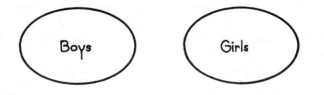

Other sets have some of their members in common and are called MEET sets. Sets which meet can be found in the classroom by such activities as sorting brown-haired children and those who wear glasses.

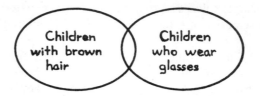

Some sets have all members in common and are called EQUAL sets. Equal sets are those sets consisting of exactly the same elements but named in a different way.

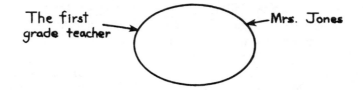

3. *Set-Operation Activities.* Children may deal with set operations like intersection, union, and negation, but primarily at an intuitive level. For example, children who have just sorted brown haired children and children who wear glasses can be asked who would be members of BOTH sets (intersection) and who would be members of EITHER set (union).

Children also find that they can sort sets into complementary classes through negation: square-not square; green-not green; thick-not thick; smooth-not smooth.

To conclude, prenumber experiences broaden the experiential base from which young children can draw as they abstract number concepts from their environment. While prenumber experiences with concrete objects probably won't speed up cognitive development, their incorporation into the primary curriculum assures that each child has had the concrete environmental interaction necessary in the formulation of the concepts leading to the abstraction of number.

THE LEARNING OF NUMBER

A child who can conserve, classify, seriate, and demonstrate various other abilities as described earlier is prepared to learn numbers. Because these abilities are not arrived at until about the age of seven, number learning prior to that stage of maturation is not complete and understanding can be achieved only up to a point. Once children arrive at the concrete operations stage, however, they are not deceived by their perceptions. They can focus on more than one attribute simultaneously and are ready to abstract number from their environment.

Cardinality and Ordinality

Cardinality and ordinality refer to quantity and order, respectively. The cardinality of a given finite set is its number property; cardinality answers the question, "How many?" Ordinality, on the other hand, is concerned with position and answers the question, "Which one?" For example, suppose cups are arranged on a table. When asked how many cups are on the table, the child answers, "Four." This is the cardinality, or the total number property, of the set. On the other hand, when asked which cup belongs to Mary, the child responds, "The third one." This is the ordinal usage of number. In this case, relative position within the set is important.

Counting is inherent in both usages of number. Counting may be either rote or rational in nature.

Rote counting refers to the ability to recite number names in sequence but without understanding. For example, a child may be able to recite number names to ten and yet still not be able to select five blocks from a set. Most children enter school with at least a rote knowledge of some number order; that is, they can count to a given number on request with perhaps a few inadvertent permutations. They have learned such number songs as "Ten Little Indians" and such number poems as "One, Two, Buckle My Shoe." These rote counters are beginning to understand that there is a pattern used to name numbers and they are memorizing some of the sequence.

Rote counting, while necessary to number learning, is not sufficient. Children must also develop rational counting ability; that is, they must develop understanding of the enumerative process. To do this, children build upon their early experiences in comparing sets and matching sets one-to-one. They begin to refine their broad initial quantitative set comparisons which led them to conclude that some sets were "more than," "less than," or "equivalent to" other sets. They develop a "one-more" concept in the building of number sequences. What began as a matching of objects one-to-one progresses to a matching of the set of counting numbers {1, 2, 3, 4, . . . } with the set to be enumerated.

Initial counting activities should involve only a few objects and should begin with an intuitive notion of "one." Most children will also recognize sets of two elements. From this point on, numbers can build, one upon the other, using the one-more concept.

Consider an example. You, the teacher, begin at the flannel board with two figures in one row and a like set below them. The children confirm that each is a set of two. Then you place one more figure beside the second set (optionally of a different color) and you ask how many are now in that set. (Three) Count together the objects in the newly formed set. Have the children take three objects from their individual "set-boxes" and place them on their desks and count them, pointing to each member of the set as they count. Be sure that you have plenty of sets of three positioned around the room and ask children to identify various sets of three which they find, each time verifying by counting that there are indeed three in the set.

Other numbers should be approached similarly with plenty of manipulative, hands-on experience in determining the number of the set involved.

Many materials are available to reinforce the one-more concept of counting; you are only limited by your imagination. Counting frames, beads, and number rods are among commercially available items. (Figure 3.) Beans, bottle caps, and buttons can serve the same purpose at little or no cost.

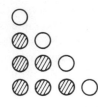

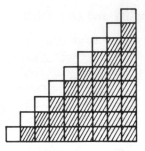

Figure 3.

Zero should be introduced only after children have learned at least a few of the counting numbers. It is a more difficult concept to understand, but children can learn about it well enough to use it. It should be approached as the number (cardinality) of the empty set and can be illustrated in many ways to children, who then enjoy making up their own "empty sets" with zero objects in them. You can begin with a cookie jar with perhaps three cookies in it. Remove one cookie at a time, each time asking "How many cookies are in the jar?" When there are no cookies left, show the children the empty jar and repeat the question. Answers like "None" and "It's empty" are fine. Explain that zero is the number that tells how many are in the empty set. The concept can be reinforced with practical examples such as the number of objects in an empty shoebox or whimsical examples such as the number of E.T.'s in school.

Reading and Writing Number Symbols

Numbers are concepts. They are abstractions existing only in the mind. Numerals are names and symbols given to represent these numbers. Numerals provide a way to communicate about and record numers. Each number can have many different names, or numerals. Just as a woman can be variously known as Mrs. Jones, Sara, Mom, Mommy, Honey, or Aunt but still be the same person, so also can the quantity, *****, be known as five, 5, V, 10/2, 4 + 1, and so on. So, numerals are what we see, hear, speak, or write as we communicate about quantitative abstractions called numbers. Each number has many numerals which may represent it. Children need to know how to read and write these numerals.

Once children begin to enumerate sets, they can also learn to read the numerals associated with the sets. For example, as children learn to associate the oral word "three" with the appropriate quantity, they can also associate the symbol "3" with that quantity. Because the learning of ten different symbols and their related word symbols is not easy, it is recommended that charts be kept readily visible in the classroom for reference. As each number is learned, its chart can be placed for display. Figure 4 illustrates the first four units of such a chart sequence. (Note that this sequence includes a chart for zero. While it is not a part of the counting sequence, it is a number symbol to be learned.)

Figure 4.

Reading practice and symbol recognition can take many different forms. Here are a few examples.

1. Using magnetic set strips and magnetic numerals, begin by placing the strips in sequence and have the children place numerals in their correct positions. (Figure 5.) Vary the activity by having the children supply the correct set strip for the given symbol or by beginning within the sequence and working in either direction.

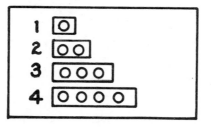

Figure 5.

2. Using stickers and paper plates, make number-match puzzles as illustrated in Figure 6. The paper plates are cut in two parts and the children match the numeral with its appropriate quantity.

Figure 6.

3. Worksheets and textbook activities which provide practice in numeral identification are plentiful. Typically, they require either figure recognition for a quantity or vice versa.

Draw a ring around the correct numeral for the set.

Which set does the following numeral represent?

Not only must children be able to read numerals but they must also learn how to write them. Symbol writing should be carefully taught. Children should know each move necessary in writing every numeral. Otherwise they might very well write eight as two circles, 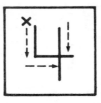, and five as a single move resembling an S. Demonstrate the movements and the rhythm of numeral writing at the chalkboard. Describe each movement as you make it. Let several children practice at the chalkboard at a time as you observe their movements. Introduce only one symbol at a time and build the repertoire of symbols as they learn to enumerate sets. Some activities which facilitate numeral writing follow.

1. Place a chart like the one below beside a sand board (a container of sand). The children make a numeral like the one on the chart by marking with their fingers in the sand. (Note the arrows and the beginning "x" on the chart.) Erasing and practice are simple with sand, and the child's tactile sense is incorporated in the learning.

2. Use commercially available, or teacher made, numerals made of sand paper or velour and mounted on stiff backing and allow the children to trace these figures with their fingers. Again the materials are of a kinesthetic type.

3. Paper and pencil activities, such as those given below, can be found in abundance.

Write the numeral for the set   Trace the numeral below
and then write it in the blank.

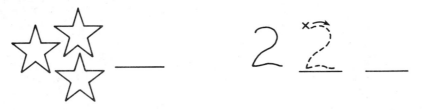

Selected Number Abilities and Related Activities

As children learn about number, they need practice activities. A brief summary of representative number abilities and related practice activities and games is provided below. Two words of caution should be mentioned regarding the selection and use of games: (1) Be sure that the game or activity you select is suited to your specific needs; a game ill-suited to a particular purpose is wasteful. (2) Also be sure that the activity parallels each child's ability. A game which is beyond a child's capability at a given point can be detrimental psychologically and emotionally and, at the same time, promotes no math learning. The games described are recommended because they can involve few or many children and they do provide practice at various stages of number learning.

1. Ability to count by rote.

   Example: Play the game, "Buzz-Buzz." At least four or five members of the class form a circle and count by turns. A certain digit is agreed upon. When that digit is a part of a number reached in the counting process (or a multiple of that digit is a variation of the game), the child counting says, "Buzz," instead of that number. For example, if the digit is 2, the counting goes "1, buzz, 3, 4, 5, 6, 7, 8, 9, 10, 11, buzz, . . ."

   Example: Recite nursery rhymes, children's songs, and finger-plays involving number. "Chickadees," "One Little Brown Bird," and "Ten Little Indians" are just three of the many available.

2. Ability to count rationally.

   Example: Supply the child with various sets and have him determine their respective number properties. (How many beans are in this cup? How many beads on this string? etc.)

3. Ability to associate sets with a specific numeral.

   Example: Play "Ice Cream Cone." Make 11 felt "cones" to be used on a flannel board and number them from 1–10. Also make 11 pieces of "ice cream" with dots on them from 0–10. Each child matches his or her "ice cream" with appropriate "cones."

   Example: Play the game, "Bounce-the-Ball." One child stands in front of a group of 2 to 10 and bounces the ball any numer of times from 1–10 while the others listen. The child who bounced the ball asks another player to tell how many times the ball was bounced. The child who gives the correct number is permitted to bounce the ball next.

4. Ability to reproduce a set of a given number.

   Example: Ask the child to hand you three crayons, four books, etc.

   Example: Play "Card Match" with from one to four children. Remove face cards from an ordinary deck of cards or make a set of your own from 3 × 5 cards. Give each child a random assortment of a single suit. (Each player now has an assortment of 10 cards, each with a numeral and the corresponding number of figures on it.) One child is leader and places the card of his choice on the table for everyone to see. The other players must find the card which matches the card on the table in their own suit and place their corresponding card on the table also. Players check to see that all choices were correct. Players take turn being leader.

5. Ability to compare sets to find out how many.

   Example: Ask children lined up for an activity how many more children are in Line 1 than Line 2?

   Example: Play the card game, "War." Remove the face cards from an ordinary deck of playing cards. Shuffle and separate the deck into two equal piles, face down in front of each of two players. The two players each turn their top card over simultaneously. The winner of the play is the one with the higher valued card, and he takes the "trick." Two equal-valued cards mean "War." Two more cards are dealt face down and the subsequent card is turned up. The winner of this pairing wins all cards in that play. The child with the most cards at the end of play is the game winner.

6. Ability to recognize numerals.

Example: Play the game, "Bingo." Prepare cards on which appear various assortments of six of the numerals 1–10. The leader calls a numeral from 1–10, being careful to remember the numbers he has called. Each player places a bean on the numeral called if it appears on his card. The first child to cover all numbers on his card calls "Bingo" and then becomes leader of the next game.

Example: Play "Number Jump." You will need at least five floor tiles, each with a numeral painted on it. Scatter the tiles on the floor all within jumping distance of each other. Call a number and have the child jump on the appropriate tile. If correct, give another number until he or she misses or jumps through all five tiles. (If a child misses a given numeral identification, make a mental note so that you can help the child correctly identify that numeral next time. Remember that a game atmosphere is not fun for a child meeting failure.)

7. Ability to group objects to help determine a number property.

Example: Grouping objects and skip counting are preludes to multiplication. Present the child with sets such as the groupings of two below and have him count "2, 4, 6, 8" to determine the number property.

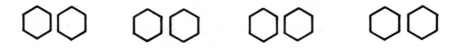

8. Ability to arrange numerals in order.

Example: Given a scrambled set of five cards, each with a single numeral 1–5 on it, the child is asked to rearrange them in proper order.

Example: An extension of the previous activity can also be done with four children and a deck of playing cards with face cards removed. Give each child one suit in random order and have him or her arrange his suit in proper sequence. At one glance you can tell who is ordering correctly and who needs help.

Example: Play "Bean Bag Toss." For this game you will need bean bags and floor tiles each with a number 1–10 painted on it. (The same tiles may be used for "Number Jump" described earlier.) Place the tiles on the floor in scrambled order. Have the child toss bean bags on the tiles according to correct numerical order. With each game the child tries to better his previous record.

9. Ability to supply missing numerals in a sequence.

Example: Practice with the activity, "Neighbors." One child writes a numeral on the chalkboard and says, for example, "I am 12. Who are my neighbors?" Another child comes to the board and writes 11 and 13 on appropriate sides of 12. The activity continues with either the teacher or children selecting numerals for which to determine "neighbors."

Concrete-To-Abstract Continuum

As is apparent from the previous discussion, activities for number learning are abundant. But which ones are appropriate for a given child at a particular point in his learning? Young children in any one classroom may be at a wide variety of points along their continuum of learning for a given concept. Some may need extensive work at the concrete level, others may be functioning at the semi-concrete level as they learn a given number concept, and still a few others may be able to deal with the same concept at the abstract level. Any math topic can be approached at any level of procedure depending on the needs of the individual child. It is up to the teacher to determine at what point along the continuum the child is functioning and to select those activities which are appropriate for a given child at a certain point along that continuum.

The key is to maintain a basic pattern of activity in moving from the concrete to the abstract; then variations can be formulated for any specific mathematical concept. For example, let's summarize previous discussions and simultaneously establish a pattern of procedure which may be followed in the teaching of any number—four, for example. The diagram in Figure 7 illustrates movement along the concrete-to-abstract continuum as the child is helped to learn the cardinality of four.

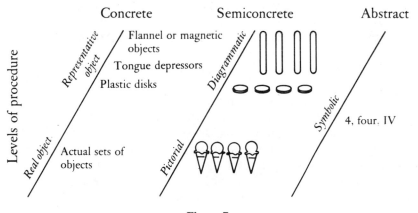

Figure 7.

Movement begins at the lower left and proceeds up each diagonal; this movement need neither be rigid nor uniform for all children. Some children will need numerous activities on each diagonal as they progress to the abstract level on the right; others will be able to proceed directly from left to right by doing only a few activities on each diagonal. Note too that some activities may involve elements of both the concrete and the abstract. Do not be concerned with this as you plan; the important consideration is to include activities at each level.

Basically, at the concrete level you and your students are manipulating actual objects. Remember that the child does not learn directly from the objects themselves but instead from actually working with the objects. The first level of procedure at the concrete end of the continuum involves real objects. You may have the child bounce a ball four times, place four milk cartons on the table, select four crayons, or bring four books to you. The only difference occurring, then, at the representative object level is that small disks, popsicle sticks, or whatever separate, discrete objects are available may be used. Now the child must make one more step in the abstraction of the number four. He must generalize that four is a property independent of the type of objects involved. At all levels within this stage, however, the child can touch and manipulate objects, whether real or representative.

The next diagonal, which represents the semiconcrete stage, is an interim stage during which pictures or diagrams on the printed page may be involved. Instead of placing four milk cartons on his desk, the child circles a picture of four milk cartons on a sheet of paper or perhaps draws a set of four milk cartons. These are typical activities at the pictorial level of the semiconcrete stage. At the diagrammatic level the child does the same kind of paper and pencil activities as at the pictorial level but instead selects, identifies, and matches representative figures like tally marks, dots, squares, and so on. Note that these semiconcrete activities are not the same as actually manipulating objects; paper work is important, but remember that it is an intermediate step and not the beginning point. Basically, the pictorial and diagrammatic levels parallel the real object and representative object levels with the limitation of being placed on paper or on the chalkboard instead of having the appeal of various senses other than visual. Also movement associated with joining and separating is missing.

The last diagonal represents the abstract level. A child at this point is ready to deal with the symbol for four. He must be able to respond, not only to the audio "four," but also he must recognize "4" and "four" as symbols to attach to that particular number property on which he has been working.

Activities just summarized in the learning of four may be generalized to the learning of any number necessary in initial learning situations. Also, these same activities could be used in a sequence beginning at any level for remediation. A teacher who has the general sequence of the continuum well in mind is ready to help a child at any level progress to an understanding of number by incorporating activities suited to that level.

SETS OF NUMBERS

The concept of set has been integral to discussion of prenumber experiences and the learning of number. Now sets will be incorporated on a more sophisticated plane as discussion turns to different sets of numbers.

Attention to this point has been directed at the set of counting numbers and, with zero, the set of whole numbers. When children extend their investigations to other sets of numbers, as much continuity as possible should be maintained. Number systems build, one upon the other, as illustrated in Figure 8.

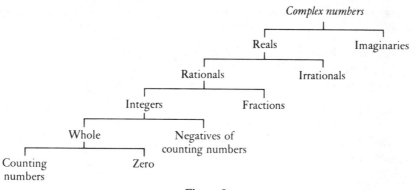

Figure 8.

Using the set operation of union to explain, the union of the counting numbers and zero is the set of whole numbers; the union of whole numbers with the negative counterparts of the counting numbers is the set of integers; the union of the integers with fractions is the set of rational numbers; the union of the rational numbers with the irrational numbers is the set of real numbers; and the union of the real numbers with the imaginary numbers is the set of complex numbers.

Although elementary school children do not work with the complex number system, they are familiar with the real numbers through exposure to the irrational number π. All other number systems, including the rationals, are commonly studied in varying degrees in the elementary school curriculum. It is desirable, therefore, for the children to make note of their expanding repertoire of number systems.

Noting different number systems will aid you, the teacher, too. No longer should a teacher find himself or herself stating this inaccuracy to a first-grader: "You CANNOT subtract seven from four, Johnny." Instead, the statement can be prefaced with a qualification about the set of numbers being used, the whole numbers in this case. You can then cope more easily with the situation which arises when Johnny checks temperatures during the winter and finds that the thermometer reading went down seven degrees after having been at four above zero. He sees that the temperature is three degrees below zero, or negative three. With this set of numbers, the integers, the problem of subtracting seven from four produces a very correct answer of -3.

CHAPTER KEY POINTS

1. Children at the elementary school level cannot be expected to learn abstractly. They must relate what they learn to the physical world and they rely heavily upon their senses in their learning.

2. Prenumber experiences are important preludes to number learning. Such experiences relate to abilities associated with the concrete operations stage of development and include matching objects, conserving discontinuous quantities, reversing, seriating, comparing sets quantitatively, and comparing sets qualitatively.

3. Qualitative set comparisons involve sorting activities, set-relations activities, and set-operations activities.

4. Children must learn both cardinal and ordinal uses of number. The cardinality of a given finite set is its number property; cardinality answers the question, "How many?" Ordinality is concerned with position and answers the question, "Which one?"

5. Rote counting refers to the ability to recite number names in sequence through memorization and not understanding. Children who can count by rote are beginning to realize that there is a sequence used to name numbers but they don't necessarily know how many objects any given number represents.

6. Rational counting involves an understanding of the enumerative process on the part of the counter. Children who have learned to count rationally have built their understanding upon early experiences in matching and comparing sets. They have developed a "one-more" concept in the building of number sequences.

7. Numerals are the names and symbols used to communicate about the abstract concept of number. Numerous activities are available to help children read and write numerals associated with specific quantities.

8. As children develop necessary understandings about numbers, they need to practice what they have learned. This practice can assume many forms, two of which are activities and games. These should be selected according to specific needs and not randomly. Games can be found which provide pleasant practice in such activities as rote and rational counting, identifying sets with a specific number in them, reproducing sets of a given number, comparing sets to find out "How many more?", recognizing numerals, grouping objects to determine number property, arranging numerals in order, and supplying missing numerals in a given sequence.

9. The pattern followed in the concrete-to-abstract continuum provides a consistent sequence which can be used in helping any child to learn a given number concept. The teacher can select from a variety of activities at a given level of procedure for a specific child at a specific stage in his or her learning of a number concept and then proceed through various degrees of abstraction appropriate to the child's need. The continuum provides direction for both initial learning and remediation.

10. As children expand their knowledge of number, they also expand the repertoire of number systems within which they can work. Elementary school children commonly have experience with the sets of counting numbers, whole numbers, integers, and rational numbers. Work with the real numbers is usually limited to the introduction of the irrational number of pi.

Laboratory 6

Developing Number Concepts

Regardless of the level at which you, as teacher, are going to work with a child, you should have a basic knowledge of a child's initial mathematical learning related to the development of number concepts. The following exercises are designed to acquaint you with various instructional materials which may be used with the child in the classroom to develop number concepts.

I. *Objectives:* Upon completion of these laboratory exercises, you should be able to do the following:

    A. Identify basic learning which a child must possess in order to demonstrate understanding of numbers and numerals. (Chapter Competency 6–A)

    B. Describe instructional aids and activities which will facilitate a child's learning of number concepts. (Chapter Competencies 6–B and 6–C)

II. *Materials:* Any kindergarten or first-grade teacher's edition of an elementary mathematics textbook series, set of attribute pieces consisting of three shapes (square, triangle, circle) with two sizes for each shape. There should be one of each size and shape in each of the following colors: red, yellow, blue, green, and white.

III. *Procedure:*

    A. Read Chapter 6 of *Helping Children Learn Mathematics.* If you have any questions, consult your instructor.

    B. Choose a primer or first-grade elementary text (teacher's edition) and along with several classmates, examine how number concepts are developed. Items 1 and 2 which follow will aid you in your examination.

        1. Give the bibliographical information for the text which you have chosen. How is number introduced? Is study with sets involved? What types of activities are used to introduce number? Do the suggested activities feature child involvement? How are cardinality and ordinality introduced?

        2. In Chapter 2 both process- and product-oriented approaches to learning were discussed. What elements of each viewpoint do you find in your examination of the text? Is there any reference to readiness? Are there any activities to determine each child's ability to conserve or seriate number or perform other tasks related to the stage of concrete operations? Compare your responses to these questions with some classmates who examined a different textbook series to learn in what ways your findings were similar or different.

    C. Identify three manipulative aids which you would like to have in your classroom for helping children learn the fundamental aspects of "number."

    D. Describe briefly three activities which you might use to involve children in PRACTICING numeral identification, cardinality, and ordinality (one activity for each area). Give the objective(s) for each activity which you describe.

E. List five activities that you would expect a child to be able to do to indicate an understanding of "six."

F. Design an instructional strategy which you would use to help a child learn the concept of number. Why did you choose this strategy? Were any of your decisions based upon the work of Piaget, Bruner, and/or Gagné? If so, in what way?

G. Attribute pieces are fundamentally a set of assorted geometric plastic shapes with varying characteristics (attributes). Because the attributes are carefully controlled according to shape, size, color, and thickness, the pieces are useful in developing number concepts. Children usually want to start grouping them in various ways and this desire leads to a suitable beginning in sorting and classifying. Activities in which patterns are formed are followed by increasingly more complex sequences. The pieces are useful in later set work, in geometry, and in probability. Some activities follow which will offer you some practice with the pieces.

    1. Begin with the large red circle. Place next to it all the pieces which differ from it ONLY in color. Must the pieces be large? Must they be circles? Can they be red? How many pieces differ ONLY in color?

    2. Begin again with the large red circle but this time find those pieces which differ only in shape. How many did you find?

    3. Repeat the procedure finding those which differ only in size.

    4. Altogether, how many blocks differ from the large red circle by ONLY one attribute? Suppose we had begun with a different block. How many of the remaining twenty-nine blocks would have differed from that block by one attribute only? (Try to visualize the situation; if you are having difficulty, repeat the above activities with a different initial piece.)

    5. Start again with the large red circle. How many pieces differ from it in size and shape? in size and color? in shape and color? Notice that we are searching for two-attribute differences. Altogether, then, how many pieces differ from a given piece by two attributes?

    6. For any given block, how many of the remaining twenty-nine blocks differ by three attributes?

    7. To build a one-difference sequence, blocks can be arranged in a line, each block different from the one to the immediate left by exactly one attribute. Consider the following four blocks of a one-difference sequence and decide what blocks could be placed after the small yellow triangle.

8. Examine the four blocks in the following sequence and again decide what blocks could be placed after the large red square.

9. Use what you learned above to design a four-block sequence in which there will be four possible blocks for the fifth position.

10. Arrange sixteen blocks on a four-by-four grid so that blocks adjacent horizontally are one attribute different and blocks on the vertical are two attributes different.

7
Numeration

Teacher Competencies

After studying Chapter 7 and completing Laboratory 7, you should be able to achieve each of the following:

A. Given a selected concept or skill in the area of numeration, design foundational activities which may be used in the acquisition of that concept or skill. (Part Competency III-A)

B. Given a selected concept or skill in the area of numeration, identify activities which may be used to develop proficiency in the use of that concept or skill. (Part Competency III-B)

C. Given a selected concept or skill in the area of numeration, identify and/or demonstrate the use of selected instructional aids which might be used to help a child learn that concept or skill. (Part Competency III-C)

Numeration is the system of assigning numerals to numbers. When one speaks of a given numeration system, he is referring to the sounds and symbols incorporated in identifying various quantities according to the given system. The numeration system most commonly used today is the Hindu-Arabic system, a base ten system using positional, or place, value.

A thorough understanding of this system is a major goal of elementary school mathematics instruction. Too often, however, the instruction does not meet its intended goal with numerous problems awaiting both the teacher and the student who have dealt with the topic superficially.

Because the teaching of basic sounds and symbols associated with various numbers was covered at length in a previous chapter, discussion at this point will revolve around the following question: How can you, as teacher, provide a learning environment which will facilitate the development of an understanding of the structure of our system of numeration? First, we'll explore the possibilities related to a developmental sequencing of activities.

THE HINDU-ARABIC NUMERATION SYSTEM: A DEVELOPMENTAL APPROACH

The importance of work at the concrete level cannot be overemphasized. Structural understanding of the Hindu-Arabic system, which is facilitated by work at the concrete level, is fundamental to subsequent work in such areas as doing written and mental computation, dealing with large numbers, and comprehending certain algebraic concepts. Forced abstractions too early can result in such sing-song efforts as "this is the one's place, this is the ten's place, this is the hundred's place, . . ." The words are correct, but the understanding may be deficient, and new math is turned into new rote.

This is not meant to imply that practice on paper and oral practice are undesirable; they are indeed vital at a given point. Whether a child should be working at the concrete level, at the abstract level, or at some interim level is dependent on a variety of factors, not the least of which are his developmental stage and his point of progress through the logical sequencing of the content of numeration.

Consider the chart in Figure 1, describing alternatives from which you might choose to help a child better understand place value. Before dealing with specific examples, examine the chart generally. There are three diagonals placed under three general headings: concrete, semiconcrete, and abstract. On the left is a signification of "levels of procedure," each described by the titles written on the diagonals, e.g., real object, representative object. By proceeding upward on each diagonal one encounters activities involving somewhat more advanced levels of thinking than that which preceded each. This does not imply that you need only begin with a child at the lower left and end at the upper right in order to succeed in teaching place value to every child satisfactorily. It does provide a sample framework for moving from the concrete to the abstract in place value work, and it should represent some of the considerations that a teacher might have made in planning which manipulative devices and which workbook activities would be appropriate for a given child, whether planning initial learning experiences or remedial ones.

Let us consider what might be done for Ann, a child at the primary level who does not yet fully comprehend the concept of place value. The teacher decides to involve Ann actively at the concrete level as indicated on the left diagonal of the chart. The following points are salient. There are a variety of concrete materials available, they themselves differing in degree of abstraction. For example, one may begin at the real object level where the actual objects are there for manipulation, whether they be marbles, theater tickets, elephants, or ice cream cones. Or, because of some obvious disadvantages sometimes associated with the use of real objects, one might use representative objects, thereby introducing an element of abstraction in having a circular disk or a tongue depressor stand for an ice cream cone.

In any case, at this stage Ann has all the objects before her, i.e., per the chart, 24 objects to manipulate and group. Although any discrete objects could be used for grouping purposes, straws, tongue depressors, and popsicle sticks grouped with rubber bands or twistems have been used with success. She may initially identify the number of objects by establishing a one-to-one correspondence between the set of counting numbers and the objects before her; or more simply stated, she may count them, which is a perfectly justifiable technique. Counting does not, however, indicate an understanding of place value. If, on the other hand, Ann were to collect the objects into groups of ten, finding that she had two groups of the base and four which could not be grouped, she would

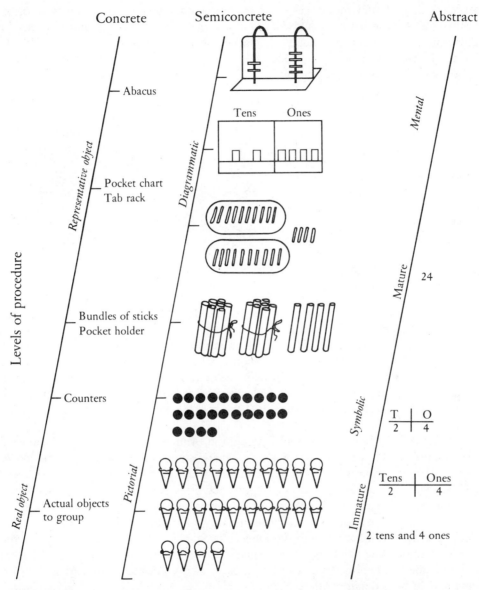

Figure 1. Place value (Example: 24).

be exhibiting initial efforts into the place value concept. Thus far Ann would always be dealing with the actual number of objects whether they had been grouped in certain ways or not.

An intermediary device which combines some of the elements of grouping with those which follow in the sequence of the place value chart is a kit of *base ten blocks* (see the next illustration). Although variations exist in basic dimensions and in materials, structurally the kit may be described as consisting of numerous pieces which may be combined into various powers of the base—ten, in this case. A base ten kit would consist of a large quantity of tiny unit cubicals (units); rectangular blocks representing ten cubicals placed end to end (longs); large square blocks representing ten rectangular blocks placed side by side (flats); and cubical shapes representing the large square blocks stacked ten deep (blocks). The blocks are notched to resemble units joined together.

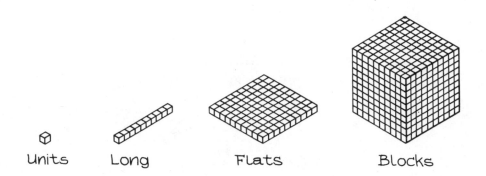

Units   Long   Flats   Blocks

Several valuable activities in numeration can be derived from the use of these blocks. At this point all of the units are before the child, but now the groupings have already been made. Ann can trade ten of one unit for one larger block in the next higher unit, an activity similar to those described a little later but which still involves all of the objects whether combined or not. She can determine for herself that 123 can be made of 123 units; 12 ten blocks and 3 units; or 1 hundred block and 2 ten blocks and 3 unit blocks. She can build 2435 and see for herself that although the face value of "2" is less than "5," the position which "2" occupies gives it a much greater value.

As mentioned briefly in the preceding paragraph, Ann might then be ready to move up the levels of procedure at the concrete stage to a point whereby one object in a certain position "stands for" so many in another position. Instead of bundling sticks or stacking disks into groups of ten, she would be engaged in *exchanging,* or *regrouping,* activities. It is through these types of activities that Ann can learn that just as 10 ones may be grouped into one bundle of ten, so also may 10 ones be exchanged for their equal, 1 ten, coded in a way other than bundling or grouping. Perhaps initially the coding would be by color: 100 blue disks equalling 10 white and 10 white equalling 1 red. Perhaps the coding would be through coins. Finding that 16 pennies are equivalent to 1 dime and 6 pennies often provides motivation where it has been lacking. At some point, however, the coding should be through position.

Numerous devices are available commercially, but reasonable facsimiles can be easily made by the teacher and often serve the purpose well. Juice cans or milk cartons (tops removed) labeled "ones," "tens," and "hundreds" and placed side by side can serve as holders for straws, popsicle sticks, or tongue depressors. As ten are accumulated in a box they are removed and *exchanged* for a *single* stick in the next container to the left.

Another easily made device which proves useful at this stage is the *pocket chart*. Again, if purchasing enough pocket charts for the entire class is prohibitive, a simple fold in the bottom of an opened manilla folder with some strategically placed staples can form a pocket chart. Having the children then cut tabs makes short work of the project. The basic procedure remains the same as in working with the cans insofar as when 10 tabs are accumulated in one pocket, they are removed and exchanged for 1 tab in the next pocket to the left.

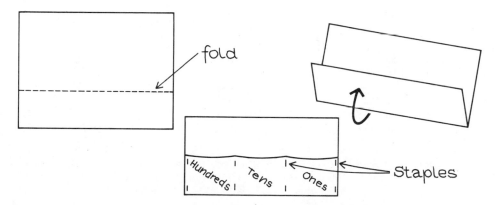

A primary tool in the teaching of numerations is the *abacus*. An 18– or 20–bead abacus is extremely useful in teaching regrouping and in later work in addition and subtraction. Since the abacus consists only of disks, wires, and a frame, the child must not only perform the exchanging correctly, but must also know which wire represents which positional value.

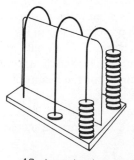

18–bead abacus

Mention should be made here about the possible confusion which Ann might have in doing numeration activities. In mathematics, unlike in reading, the child is asked to work from right to left. The teacher should be aware that this manipulation is opposite of that asked of the child at other times.

At each point described in the concrete level, the teacher may ask Ann either to picture on paper the work she has just done or to interpret the same in a diagram provided. Such products are pictured on the middle diagonal of the place value chart (Figure 1) and are labeled "semiconcrete." The pictorial stage parallels the real object stage, and the pictures look as realistic as possible; the diagrammatic stage similarly parallels the representative object stage, and various marks are made to represent objects. None of the diagrams in the chart have really shown the action involved in the regrouping process. Actually, no marks on paper can do this as effectively as working with the objects themselves; marks on paper only illustrate the action that has been performed or visualized (they *record* the action). Action can be illustrated to some degree by the use of arrows. For example, perhaps 13 beads are placed in the one's position on the abacus, and the child is asked to show how this would look if regrouping were done. She might illustrate it as follows:

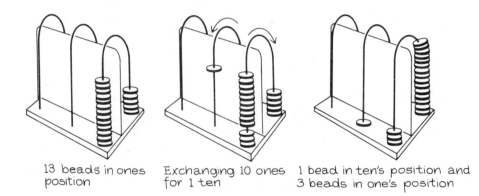

13 beads in ones position

Exchanging 10 ones for 1 ten

1 bead in ten's position and 3 beads in one's position

To a child who has had sufficient practice with manipulating real objects, the picturing of the action should not be too difficult. Again, however, such picturing activities should only follow and supplement actual regrouping work with the tangible, concrete objects; they should not be used in lieu of the concrete activities.

Stress has been given to the ten's and one's exchanges, but little mention has been made of exchanges of greater values at both the concrete and the semiconcrete levels. To generalize the base ten-place value idea, Ann should be able to see for herself, with the teacher's guidance and with ample concrete practice, that each position is ten times greater in value than that to its right. Also, in time she should be able to interpret 257 not only as 2 hundreds 5 tens and 7 ones, but also as 25 tens and 7 ones or even as 1 hundred 15 tens and 7 ones. Such versatility in interpretation may test a primary level teacher's patience, but the results of these efforts are of inestimable value in later work with the basic operations.

Lastly, the child may need some immature forms of recording the numeral before the mature form (24) is understood. A few of these forms are indicated on the right diagonal of the place value chart and are labeled "abstract." Perhaps writing the numeral completely with place value names will help (2 tens and 4 ones). When Ann discovers that the pattern for naming remains invariant, however, she will want to devise a simpler technique for recording the number. Perhaps a grid form is the choice:

Tens	Ones
2	4

Another abbreviated form may then evolve:

T	O
2	4

Ultimately the positional notation evolves, and Ann decides that she could just as well write 24 as long as the meaning is clear.

To summarize, not all of these activities will be necessary for a particular child; on the other hand, many more activities of a similar nature may be imperative for another child. Again, it is your responsibility as teacher to decide the proportionate doses necessary for each of your students. Using the laboratory or active-learning approach, you will find that you are guiding the learning of each child as he proceeds at his own optimum rate.

HISTORICAL AND NONDECIMAL APPROACHES TO NUMERATION

Some teachers will decide not to proceed beyond the teaching of the base ten-place value developmental approach described in the preceding section. Reasons for such a decision usually revolve around one of these three arguments: (1) the belief that most people have little or no need for a system other than the one used commonly in society today; (2) the belief that the pupils would be inept or become confused; or (3) the belief that the teacher's own ability to diversify instruction in the area is inadequate.

Given special circumstances, the choice of these teachers might be appropriate. Certainly, the ultimate decision as to whether or not to incorporate variations in the teaching of numeration is the teacher's. Under appropriate circumstances, however, we would suggest varying degrees of the alternatives discussed in the next section.

Historical Approach

In opting to use the historical approach as a way of varying instruction, the teacher opens several methods for active learning situations and for creating interest.

Whether the class studies only one alternative system or several is relatively unimportant. Regardless of the choice, however, several important conclusions should be reached: (1) numeration systems are a product of man and were devised by him as the need arose; (2) not all numeration systems are alike structurally, but some similarities can be found; and (3) the Hindu-Arabic system offers certain advantages over other historical systems.

The historical approach could be concisely presented by simply having the child memorize these three points and complete a couple of workbook pages in Roman numerals. But how useless! The points above are only *representative* conclusions that the teacher would like the student to reach after reading about other systems and experimenting with other systems on *both* a concrete and an abstract level. Through the teacher's guidance and provision of a proper learning environment, the child learns to compare and contrast the structure of other systems with his own, thereby finding that number can be, and has been, approached in a variety of ways. He finds that just as languages other than his own exist, so also do other number systems exist. By providing the proper learning environment, the teacher helps the child to arrive at his *own* conclusions.

Although numerous writings on the history of mathematics exist on both an elementary and an adult level, brief mention should be made here of some historical options that are available.

Early Man.   Most young children enjoy the study of early man and his initial efforts in the development of number. Because early man lived prior to written historical accounts, much of what is described is conjecture. Historians, however, agree with the conclusions. They believe that as early man accumulated more possessions and traded more goods with his companions, he developed a need for number to keep account of possessions. He used a one-to-one notion initially. In keeping count of his sheep, for example, he matched them one-to-one with another set—perhaps pebbles or notches on a stick. By matching them later, he could determine whether he had more, fewer, or the same as before. As his flock increased in size he may have decided to streamline his work and decrease the number of pebbles he needed. He discovered that he himself always carried a set of counters with him in the form of fingers. He could match sheep with fingers; after using all of his fingers, he could make a notch or represent this with a single stone, thereby grouping at ten and providing a beginning for our base of ten.

Egyptians and Babylonians.   The Egyptian system and the Babylonian system are interesting insofar as they are repetitive and additive in nature, and each provides a contrast with the positional characteristics of the Hindu-Arabic system. Also of some interest are the symbols incorporated by each system. Man, quite logically, chose symbols which were easily made by the writing tools he used. The Egyptians used a brush-type stroke on papyrus and so developed the following numerals:

Number represented	Symbol	Name
1	/	Staff
10	∩	Heel bone
100	9	Scroll

Note that the symbols pictured objects familiar to a sheepherding group of people. The Babylonians, unlike the Egyptians, recorded numerals with a stylus on clay, and so they evolved a very natural wedge-shaped character.

Number represented	Symbol
1	V
10	<

Both systems used repetition extensively. In recording 24, for example, they would write:

Egyptians	Babylonians
∩∩ ////	< < V V V V

By repeating each symbol enough times and then totaling the result, they would arrive at the intended number. Notice, however, that these systems were used only to record numbers and not to perform operations. A few sample problems done by the children investigating the systems should result in their concluding that adding and subtracting are at least performable but that multiplying and dividing are very unwieldly in these systems. How then did these people do basic operations? They used calculating devices much like those the children use today, major differences occurring only in the way the numbers are recorded. Some experimentation with historical calculating devices like the sand board or counting board usually leads to fruitful observations about the systems.

Greeks.   At one point in their history, the Greeks used their alphabet symbols as their numerals, too, and it was the individual's decision whether the symbol was related to a number or an object or a person. This situation led to all sorts of fascinating results. Because now a number could be assigned to any object or person, people began to attach mystical significance to certain numbers. Studies in numerology and gematria were undertaken and in fact still remain today. References to such can be found in the Bible. Further reading and experimenting in this historical-mathematical area might stimulate motivation in some students. They could explore such questions as: "What complications could arise today if we used the same symbols for both our alphabet and our numerals?" and "Are there any advantages to such a system?"

Romans.   The Roman numeration system is still the most commonly taught alternative system, possibly because it is still used on preface pages in books, cornerstones of buildings, and certain outline forms. Certainly it is not taught because of being totally unique in its structure. It is basically a base ten system, but it has the additional feature of "half-way" grouping points. Recall that it looks like this:

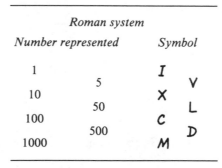

Roman system

Number represented		Symbol	
1		I	
	5		V
10		X	
	50		L
100		C	
	500		D
1000		M	

Although there have been a number of conjectures about the origins of the symbols I, V, and X, the tally notion seems most logical. Initially, the Romans merely tallied to arrive at the appropriate number, but to help keep track they crossed through the tally with a cross (X) to symbolize ten. Five is half of ten (V). Later symbols appear to be the first letter of the identifying word e.g., C represents *centum* and M represents *mille*. Initially the system was repetitive and additive only in nature. The subtractive form was a later invention of clock makers who encountered difficulty placing IIII and VIIII on a clock face. They introduced the notion of placing a lesser valued symbol to the left of a higher valued symbol to represent a subtractive situation. Then IV would be one less than five and IX would be one less than ten—much shorter than the additive forms and the clocks would be more symmetrical in appearance. Once again the student might explore such questions as: "Why don't we use the Roman system today?"; "How did it prove satisfactory to the Romans?"; and "If you had been a Roman, what materials might you have wanted available in order to do your arithmetic?"

Hindus-Arabs. The Hindu-Arabic system, described in detail earlier, originated with the Hindus in Asia. Actually the Hindus had developed the system of place value, had invented the zero, and had developed the symbols. They were very advanced people in terms of mathematical ability. The Arabs were the ones who, through their conquests, adopted the system and spread it into Western Europe. At first the system met with much opposition in Europe, however, and laws were even passed forbidding its use. Ultimately, of course, it was accepted and was in use when Columbus discovered America. Children investigating the system can be asked to ponder and explore the following: "Why was this system finally used in preference to others?"; "In what ways is the Hindu-Arabic system better?"; and "How might it still be improved?"

These are only representative samples of historical numeration schemes. Perhaps your students will want to study other systems. The Chinese and Mayans had numeration systems often described in literature, but what about the American Indian or the African native? Did he have a numeration system? Whatever system is studied, the historical approach should proceed on an active, experimental, investigative, comparative plane.

Nondecimal Basal Systems Approach

Another variation in the teaching of numeration is the nondecimal basal systems approach. The teaching of number bases can proceed along any of several dimensions. The selection is highly dependent on the teacher's reason for teaching nondecimal systems.

If number bases are taught only because they are found in the children's text or because they are part of "new math," then the teacher approaches the topic abstractly. The children are taught the mechanics of converting from one base to another, usually to and from base ten. Once they have mastered the conversion technique, the "how to," it is assumed that they understand that which is salient to number bases. This approach is often used, or perhaps better stated, mis-used. On the other hand, the teacher might reason thusly and so act differently if he asks himself, "*why* were number bases included in many modern mathematics programs?"

Ten, the collection point of the Hindu-Arabic system, is really an arbitrary selection, probably having been used simply because man was born with that number of fingers. Other systems using the same basic structure but with differing collection points, or bases, might serve some purposes more satisfactorily than the system with a base of ten. In fact, this is true; in computer work a collecting point of two is used (to relate to on-off electrical currents and yes-no decisions); a carpenter essentially uses a base of twelve when using inches and feet; a stockbroker uses a base of eight in noting market returns; and packagers who crate in dozens and gross often use a base twelve system with success.

"But," the teacher reasons, "even though such bases may have uses in certain occupations, why should the majority of children be exposed to such varied base systems?" The reasons are similar to those given for teaching historical systems; namely, alternative systems provide opportunity to study the Hindu-Arabic system in relation to another system and to see its structure and its characteristics against a variable background. With nondecimal systems, the comparative possibilities are even greater than with historical systems because the basic structure is the same; the place value concept remains the same; the pattern for naming can remain the same; and the techniques for the basic operations parallel those used in the Hindu-Arabic system.

Study of nondecimal systems, then, can help a person to figuratively step back from the system with which he has become so familiar and study it from a new perspective, thereby becoming aware of properties that were so close to him that he could not see them. A developmental approach much like that described in the section entitled "The Hindu-Arabic Numeration System: A Developmental Approach" is quite valuable in generalizing the place value concept when a nondecimal base is used. Grouping activities followed by exchanging activities in nondecimal bases have provided enlightening experiences for both children and adults. Simple counting exercises in a base other than ten illustrate the pattern used in naming numbers. The number-numeral distinction becomes clearer as children see names varying as the grouping point varies. Building addition and multiplication tables helps generalize the technique of building base ten tables. Performing simple operations not only clarifies patterning in this area, but often the basic properties of commutativity, associativity, and distributivity are made apparent.

If any of these benefits are not clear to you, the teacher, you should select a base other than ten and, using selected manipulative aids, actually proceed from the concrete to the abstract just as you would ask the child to do in base ten. Four would be a good base to begin with. Counters and a pocket chart might be used for manipulative devices; the collecting idea is predominant with counters, and exchanges are the keynote with the pocket chart. Then ask yourself the same kinds of questions that you would ask of your own pupils in base ten. Proceed to answer the questions using the same techniques as you would expect your pupils to use.

A number of revelations may arise. You may find that you are drawing on your own reservoir of memorized facts instead of trying to know what thought you are expecting of the pupil. Of course, since you are not a child, you cannot be expected to think as a child. With activities such as those just described, however, you may begin to know what kinds of thought are required in learning base and place value. When you encounter pitfalls in your developmental approach to a nondecimal numeration system, you might expect the same kind of difficulties to occur with your pupils in base ten work because structurally the systems parallel. Another advantage to associate with your actually following a developmental approach to numeration systems with place value is your discovery of numerous possibilities for laboratory activities no matter which base is used.

Since the possibilities are endless in teaching nondecimal systems, you should examine several before deciding on any one course of action. Familiar symbols with coding might be used; familiar symbols but with different sounding names might be used; or totally unfamiliar symbols can be used. Whatever nondecimal base system you may decide to teach, the most important point is that structure and pattern remain the key.

CHAPTER KEY POINTS

1. Numeration is the systm of assigning numerals to numbers. The numeration system most commonly used today is the Hindu-Arabic system, a base ten system using positional, or place, value.

2. Teaching the structure of our numeration system may be one of the most fundamentally important tasks of the elementary teacher; and it can be one of the most rewarding if approached developmentally.

3. Real objects, counters, base ten blocks, bundles of sticks, pocket charts, and abaci are among the real and representative objects available to help children learn numeration at the concrete level. There should be ample opportunity to group these various objects according to place value. Also ample practice is needed in exchanging and regrouping between and among the various positional values.

4. As the child moves into more abstract stages in numeration he or she may picture or diagram the situation under discussion.

5. Among the immature forms of recording numerals are the use of written words and place value grids. Finally, the symbols themselves are sufficient to assign sufficient meaning for the child.

6. Using a historical approach in teaching numeration offers variety. Whatever system(s) are chosen for study, these conclusions should be reached: (a) numeration systems are man made; (b) not all numeration systems are structurally alike, but there are some similarities; and (c) the Hindu-Arabic system offers certain advantages over certain other systems.

7. Nondecimal basal systems can offer numerous advantages to learners of any age if approached on a developmental level.

Laboratory 7

Numeration

The power of the Hindu-Arabic numeration system lies in the base-place characterization of its foundation. A child's success in later work with fundamental operations is dependent upon an understanding of numeration properties. The following exercises are designed to provide you with an opportunity to work with numeration systems other than base ten. All of these exercises may be adapted to base ten to help a child who is having difficulty with numeration.

I. *Objectives:* Upon completion of these laboratory exercises, you should be able to do the following:

    A. Describe a general sequence of activities which may be used when helping a child learn the Hindu-Arabic system of numeration. (Chapter Competencies 7–A and 7–B)

    B. Identify and correctly manipulate aids which may be used in the learning of numeration. (Chapter Competency 7–C)

II. *Materials:* Popsicle sticks and rubber bands (straws or tongue depressors may also be used); multibase blocks (available from Creative Publications, P.O. Box 10328, Palo Alto, CA 94303); abacus

III. *Procedure:*

    A. Read Chapter 7 of *Helping Children Learn Mathematics.* If you have questions, consult your instructor.

    B. It was suggested in the text that every prospective teacher of elementary school mathematics should relate as much as possible to what he is asking of his students. Unfortunately, when working with the base ten numeration system, we find that responses come automatically so that it becomes very difficult to realize that a child might not be able to comprehend work with the Hindu-Arabic system of numeration. In order to help you relate to the possible problems of your students, the following exercises are concerned with bases other than ten.

        1. Using popsicle sticks and rubber bands, count out 100_{four} sticks.

        2. Write the numerals from 1_{four} to 100_{four}

        3. Solve the following problems which are in base four, using popsicle sticks. Try to perform the operation without converting back to base ten.

$$21 + 3 = \underline{\hspace{1cm}} \qquad 101 - 23 = \underline{\hspace{1cm}}$$
$$11 - 3 = \underline{\hspace{1cm}} \qquad 3 \times 3 = \underline{\hspace{1cm}}$$
$$3 + 2 = \underline{\hspace{1cm}} \qquad 2 \times 12 = \underline{\hspace{1cm}}$$
$$10 - 2 = \underline{\hspace{1cm}} \qquad 3 \times 12 = \underline{\hspace{1cm}}$$

        4. Repeat Exercises 2 and 3 using an abacus.

5. Complete the following addition and multiplication tables in base four.

+	0	1	2	3
0				
1				
2				
3				

×	0	1	2	3
0				
1				
2				
3				

6. Repeat Exercises 1 through 5 using the same numerals but in base six.

C. Work in other base systems may also be done using multibase blocks as shown below. Sugar cubes glued together may be used if the multibase blocks are not available.

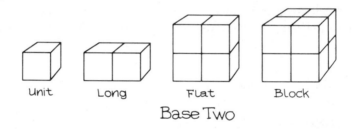

Unit   Long   Flat   Block

Base Two

To help familiarize you with multibase blocks, here is a simple game which you can play with some other classmates. You may use the blocks from any base except base ten. Play begins with each player rolling two dice; the player with the highest sum begins the game. The first player rolls the two dice (use only one die if the base two or base three blocks are used). Take from the pile of blocks the number of units, longs, flats, and blocks represented by the sum on the dice using the fewest number of pieces possible. Record the number of each piece used on the table which follows. If another player spots a mistake, he may challenge and if correct, the player making the mistake scores nothing for that round. If an incorrect challenge is made, the player who makes it loses his next turn. The first player to complete five successful turns signals the beginning of the final round, and each player gets one more turn. The player with the highest total wins the game.

Tosses	B	F	L	U
1				
2				
3				
4				
5				
Total				

D. What are three activities that you would expect a child to be able to do to exhibit un-derstanding of the number 24?

E. Identify five aids which you feel would be helpful to a child learning place value and describe the particular value of each.

F. You, as an adult, have been asked to respond briefly to some exercises in numeration systems other than base ten. Do you think that children should learn systems of numer-ation other than the Hindu-Arabic system or systems other than base ten? Why or why not?

8
Addition and Subtraction of Whole Numbers

Teacher Competencies

After studying Chapter 8 and completing Laboratory 8, you should be able to do the following:

   A. Given a selected concept or skill in the area of addition and subtraction of whole numbers, design foundational activities which may be used in the acquisition of that concept or skill. (Part Competency III-A)

   B. Given a selected concept or skill in the area of addition and subtraction of whole numbers, identify activities which may be used to develop proficiency in the use of that concept or skill. (Part Competency III-B)

   C. Given a selected concept or skill in the area of addition and subtraction of whole numbers, identify and/or demonstrate the use of selected instructional aids which might be used to help a child learn that concept or skill. (Part Competency III-C)

Whole numbers can be added, subtracted, multiplied, and divided; that is, operations can be performed on whole numbers. Permeating these various operations on whole numbers are basic properties which provide the foundation for algorithms associated with the operations. Operations and properties associated with whole numbers are highly interrelated, as subsequent discussions in this chapter and the next will reveal. There are also facets of each, however, which may best be emphasized in separate study. This chapter deals with addition and its inverse, subtraction.

The addition of whole numbers relates to the physical activity of joining sets of objects. After the child has had sufficient practice joining sets of three with sets of two, for example, he or she finds that the resultant set is five, regardless of the type of object being used. This situation may be related to the set operation of union and symbolized thusly when disjoint sets are used: $N(A) + N(B) = N(A \cup B)$. Translated, the equation states that the number property of set A plus the number property of set B is equal to the number property of the set representing the union of A and B. Notice that numbers ONLY are added, not sets. Sets may have an operation called union performed on them, or groups of objects may be joined, but sets are never referred to as having been "added." Notice also that addition is a binary operation; that is, exactly two numbers (addends) are operated on (added) to give another number (sum).

Subtraction is the inverse of addition. It is used to find a missing addend when the sum and one addend are known. Since addition relates to the physical activity of putting together or joining, then subtraction must relate to the physical activity of taking apart or separating. Also, comparison situations relate to subtraction.

An addition fact is comprised of a pair of single-digit addends and their sum; for example, $1 + 4 = 5$ is an addition fact because it is made up of the single-digit addition combination $1 + 4$ and the sum 5. Some addition situations involve more complicated numbers and so step-by-step computational procedures must be used to solve them. Such procedures are called algorithms (or algorisms). An addition algorithm would be used to solve this problem: $465 + 897 = x$.

Similarly, subtraction facts parallel the inverse situations described by addition facts; $6 - 2 = 4$ and $17 - 9 = 8$ are examples of subtraction facts. Subtraction algorithms are step-by-step computational procedures used to find answers to multi-digit subtraction problems like $45 - 36 = x$ and $731 - 24 = n$.

Now that abstract interpretations and terminologies for addition and subtraction have been provided, let's examine ways in which to help children learn properties, concepts, facts, and algorithms associated with each of these operations.

BASIC PROPERTIES

Basic properties of addition and subtraction play a fundamental role in helping children learn basic facts and algorithms. In fact, properties can be powerful mathematical tools at all levels when taught in a functional way from the beginning. While children may not learn formal words and formulas for commutativity, associativity, closure, and the existence of identities and inverses, they can understand the fundamental concepts involved.

Commutativity

Commutativity can be made real for even very young children. Upon working with two sets, they find that whether they join the first set with the second or the second set with the first, the resultant set is the same. As they assign numbers to these sets they also learn that the sum of these numbers is the same regardless of the order in which they are added; e.g., $2 + 3 = 3 + 2$.

Commutativity can be shown and verified in many ways. Trays, paper plates, sheets of paper, or floor tiles can be divided in half by marking through the center. Objects can be placed on either side and the corresponding number sentence recorded. Then by rotating the tray, tile, plate, etc., a half turn the objects have been "commuted" and the new number sentence can be recorded.

2 + 3 = 5   3 + 2 = 5

The same results can be obtained through the manipulation of a variety of other learning aids from dominoes to clothespins on a hanger. Each manipulation should result in a restatement or recording of the corresponding number sentence.

Commutativity is a valuable tool because it significantly reduces the number of addition facts to be learned. For example, if 3 + 4 = 7, then 4 + 3 = 7 also, and the 100 basic addition facts are reduced by almost a half (the doubles not having commutative pairs).

Some operations are NOT commutative. Subtraction is not commutative for example; that is, a − b ≠ b − a, when a and b are not equal. Again, children should be allowed to test commutativity themselves with real or representative objects; otherwise they may just be memorizing words.

As work with commutativity progresses, you might hear from one of your students that his older sister commutes to school in another town and he has decided that this means that the trip is the same whether she is going to or coming home from school. Such insights into the fundamental idea involved in commutativity should make you feel secure that this child will be able to use the property now and to understand it later if he proceeds in the more exacting aspects of mathematics. While commutativity is a difficult concept for many, it is one which can be approached concretely and by doing so provide foundational experiences for building later understanding.

Associativity

Associativity is a simple property which is too often misunderstood. Basically, think in terms of three entities and one operation. If the operation involves only two entities at a time, naturally it is impossible to deal with three simultaneously; they must be considered two at a time. If the associative property holds for the given operation, then a person can group either adjacent pair, determine that result, and then operate on that result with the remaining entity; the same final answer is found either way.

Consider three piles of bottle caps and an operation called joining. If you join the first pile and the second and then join that pile with the third, the resultant pile is exactly the same as if you had joined the second and third piles initially and then joined that pile with the first. If you were to assign numbers to these three piles and then to add these numbers as they related to the groupings, you would find that addition is also associative on the set of whole numbers as illustrated below.

$$(1 + 2) + 3 = 1 + (2 + 3)$$
$$3 + 3 = 1 + 5$$
$$6 = 6$$

Subtraction is not associative. That is, you will not get the same result with $(5 - 3) - 1$ as with $5 - (3 - 1)$ as illustrated. (Remember that parentheses tell you to perform the operation within them first.)

$$(5 - 3) - 1 \neq 5 - (3 - 1)$$
$$2 - 1 \neq 5 - 2$$
$$1 \neq 3$$

The value of associativity becomes apparent when doing multi-digit addition. In fact, it is because of associativity and the existence of place value in our number system that columnar addition is possible. Consider $23 + 5$ as an example. The simple solution at the left is only possible because of the reasoning, which holds for every similar addition problem, given at the right.

$$
\begin{array}{l}
23 \\
+\ 5 \\
\hline
28
\end{array}
\qquad
\begin{array}{ll}
23 + 5 = (20 + 3) + 5 & \text{Renaming} \\
\quad = 20 + (3 + 5) & \text{Associativity} \\
\quad = 20 + 8 & \text{Renaming} \\
\quad = 28 & \text{Renaming}
\end{array}
$$

Commutativity and associativity combine forces to permit the standard addition algorithm to be effective. Most of the time we use the addition algorithm without even consciously referring to the properties which allow us to do so. Again, each time we do a problem like the one at the left, it is because of reasoning such as given at the right.

$$
\begin{array}{l}
24 \\
+51 \\
\hline
75
\end{array}
\qquad
\begin{array}{ll}
24 + 51 = (20 + 4) + (50 + 1) & \text{Renaming} \\
\quad = [(20 + 4) + 50] + 1 & \text{Associativity} \\
\quad = [20 + (4 + 50)] + 1 & \text{Associativity} \\
\quad = [20 + (50 + 4)] + 1 & \text{Commutativity} \\
\quad = [(20 + 50) + 4] + 1 & \text{Associativity} \\
\quad = (20 + 50) + (4 + 1) & \text{Associativity} \\
\quad = 70 + 5 & \text{Renaming} \\
\quad = 75 & \text{Renaming}
\end{array}
$$

Commutative and associative properties are also basic to mental calculations in addition. "Doing problems in your head" is a valuable tool in daily living. A person who adds mentally picks "easy" combinations which are possible because of these basic properties. Here are some examples.

1. When adding $7 + 2 + 3$ a mental note of 7 and 3 gives a grouping of 10. Then an easy $10 + 2$ is all that remains. (Some educators have not approved of this technique because of the possibility of an addend being inadvertently omitted. Others contend that if the properties hold and the person can do the addition easily, there is no real reason to disallow the technique.)

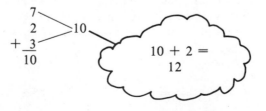

2. Similarly, 175 + 289 + 11 becomes easier when you group 289 and 11 first to get 300 and then are left with the simpler 175 + 300 to total.

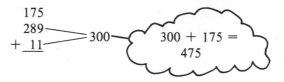

Identities and Inverses

Two additional properties should be a part of each child's mathematical repertoire: the existence of an identity element and an inverse element.

Identities vary with the operation involved, but operating with an identity always results in no change in the original entity. If i is the identity for the operation $*$, then operating on a with i produces no change in a, or $a * i = i * a = a$. Zero is the identity for addition because the child finds that adding zero to any whole number results in that same number. (On a clock the identity is 12. Why?)

Existence of an identity element for addition again reduces the number of facts which a child must learn. Actually, knowledge of the identity, coupled with commutativity described earlier, reduces the number of facts to be learned from 100 to a much more manageable 36.

Does subtraction have an identity element? Try some examples: $2 - 0 = 2$, $131 - 0 = 131$, and $5 - 0 = 5$. At this point subtraction may seem to have 0 as its identity. But what about $0 - 2$? $0 - 131$? and $0 - 5$? These examples show that there is no identity for subtraction because there is no number for which $a - 0 = 0 - a = a$. (Subtraction does have a right hand identity element, however, as illustrated in the first set of examples given.)

Inverse elements are even more complex for they vary even within the operation. Basically, if two numbers are paired so that when they are operated on, the identity to that operation results, then each of the numbers is the inverse of the other. Consider addition with its identity, zero. What pairs of numbers can be added to produce zero? Each number and its negative counterpart, of course! But the set of whole numbers does not include negatives; therefore, additive inverses do not exist in the set of whole numbers. The set of numbers would have to expand to the integers for additive inverses to exist. This discussion leads to our next property: closure.

Closure

We speak of sets being closed with regard to an operation. For example, when we take any two whole numbers and add them, the sum will ALWAYS be a whole number. Therefore, the set of whole numbers is closed with regard to addition.

The same does not hold for subtraction. While there are whole numbers which when subtracted yield a whole number difference, there are others which do not. For a property to hold, it must hold for every member of a given set, not just some. Lack of whole number closure with respect to subtraction can be a problem for some children, so once again the concrete level must be given priority. (Refer to "Sets of Numbers" in Chapter 6.)

DEVELOPMENTAL SEQUENCING AND MATHEMATICAL SEQUENCING

Sequencing of addition and subtraction follows two planes, one child oriented and the other subject oriented. The child oriented sequencing follows developmental patterns and is used primarily in the teaching of each specific facet of a topic. The subject oriented sequencing is that which involves a logical ordering of a mathematical topic, addition for example, from its most simple elements to a generalized concept.

Developmental Sequencing

We begin discussion of developmental sequencing with an example using a sample concrete-to-abstract sequencing chart (Figure 1) for the learning of basic addition facts. Remember that movement proceeds from left to right and up each diagonal.

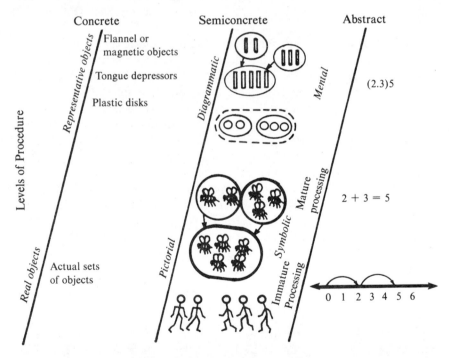

Figure 1. Learning sequence chart.

Concrete. Note that many of the manipulative aids cited at the concrete level in Figure 1 were also cited in prior chapters related to the learning of sets and numbers. The major differences occur only in the action being performed with the objects—joining, in this case. Remember that it is the manipulation of the objects and not the objects themselves that is important. You, as teacher, may demonstrate at times, but pupils should actually do the work themselves. The BEST tools to show the action are the actual objects or representative objects. First, like objects may be joined; later, unrelated objects should be joined. The familiar phrase, "You can't add apples and bananas," finally should have disappeared.

Semiconcrete.   At the semiconcrete level, some problems may arise in trying to show the joining concept on paper. The transition to paper is important, however, and can be arrived at in various ways. Note on the chart in Figure 1 that at the pictorial level the joining idea can be conveyed by showing two people walking toward three people and the teacher asking how many people will then be in the group. Some prefer to draw each set and, by use of their hands, depict the action. Also, the use of rings and arrows may help; for example:

Some teachers object to this last technique by arguing that the movement is not actually shown and that altogether ten objects are seen instead of the five that there really are. All techniques must be accompanied by communication; some techniques require more discussion than others; some lend themselves better to symbolic interpretation than others. You and your students should use the one with which you feel most comfortable.

Abstract.   At the immature processing level, as noted on the sequencing chart, numerals and diagrammatic devices join forces in such combinations as the number line. Finally, as the children move further up the diagonal at the abstract level, they begin to use the numbers totally without need for more concrete referents. Work then progresses on paper or mentally.

Again, not every child will proceed through the learning sequence in the same way or with the same speed. The chart in Figure 1 is only a guide. It can be adapted to any subtopic in addition or subtraction. Children who exhibit facility and work their way through the concrete-to-abstract stages with expediency should be allowed to proceed more rapidly and at their own level. It is possible that in their development they have already experienced the concrete aspects of the operation and are indeed ready to proceed. Check each child's work at all stages, however, because some children become good "numeral flippers"—that is, they can memorize facts quickly or they have had basic facts drilled into them. It is quite possible, though, that they are not adept at translating these facts into problem situations.

Mathematical Sequencing

Recall that developmental sequencing is usually applied to a specific mathematical topic to be learned. Now let's examine sequencing from a broader perspective, that of logically ordering topics in a particular phase of mathematical study from the most simple elements to a generalized concept. Again, some variation is possible, but basic patterns are constant. Study the flow chart in Figure 2 which illustrates a possible mathematical sequencing from simple set concepts to a generalized algorithm in addition.

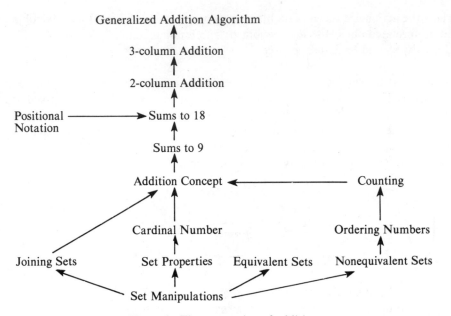

Figure 2. The sequencing of addition.

It is not necessary to memorize such a sequence, for more elaborate scope and sequence charts are available through textbook companies. Indeed, what is a basal mathematics series itself but a highly refined description of scope and sequence in elementary school mathematics. Because you will be confronted with some decisions relative to sequencing, however, you should study the flow chart carefully and decide for yourself if any topics could be rearranged or completely omitted or if any other topics should be included for better understanding. These are the types of decisions about sequencing with which you will be confronted when teaching, whether you are using no text, one text, or several texts.

To conclude, any type of addition or subtraction problem can be approached developmentally at any point on a concrete-to-abstract continuum. Also, addition and subtraction can be sequenced from their most basic relationship to sets to their more complex, generalized algorithms. These two sequential aspects of addition and subtraction will enable you to develop a fundamentally sound learning plan for your students. Equally as important, however, is that you will also be able to determine specific points of learning difficulty for individual children and be able to prescribe logically sequenced activities at the appropriate developmental level for these children.

LEARNING BASIC FACTS

Now let's expand upon the sequencing just described as we examine addition and subtraction from initial learning experiences to mastery of basic facts.

Initial Learning Experiences

The concrete-to-abstract continuum provides a structural foundation from which to build a variety of suitable experiences for children learning addition and subtraction facts. Basically, it is a matter of organizing a variety of materials and activities at each level on the continuum for a given topic. Some of these materials and activities were illustrated earlier in the discussion of developmental sequencing.

Concrete.   Children who have been working successfully with various sets and determining cardinality and ordinal usages, can begin joining sets. Remember to start at the concrete level with real objects and realistic situations. You may begin with crayons, books, dolls, blocks, finger paint cups, or any other real objects in the classroom, including the children themselves. For example, start with a set of two blocks and a set of three blocks. Have the children identify the number of each set. Join the two sets, and then have the children determine the total number.

In moving to representative objects the children are beginning to abstract the operation from the movement of the objects. They find that whether they join tongue depressors, magnetic figures, bottle caps, or plastic discs, a set of two and a set of three make a set of five.

Throughout the concrete stage be sure to use clear terminology, at first emphasizing the objects and the action and then moving slowly to the numerical generalizations.

Because subtraction is the inverse of addition—that is, because subtraction "undoes" what addition does—most of the activities associated with addition apply equally well to subtraction. Manipulative aids used to illustrate the joining process of addition may also be used to illustrate the separating process of subtraction. Of course, there are differences too, and these will provide the basis for the following discussion.

While addition is associated with the singular physical situation of joining, subtraction relates to several physical situations. The most commonly thought of subtraction situation is that of "take-away." Equally as important, though, is the "missing addend" situation. Some teachers would also include the "comparison" situation. Although each of these situations involves a sum, a known addend, and an unknown addend and so can be recorded in any of the conventional subtractive forms, each relates to a different type of real life situation and so would be treated differently at the manipulative level. Although the names associated with the various subtractive situations are relatively unimportant, it is advisable that the child recognize different physical situations related to subtraction. The following three examples illustrate the different subtraction situations.

1. Bobby had 7 pennies. He gave 2 pennies to Ben for bubble gum. How many pennies did he have left? (This is perhaps the most simple subtractive situation in which we begin with a total amount and "take-away" a given number as shown.)

2. Sally has 3 pennies. She needs 5 pennies. How many more pennies does she need? (In this situation, the sum and one of the addends is known. There is a "missing addend.")

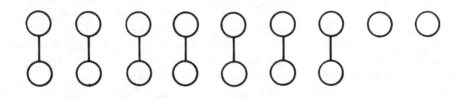

3. An eraser at one store costs 9 pennies. At another store it costs 7 pennies. What is the difference in the cost of the erasers? (In this situation two quantities are being compared.)

In conclusion, perhaps more commercially-prepared and teacher-made concrete aids are available for learning basic addition and subtraction facts than for any other mathematical area. In addition to aids already mentioned are the flannel board, magnetic board, colored rods, counting frame, bead wire, unifix cubes, perception cards, counting man, and abacus. The list could go on indefinitely. While each aid has its own special advantages all are based on the idea of discrete objects which can be joined or separated.

Semiconcrete. At the semi-concrete stage the children use and interpret pictures and diagrams which depict the action of the operation. Some illustrations suit the purpose better than others. (Notice that different illustrations were used to describe manipulations associated with various subtractive situations given earlier.) Care should be taken to communicate the actions and numerical counterparts effectively. Study the illustrations below. Which is least effective in communicating the take-away subtractive situation?

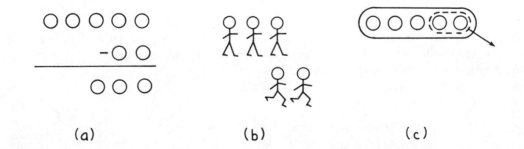

Illustration (a) is least effective. Illustrations (b) and (c) show 5 figures altogether and each shows a set of 2 being separated from the set. On the other hand, Illustration (a) shows figures being subtracted. Remember that numbers are subtracted; figures and objects are not, so the subtraction sign should not be included at all. Also, the illustration is unacceptable for the take-away aspect of subtraction because there is no separating action shown. The figure could be adapted for purposes of showing the comparison aspect of subtraction, however. Consider this form which would be a suitable representation of a comparison problem.

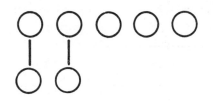

Abstract. At the immature processing level, as noted on the developmental sequencing chart, numerals and diagrammatic devices join forces in such combinations as the NUMBER LINE. Used at the appropriate time and for the proper illustrations, the number line can prove an invaluable tool. It is not a panacea, however, as it does not work well for every operation and more importantly it cannot teach by itself. Instead it is a TOOL to be used by teacher and pupil. The following points should help you to use the number line effectively.

1. A number line is a calibrated segment of a line. Structurally the calibrations should be uniform in length, and any omissions should be marked with ellipses. All number lines should have a zero point from which to begin. Numerals should be recorded below the calibrations.

$$\longleftrightarrow \atop 0 \quad 1 \quad 2 \quad 3 \quad 4 \quad 5 \quad 6$$

2. Children should always start at the zero point in their calculations. Most important, too, they should count spaces, or jumps, on the number line and not the calibrations. Some children who count calibrations starting at zero are "one off" in their calculations. Recording the maneuvers can assume many forms:

3. Although the number line can be an effective tool, it can be misused. It should not be required of the child to the point of tedium; that is, if the child can demonstrate an understanding of the maneuvers involved and can arrive at the desired answer without repeated use of this crutch, then he or she should be allowed to do so. Too often children find themselves solving the problem symbolically first and then backing up to the number line stage merely to record the problem and solution. Because the number line is not integral to the solution and is amended only as an after-thought, many times the actual problem is not shown properly by the number line representation, as will be noted in division. Use the number line whenever it will be helpful. Be certain, though, that it truly represents the problem as stated and that it is being used at the appropriate stage for the child.

Another aid similar to the number line is the addition/subtraction slide rule. It is made of a folded sheet of paper and a paper strip, each of which has been calibrated as shown.

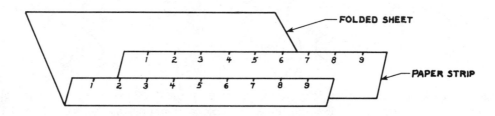

The paper strip can be moved left or right along the fold line to illustrate various sums or differences. For example, the sum of 2 and 3 can be found by aligning the left edge of the paper strip with 2, the first addend. Then locate 3, the second addend, on the paper strip. The sum is the number directly below the 3 on the folded sheet. To subtract, begin by aligning the sum (folded sheet) and the known addend (paper strip); then note the difference which is the number on the folded sheet directly under the left edge of the paper strip. Also, two rulers aligned parallel to each other on a flat surface effectively function the same as the slide rule.

Addition facts with sums between 10 and 18 often have the concepts of ten and place value stressed through various aids. For example, a ten-grid and plastic discs (or drawn circles) can be used to help solve this problem:

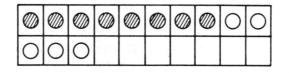

$$8 + 5 = ?$$
$$8 + (2 + 3) = ?$$
$$(8 + 2) + 3 = ?$$
$$10 + 3 = ?$$
$$13 = ?$$

Notice that 8 discs are placed on the grid followed by 5 discs, 2 of which complete the ten pattern and 3 of which will form the units portion of the solution. In this way 13 is visualized as a 10 and a 3 rather than as 13 ones.

As work at the immature processing level is completed the child moves into mature processing levels and deals with addition and subtraction facts directly.

Coordinating Initial Learning Experiences.   How might all these different facets and levels of learning activities be emphasized and coordinated? Certainly, neither you nor your students would care to go through all activities using every aid for each of the 100 addition facts and their subtraction counterparts.

First, consider an illustration of activities from various levels and stages on the learning sequence chart and see how a child can naturally progress from one to the other. Perhaps Johnny is working on facts with sums of five. His activities might include the use of objects as simple as a TV dinner tray and five lima beans. The dinner tray is divided thusly:

A set of two beans and a set of three beans may be placed in the small compartments on the tray

and then joined in the large compartment to produce

Johnny may then sketch a diagram of his work, such as

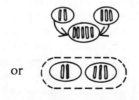

or

and then record his findings in the form $2 + 3 = 5$. Each of the stages has been incorporated in this sequence of activities. He can then proceed with zero beans and five beans and one bean and four beans in the various positions until he has exhausted the possibilities. He is finding that there may be many names for a number. In this case, he is finding that 5 can also be named $0 + 5$, $1 + 4$, $2 + 3$, etc. Actually, he can be said to be using a missing addend concept of subtraction in his work since he is starting with the desired sum and examining various components. Such activities should be encouraged because, as mentioned earlier, the integrated approach to operations is a desirable one.

Notice that Johnny need not be totally involved with just one fact but may be learning several at a time. His work should lead him to discover sequences and patterns because isolated facts are often difficult to remember. Activities involving families of facts, such as described earlier with beans and dinner trays, help in leading children to discover patterns of addition facts associated with a specific sum.

Using an active, coordinated, concretely oriented approach to initial fact learning alleviates many problems associated with initial number learning. With the hands-on approach children can more readily relate a situation to its mathematical counterpart. Still, however, there comes a time when these children need to practice the facts. They need to commit the facts to memory for quick recall in calculations.

Practice Activities

Practice can assume many forms from flash cards to board races to Bingo to card games to worksheets. Sources for practice activities and materials and games are abundant. Entire books have been written describing practice activities in mathematics. Textbooks and workbooks are also good practice sources. Suggestions are included in every issue of the *Arithmetic Teacher* and other journals. Also, software for drill-and-practice is burgeoning in the computer field.

In fact there is such an abundance of possibilities that the real challenge becomes more a matter of making a prudent choice. Some general guidelines may help make this choice easier:

1. The activity must serve a specific mathematical function. Whenever a game, activity, or worksheet is selected it must be chosen because it best satisfies a particular mathematical need or objective.
2. The practice must also be appropriate for the children involved. After initial learning, it is seldom that an entire class will profit maximally from any one learning activity because children will be at different points along the continuum. One learning activity, while being suitable for a few in the class, might be too advanced for some and too simple for others. Continuously exposing an academically talented child to nonchallenging practice activities can produce boredom or perhaps discipline problems. On the other hand, exposing a child who is not yet ready for a given problem situation to certain defeat can produce discouragement, dislike, or perhaps again, discipline problems.
3. There should be variety in time, materials, and procedures for practice. Even the most interesting form of practice can pale when done to the exclusion of all else. Even practice at a computer can become dull and tedious when used exclusively.

The advent of copying devices has become something of a double-edged sword in this respect. On one hand it has provided the teacher with a ready supply of worksheets which when used properly are valuable; on the other hand, these worksheets have often become "seatwork," assigned to keep children "busy" whether they need the practice or not.

While practice need not be entertaining, it should be varied sufficiently to be interesting for each child, be selected for a particular purpose, and serve the needs of certain children.

Use the guidelines just described to determine relative merits of the following practice possibilities for four children who need to work on facts through sums of 18.

Worksheets.   Worksheets have many advantages. They usually have been designed by specialists to suit a specific purpose. They are readily available. When you check them yourself you may diagnose error sources for particular children. Also you know exactly which problems have been worked by each child. On the other hand, sometimes worksheets are poorly selected. Also, many children tire of worksheets and direct their energy toward "getting the page done" more than to "getting the work right." The effectiveness of worksheets diminishes when they are used too often.

Board Races.   When you send children to the board to practice, you are usually looking for both accuracy and speed. As with worksheets you can see immediately who is and who is not having difficulty, and you get that information right in class. Unfortunately, this immediate feedback for you can become embarrassing and even humiliating for the child whose difficulties are being exhibited before other class members. In addition, it is possible that the speed factor is compounding any other problems.

Mail Delivery.   This activity involves a "mail carrier" who has envelopes, each address with a number combination, such as $3 + 4 = ?$. Attached to a bulletin board are sack "houses," each with a single-digit sum printed on it. The mail carrier delivers his envelopes to the proper house; for example, "$3 + 4 = ?$" must be delivered to "7." The other players decide if the mail has been delivered correctly. This activity provides variety, it involves practice for specific facts, and it puts less pressure and more pleasure on the young learner.

Octopus.   An octopus is drawn on a cardboard square and its tentacles numbered 2 through 9. One child picks a number card to be placed on the body and the other children try to "keep the octopus in his cage" by adding the number on each tentacle to the number on the body. This activity provides practice on specific facts, offers variety, is interesting, and can be used easily with four children.

Old Sum.   Old Sum is a card game. The teacher makes "cards," some with addition combinations and others with corresponding sums. One card, however, has "OLD SUM" written on it. The rules for playing the game parallel Old Maid. Because it is a card game, the children will probably elect to continue to play until you call "time." Since you have selected the deck of cards they are using, you know that the facts they are working on are the ones they need; that they are all working numerous examples; that the learning is pleasurable for them; that they are each checking the solutions of the others; and that you can determine their individual progress by observing their game, briefly questioning each later, or by having them complete a written quiz. (A regular deck of cards with the face cards removed can be used in many ways to teach all four operations. Variations of War and Rummy offer many options.)

Obviously, some choices are better than others for a given purpose and for specific children at a given time. Appropriate choices can mean time well spent for each child.

DEVELOPING THE ALGORITHMS

Armed with understanding of the concepts of addition and subtraction and with the knowledge of basic facts, children are ready to learn generalized algorithmic forms for each operation.

In early learning situations the horizontal form of addition and subtraction problems is useful because it relates directly to mathematical statements describing manipulative actions. As children prepare to learn addition and subtraction algorithms, however, they need to learn the vertical forms. One way to help children make such a transition involves a cardboard square (or rectangle) and clothespins. Begin with a horizontal placement with clothespins showing the two addends. Then rotate the cardboard a quarter turn to illustrate the vertical counterpart.

Addition Algorithms

Children need to learn vertical procedures for columnar addition and additions with and without regrouping.

Columnar Addition.　Addition problems with three or more addends confuse some children. The fact that the addends must still be taken two at a time—addition being a binary operation—can elude the children. In approaching such problems generally, time should be devoted to the use of counters such as plastic discs, beans, buttons, etc. Children should be presented with a multiaddend problem situation such as this:

> Mary has a fish tank with 3 tropical fish in it. She bought 2 guppies and a beta and put them in her tank. How many fish are in her tank now?

Ask the children to describe and demonstrate with their counters how the problem might be solved. By actually doing the problems, they find that there are intermediate sums (often called hidden sums) to be found. The task then becomes one of how to record the problem on paper. They might proceed with any of the following:

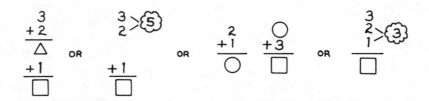

Any of the methods would be acceptable, although some are more conventional than others. The point is that each child understands that the problem must be done in parts and that there are intermediate steps to be taken. By the way, remember that the associative and commutative principles are an integral part of these additions. Also note that children with a primarily concrete background and with an understanding of properties might be able to solve a multiaddend problem directly and with complete understanding at the symbolic level. It is up to each child and his or her teacher to decide at which stage the work should proceed.

Addition without Regrouping. Addition types which involve more than one digit in at least one addend require that a sound foundation have been laid in the study of place value. A child who does not understand the meaning underlying positional values cannot be expected to understand multicolumn addition. On the other hand, a child who does understand both base value and place value should be adequately equipped to proceed with multicolumn addition. As with all areas of mathematical learning discussed to this point, however, total familiarity of the mathematics involved at the concrete and semiconcrete stages is recommended before symbolic efforts are made.

Because of the dependence of multicolumn addition upon an understanding of place value, virtually all of the manipulative aids used in the learning of numeration can and should be used in addition too. The abacus, the tab rack, the pocket chart, base ten blocks, and even straws and tin cans can help the child with this aspect of addition.

Introductory work in multicolumn addition might best be done with aids which actually show the number of units involved in the various positions rather than those aids which require that the child abstract the place value concept from the position itself. For example, these aids actually allow the child to see and feel the quantity represented by 23:

The following aids require that the child have already abstracted the positional value in their representations:

To illustrate how these kinds of aids may be used let's work from a sample problem situation: Lori has 23 pencils. Billy has 14 pencils. How many pencils are there altogether?

Ask for suggestions about how to solve the problem. Some children might want to count the pencils to find the answer. Accept this as one solution and try it even though it takes awhile. After an effort or two by counting, suggest that there may be easier ways to find answers to questions like these. One way is to bundle, or group, all tens so that they need not be recounted each time. Lori's pencils and Billy's pencils are now grouped this way.

LORI'S PENCILS 23   BILLY'S PENCILS 14

Join the single pencils and the ten-groups of pencils in separate piles and identify the total number: 3 groups of ten and 7 ones or 37.

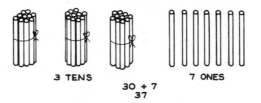

3 TENS   7 ONES

30 + 7
37

Remember to work from right to left starting with the units position. Also emphasize how much easier it is to identify values when the tens are grouped. (Note yourself how little meaning any of this discussion would have for a child who is not yet conserving numerousness. These activities must be reserved for conservers or the children are being asked to memorize instead of understand.)

After children practice joining sets in which the tens groups are bundled, they can turn to more abstract manipulations on the tab rack or the abacus, for example. In these instances the tens are no longer bundled but are represented instead through position. Using the example 23 + 14 again, we can turn to the tab rack for solution. (Be careful in illustrating subtraction on the tab rack. The "take-away" manipulation must be maintained.)

TENS	ONES
⊓⊓	⊓⊓⊓
⊓	⊓⊓⊓

SHOWING
23
+ 14
⎡⎤⎡⎤

TENS	ONES
⊓⊓	
⊓	
	⊓⊓⊓⊓⊓⊓⊓

GROUP ONES
23
+ 14
⎡⎤7

TENS	ONES
⊓⊓⊓	⊓⊓⊓⊓⊓⊓⊓

GROUP TENS
23
+ 14
37

Notice that in this discussion each successive aid has been a little more abstract in its orientation and moves the child one step closer to total symbolic work.

As children move to immature forms at the symbolic level to describe on paper what they have done with aids, they might use such additive forms as these, arriving finally at (e) the mature form of the addition algorithm requiring no regrouping.

(a)   2 tens and 3 ones
       1 ten and 4 ones
       3 tens and 7 ones or 37

(b)   20 + 3
       10 + 4
       30 + 7 or 37

(c)
T	0
2	3
+1	4
3	7

(d)   23
       +14
          7
         30
         37

(e)   23
       +14
         37

Obviously, teachers could simply tell children to keep their "columns straight" and "add each column" without using any of the aids described. Unfortunately, children need concrete referents upon which to draw to build understanding of the number operation and the real-life situations requiring that operation. Such well intentioned teaching of "short cuts" as mentioned above end up costing too much in lack of understanding now and in reteaching later.

Addition with Regrouping.   Basic patterns of progress remain the same when dealing with additions involving regrouping. However, extra manipulations and illustrations are needed when regroupings are necessary as a result of the joining process. Consider the illustration of 37 + 25 on the 20–bead abacus.

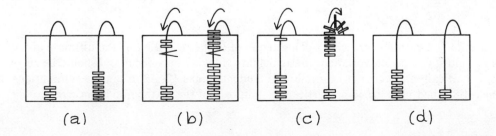

(a)   (b)   (c)   (d)

In illustration (a), three beads are drawn forward in the ten's column and seven beads are drawn forward in the one's column. In illustration (b), the second addend is represented by being drawn forward. In additions involving no regrouping, the addition is complete and the final answer need only be interpreted. In the problem being illustrated, however, there are 12 beads showing in the one's column, and regrouping is necessary as shown in illustration (c) where 10 beads are being exchanged for one bead in the next column to the left. Finally, in illustration (d) the answer of 62 is shown.

Those teachers who would prefer to make the manipulation parallel even more closely the addition algorithm should have their students add all the ones first and regroup, then add the tens and regroup, and so on. Then the preceding illustration would change accordingly.

Also immature forms of addition at the symbolic level are varied. Some that you might include for children are shown here:

(a)
3 tens and 7 ones
2 tens and 5 ones
5 tens and 12 ones or 5 tens and 1 ten and 2 ones
or 6 tens and 2 ones

(b)
$30 + 7$
$\underline{20 + 5}$
$50 + 12$ or $50 + 10 + 2$
or 62

(c)

T	0
1	
3	7
2	5
6	2

(d)
$$\begin{array}{r} 37 \\ \underline{+25} \\ 12 \\ \underline{50} \\ 62 \end{array}$$

(e)
$$\begin{array}{r} {}^{1}37 \\ \underline{+\ 25} \\ 62 \end{array}$$

(f)
$$\begin{array}{r} 37 \\ \underline{+25} \\ 62 \end{array}$$

The form in (f), with no "crutches" being required in the recording, is the ultimate aim of most teachers and students, but variations in each child's thinking may occur and should be encouraged if mathematically correct. For example, if a student thinks 12, 42, 62 in his summations, he or she has still relied upon basic properties for addition and the mathematics is correct.

Subtraction Algorithms

The similarities between the learning continuum of addition and that of subtraction are numerous; the only basic differences lie in the "undoing" of the action. When the child is learning to do multicolumn subtraction, he or she will still use such devices as the abacus or the pocket chart just as was done in multicolumn addition. The difference, again, is that beads are being removed in the "take-away" situation and any regroupings are made in the opposite direction of addition groupings.

At the semiconcrete level the same disadvantages apply as with addition. Again, the communication at this level is important to help explain the action of the picture or diagram. However, the diagrams can help complete the subtractive picture. Consider solving $43 - 18 = ?$ by diagramming moves on an abacus. As with addition, diagram (a) shows the initial number placement. Diagram (b) shows any regroupings necessary, while diagram (c) shows the operation being performed. Diagram (d) shows the result.

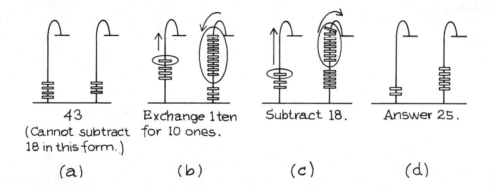

43
(Cannot subtract
18 in this form.)

(a)

Exchange 1 ten
for 10 ones.

(b)

Subtract 18.

(c)

Answer 25.

(d)

The same types of immature algorithmic forms may be used as were used with addition. For example, the grid form still is useful.

Tens	Ones
^{3}4	^{1}3
− 1	8
2	5

At more advanced stages, numerous subtraction methods have been used. Two of the most commonly known methods are the decomposition method and the equal additions method. Let us examine the two methods via an example: $246 - 187 = ?$

The DECOMPOSITION METHOD is based upon the familiar "borrowing" idea, today more commonly referred to as regrouping.

3_1
246
− 187

Examination of the one's column reveals that regrouping is necessary before the subtraction can be performed. Decomposition requires that a ten be exchanged for its equivalent, 10 ones. This leaves the problem as shown at the left.

3_1
246
$-\ 187$
9

Subtraction of the ones leaves 9 ones.

13_1
246
$-\ 187$
9

A similar problem is confronted when the ten's column is to be subtracted, and so 1 hundred is exchanged for 10 tens, leaving the problem as such.

13_1
^{1246}
$-\ 187$
59

Thirteen tens minus 8 tens leaves 5 tens.
Moving to the hundred's column we find that the subtraction may be performed without any further regrouping and zero results in that step of the operation. The result is 59, as shown above.

The EQUAL ADDITIONS method has a slightly different basis. Before moving to the example, think first about a number line. Consider two numbers on the line. Find the difference. Now think of any other number. Add this number to both numbers on the number line. Find the difference between these two sums. Is this difference the same as the first difference you found? Of course it is. Can you tell why? Let's try some other number pairs:

$$\begin{array}{cccc}
6 & 9 & 6 & 16 \\
-\ 4 \quad (\text{add } 3) & -\ 7 & -\ 4 \quad (\text{add } 10) & -\ 14 \\
\hline
2 & 2 & 2 & 2
\end{array}$$

We conclude that adding equal numbers to the subtrahend and minuend does not affect the difference. The equal additions method utilizes this finding. Specifically, it capitalizes on the exchange values for the various powers of ten. Let us now examine the reasoning used in solving the example using the equal additions method.

$2\ 4\ ^16$
$-\ 1^9 8\ 7$
9

To enable subtraction in the one's column, 10 must be added to both numbers. The key, though, is to add the ten in the form of 10 ones to the top number (minuend) and in the form of 1 ten to the bottom number (subtrahend), leaving the problem in the form at the left. Again, 9 is the result.

$^12\ ^14\ 6$
$-\ ^21\ ^98\ 7$
$5\ 9$

To continue with the next step of the algorithm, it becomes necessary to add 1 hundred to both numbers in the form of 10 tens and 1 hundred in their respective places. Subtracting, we again find 59 to be the difference.

The equal additions method was often taught decades ago. The process is easy to do once mastered. However, the decomposition method has gained prominence because it has been found that most children understand it better.

I. What would you do if two of your students were solving problems this way?

a.
$$\begin{array}{r} 26 \\ + \ 18 \\ \hline 314 \end{array} \qquad \begin{array}{r} 46 \\ +69 \\ \hline 1015 \end{array} \qquad \begin{array}{r} 21 \\ +37 \\ \hline 58 \end{array}$$

b.
$$\begin{array}{r} 106 \\ - \ 48 \\ \hline 142 \end{array} \qquad \begin{array}{r} 45 \\ -13 \\ \hline 32 \end{array} \qquad \begin{array}{r} 72 \\ -28 \\ \hline 56 \end{array}$$

c. $4 + \boxed{12} = 8$ $\qquad$ $\boxed{4} - 2 = 6$ $\qquad$ $2 + \boxed{7} = 5$

CHAPTER KEY POINTS

1. Children can learn fundamental concepts associated with commutativity, associativity, closure, and the existence of identities and inverses.

2. Addition and subtraction can be sequenced according to developmental patterns and according to a logical ordering of mathematical topics from the most simple elements to a generalized concept.

3. The concrete-to-abstract continuum provides a structural foundation from which to build a variety of suitable experiences for children learning to add and subtract.

4. Addition relates to the physical action of joining. Subtraction relates to three physical actions: separation, finding the missing addend, and comparison.

5. Some difficulties may be encountered when picturing action at the semiconcrete level. Communication is vital at this point.

6. The immature processing level offers a variety of aids which help the child relate more physical situations to their symbolic counterparts on paper. The number line is one such aid.

7. Practice activities should serve a specific mathematical function, be appropriate for the children involved, and offer variety.

8. Numerous aids are available to help children learn addition and subtraction algorithms. These aids are varied in the degree of abstraction necessary to solve problems with them but all serve equally well for either operation.

9. Subtraction algorithms can be taught using either the decomposition method or the equal additions method.

Laboratory 8
Addition and Subtraction of Whole Numbers

Fundamental importance must be attributed to the learning of operations and properties associated with whole numbers. Such learning is basic to most subsequent mathematical endeavors.

The following laboratory activities are designed to supplement your study of Chapter 8 insofar as you will gain proficiency in working with aids and activities which are related to addition and subtraction of whole numbers.

I. *Objectives:* Upon completion of these laboratory exercises, you should be able to do the following:

 A. Demonstrate how colored rods may be used to illustrate addition and subtraction of whole numbers and related properties. (Chapter Competencies 8–A, 8–B, 8–C)

 B. Use such aids as the abacus and the number line to solve addition and subtraction problems. (Chapter Competency 8–C)

 C. Design a sequence of activities from the concrete to the abstract which would be suitable for learning an addition or subtraction topic. (Chapter Competency 8–A)

 D. Describe problem situations associated with each of three subtraction types. (Chapter Competency 8–B)

 E. Solve subtraction problems using decomposition and equal-additions methods. (Chapter Competency 8–B)

II. *Materials:* Cuisenaire rods (available from Cuisenaire Company of America, 12 Church Street, New Rochelle, New York 10805)[1], Modern Computing Abacus, base ten blocks

III. *Procedure:*

 A. Read Chapter 8 of *Helping Children Learn Mathematics*. Consult your instructor if you have any questions.

 B. Colored rods provide one concrete way to consider addition and subtraction of whole numbers. For these exercises you will use a particular set of colored rods called Cuisenaire rods. A set of these rods uses the following colors:

 W—White   DG—Dark green
 R—Red   BK—Black
 LG—Light green   BR—Brown
 P—Purple   BL—Blue
 Y—Yellow   OR—Orange

   1. Place the set of rods in front of you and examine them. What characteristics of the rods do you see? List them.

---

1. A set of rods can be constructed from colored paper, cardboard, or wood. They should be cut to scale as follows (lengths in desired units): W-1, R-2, LG-3, P-4, Y-5, DG-6, BK-7, BR-8, BL-9, OR-10.

2. A train is an ordered set of rods laid end-to-end. Can you find a train of two rods length which has the same length as the DG rod? What is it? What different trains of two rods could also be used? List all of them. (Remember that order makes a difference.)

3. Do the same for the OR rod.

4. Addition and subtraction may be illustrated using trains. Using your rods, fill in the blanks with the name of a colored rod that will correctly complete the sentence.

 a. R + W = _____   e. Y + _____ = BL
 b. Y + W = _____   f. _____ + R = OR
 c. LG + R = _____   g. P + _____ = DG
 d. BK + R = _____   h. BL + BK = OR + _____

5. Follow the same instructions for this exercise as you did in Exercise 4.

 a. R − W = _____   e. _____ − R = Y
 b. OR − DG = _____   f. P − LG = _____
 c. BR − _____ = P   g. W + R = _____ − P
 d. _____ − Y = W   h. DG − _____ = LG

 6. Show how the rods might be used to illustrate the additive identity, commutativity, and associativity.

C. Use the abacus to solve the following problems. Describe each move. Remember that the terms "exchange" and "regroup" are preferable to "carry" and "borrow" insofar as they describe the processes more accurately. Also, "join" and "separate" relate to "add" and "subtract," respectively, at the concrete level.

a.	b.	c.	d.	e.	f.
462	7	56	27	45	1006
+ 35	+8	+48	− 4	−29	− 238

D. Use base ten blocks to solve the problems in part C. What similarities/differences are there in the use of the two types of aids to solve the problems?

E. Solve the following problems on the number line.

 a. 3 + 5 = _____   d. 8 − 2 = _____
 b. 0 + 7 = _____   e. 12 − 6 = _____
 c. 21 + 5 = _____   f. 23 − 4 = _____

F. A concrete-to-abstract continuum model was provided for you illustrating addition. Produce a similar model for the "take-away" situation in subtraction by showing a sequence which could be used in the teaching of that topic.

G. Describe problem situations which would be meaningful to a child and which illustrate each of the following subtraction types: take-away, missing addend, comparison.

H. Solve the problem below (showing "crutches") by the decomposition method and by the equal-additions method.

$$\begin{array}{r} 435 \\ -287 \\ \hline \end{array}$$

9
Multiplication and Division of Whole Numbers

Teacher Competencies

After studying Chapter 9 and completing Laboratory 9, you should be able to do the following:

    A. Given a selected concept or skill in the area of multiplication and division of whole numbers, design foundational activities which may be used in the acquisition of that concept or skill. (Part Competency III-A)

    B. Given a selected concept or skill in the area of multiplication and division of whole numbers, identify activities which may be used to develop proficiency in the use of that concept or skill. (Part Competency III-B)

    C. Given a selected concept or skill in the area of multiplication and division, identify and/or demonstrate the use of selected instructional aids which might be used to help a child learn that concept or skill. (Part Competency III-C)

Multiplication at the elementary school level relates most often to the joining of equivalent sets or the repeated use of equal addends. The most commonly accepted terms for multiplication are "factor times factor equals product," in which the first factor indicates the number of groups (multiplier) and the second indicates the number in each group (multiplicand).

There are other interpretations of multiplication. One alternative interpretation is that the first factor is the operand (multiplicand) and the second factor is the operator (multiplier). This interpretation parallels more closely the horizontal division counterpart in which the second term is also the operator. If this interpretation is used, the multiplication is expressed as "factor multiplied by factor equals product."

For purposes of this discussion the first multiplicative interpretation will be used. Of course, as children move more into abstract stages of multiplicative learning, such distinctions become less important and commutativity is easily applied to provide ease in operating.

Division may be interpreted as the inverse of multiplication or as repeated subtraction of equal numbers. Division may be expressed in several forms, two of which are a$\overline{)b}^{\,c}$ and b ÷ a = c. In these cases a is called the divisor, b is the dividend, and c is the quotient. The fractional form b/a sometimes best expresses a division situation. When a missing factor is needed, division may best be expressed as □ × a = c or a × □ = c.

RELATIONSHIPS AMONG OPERATIONS

Mention was made earlier about the interrelationships which exist among the various whole number operations. Because of these relationships much of the discussion of multiplication and division is an extension of discussion in the previous chapter about addition and subtraction. To place these operational interrelationships in perspective consider the following diagram:

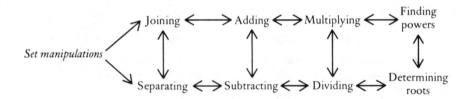

Begin at the left of the diagram and think back to basic movements of objects. One such set manipulation is joining. Joining relates to the number operation called addition. When equivalent sets are joined, or when equal numbers are added, multiplication results. Successive multiplications of the same factor can be written as a power. And so all operations on the upper horizontal level on the diagram are related.

Begin at the left again with set manipulations and this time consider separating sets of objects. Separating sets relates to the number operation called subtraction. Repeated subtractions of equal numbers is division, and repeated divisions by the same number may result in the extraction of roots.

Now consider the vertical arrows. Each arrow connects inverse operations: joining and separating, adding and subtracting, multiplying and dividing, powers and roots.

Undoubtedly, relationships which exist between and among the various operations are many. Similarly, properties which were discussed with respect to addition and subtraction may also be discussed as they relate to multiplication and division.

BASIC PROPERTIES

Commutativity, associativity, closure, and the existence of identities and inverses relate to multiplication and division much as they did to addition and subtraction. Also appropriate to the topic at this point are distributivity and the particular case of zero in multiplication and division.

Commutativity

If 3 sets of 2 objects are joined, the answer is the same as if 2 sets of 3 objects had been joined, or in the set of whole numbers, $3 \times 2 = 2 \times 3 = 6$. Because this works for any whole number, the commutative property of multiplication exists for the set of whole numbers. The property can be shown by various means, one of which is the use of rods as in the following illustration.

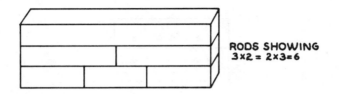

RODS SHOWING
$3 \times 2 = 2 \times 3 = 6$

As with commutativity in addition, commutativity in multiplication substantially reduces the number of basic facts to be learned.

Commutativity does not hold for division however. A property does not hold if even one counterexample can be found. For example, $6 \div 2 \neq 2 \div 6$; this constitutes a counterexample and commutativity does not hold.

Associativity

Multiplication of whole numbers is associative; division is not. For example, using the general form, $(a \times b) \times c = a \times (b \times c)$, try to think of even one selection of whole numbers for which the equality will not hold. Impossible; therefore, the property holds. On the other hand, associativity does not hold in division; that is, the groupings do make a difference in the final quotient. Associativity of multiplication can be shown with real objects, with blocks or rods, and on paper. An example follows showing associativity using $(2 \times 3) \times 4$ and $2 \times (3 \times 4)$.

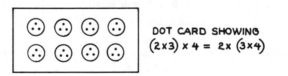

DOT CARD SHOWING
$(2 \times 3) \times 4 = 2 \times (3 \times 4)$

Distributivity

Distributivity is interesting insofar as it involves two operations instead of one. The student of sets finds that union distributes over intersection and also the converse. In dealing with whole number operations, however, one finds that although multiplication distributes over addition, the converse does not hold true.

New learners tend to have difficulty with the distributive property. Sometimes they confuse distributivity with associativity for no apparent reason. This confusion tends to occur when learners have been exposed to the general formulas and little effort has been made to understand exactly what is involved. Instead, there should be plenty of exposure to problems exhibiting the distributive property of multiplication over addition, or a × (b + c) = (a × b) + (a × c). An understanding of the property is important to later understanding of algorithms and of still later work in algebra. It also proves helpful in mental calculations as will be seen later.

Basically, distributivity allows you to examine a problem in different ways. For example, consider the problem, 2 × 7 = □. It can be represented by an array of dots (2 groups of 7). The product is 14.

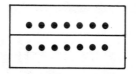

While the preceding problem could be solved without difficulty as shown, it is also possible to view it from various distributive perspectives and solve it in other ways. Consider 2 × 7 = □ again, but this time note how the same problem can be taken in parts for solution.

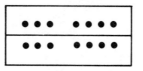

In the preceding diagram the dots are viewed as 2 × (3 + 4); that is, the 7 factor is now shown as 3 + 4 and there are 2 of these groups. Now study the following diagram.

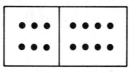

Now the multiplication itself is taken in parts and the same 14 dots are viewed as (2 × 3) + (2 × 4).

To summarize, the problem remained throughout one of 2 × 7 = 14. However, the problem could be solved in different ways because multiplication distributes over addition. Let's verify that the equality holds numerically.

$$
\begin{aligned}
2 \times 7 &= 2 \times (3 + 4) \\
&= (2 \times 3) + (2 \times 4) \\
&= 6 + 8 \\
&= 14
\end{aligned}
$$

Exposure to the distributive property should not only take the form of working number problems, but also examining problem situations which involve basic distributive principles. For example, if there are three boys and seven girls at a table in class and you are passing two papers to each, pose this question: "If I were to pass two papers each to the girls at this table and then two papers each to the boys, would I not have passed two papers to everyone at this table?" When they concur, ask them if this could be pictured on the chalkboard. In effect, the situation looks like this mathematically: $(3 \times 2) + (7 \times 2) = (3 + 7) \times 2$. Using commutativity, we get the more familiar $(2 \times 3) + (2 \times 7) = 2 \times (3 + 7)$ or 2×10. Whenever possible, such relationships should be demonstrated so that there will be more substance to the property than a mere formula.

Closure

To determine if the set of whole numbers is closed with respect to multiplication, think of a pair of whole numbers and determine if their product would also be a whole number. Would this always be the case; that is, would any pair of whole numbers yield a whole number product? Yes, so there is closure for multiplication in the set of whole numbers. Children can come to this same conclusion by doing the same kinds of activities as just described. Using similar techniques, check for closure in division of whole numbers. It will become apparent that the set of whole numbers is not closed with respect to division. For example, while $9 \div 3 = \square$ and $4 \div 2 = \triangle$ yield answers in the set of whole numbers, $3 \div 9 = \bigcirc$ and $2 \div 4 = \triangledown$ obviously do not.

Identities and Inverses

Recall that operating on an entity with an identity element results in no change in the original entity. As children practice using one as a factor, they find that it indeed constitutes the identity element for multiplication. By relating division to its multiplicative counterparts, they also find that dividing a number by one results in a quotient equal to the number divided. As with subtraction, however, while $3 \div 1 = 3$, $1 \div 3 \neq 3$, and division has no i for which $a \div i = i \div a = a$.

To determine an inverse, one must locate two whole numbers which can be multiplied to give the multiplicative identity, or one. Such cannot be found in the set and so multiplicative inverses do not exist in the set of whole numbers. (However multiplicative inverses do exist when the set of numbers expands to the rationals; at the elementary school level these inverses are often called reciprocals.)

Zero as a Factor

Zero as a factor in multiplication can be approached intuitively with children through hypothetical situations. For example, tell the children that you are thinking about sets of pink elephants in the classroom and that you have four of these sets. How many sets? (4) How many pink elephants are actually in each set? (0) How many pink elephants are in 4 sets? (0) Now write the number sentence for this situation: $4 \times 0 = 0$. Often the children want to extend this exercise by finding their own empty sets and considering various groups of these, always arriving at zero.

It is also possible to think about zero groups of a given set of objects. Some educators would prefer that multiplications with zero as a factor be done using cartesian products as illustrations. Whatever technique is used to promote understanding that zero as a factor produces a product of zero, one positive effect is another reduction in the number of basic multiplication facts to be learned.

Division may involve zero in the dividend, the divisor, or both. The problem $0 \div b = ?$, b $\neq 0$, illustrates division with zero in the dividend. To solve the problem, interpret it in multiplicative form, or $? \times b = 0$. By what number must a nonzero number be multiplied in order to arrive at a product of zero? Zero, of course, because $0 \times b = 0$. Therefore, $0 \div b = 0$ when b $\neq 0$.

When the divisor is zero, different results occur. The problem $a/0 = ?$, $a \neq 0$, interprets as $? \times 0 = a$. Now the question is, "What number can be multiplied with zero to yield a nonzero product, or a?" Because no number could give this result, we interpret division by zero in this case to be meaningless.

Zero in both the dividend and divisor yields $0/0 = ?$ and so its multiplicative counterpart, $? \times 0 = 0$. We find that any number will satisfy these sentences, and we describe the problem as ambiguous.

Basic Properties and Mental Calculations

Some readers might wonder at this time why children should bother learning such properties as just described. Among other things they are particularly helpful in calculating mentally. How much do YOU use basic properties in your calculations. Consider the following group of problems. Can you solve them "in your head"? Try each one first mentally and then compare your method of solution with that described.

1. $8 \times 3 \times 0 \times 4 = \square$

   A person used to mechanically performing operations might proceed through the entire problem before arriving at the product of 0, while a person accustomed to looking for basic property uses will see the 0 factor amid all the multiplication operations and know the answer immediately to be 0.

2. $25 \times 14 = \bigcirc$

   Again, the usual way to solve such a problem is vertically and with the aid of pencil and paper thusly:

$$
\begin{array}{r}
25 \\
\times\ 14 \\
\hline
100 \\
25 \\
\hline
350
\end{array}
$$

However, a person with an understanding of renaming and distributivity can arrive at the product quickly. Recording the possible thought sequence we have

$$25 \times 14 = \bigcirc$$
$$25 \times (10 + 4) = \bigcirc$$
$$(25 \times 10) + (25 \times 4) = \bigcirc$$
$$250 + 100 = \bigcirc$$
$$350 = \bigcirc$$

3. $5 \times 28 \times 2 =$
The usual procedure would be to multiply 5 and 28 and then to double that product; some difficult calculations are involved. The person looking for a simpler solution notes an easy combination (5×2) which will make the second multiplication (28×10) rather easy. Associativity, commutativity, and the generalization of multiplying by 10 are all involved.

4. $8 \times 251 \times \frac{1}{8} =$
Associativity, commutativity, and the multiplicative inverse help simplify this solution. Hint: $251 \times (8 \times \frac{1}{8}) =$

5. $14 \times 99 = \text{O}$
Renaming and distributivity simplify this calculation. Hint: $14 \times (100 - 1) = \text{O}$.

6. $25 \times 48 = \square$.
Renaming is basic to the simplification of this solution. Hint: $\frac{100}{4} \times 48 = \square$.

7. $11 \times 1,356,942 =$
Renaming and distributivity simplify this difficult problem so that it may be done mentally. Once you understand the principle and the procedure, it is rather simple and attracts the attention of children. Hint: $(10 + 1) \times 1,356,942 =$. What does multiplication by 10 do to each of the digits? multiplication by 1?

8. In a room there are 14 stacks of books, 25 in each stack. In a second room there are 6 stacks of books, 25 in each stack. How many books are there altogether?
The distributive property forms the basis for simplifying the word problem solution. Hint: $(14 \times 25) + (6 \times 25) = \star$.

Simplifying some calculations to the point that they can be done mentally is only one use of basic properties. Of course, as mentioned earlier, properties are used repeatedly in the learning of operations. Their use in number theory, geometry, measurement, problem solving, and other mathematical areas will become apparent in subsequent chapters.

LEARNING BASIC FACTS

Multiplication and division topics can be sequenced either mathematically or developmentally just as was done in Chapter 8 for addition and subtraction; that is, a multiplication topic can be sequenced logically from its most simple mathematical elements to its most complex forms and also any portion of the topic can be sequenced from the concrete to the abstract. In learning basic multiplication and division facts, for example, activities can be organized from the concrete to the abstract in initial learning experiences. Practice activities are also important to help promote quick recall of these facts.

Initial Learning Experiences

While multiplication and division do relate to each other, they will be examined separately.

Multiplication.   A teacher of older children is sometimes tempted to bypass the concrete stage in multiplication and proceed directly to repeated additions. It seems sufficient to illustrate the addition of 3 fours (4 + 4 + 4 = 12) and interpret the result in multiplicative form (3 × 4 = 12), but it is not. Granted, children should require little time manipulating objects in multiplicative manner, but it is the teacher's responsibility to see that EACH child readily relates multiplication to appropriate physical situations as well as to its additive counterpart. This early effort in the learning of multiplication helps to avoid confusion later on when the child begins problem solving.

Numerous concrete and semiconcrete aids are available to help build foundations in multiplication. Basically, the following aids relate to multiplicative concepts associated with repeated additions as described earlier, to arrays, and to Cartesian products.

Returning to the example of 3 × 4 = ?, consider the following various options to facilitate understanding. Of course, at the most fundamental level real and representative objects can be grouped and counted or added. At first the objects may be arranged more or less at random as they are grouped. These same groupings can be shown at the semiconcrete stage using pictorial or diagrammatic schemes to represent the concrete objects. For example, the diagram below shows 3 groups of 4, or 3 fours, or 3 × 4.

* * * *   * * * *   * * * *

The number line parallels this repeated additions concept at the immature processing level. For example:

Remember, of course, that multiplication still requires that the jumps begin at zero and that each jump must be of a given equal length. The problem 3 × 4 = ? would be pictured by 3 jumps of 4 units per jump landing finally at 12.

The number line is useful as children begin skip counting in their multiplication work. (Skip counting is a process of starting at a given number and calling every second, third, fourth, etc., number while skipping those in between. Starting at zero and calling every second number leads to the multiples of two, for example.)

Also helpful in skip counting is a hundred board. A hundred board is a 10 × 10 chart containing the numerals consecutively arranged from 1 to 100 and of a form whereby certain numerals can be covered, turned around, or hidden in some other way. Various patterns in multiplication can be found: odds and evens, ten patterns, etc.

Multiplication can also be shown as an array of objects (concrete) or pictured in array form (semiconcrete). The following diagram shows 3 × 4 as it might be in an array.

Notice that there are 3 rows with 4 stars in each row, or 3 fours. If the diagram were rotated or if loops had been placed vertically, the picture would show $4 \times 3 = 12$, or 4 groups of three equal 12, thereby illustrating commutativity once again.

A pegboard and golf tees also provide a means of illustrating different arrays. The pegboard can be of any size although commonly a 10×10 array of holes is recommended. (Some prefer a larger size and simply tape off a 10×10 section. This allows extra room in which to insert inverted golf tees at the corners to "lift" the pegboard surface slightly.) Then the array can be illustrated by placing the appropriate arrangement of golf tees in the holes.

Array cards with dot patterns are easily made and are helpful for children learning facts. Consider facts in which 4 is a factor. A dot pattern card like the following can be made.

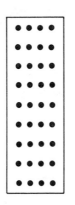

By placing a sheet of paper over the rows and moving it down one row at a time, the four-facts are revealed and can be recorded as shown:

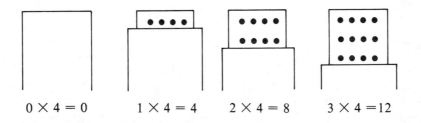

$$0 \times 4 = 0 \qquad 1 \times 4 = 4 \qquad 2 \times 4 = 8 \qquad 3 \times 4 = 12$$

The same array card can be folded instead so that one line of figures is revealed at a time. Also, egg cartons can be cut into 1×4 unit shapes to provide a more concrete orientation to the same idea. As each successive strip of four is placed into an array format, it can be interpreted multiplicatively.

Squared (or graph) paper also provides a grid upon which arrays may be drawn. Such work with grids provides excellent foundational work for the study of area later. Similarly, once again the unit blocks form a base ten set of blocks (or the white cubes from Cuisenaire rods) form a more concrete orientation to the same idea. As children line up a 3 × 4 array of unit blocks or shade in a 3 × 4 array of squares, they can count, add, or multiply to find 12.

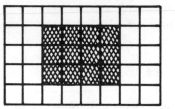

Finally, Cartesian products offer yet another interpretation of multiplication situations. While their use is limited at the elementary school level, still fundamental understandings can be developed. Situations involving matching of possible combinations utilize the Cartesian (or cross) product idea. For example, you could ask your class how many possible different outfits Rich would have to wear if he had two pairs of pants (blue and brown) and three shirts (striped, plaid, and checkered). To solve this problem, the children could match each pair of pants to each shirt. This could be accomplished in an orderly manner via the following diagram. Note that 2 × 3, or 6, combinations are found.

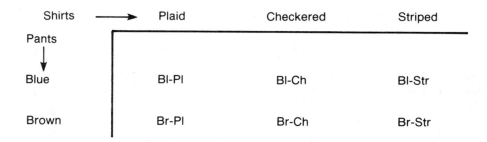

Division.   Recall that a generally accepted interpretation of multiplication of whole numbers is factor (number of groups) times factor (number in each group) equals product. When dividing, the product and one factor are known, and either the number of groups or the number in each group is to be determined. At the abstract level the two division situations become rather obscure, but at the concrete level—the point at which children learn the physical situations associated with a given operation—the differences should be known and experienced. There are names associated with each situation, partitive division and measurement division, and for purposes of this discussion the names will be used. It is not necessary, however, for children to use the names; it is only important that they be able to cope with each situation. Let us consider similarities and differences so that you, the teacher, will be able to provide experiences related to both types. We will illustrate via the sentence, 6 ÷ 2 = □. The two possible interpretive options are discussed in the following paragraphs.

Consider the interpretation, □ × 2 = 6. We are trying to find how many sets of 2 are contained in 6. How can we best arrange tongue depressors, for example, to show this situation?

First, obtain six tongue depressors; then lay them down two at a time until none are left. The number of groups of 2 resulting is the answer we are looking for. So we have

or three groups of 2. When we know how many are in a group and are determining the number of groups, we are involved in the *measurement* aspect of division.

Now consider $2 \times \square = 6$. The product and the number of groups are known, but we do not know how many are contained in each group. How can we best arrange tongue depressors to show this situation? Of course, designate two piles and dole out tongue depressors, one at a time, to each pile until there are none left. The number in each pile tells how many per group. This division is called *partitive*.

Referring to the basic manipulative differences of each situation, let us investigate two word problems to see how their respective diagrams would compare.

Word problem 1: Mary gave her friends six hair ribbons. If she gave each friend two ribbons, how many friends received ribbons?

Because we are trying to determine the number of groups (friends), we are dealing with the measurement aspect of division, or in this case, $\square \times 2 = 6$. Of course, we could actually simulate the situation and pass out ribbons two at a time to see how many people get ribbons.

The problem could also be pictured satisfactorily.

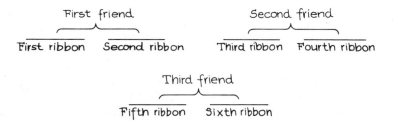

Notice that the number line representation parallels the above depiction closely.

In a sense we have been measuring off a certain number of units at a time in an effort to determine how many groups of these units are contained in the total; hence, we are using measurement division. If we were to use only numerical operations, we could arrive at the answer by repeated subtractions of 2, or $6 - 2 = 4, 4 - 2 = 2, 2 - 2 = 0$.

Now let us change the problem situation so that it relates, not to measurement, but to partitive division. The number of groups is known, but the number per group is not. Consider this problem.

Word problem 2: Mary gave her friends six hair ribbons. If she gave an equal number of ribbons to each of two friends, how many ribbons did each friend receive?

Visualize the action of the problem. We see the situation as $2 \times \square = 6$, a partitive division. Mary can give her friends the ribbons one at a time until she is out of ribbons; that is, she may give each of her friends a ribbon, then she may give each of them another ribbon, and so on, until she has none left to give away. A possible representation for the partitioning would be

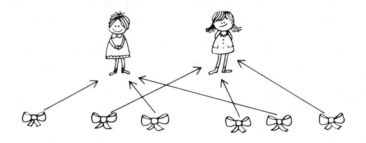

Notice that if Mary were looking for a solution, she could not be expected to begin by passing out three ribbons to each friend, for to do so would indicate that the problem had already been solved—a "cart-before-the-horse" situation of sorts. Similarly, if the number line were to be used to *help solve* the problem and the teacher were to illustrate this way

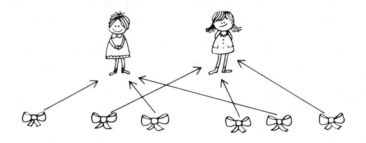

then the teacher is not thinking about the sense of the problem and the child is learning, erroneously of course, that one must know the answer before beginning to use diagrams. He soon thinks, "why should I even bother to diagram the problem if I already know the answer?" If one knows the answer to begin with, then indeed the aids and diagrams are superfluous. Use the aids and diagrams; do not tag them on as afterthoughts which may not even represent the problem.

Thus far, we have been dealing with simple interpretations of division at the concrete and semiconcrete levels. Another aspect of division involves remainders. Divisions with remainders may be dealt with in any of four ways, depending upon the nature of the problem or upon agreement between you and the learner. Consider the division problem: $17 \div 3 = ?$

First, the remainder may be expressed in fractional form, as with

$$5\frac{2}{3}$$
$$3\overline{)17}$$

Second, the remainder may be expressed as part of the number sentence associated with the problem, or (3 × 5) + 2 = 17.

Third, the remainder may be dropped. For example, if children are asked how many egg cartons will be filled when Farmer Jones has 38 eggs, they can correctly respond "3," rightfully ignoring the remainder.

Fourth, the quotient may be increased by 1. For example, if a child is asked the number of benches required at a meeting of 17 people if 3 people can be seated at each bench, he or she can correctly respond "6." Notice that the answer should relate to the sense of the problem whenever such is known. When the problem situation is not known and divisions with remainders are being practiced, you and the students may agree on whatever of the preceding forms you prefer. While it is used in some elementary mathematics texts, the authors do not recommend this option:

$$\overset{\displaystyle 5R2}{3\overline{)17}}$$. The quotient 5 R 2 is not a number and so is mathematically incorrect.

Practice Activities

After initial concrete and semiconcrete experiences, there are a great many approaches to the practice of multiplication and division facts. By this time most students enjoy manipulating numbers as well as objects. They have searched for patterns in other number operations and now find that multiplication is replete with patterns. Multiplication of nines, for example, holds many patterns.

1 × 9 = 9	6 × 9 = 54	The one's digits decrease by 1 when proceeding down the
2 × 9 = 18	7 × 9 = 63	product column while the ten's digits increase by 1. Each
3 × 9 = 27	8 × 9 = 72	product has a digital sum of 9. The digits in the product
4 × 9 = 36	9 × 9 = 81	reverse order as one proceeds from 5 × 9. There are more
5 × 9 = 45	10 × 9 = 90	patterns. Can you find them?

In fact, the entire multiplication table abounds in patterns. Study the following multiplication table and find as many patterns as you can.

×	0	1	2	3	4	5	6	7	8	9
0	0	0	0	0	0	0	0	0	0	0
1	0	1	2	3	4	5	6	7	8	9
2	0	2	4	6	8	10	12	14	16	18
3	0	3	6	9	12	15	18	21	24	27
4	0	4	8	12	16	20	24	28	32	36
5	0	5	10	15	20	25	30	35	40	45
6	0	6	12	18	24	30	36	42	48	54
7	0	7	14	21	28	35	42	49	56	63
8	0	8	16	24	32	40	48	56	64	72
9	0	9	18	27	36	45	54	63	72	81

How many patterns did you find? Some patterns are quite simple; others prove more elusive. For example, study the one's digits in the seven's column in relation to the one's digits in the three's column. What do you see? How about the two's and the eight's column? Do any other pairs of columns work this way? Why is the five's column so simple to remember? And how about certain diagonals? Don't forget corresponding rows and columns. Can you determine why certain sequences form patterns?

Finger multiplication is also universally liked by children. Of course, such multiplication is in no way intended to replace more conventional forms, but it can revive an otherwise waning interest and provide practice. There are several forms, one of the more simple of which capitalizes again on the multiplication of nines. Hold up your hands before you, fingers spread wide. Number your fingers, left to right, from 1 to 10. Then simply bend the finger associated with the factor to be used with nine. The ten's position is shown by the fingers to the left, while the one's position is shown by the fingers to the right. For example, multiply 3 and 9. Bend the third finger from the left, thusly:

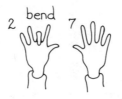

The product of 27 is shown directly. Using a different technique, all multiplications from 5 through 10 can be shown by your fingers. (Actually, finger multiplication can trace its antecedents to the Middle Ages. Any good history of mathematics text will describe the rather simple technique.)

Also, games and activities as described in the previous chapter can be adapted to multiplication and division practice. Card games, bingo variations, worksheets, multiplication wheels, etc., can all serve to provide practice. Each practice activity should still follow the same guidelines as described in Chapter 8.

DEVELOPING THE ALGORITHMS

Following initial learning experiences with multiplication and division, work can begin with the related algorithms.

Multiplication

Practice at this level should begin with multiplying by a one-digit number without regrouping. As always relate the operation to a realistic problem situation. For example, present the following problem to the class:

> I have three boxes of pencils. Each box contains 12 pencils. How can I determine the number of pencils there are altogether?

You might get a variety of solution possibilities, each of which should be considered. One child might suggest actually counting the pencils. (Note that while this is a most primitive form of solution, the child making the suggestion at least has a plan of attack which will work. The child is actively searching for an answer and this is good.) Another child might say that it would be better not to have to unwrap the boxes and that the numbers in each box could be added ($12 + 12 + 12 = 36$). Still another child might observe that this is much like multiplication because the problem involves repeated additions. You might note at this point that the problem could be written in this way: $3 \times 12 = ?$ Of course, it is possible that these suggestions are not offered, and you may have to do some prompting to arrive at the point in which algorithms are recognized as playing an important part.

Array cards, Cuisenaire rods, or pegboard grids can help children visualize the situation in an orderly fashion. Basically, the plan is to express the multiplicand in expanded form and use the distributive principle to multiply the problem in parts. Here is how the problem would be shown using array cards or rods:

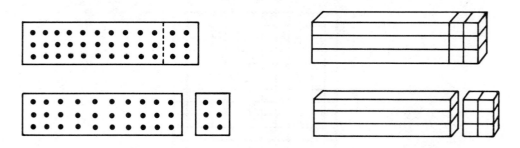

Each pair of preceding diagrams illustrates the mathematics which forms the basis for the algorithm:

$$3 \times 12 = 3 \times (10 + 2)$$
$$= (3 \times 10) + (3 \times 2)$$
$$= 30 + 6$$
$$= 36$$

Vertically, the problem looks like this:

$$\times \frac{\begin{array}{r} 10 + 2 \\ 3 \end{array}}{30 + 6 = 36}$$

Pocket charts, abaci, etc., have limited use at this point. They can be used to show that place value does indeed play a role at this point, however, as shown below:

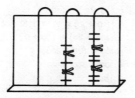

3 groups of 12

As children gain understanding of multiplication by a one-digit number without regrouping they can expand their knowledge to similar situations which require regrouping. Again, the same basic pattern as considered above can be used with the added necessity for regrouping.

Children need also to be able to generalize the results which accrue following multiplications involving a factor of 10, 100, 1000, etc. For example, after practicing the addition of 2 tens, 3 tens, 4 tens, etc., they should conclude that multiplying with 10 as a factor in effect results in the annexation of a zero to the other factor as product. Other similar conclusions can be related to multiplications with other powers of ten.

At this point children can begin study of multiplications involving 2 two-digit numbers as factors. Once again arrays illustrating the components of the problem provide excellent foundations for understanding the algorithmic forms. The array for $12 \times 13 = ?$ is shown below:

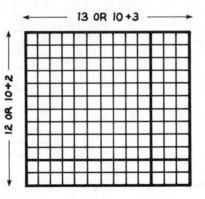

The information given above can be capsulized in the chart below:

	10	3
10	10 x 10 (100)	10 x 3 (30)
2	2 x 10 (20)	2 x 3 (6)

The horizontal format below illustrates that renaming, distributivity, and associativity play integral parts in the algorithm.

$$
\begin{aligned}
12 \times 13 &= (10 + 2) \times (10 + 3) \\
&= [(10 + 2) \times 10] + [(10 + 2) \times 3] \\
&= (100 + 20) + (30 + 6) \\
&= 100 + (20 + 30) + 6 \\
&= 100 + 50 + 6 \\
&= 156
\end{aligned}
$$

Still, however, the vertical algorithm is the ultimate aim for each child. The following three vertical forms of a problem involving regrouping illustrate how the algorithm can be made meaningful. (Notice that none of the illustrations involve rote rules of "how to get the answer." Each instead relies heavily upon fundamental understanding of the procedure itself.)

$$
\begin{array}{r}
60 + 7 \\
\times\ 30 + 2 \\
\hline
14 \\
120 \\
210 \\
1800 \\
\hline
2144
\end{array}
\qquad
\begin{array}{r}
67 \\
\times\ 32 \\
\hline
14 \\
120 \\
210 \\
1800 \\
\hline
2144
\end{array}
\qquad
\begin{array}{r}
67 \\
\times\ 32 \\
\hline
134 \\
2010 \\
\hline
2144
\end{array}
$$

All that is left is to generalize the algorithm using the same kinds of procedures as described earlier. The only additional intermediate step required is that of using "crutches" to indicate regrouping in the shortened form as shown in the following illustrations:

(a)
$$
\begin{array}{r}
26 \\
\times\ 38 \\
\hline
48 \\
160 \\
180 \\
600 \\
\hline
988
\end{array}
$$

(b)
$$
\begin{array}{r}
1 \\
\not{4} \\
26 \\
\times\ 38 \\
\hline
208 \\
78 \\
\hline
988
\end{array}
$$

The multiplication algorithm is not easy and there are numerous points at which errors can occur. It is particularly necessary for you to observe each child at work and to study error patterns in their assignments yourself so that you can correct any procedural problems before they become habitual and compound what might initially only be minor difficulties.

Division

Division methods and division forms have improved greatly during the past two decades. Basically, most methods being advocated currently relate to the entire division problem, whereas formerly children had to memorize a seemingly piecemeal procedure for division. All too often, neither the teacher nor the pupils understood exactly what they were doing; they simply labored over the repeated steps until the answer was obtained.

Remember that division may be either partitive or measurement in nature. If the division problem being worked relates to a particular situation, then the reasoning process alters according to whether it is the number of groups or the number in each group to be found.

Consider $26 \div 2 = \square$ as a measurement type of division problem; that is, the number in each group is known and the number of groups is sought. Use 26 toothpicks and divide (separate) them into groups of 2 as shown.

// // // // // // // // // // // // //

We find that 26 toothpicks can be divided into 13 groups of 2.

Now translate the same problem situation into numerical form by using the reasoning which follows:

$$
\begin{array}{r|l}
2\overline{)26} & \\
\underline{20} & 10 \times 2 \\
6 & \\
\underline{6} & \underline{3} \times 2 \\
0 & 13 \\
\end{array}
$$

Measurement division question: How many groups of 2 are contained in 26? Will there be at least 10 groups? (Yes, because $10 \times 2 = 20$ and 20 is less than 26.) Remove 20 from the original 26 by subtracting. Now how many groups of 2 are contained in the 6 which remain? (There are 3 groups of 2 because $3 \times 2 = 6$.) Altogether, how many groups of 2 were contained in 26? ($10 + 3$ or 13)

Consider $26 \div 2 = \square$ again, this time from a partitive standpoint. Now the 26 toothpicks are to be divided into two groups in order to determine the number in each group as shown.

/////////   ///
/////////   ///

Translate the preceding partitive problem situation into numerical form by using the reasoning which follows. Then compare the form with that which showed measurement.

$$
\begin{array}{r|l}
2\overline{)26} & \\
\underline{20} & 2 \times 10 \\
6 & \\
\underline{6} & 2 \times \underline{3} \\
0 & 13 \\
\end{array}
$$

Partitive division question: How many will be in each group when 26 is divided into two groups? Reasoning: Are there at least 10 in each group? (Yes, because 2×10 equals 20 and 20 is less than 26.) Might there be 20 in each group? (No, because 2×20 is 40 and there are not 40 toothpicks altogether.) As before, remove the set of 2×10 or 20 from the original amount of 26 and determine how the difference, 6, might be partitioned into two sets.

Actually, the form would remain the same for both division situations if only the factor were recorded at the right and not the entire multiplication as follows:

$$
\begin{array}{r|l}
2\overline{)26} & \\
\underline{20} & 10 \\
6 & \\
\underline{6} & \underline{3} \\
0 & 13 \\
\end{array}
$$

Traditionalists still often prefer that the quotient be written above the dividend. This presents no real problem for a child who understands the reasoning above. Study the algorithmic forms which follow and note how the same reasoning can be used with what approaches the traditional pattern of recording.

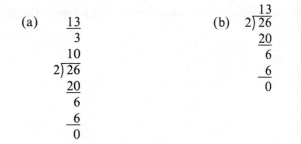

(a)
$$\begin{array}{r} 13 \\ 3 \\ 10 \\ 2\overline{)26} \\ \underline{20} \\ 6 \\ \underline{6} \\ 0 \end{array}$$

(b)
$$\begin{array}{r} 13 \\ 2\overline{)26} \\ \underline{20} \\ 6 \\ \underline{6} \\ 0 \end{array}$$

In example (a) the factors are recorded above rather than at the right. In example (b) the child records a 1 in the ten's position thereby using place value in lieu of recording a 10. Then the 3 is recorded directly in the one's position at the appropriate point in the solution.

Although variations may exist in the form, procedures which require regrouping follow much the same pattern. Multiplication and subtraction are still integral to the work as are approximation, estimation, and basic principles. Relate the following problem at the left with its vertical algorithmic counterpart at the right and note how regrouping is incorporated.

$$
\begin{aligned}
48 \div 3 &= (30 + 18) \div 3 \\
&= (30 \div 3) + (18 \div 3) \\
&= 10 + 6 \\
&= 16
\end{aligned}
\qquad
\begin{array}{r}
16 \\
3\overline{)48} \\
\underline{30} \;\; 10 \\
18 \\
\underline{18} \;\; \underline{6} \\
0 \;\; 16
\end{array}
$$

The measurement (subtractive) process described earlier in division is particularly valuable for students who are at various stages in developing facility with the algorithm. Consider $156 \div 4 = \square$ and note how the reasoning as previously described can be used from the most simple beginnings to its more sophisticated forms.

A simple, but workable, solution might be the following one by a student who only used multiples of four through 4×10.

$$
\begin{array}{r}
39 \\
4\overline{)156} \\
\underline{40} \;\; 10 \\
116 \\
\underline{40} \;\; 10 \\
76 \\
\underline{40} \;\; 10 \\
36 \\
\underline{20} \;\; 5 \\
16 \\
\underline{16} \;\; \underline{4} \\
0 \;\; 39
\end{array}
$$

A student who feels more secure with the problem may produce this solution:

$$
\begin{array}{r}
39 \\
4\overline{)156} \\
\underline{80} \quad 20 \\
76 \\
\underline{40} \quad 10 \\
36 \\
\underline{36} \quad \underline{9} \\
0 \quad 39
\end{array}
$$

A student who can do the following is rapidly gaining an understanding of division.

$$
\begin{array}{r}
39 \\
4\overline{)156} \\
\underline{120} \quad 30 \\
36 \\
\underline{36} \quad \underline{9} \\
39
\end{array}
$$

Moving on to more traditional forms, we find

$$
\begin{array}{r}
\underline{39} \\
9 \\
\underline{30} \\
4\overline{)156} \\
\underline{120} \\
36 \\
\underline{36}
\end{array}
\quad \text{or} \quad
\begin{array}{r}
39 \\
4\overline{)156} \\
\underline{120} \\
36 \\
\underline{36}
\end{array}
$$

Hopefully, a child well based in the division process could overestimate, as well as under-estimate, his answer and still be able to correct himself as in the following:

$$
\begin{array}{r}
39 \\
4\overline{)156} \\
\underline{160} \quad 40 \\
-4 \\
\underline{-4} \quad \underline{-1} \\
39
\end{array}
$$

Zero in the quotient becomes less of a problem than formerly because the problem is viewed as a whole in this type of division. Consider this problem as an example:

$$
\begin{array}{r}
407 \\
7 \\
400 \\
6\overline{)2442} \\
\underline{2400} \\
42 \\
\underline{42}
\end{array}
$$

There is no longer a need to "bring down the next number" and so the problem proceeds in a more natural fashion with the zero being part of the problem rather than a "special case."

Finally, how might such techniques as described above be incorporated when dealing with more complex division problems? Consider the following options with $1512 \div 24 = \square$.

$$
\begin{array}{lll}
\text{(a)} \quad \begin{array}{r} 63 \\ 24\overline{)1512} \\ \underline{480} \quad 20 \\ 1032 \\ \underline{480} \quad 20 \\ 552 \\ \underline{480} \quad 20 \\ 72 \\ \underline{48} \quad 2 \\ 24 \\ \underline{24} \quad \underline{1} \\ 63 \end{array}
&
\text{(b)} \quad \begin{array}{r} 63 \\ 24\overline{)1512} \\ \underline{1200} \quad 50 \\ 312 \\ \underline{240} \quad 10 \\ 72 \\ \underline{72} \quad \underline{3} \\ 63 \end{array}
&
\text{(c)} \quad \begin{array}{r} 63 \\ 24\overline{)1512} \\ \underline{1440} \quad 60 \\ 72 \\ \underline{72} \quad \underline{3} \\ 63 \end{array}
\end{array}
$$

Once more, the same reasoning applies as earlier and the algorithmic form on the right is rather simple. If shortened forms are desired, it is a matter of extending the reasoning while incorporating the place value concept more.

Certainly, division is the most complex of the operations. The subtractive method just illustrated is helpful, however, in terms of understanding. The child must estimate and approximate, know basic facts, and understand the properties associated with the techniques. Above all, though, at whatever level the child is working, he or she must know what is being done in terms of understanding the method of solution.

BEYOND THE BASICS

Both multiplication and division offer a wide range of activities which can stimulate interest and diversify learning beyond the basic standard algorithms. Some representative variations incorporating patterns and historical techniques follow. They allow the child to work with multiplication and division facts while investigating beyond the basics of the operations.

Multiplication patterns can be found in many sequences. Consider the following sequence. Why does it work?

$$
\begin{array}{l}
1 \times 1 = 1 \\
11 \times 11 = 121 \\
111 \times 111 = 12321 \\
1111 \times 1111 = 1234321 \\
11111 \times 11111 = ?
\end{array}
$$

Generalizations prove interesting to some older children. Do you remember the algebraic equation, $(n - 1)(n + 1) = n^2 - 1$? This generalization has usefulness in multiplying two numbers which differ only by two units, like 9 and 11. Simply square the number between the two and subtract one from that product, or $9 \times 11 = 10^2 - 1 = 100 - 1 = 99$. The benefit is greater, perhaps, in finding the product of 19 and 21. Square twenty ($20^2 = 400$) and subtract one ($400 - 1 = 399$). The answer is 399. Many more generalizations can be investigated. Industrious students may also want to investigate *why* the generalizations work.

Historical side trips in multiplication provide practice in both multiplication and addition, reinforce the idea that "there is no *one* way" to do mathematics, and reconfirm the notion that all techniques still are based on certain fundamental properties.

The lattice, or *gelosia,* method of multiplication is illustrative. Study 23 × 35 in lattice form.

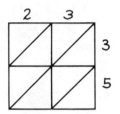

The solution is as follows:

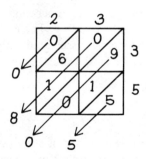

The answer is 805. What are the key elements to this solution? First the rectangle, which is a square in this case, has been divided into cells, and each cell has been divided by a diagonal. The intent is very similar to the reasoning underlying the use of straight columns in algorithms of today. Close examination of the longer diagonals reveals the positioning of ones, tens, hundreds, and so on, moving from the lower right in a clockwise direction. Partial products are recorded in individual cells, and the structuring of the cells allows the automatic incorporation of the distributive principle. Summing each diagonal gives the product. The child who needs practice in finding partial products should be encouraged to do some lattice multiplication. The student who is in need of horizontal enrichment may also be encouraged to do lattice multiplication.

A variation of the lattice method lies in the use of Napier's bones, or Napier's rods. Each rod has basic multiples of a given number listed vertically on it, and there are rods for multiples of one through nine, plus an index rod. The rods are arranged so that one factor shows across the top and the other is found by means of the index. Using renaming, distributivity, and principles of multiplying by powers of ten, one can total the diagonals and arrive at the product. Notice the similarity to the lattice solution of the problem given previously.

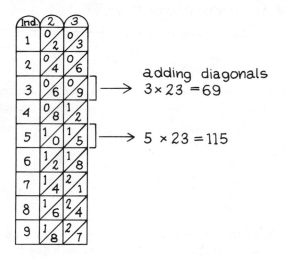

adding diagonals
$3 \times 23 = 69$

$5 \times 23 = 115$

But the problem is 35×23 or $(30 + 5) \times 23$, and so we must multiply 23×30, not 3. This simply involves the annexation of zero, and so we are left with the summation:

$$
\begin{array}{r}
690 \\
+115 \\
\hline
805
\end{array}
$$

Egyptian doubling also gives practice with addition, multiplication, and the use of basic principles, particularly renaming and distributing. To solve 35×23 by Egyptian doubling, we begin with one and start doubling until we have enough digits from which to make a sum totaling one of the factors, for example, 23.

$$
\begin{array}{r}
1 \\
2 \\
4 \\
8 \\
16
\end{array}
$$

We may stop here because we can select from among these numbers those which would total 23, namely $1 + 2 + 4 + 16$. Mark these in some way. Now turn to the other factor and, starting with that number, double.

$$
\begin{array}{rl}
\checkmark\; 1 &—\; 35 \\
\checkmark\; 2 &—\; 70 \\
\checkmark\; 4 &—140 \\
8 &—280 \\
\checkmark 16 &—\underline{560}
\end{array}
$$

The final step is to total those numbers on the right which correspond to the marked numbers on the left, or $35 + 70 + 140 + 560 = 805$.

All that has been done was to rename 23 as $1 + 2 + 4 + 16$ and to use the distributive principle. Relate the following to what was just illustrated.

$$35 \times 23 = 35 \times (1 + 2 + 4 + 16)$$
$$= 35 + 70 + 140 + 560$$
$$= 805$$

The Egyptian system of doubling could similarly be used for division. To divide 805 by 35, for instance, the divisor would be doubled and redoubled until there are sufficient addends to total the dividend.

$$35$$
$$70$$
$$140$$
$$280$$
$$560$$

We may stop doubling here because we can select from these numbers those which would total 805. Mark these and make another column beginning with one and doubling as below:

1	35 ✓
2	70 ✓
8	280
16	560 ✓

Now we total those numbers opposite the ones we checked earlier as components of 805. These are $1 + 2 + 4 + 16$, or 23. Compare the procedure in this division problem with those given earlier for the corresponding multiplication problem. Notice how similar the procedures are.

The above variations are only a sampling of those from which to choose, but they illustrate that basic operations can be interesting to study at many levels.

CHAPTER KEY POINTS

1. Numerous interrelationships exist among various operations. Because of the interrelatedness of the operations, many parallels can be found in teaching methods associated with the operations.

2. Children can learn fundamental concepts associated with commutativity, associativity, distributivity, closure, the existence of identities and inverses, and multiplications and divisions involving zero.

3. Multiplication and division topics can be sequenced either mathematically or developmentally just as addition and subtraction can also be.

4. Multiplication can be approached as repeated additions, as arrays, or as Cartesian products. The interpretation emphasized is that of factor (number of groups) times factor (number in each group) equals product. The approach used is dependent upon the problem situation involved.

5. Division, on the other hand, involves finding the missing factor when one factor and the product are known. The division, therefore, might involve finding the number of groups or the number in each group, depending upon which factor is unknown. At the abstract level the differences become obscure, but children should have experience with each situation, commonly called measurement division and partitive division.

6. The number line, the hundred board, array cards, pegboards and golf tees, egg cartons, and graph paper are typical aids to facilitate learning of the basic facts in multiplication and division. Common to both operations also are whatever real or representative objects which may be used in joining or separating like groups of objects.

7. Practice activities include pattern searches and historical variations as well as variations of games, worksheets, and boardwork as described in Chapter 8.

8. Numerous aids and techniques are available to facilitate understanding of the multiplication and division algorithms. Such aids and techniques include the use of real and representative objects, array cards, Cuisenaire rods, pegboard grids, and diagrams. Fundamental to the teaching of the algorithms is an understanding of the reasoning behind each.

9. Both multiplication and division offer a wide range of activities which can stimulate interest and diversify learning beyond the basic standard algorithms. Patterns, generalizations, lattice multiplication, Napier's bones, and Egyptian doubling are examples of such diversions.

Laboratory 9

Multiplication and Division of Whole Numbers

The following laboratory activities are designed to supplement your study of Chapter 9 insofar as you will gain proficiency in working with aids and activities which are related to multiplication and division of whole numbers.

I. *Objectives:* Upon completion of these laboratory exercises you should be able to do the following:

    A. Demonstrate how colored rods may be used to illustrate multiplication and division of whole numbers and related properties. (Chapter Competencies 9–A, 9–B, and 9–C)

    B. Use such aids as arrays and number lines to solve multiplication and division problems. (Chapter Competency 9–C)

    C. Use alternate algorithms in the solution of multiplication and division problems. (Chapter Competency 9–B)

    D. Describe and illustrate problem situations indicative of the measurement and partitive aspects of division. (Chapter Competencies 9–A and 9–B)

II. *Materials:* Cuisenaire rods (available from Cuisenaire Company of America, 12 Church Street, New Rochelle, New York 10805), discrete objects to group (toothpicks, popsicle sticks, etc.), Napier's bones

III. *Procedure:*

    A. Read Chapter 9 of *Helping Children Learn Mathematics*. Consult your instructor if you have any questions.

    B. Review the use of colored rods in addition and subtraction (Laboratory 8, III B). Extend your knowledge of the rods by working the following exercises in multiplication and division:

        1. Could you use a train to show multiplication? How? Give an example.

        2. Could you write R + R + R using the operation sign for multiplication? How? Complete these sentences:

            a. _____ $\times$ R = DG   d. 5 $\times$ P = _____ + _____

            b. 4 $\times$ W = _____   e. _____ $\times$ DG = OR + BR

            c. 2 $\times$ _____ = OR + P   f. _____ + _____ + _____ = BL

        3. Another way of illustrating multiplication is to use the "cross" method. Suppose we wish to find R $\times$ Y which may be shown by

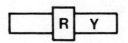

The rectangle can be completed by

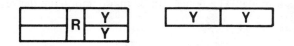

so that R × Y = Y + Y = OR. Complete these sentences:

a. R × LG = _____

b. LG × _____ = OR + R

c. BL × W = _____

d. Y × R = _____

e. P × P = OR + _____

f. BK × LG = OR + _____ + ___

4. Just as multiplication can be shown as repeated addition, division can be shown as repeated subtraction. For example, consider the DG rod. What trains can be made so that all rods in the train are the same color? (Your trains may have more than two rods in them.) Draw a diagram of what you have found.

You should have found three trains. These results may be summarized as:

DG = LG + LG or DG ÷ LG = 2 or R

DG = W + W + W + W + W + W or DG ÷ W = 6 or DG

DG = R + R + R or DG ÷ R = 3 or LG

Using your rods, complete the following sentences:

a. BL ÷ LG = _____

b. OR ÷ R = _____

c. P ÷ R = _____

d. BR ÷ P = _____

5. Show how the rods might be used to illustrate multiplicative identity, commutativity, associativity, and distributivity.

C. Use the number line to solve the following problems:

a. 2 × 4 = _____

b. 4 × 2 = _____

c. 6 ÷ 3 = _____

d. _____ × 3 = 12

D. Arrays may be formed using geoboards, dot matrix cards, paper grids, etc. Using whichever aid you prefer, illustrate the solution of the following problems with arrays:

a. 13 × 4 = _____

b. 12 × 14 = _____

E. Division situations may be either partitive or measurement in type.

a. Using the problem 13 ÷ 4 = _____, describe a partitive division situation which would be meaningful to a third grade child.

b. Illustrate this situation using objects.

c. Diagram this same partitive situation.

d. What should be done with the remainder according to the problem you described?

e. Repeat all of the above activities using a measurement division situation.

F. Using whatever discrete objects you selected to group (toothpicks, popsicle sticks, etc.), illustrate the following division problem and solution using the subtractive (measurement) method. Show the related algorithmic solution on paper. Try the solution using the partitive approach.

$$12)\overline{156}$$

G. The use of the lattice method and Napier's bones (rods) was described as a historical variation of the multiplication algorithm. Make your own set of "bones" using the diagram given as a model. The bones can be made on tongue depressors or on paper strips.

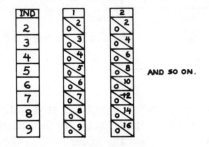

AND SO ON.

Examine each bone, or rod, carefully. What is contained on each? The Index rod is the only rod without diagonals. Why are the diagonals necessary? Show 4 × 8 using the rods. How can the rods be used to show 20 × 8? Now combine the rods to show 24 × 8. Use the rods to solve 34 × 57. Can the rods be used for three-digit factors? What basic properties are apparent in this procedure? What advantages/disadvantages might be associated with the teaching of this procedure? How and with whom might such a study be valuable?

H. Use Egyptian doubling to illustrate 25 × 32.

10
Operations and Properties
Associated with Rational Numbers

Teacher Competencies

After studying Chapter 10 and completing Laboratory 10, you should be able to achieve each of the following:

   A. Given a selected concept or skill in the area of operations and properties associated with rational numbers, design foundational activities which may be used in the acquisition of that concept or skill. (Part Competency III-A)

   B. Given a selected concept or skill in the area of operations and properties associated with rational numbers, identify activities which may be used to develop proficiency in the use of that concept or skill. (Part Competency III-B)

   C. Given a selected concept or skill in the area of operations and properties associated with rational numbers, identify and/or demonstrate the use of selected instructional aids which might be used to help a child learn that concept or skill. (Part Competency III-C)

The study of the operations and properties associated with rational numbers is perhaps one of the most difficult and frustrating experiences for children who are learning mathematics. The unusual form of the numbers themselves and the resulting confusion with the computational algorithms, which are distinct from the algorithms of whole numbers, seem to create the most difficulty for children. Because rational numbers in the form of fractions and decimals are an important part of everyday life, careful development of the rational numbers is of utmost importance.

   Our discussion begins with the concept of a rational number and proceeds to sections concerned with operations and properties relating to two forms of rational numbers—fractions and decimals. Appropriate activities at different levels of the learning continuum discussed earlier are included. The concluding section focuses on percents, an application of rational numbers involving both fractions and decimals.

RATIONAL NUMBERS

An obvious reason for discussion of rational numbers in a child's study of mathematics is the need to describe certain mathematical situations which cannot be described through the use of whole numbers. Questions such as "what is the cost of $2\frac{1}{2}$ pounds of steak at that price?" and "what part of the candy bar is left?" cannot always be answered with the use of a member of the set of whole numbers. Therefore, children should be asked questions such as the preceding ones, and they should be helped to develop ways of answering them. Such activities should develop a child's motivation to study a new mathematical idea—the idea of numbers of the form

$$\frac{a}{b} \text{ when } b \neq 0 \text{ and } a \text{ and } b \text{ are whole numbers.}$$

Numbers of this form are called *rational numbers*. Two forms of rational numbers to be discussed in the remainder of the chapter involve numerals such as $\frac{1}{4}$, $\frac{9}{5}$, $\frac{6}{2}$, and $\frac{2}{3}$ and numerals such as .27, .002, and 3.1. The former are called *fractions* and the latter *decimals*. Decimals are special kinds of fractions; the distinction has been made between the two forms to facilitate discussion of the properties and algorithms associated with each. It should be noted that discussion in this chapter will be concerned only with nonnegative rational numbers.

FRACTIONS

Introducing the Meaning of Fractions

Elementary teachers of the primary grades are very concerned with developing the child's understanding of the concept of number. Experiences relating the spoken word to the written symbol are considered to be imperative if a child is to become proficient in his or her use of mathematics. Similar care should also be taken to develop the child's understanding of fractions.

A child's experiences with fractions in the elementary school should begin during the primary grades. Since most children have an intuitive feeling for or knowledge of fractions as parts of a whole, this meaning should be developed first. Referring to experiences which children have had in earlier years, such as "divide the candy bar into two parts, one for you and one for Billy," you, as teacher, can develop the notion of parts of a whole. Another good approach to the "parts-of-a-whole" idea is to use paper folding. The child can be given a circle or a strip of paper and asked to fold it so that he has two parts which are the same size or four parts the same size. The child could also try to fold the strip into thirds, an activity which could not be easily accomplished with the circle. Such activities would be considered concrete in nature.

On the semiconcrete level, the child can be given circles or strips of paper with the parts already drawn on them and asked to color in various fractional parts.

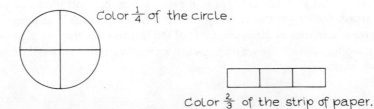

Color $\frac{1}{4}$ of the circle.

Color $\frac{2}{3}$ of the strip of paper.

On the abstract level, the child may be asked to write a numeral which represents a given shaded region of a figure. Time should also be spent discussing the meaning of the symbol; for example, $\frac{1}{4}$ means "one of four parts" and $\frac{2}{3}$ means "two of three parts."

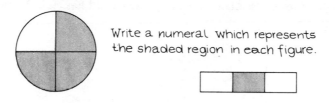

Write a numeral which represents the shaded region in each figure.

These activities should begin with relatively simple fractions such as halves, thirds, and fourths since they are more familiar to the child. Care should be taken to help the child realize that each part in a figure used in such activities is the same size as corresponding parts. This can be done by cutting the figure in various parts and placing the parts on top of each other.

After children have developed an understanding of fractions as parts of a whole, they should be introduced to three other meanings of the fraction symbol with which they should be familiar before leaving elementary school.

One meaning of the fraction symbol is that it represents a part of a collection or set of objects. A good way to begin study of this meaning at the concrete level is to give the child a collection of objects and ask him to group the subset of objects which represents a requested fractional part of the set. For example, he might be asked to look at a set of four books and to show you $\frac{1}{2}$ or $\frac{1}{4}$ of the books in the set. On the semiconcrete level, he may be shown a picture of a set of objects and asked to encircle $\frac{1}{2}$ or $\frac{1}{4}$ of the objects in the set. At the abstract level, he could be given a picture of a set of objects with part of them encircled and asked to write a numeral which represents the encircled objects as a part of the set.

A second meaning of the fraction is that a fraction represents the quotient of two whole numbers. Relating this meaning to the child's experiences with division of whole numbers will provide additional activities to reinforce this meaning.

The third meaning of the fraction is that it represents a ratio or a comparison. Problems such as comparing the number of girls in the class to the number of boys will provide meaningful activities.

Children should be given varied problem situations involving the different meanings of the fraction symbol. Initially these problems may be verbal in nature and then gradually move toward the more abstract written form. These types of problems will also provide additional opportunities to help children develop problem-solving skills.

Renaming Fractions

A powerful mathematical notion is that of renaming numbers in forms that are more appropriate for solving a problem. We have seen that whole numbers can be named in many ways. The idea is perhaps even more useful in the study of fractions because it has direct application in the computational algorithms for fractions as well as in the study of fractions themselves.

A child who has studied the renaming of fractions should be able to write different names for a given fraction, determine whether two fractions represent the same number, and write the simplest name for a given fraction. There are many activities which you might use to help a child achieve these objectives. On the concrete level, the activity may be as simple as covering the same area with different pieces of material or paper. Suppose a child has eight blocks, all the same size, in front of him.

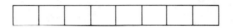

He may be asked to cut out pieces or strips of paper so that he can cover all eight blocks with four pieces of paper all the same size. Using different colors, the same task can be performed using two pieces of paper, eight pieces of paper, and finally, one piece of paper. Placing the pieces of paper side-by-side as in the following diagram, the child can see that certain sets of equal-length pieces of paper have the overall length and hence can represent the same thing.

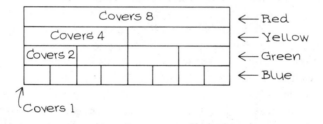

As a result of this activity, the child can see that one red strip has the same length as two yellow strips, as four green strips, and as eight blue strips. He can also see that four blue strips have the same length as one yellow strip and so forth until he has found every possible equality. These relationships should then be expressed in fractional form. You should verify that the preceding statements are true by using colored strips of paper and writing the corresponding fractions. Other fractions can be studied in a similar manner simply by altering the number of blocks in the beginning of the activity.

Another technique which may be used to demonstrate the same idea is that of paper folding. Rectangular strips or circles of paper may be folded to show congruent parts as in the preceding diagram. Either ordinary or waxed paper may be used. The advantage of waxed paper is that the subdivisions are clearly visible when the paper is folded. Ordinary paper, on the other hand, is less expensive. Either way, the notion of equal or congruent parts ($\frac{2}{4} = \frac{1}{2}$, etc.) becomes clearly visible. Folding also helps to show different names for the same fractional values. A piece of waxed paper folded once will reveal $\frac{1}{2}$ and folded again will show that $\frac{2}{4} = \frac{1}{2}$.

On the semiconcrete level, the child may use line segments placed side-by-side and divided into different parts for purposes of comparison. The points on the line segments should be labeled so that different equalities may be easily recognized.

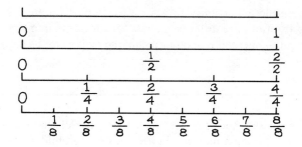

Another activity at this level may ask the child to shade in areas of a given figure to show number equalities.

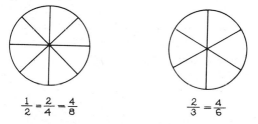

Shade in the figures below to show the equalities represented by the equations.

$$\frac{1}{2} = \frac{2}{4} = \frac{4}{8} \qquad \frac{2}{3} = \frac{4}{6}$$

On the abstract level, equality and other names for fractions can be considered through the use of the product of the fraction and 1. There are many names for 1, and the child should begin by writing as many different names for 1 as he can. He is then ready to consider taking a fraction and writing other names for it. To do this, he must consider problems

$$\frac{1}{3} \times \frac{2}{2}, \frac{1}{3} \times \frac{3}{3}, \text{ etc.}$$

and explore these products to see that

$$\frac{1}{3} \times \frac{3}{3} = \frac{1 \times 3}{3 \times 3} = \frac{3}{9}.$$

If two fractions are equivalent, then the name of each can be expressed as the name of the other, using multiplication by a form of 1.

In a similar fashion, the child can write the simplest name for a fraction by finding the greatest common divisor of the numerator and denominator and dividing each by that number. His reasoning might proceed like this:

I want to find the simplest name for $\frac{3}{9}$. The greatest common divisor of 3 and 9 is 3. So if I divide both the numerator and denominator by 3, then I will have $\frac{1}{3}$ which is the simplest name for $\frac{3}{9}$.

The child should have ample opportunity to write the simplest name for a given fraction and determine whether two fractions are different names for the same number.

The cross-multiplication method is another technique which can be used to check the equality of two fractions.

$$\frac{a}{b} = \frac{c}{d} \text{ if and only if } a \times d = b \times c.$$

This method should be related to the previous one through use of the renaming of both fractions to determine if they name the same number. For example, the child might solve the problem of equality of $\frac{2}{4} = \frac{3}{6}$ in the following way:

Well, $\frac{2}{4} = \frac{3}{6}$ because $2 \times 6 = 3 \times 4$; this is also because both fractions can be renamed in simpler form, namely $\frac{1}{2}$. I can also prove that $\frac{2}{4} = \frac{3}{6}$ if I rename both fractions so that they have the same denominator by using a common multiple of 4 and 6. If I use 12 as the common multiple, then $\frac{2}{4}$ can be renamed as $\frac{6}{12}$ and $\frac{3}{6}$ can be renamed also as $\frac{6}{12}$. So again, $\frac{2}{4} = \frac{3}{6}$. Now I have several ways that I can check to see if two fractions are equal to each other.

During this process you should provide practice and ask questions which will stimulate the child to reach the desired conclusion. Hence, knowledge of how to recognize and use fractions with the same name is a basic need of all children if they are to understand and manipulate fractions.

Ordering Fractions

As the child learns to manipulate fractions, it is also important for him to be able to order fractions. The comparison of two or more fractions to determine which has the greater or greatest value is not intuitively obvious to the child. If you ask him to tell you which is greater, for example, $\frac{1}{3}$ or $\frac{1}{4}$, he will probably say that $\frac{1}{4}$ is greater. In order to correct this misconception, the child will need to work with activities which illustrate the comparison of fractions.

On the concrete level, such comparison might be illustrated with the use of two congruent geometric shapes such as two circles or two rectangles. As in the preceding example using $\frac{1}{3}$ and $\frac{1}{4}$, he could cut one figure into thirds and one figure into fourths. Comparing the sizes of the pieces of the two figures, the child would see that $\frac{1}{3}$ has a greater area than $\frac{1}{4}$.

A semiconcrete-level activity might involve the use of a number line. To compare two fractions, each can be plotted on the number line to see which one lies to the right, indicating that its value is greater. The example with $\frac{1}{3}$ and $\frac{1}{4}$ might be shown as follows:

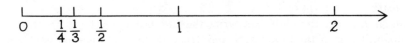

Since $\frac{1}{3}$ lies to the right of $\frac{1}{4}$, $\frac{1}{3}$ is greater.

On the abstract level, the comparison of numerators of two fractions with equal denominators may prove meaningful to the child. As above, $\frac{1}{3} = \frac{4}{12}$ and $\frac{1}{4} = \frac{3}{12}$. Since $4 > 3$, $\frac{1}{3} > \frac{1}{4}$.

Let's see now how the ideas just discussed may be used to develop the algorithms associated with fractions. Addition and subtraction are developed first; specific examples are provided to illustrate the process to be used in developing the general case. A similar technique of development is used in all of the remaining sections of this chapter.

OPERATIONS AND PROPERTIES

Addition and Subtraction of Fractions

In the previous chapter, addition was described as the joining of sets to make a new set. Children will be tempted to use the same reasoning with fractions, but they will soon discover that the process is not so simple.

Early experiences with addition of fractions should begin with work with fractions which have like denominators in a problem such as the following:

Johnny's mother gives him $\frac{1}{3}$ of a candy bar. She gives his sister Mary $\frac{1}{3}$ of the same candy bar. How much of the candy bar will they have eaten? How much will be left for their brother David?

As the children work with the problem, they will be able to see that together Johnny and Mary will eat $\frac{1}{3} + \frac{1}{3}$ or $\frac{2}{3}$ of the candy bar and that there will be $\frac{1}{3}$ of the candy bar left for David. Problems of this type enable children to manipulate the fractions with a minimum of difficulty; this is a valuable asset when they encounter problems with fractions whose denominators are different. At the same time, this type of example affords them the opportunity to work at the concrete level by manipulating a representation of the candy bar (or the real object itself).

At the semiconcrete level, problems may be posed for the child in which he is requested to solve a problem using pictures and/or diagrams. For example, he might be asked to solve the problem stated previously by shading in the region which represents the candy which Johnny and Mary have eaten as shown in the following diagram; the same diagram shows the part of the candy bar which is left for David.

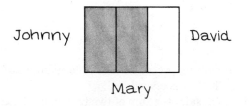

The child might also solve the problem using the number line.

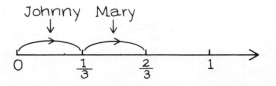

Moving to the abstract level, the child is then ready to consider the problem of

$$\frac{1}{3} + \frac{1}{3}$$

and to work with the formal operation of addition of fractions to realize that

$$\frac{1}{3} + \frac{1}{3} = \frac{1+1}{3} = \frac{2}{3}$$

A difficulty which some children encounter in early work with the addition of fractions is that they may add both the numerators and denominators of the fractions involved. For example, $\frac{1}{3} + \frac{1}{3}$ may be incorrectly added in the following way:

$$\frac{1}{3} + \frac{1}{3} = \frac{1+1}{3+3} = \frac{2}{6}$$

A technique which might be helpful to children with the above difficulty is to rewrite the problem

$$\begin{array}{r} 1 \text{ third} \\ + \ 1 \text{ third} \\ \hline 2 \text{ thirds} \end{array}$$

where "thirds" is emphasized as the name of the fractions involved in the problem.

Initial development should include examples which have solutions less than or equal to 1. As the child becomes proficient with these examples, he may be introduced to examples which have solutions greater than 1. To help him in this endeavor, he should be provided with various exercises related to the concept of a mixed number. For example, he should understand that the mixed number $1\frac{1}{2}$ can be written as

$$1 + \frac{1}{2}.$$

Using the renaming of 1, this number can be rewritten as

$$\frac{2}{2} + \frac{1}{2}.$$

Using the procedures just discussed,

$$\frac{2}{2} + \frac{1}{2} = \frac{2+1}{2} = \frac{3}{2}.$$

The child should utilize this renaming procedure until the manipulation causes him no difficulty, regardless of the direction in which it is considered.

The child is now ready to consider the sum of two fractions whose denominators are different numbers, such as

$$\frac{1}{3} + \frac{1}{4}.$$

This problem might be presented in the following way:

If Mary has eaten $\frac{1}{4}$ of the candy bar and Judy has eaten $\frac{1}{3}$ of the candy bar, what part of the bar has been eaten?

At first, the child will probably state that such a problem cannot be solved. However, actually measuring $\frac{1}{4}$ and $\frac{1}{3}$ of the candy bar and placing the pieces end-to-end and comparing them with the length of the original candy bar should convince him that the problem is possible to solve. He may wonder, though, how the amount of the candy bar which has been eaten can be represented by a number. At this point, he is ready to explore possible ways of writing the numbers so that they have like denominators since he now knows that it is possible to add those kinds of fractions. This discovery provides the springboard to refer back to the renaming idea. Is it possible to rename both $\frac{1}{3}$ and $\frac{1}{4}$ so that they have denominators that are the same? Is there more than one number which could be used in the denominator?

As the child realizes that the answer is "yes," ask him what number can be used. How can thirds and fourths be renamed so that they have a common name? What about a common multiple such as 12, 24, or 36? Could both numbers, $\frac{1}{3}$ and $\frac{1}{4}$, be renamed to have 12 as a denominator? Using the equivalent fraction idea discussed earlier, we see that

$$\frac{1}{3} = \frac{\square}{12} \text{ and } \frac{1}{4} = \frac{\triangle}{12}.$$

Can we find numbers to replace $\square$ and $\triangle$? Now $3 \times \square = 1 \times 12$ which implies that $\square = 4$, and $4 \times \triangle = 1 \times 12$ which implies that $\triangle = 3$. Substituting,

$$\frac{1}{3} = \frac{4}{12} \text{ and } \frac{1}{4} = \frac{3}{12}.$$

Children should also have an opportunity to see that both 24 and 36 will also work, along with any other common multiple of 3 and 4.

Now that $\frac{1}{3}$ and $\frac{1}{4}$ have been renamed as twelfths, the child is ready to perform the operation

$$\frac{4}{12} + \frac{3}{12} = \frac{4+3}{12} = \frac{7}{12}.$$

He finds that $\frac{7}{12}$ of the candy bar has been eaten. The use of a common multiple of 3 and 4 was the key to solving the problem. By using 12 (also called the least common multiple of 3 and 4), he was able to keep the numbers as simple as possible. Of course, he could have used *any* common multiple as a denominator to solve the problem—a fact which will be especially important for the child who has difficulty with the notion of the lowest common denominator. At this point, you should help the child to realize that the product of the two denominators may *always* be used as a common denominator.

Some children will have difficulty performing the required manipulations and tying the whole process together. Hence, it may be necessary to isolate and provide practice for specific troublesome areas. Such practice, however, is meaningful if and only if the child *understands* what he must do and why he must do it.

The problem of adding fractions in the mixed form can now be solved using the ideas developed previously. For example, what is $1\frac{2}{3} + 1\frac{1}{2}$? Initially, the child can rename $1\frac{2}{3}$ as $\frac{5}{3}$ and $3\frac{1}{2}$ as $\frac{7}{2}$. Now, $1\frac{2}{3} + 3\frac{1}{2} = \frac{5}{3} + \frac{7}{2}$. Renaming again enables this solution.

$$\frac{5}{3} + \frac{7}{2} = \frac{10}{6} + \frac{21}{6} = \frac{10+21}{6} + \frac{31}{6} \text{ or } 5\frac{1}{6}.$$

Regardless of which method is used (or variations thereof), work with the addition operation should not become mechanical but instead should be carefully developed to emphasize understanding of the process. In this way, the process will become meaningful to the child.

The development of the addition process should culminate in a discussion of the general form of the algorithm. In the general form, for any two fractions $\frac{a}{b}$ and $\frac{c}{d}$,

$$\frac{a}{b} + \frac{c}{d} = \frac{ad}{bd} + \frac{bc}{bd} = \frac{ad + bc}{bd} \text{ where neither } b \text{ nor } d \text{ equals } 0.$$

In the preceding discussion, it should be noted that the algorithm renames each fraction so that they have the same denominator since bd is a multiple of both b and d.

Throughout the development of the process of addition, the properties of the operation should also be considered. The child has a prior basis for the study of these properties because of the work done with the whole numbers. Commutativity and associativity may be easily verified; the identity element for addition may create a little difficulty. However, once the child realizes that zero can always be written as

$$\frac{0}{a} \text{ where } a \text{ is any nonzero whole number,}$$

then he will probably have little difficulty manipulating it in the addition process. The verification of previously mentioned properties with fractions provides excellent review of ideas learned earlier and also helps the child realize that mathematics has a structure.

Once the child has demonstrated an understanding of the addition of fractions, he is ready to consider subtraction. As with addition, he should begin by working with problems containing fractions having like denominators. For example, recall the candy bar problem with Johnny and Mary in the previous discussion on addition of fractions.

Even though some addition is involved in the solution of the problem, the child who needs to work on the concrete or semiconcrete level can actually cut up a candy bar or a rectangle divided into three parts to physically act out the problem, or he can draw a picture to solve the problem. In either case, the child has an opportunity to become actively involved in his learning situation.

As the child proceeds to the abstract level, he will consider the manipulation of the fractions so that the above problem may be presented to him for solution in the following form:

Together, Johnny and Mary have eaten $\frac{1}{3} + \frac{1}{3}$ or $\frac{2}{3}$ of the candy bar. How much of the candy bar will be left?

$$1 - \frac{2}{3} = \frac{3}{3} - \frac{2}{3} = \frac{3 - 2}{3} = \frac{1}{3}$$

so that $\frac{1}{3}$ of the candy bar will be left for David.

The transition now to the case involving fractions with unlike denominators should be relatively easy for the child who understands addition of fractions and the initial work with subtraction of fractions. He will probably need to engage in many activities which will enable him to practice the operation; variations on activities used earlier with addition may be used at this point.

As before, the culminating activity should be a discussion of the general form of the algorithm. For any two fractions, $\frac{a}{b}$ and $\frac{c}{d}$,

$$\frac{a}{b} - \frac{c}{d} = \frac{ad}{bd} - \frac{bc}{bd} = \frac{ad - bc}{bd} \text{ where neither } b \text{ nor } d \text{ equals } 0.$$

Multiplication of Fractions

Ultimately, the multiplication of fractions should be treated as a single general case rather than as specific cases involving various combinations of whole numbers, mixed numbers, and fractional numbers. To clarify, the generalized form, utilizing one computational algorithm, should be stressed instead of having the child memorize a specific procedure for different cases involving fractional numbers. Such generalization does not preclude the use of varied physical situations and concrete objects to represent the different types of multiplication problems, however; it only means that all of the different cases can be solved mathematically with the form $\frac{a}{b} \times \frac{c}{d} = \frac{a \times c}{b \times d}$ when neither b nor d equals 0 simply by expressing all terms in their fractional form. Consider the three forms which follow and note how they all ultimately relate to the general form just given.

$$\frac{1}{2} \times \frac{3}{5} = \frac{1 \times 3}{2 \times 5} = \frac{3}{10}$$

$$5 \times \frac{2}{3} = \frac{5}{1} \times \frac{2}{3} = \frac{5 \times 2}{1 \times 3} = \frac{10}{3}$$

$$1\frac{2}{3} \times \frac{1}{2} = \frac{5}{3} \times \frac{1}{2} = \frac{5 \times 1}{3 \times 2} = \frac{5}{6}$$

However, at the elementary school level there remains the need to relate mathematics to real life situations or at least to appropriate manipulations of concrete materials. Multiplication can be interpreted in several ways, some of which lend themselves to fractional interpretations better than others. A satisfactory approach in the beginning is that of initiating work using a whole number as the multiplier and using the interpretation of multiplication as repeated addition, with commutativity being used in the solution whenever necessary. The following problems illustrate the repeated additions interpretation:

Interpret 4×3 as 4 three's or $3 + 3 + 3 + 3$,

$4 \times \frac{1}{3}$ as 4 one-thirds or $\frac{1}{3} + \frac{1}{3} + \frac{1}{3} + \frac{1}{3}$,

$4 \times 2\frac{1}{3}$ as 4 two-and-one-thirds or $2\frac{1}{3} + 2\frac{1}{3} + 2\frac{1}{3} + 2\frac{1}{3}$.

Initial examples in which the fractional value is expressed first do not lend themselves to the repeated additions interpretation and so should be disregarded until the property of commutativity is developed. It should be mentioned that mathematics educators have disagreed on the meaning of $4 \times \frac{1}{3}$ and $\frac{1}{3} \times 4$. Some believe that $\frac{1}{3} + \frac{1}{3} + \frac{1}{3} + \frac{1}{3}$ should be interpreted in multiplication to be $\frac{1}{3} \times 4$, while others feel that it should be interpreted as $4 \times \frac{1}{3}$. Because commutativity guarantees that both multiplicative arrangements give the same answer, perhaps the distinction becomes less important as one moves to the abstract forms. To be consistent with the work on whole numbers, however, we shall interpret $4 \times \frac{1}{3}$ as $\frac{1}{3} + \frac{1}{3} + \frac{1}{3} + \frac{1}{3}$, with the first factor representing the multiplier.

A more expansive interpretation of multiplication of fractions incorporates the repeated additions idea at times, but it also incorporates a variety of concrete and semiconcrete aids. Regions and line segments in the form of number lines, colored pieces of flannel, a tape measure, or, if available, colored rods of varied lengths all find use in relating fraction multiplications to their physical counterparts. Visualization and manipulation play important roles in this interpretation. Also, remember that the unit quantity involved is important.

For example, in considering $4 \times \frac{1}{3}$ and the additive idea, a number line can help the child visualize the situation in the following way:

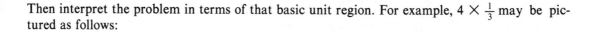

Multiplication also may be interpreted in terms of rectangular regions. Begin by deciding upon the unit region, as for example

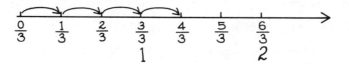

Then interpret the problem in terms of that basic unit region. For example, $4 \times \frac{1}{3}$ may be pictured as follows:

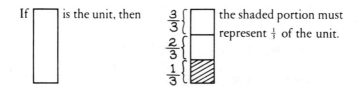

Four one-thirds could be pictured as the shaded portion of

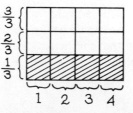

and again $\frac{1}{3} + \frac{1}{3} + \frac{1}{3} + \frac{1}{3} = \frac{4}{3}$.

The product of $\frac{1}{3} \times 4$ may be represented as follows:

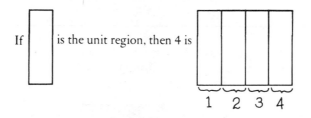

and each of these four units may be divided into thirds as

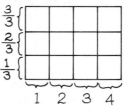

Now picturing $\frac{1}{3} \times 4$ or $\frac{1}{3}$ of 4 of the unit regions involves shading in the appropriate sections.

The shaded portion has an area of $\frac{4}{3}$ ($\frac{1}{3}$ in each of four sections). Note that the diagram appears the same as in the preceding example and $4 \times \frac{1}{3} = \frac{1}{3} \times 4$, commutativity having been illustrated.

Abstractly, $\frac{1}{3} \times 4$ may be written as $\frac{1}{3} \times \frac{4}{1}$ where $\frac{4}{1}$ is another name for 4. Experience with this idea will lead the child to see that

$$\frac{1}{3} \times 4 = \frac{1}{3} \times \frac{4}{1} = \frac{1 \times 4}{3 \times 1} = \frac{4}{3} \text{ or } 1\frac{1}{3}$$

which is the form of the basic algorithm for the multiplication of fractions.

We are now ready to consider the situation involving the product of two fractions where neither is a whole number. Suppose, for example, we wish to find the product of $\frac{2}{3}$ and $\frac{3}{4}$. This problem is perhaps best illustrated pictorially as in the preceding area relationship figures. Note that repeated addition is not applicable here. Interpreting $\frac{2}{3} \times \frac{3}{4}$ as $\frac{2}{3}$ of $\frac{3}{4}$ of the unit, we begin by shading $\frac{3}{4}$ of a unit rectangle.

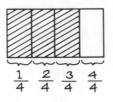

Then we determine $\frac{2}{3}$ of the shaded area. It is usually considered convenient to shade this part in the opposite direction; therefore we have the following picture:

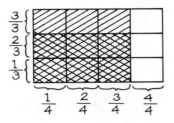

In locating $\frac{2}{3}$ of $\frac{3}{4}$ of the unit region we need only to count the small rectangles in the cross-hatched area and compare that to the total number of rectangles formed in the total unit region. There are 6 cross-hatched rectangles compared to a total of 12 small rectangles. So the solution is $\frac{6}{12}$ or $\frac{1}{2}$.

In this last example some people may wish to "cancel" because it often makes the numbers easier to work with. Note that "cancellation" is a traditional technique and is not necessary to solve the problem. If, however, you desire to use this technique in your class, be certain that the children understand what the procedure is and how it is done. Cancellation, or reduction, should not become a mechanical procedure. In the last example, traditionally the problem might have been solved in this way:

$$\frac{2}{3} \times \frac{3}{4} = \frac{2 \times 3}{3 \times 4} = \frac{{}^{1}2 \times 3^{1}}{{}_{1}3 \times 4_{2}} \longrightarrow \text{common factor of 3}$$
$$\longrightarrow \text{common factor of 2}$$

$$= \frac{1 \times 1}{1 \times 2}$$

$$= \frac{1}{2}$$

The explanation was that the threes had a common factor of 3 which, when divided into each three gave a quotient of 1. Two and four have a common factor of 2, so that $2 \div 2 = 1$ and $4 \div 2 = 2$. Hence, the numerator or product is $1 \times 1 = 1$ and the denominator product is $1 \times 2 = 2$, which gives the product of $\frac{1}{2}$.

Using the commutative property of whole numbers under multiplication, the problem might have been solved

$$\frac{2}{3} \times \frac{3}{4} = \frac{2 \times 3}{3 \times 4} = \frac{2 \times 3}{4 \times 3}$$

which, reversing the process, gives:

$$\frac{2 \times 3}{4 \times 3} = \frac{2}{4} \times \frac{3}{3} = \frac{2}{4} \times 1.$$

Now,

$$\frac{2}{4} \times 1 = \frac{2 \times 1}{2 \times 2} \times 1 = \frac{2}{2} \times \frac{1}{2} \times 1 = 1 \times \frac{1}{2} \times 1 = \frac{1}{2} \times 1 = \frac{1}{2}$$

Either way, the child should demonstrate an understanding of cancellation before he is permitted to use it. Otherwise, there is the possibility that he will incorrectly generalize the cancellation procedure to include addition and subtraction as well as multiplication. In fact, because of this abuse, many educators have recommended that the cancellation technique be dropped and the basic principle approach just described be used in all cases.

Now the child is ready to work with the general form of the algorithm in which

$$\frac{a}{b} \times \frac{c}{d} = \frac{a \times c}{b \times d} \text{ where neither } b \text{ nor } d \text{ is } 0.$$

The final type of problem concerning multiplication of fractions involves the product of two mixed numbers. This is probably best treated from the standpoint of renaming as improper fractions and application of the preceding algorithm. For example:

$$2\frac{3}{4} \times 1\frac{1}{2} = \left(2 + \frac{3}{4}\right) \times \left(1 + \frac{1}{2}\right) = \left(\frac{8}{4} + \frac{3}{4}\right) \times \left(\frac{2}{2} + \frac{1}{2}\right) = \frac{11}{4} \times \frac{3}{2}$$

Now we may proceed as with the algorithms developed previously.

$$\frac{11}{4} \times \frac{3}{2} = \frac{11 \times 3}{4 \times 2} = \frac{33}{8} \quad \text{or} \quad 4\frac{1}{8}$$

Notice that the last example can also make use of the distributive property which holds for fractions as well as whole numbers. (Children should verify that this statement is true.) It can be seen that:

$$2\frac{3}{4} \times 1\frac{1}{2} = \left(2 + \frac{3}{4}\right) \times \left(1 + \frac{1}{2}\right) = 2 \times \left(1 + \frac{1}{2}\right) \times \frac{3}{4} \times \left(1 + \frac{1}{2}\right)$$

$$= \left(2 \times 1\right) + \left(2 \times \frac{1}{2}\right) + \left(\frac{3}{4} \times 1\right) + \left(\frac{3}{4} \times \frac{1}{2}\right)$$

$$= \left(2 + 1\right) + \left(\frac{3}{4} + \frac{3}{8}\right)$$

$$= 3 + \left(\frac{3}{4} + \frac{3}{8}\right)$$

$$= 3 + 1\frac{1}{8}$$

$$= 4\frac{1}{8}$$

As a result of the multiplication algorithm, every fraction except zero (why?) can be shown to have an inverse under multiplication. This inverse is sometimes called the *reciprocal* or *multiplicative* inverse. This statement simply says that, given any nonzero fraction, there is another fraction such that the product of the two fractions gives the identity under multiplication or, in this case, 1. This property may be examined by attempting to answer the following question.

$$\frac{2}{3} \times \square = 1. \text{ What is } \square?$$

To solve the problem, the child may reason that he must find a number for both $\triangle$ and $\square$ such that

$$\frac{2}{3} \times \frac{\triangle}{\square} = 1$$

or

$$\frac{2 \times \triangle}{3 \times \square} = 1.$$

So he must find $\triangle$ and $\square$ such that $2 \times \triangle = 3 \times \square$. One such possibility is that $\triangle = 3$ and $\triangle = 2$ so that

$$\frac{2 \times 3}{3 \times 2} = \frac{6}{6} = 1.$$

Now,

$$\frac{2 \times 3}{3 \times 2} = \frac{2}{3} \times \frac{3}{2} = 1 \text{ and } \square = \frac{3}{2}.$$

Hence, $\frac{3}{2}$ is the reciprocal of $\frac{2}{3}$. This property is useful in the development of the division algorithm.

Division of Fractions

Of all the operations on fractions, division is the one that is probably least understood by both children and teachers. Perhaps this is a result of the rule of "invert the divisor and multiply" which was traditionally to be memorized. It may also be because division of fractions is used less in everyday life than the other operations on fractions.

As with multiplication, initial examples in developing the notion of division involve the use of a fraction and a whole number. We can consider the examples of $\frac{1}{2} \div 3$ and $3 \div \frac{1}{2}$.

In the first example, the operation involves the partitioning of $\frac{1}{2}$ into three equal parts and then deciding how much there is in each part. This problem may be illustrated on the concrete level by the use of paper folding. The child may take a rectangular sheet of paper and fold it in half.

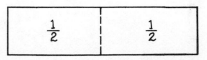

He may then fold each half into thirds so that the paper appears as in this figure:

One of the sections then represents $\frac{1}{2} \div 3$, and since there is a total of six sections.

$$\frac{1}{2} \div 3 = \frac{1}{6}.$$

The other example, $3 \div \frac{1}{2}$, may be illustrated as follows by again having the child take three rectangular sheets of paper and fold each in half.

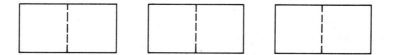

The number of "halves" may then be counted, and the child can see that there are six such halves. Hence,

$$3 \div \frac{1}{2} = 6.$$

Semiconcretely, we can refer to the pictures and diagrams used in the previous section on multiplication. In the case of the example just discussed, $\frac{1}{2} \div 3$, we could diagram the problem as follows:

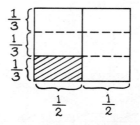

Again, using the unit rectangle, $\frac{1}{2}$ of the length of the rectangle can be represented. Then, dividing by 3 implies taking $\frac{1}{3}$; hence the shaded area is found by taking $\frac{1}{2}$ and dividing it into three equal parts, one of which represents $\frac{1}{6}$ of the unit rectangle. Hence,

$$\frac{1}{2} \div 3 = \frac{1}{6}.$$

The other situation, $3 \div \frac{1}{2}$, can be illustrated diagrammatically by choosing, this time, a rectangle which has an area of 3.

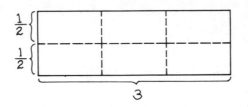

Hence, taking the number of rectangles whose area is $\frac{1}{2}$, we can see that there are six such rectangles. Since the width of the original rectangle is 1 which contains two halves, there are 2×3 or 6 of the small rectangles. So,

$$3 \div \frac{1}{2} = 3 \times \frac{2}{1} = \frac{3}{1} \times \frac{2}{1} = \frac{6}{1} = 6.$$

Note also that repeated subtraction of $\frac{1}{2}$ from 3 also gives 6.

$$3 - \frac{1}{2} = 2\frac{1}{2}$$

$$2\frac{1}{2} - \frac{1}{2} = 2$$

$$2 - \frac{1}{2} = 1\frac{1}{2}$$

$$1\frac{1}{2} - \frac{1}{2} = 1$$

$$1 - \frac{1}{2} = \frac{1}{2}$$

$$\frac{1}{2} - \frac{1}{2} = 0$$

One-half can therefore be subtracted 6 times. The use of the number line is beneficial also.

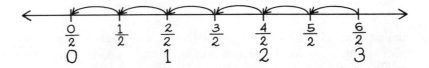

Many problems encountered by children in studying the division process stem from a lack of understanding of what division really is. As teacher, you must provide children with many such activities as just described to help alleviate problems associated with rotely memorized division rules.

We are now ready to turn to finding the quotient of any two nonzero fractions. Since the background for this situation has already been covered, it remains only to develop the base algorithm.

Consider the example of $\frac{1}{2} \div \frac{2}{3}$. Which of the previous activities may be used to find the solution to this problem? Diagrams and repeated subtraction aren't very helpful. We can think of the problem in this way. First, how many $\frac{1}{3}$'s are there in $\frac{1}{2}$? There are

$$\frac{1}{2} \times 3 \text{ thirds in } \frac{1}{2}.$$

Next, we find how many $\frac{2}{3}$'s there are in $\frac{1}{2}$

by taking $\frac{1}{2}$ of $\left(\frac{1}{2} \times 3\right)$ which gives

$$\left(\frac{1}{2} \times 3\right) \times \frac{1}{2}.$$

This last statement can, of course, be written as

$$\frac{1}{2} \times \left(3 \times \frac{1}{2}\right) \text{ or } \frac{1}{2} \times \frac{3}{2} \text{ so that we have}$$

$$\frac{1}{2} \div \frac{2}{3} = \frac{1}{2} \times \frac{3}{2},$$

a fact which will become very useful.

At this point, the child should make use of the fact that division is the inverse of multiplication. This solution of $\frac{3}{4}$ can be verified by multiplying the quotient by the divisor to obtain the dividend. In the example just completed, then, it is seen that

$$\frac{3}{4} \times \frac{2}{3} = \frac{3 \times 2}{4 \times 3} = \frac{6}{12} \quad \text{or} \quad \frac{1}{2} \text{ or, quotient} \times \text{divisor} = \text{dividend}.$$

The child is then ready to proceed to the formal algorithm or the "invert the divisor and multiply" rule which may be developed in the following way:

$$\frac{1}{2} \div \frac{2}{3} = \frac{\frac{1}{2}}{\frac{2}{3}} . \text{ To simplify this number, the child knows that}$$

$$\frac{2}{3} \times \frac{3}{2} = 1 \text{ so that} \quad \frac{\frac{1}{2}}{\frac{2}{3}} \times 1 = \frac{\frac{1}{2}}{\frac{2}{3}} \times \frac{\frac{3}{2}}{\frac{3}{2}} = \frac{\frac{1}{2} \times \frac{3}{2}}{\frac{2}{3} \times \frac{3}{2}} .$$

$$\text{Continuing,} \quad \frac{\frac{1}{2} \times \frac{3}{2}}{\frac{2}{3} \times \frac{3}{2}} = \frac{\frac{1}{2} \times \frac{3}{2}}{1} = \frac{1}{2} \times \frac{3}{2}$$

The result is that

$$\frac{1}{2} \div \frac{2}{3} = \frac{1}{2} \times \frac{3}{2}$$

and hence we "inverted the divisor and multiplied." Children should make note that the appropriate form of 1, namely $\frac{\frac{3}{2}}{\frac{3}{2}}$, was chosen because $\frac{3}{2}$ is the reciprocal of $\frac{2}{3}$, the number in the denominator.

With these facts in mind, we can now generalize about the preceding examples. They show us that

$$\frac{a}{b} \div \frac{c}{d} = \frac{a}{b} \times \frac{d}{c} \text{ where } \frac{a}{b} \text{ and } \frac{c}{d} \text{ are any two fractions and } \frac{c}{d} \neq 0.$$

If children simply memorize the "invert the divisor and multiply" rule without understanding *why,* then many of them may invert the incorrect numeral. In the preceding case, children who lack understanding tend to invert the $\frac{1}{2}$ which gives an answer that is the reciprocal of the correct answer. Children who make this error should revert to the basis of the operation until the difficulty is corrected.

In summary, alternative strategies for developing different levels of the algorithm for division of fractions have been shown. The activities used to develop these strategies are mentioned not because they exhaust all possibilities nor because they are the best ones to use, but instead to give you a basis from which to begin. In your classroom, you will no doubt develop many activities which prove to be very effective. For example, number rods (rods marked off in units) are preferred by some teachers to the use of Cuisenaire rods. The careful and logical development of the algorithm to develop understanding by children remains the most important factor in choosing activities.

With work on fractions completed, let us now turn to another form of rational numbers—decimals. The order of development will be similar to the one just completed.

DECIMALS

Developing the Meaning of Decimals

The use of money and metric measuring necessitates the child's early exposure to a special subset of the rational numbers called decimals. The study of decimals can proceed on several planes, some of which are described in the following paragraphs.

First, decimals can be related to their fraction equivalents, with similarities and differences being one basis of discussion. In this respect the child should learn that the decimal form of a fraction can always be found through the interpretation of a fraction as a division problem, e.g., $\frac{3}{4} = 4\overline{)3} = .75$. Equivalents can be found in other ways, too, e.g., $\frac{3}{4} = \frac{75}{100} = .75$. The child should learn that the decimal form usually encountered in everyday life is a terminating decimal (one which, at some point, repeats only zeros in the quotient). With respect to the notion of terminating decimal, the child should explore the fact that all fractions can be represented as repeating decimals (some group of digits in the quotient will repeat). As the child initiates investigations relative to this idea, he should be given fractions that repeat only a few digits, such as $\frac{1}{3} = .333$ . . . and $\frac{24}{99} = .24\overline{24}$. As he progresses, he may proceed to less obvious repetitions. However, the objective is not to design problems for difficulty but instead to help the child verify that all fractions can be represented as repeating decimals.

Decimals should also be dealt with as an extension of the base ten-place value notion learned earlier with whole numbers; a decimal is a fraction whose denominator can be represented as a power of ten. Basically, the same devices used to develop the base ten-place value notion of the whole numbers can be used with some modification for decimal learning. Manipulative aids like the pocket chart and the abacus may be used to advantage by simply identifying positions in tenths and hundredths as well as whole number positions. Another useful tool involves the overhead projector. By beginning with the outline of a unit region on an acetate and then by using overlays of tenths and of hundredths in conjunction with colored strips of acetate to represent different portions of the unit region, the children can actually visualize the quantities identified by various decimals.

Finally, decimals should not be taught in isolation. Instead, their study should be related to real life applications and situations. In the study of money, the child should be able to express a given quantity of money not only as dollars, dimes, and cents but also as a unit, tenths of the unit, and hundredths of the unit. Naturally, the metric system offers ample opportunity for decimal study, but then so does the English system if one considers such instruments as an odometer in an automobile or a stopwatch in timed situations.

Algorithms Associated with Decimals

Because there is such close association of the operation of algorithms of whole numbers to decimals, teachers tend to reduce study of basic operations with decimals to a three-step procedure: (1) work the problem first by ignoring the decimal points; (2) place the decimal point in the answer by following the rule appropriate to the operation; and then (3) practice. Unfortunately, such a procedure does not promote understanding, and if any area of arithmetic lends itself to being easily understood, it is operations involving decimals. Let us examine some techniques which will enable the child to work (with understanding) algorithms associated with decimals.

Addition and Subtraction of Decimals.   Traditionally, children were taught a rule by which always to add and subtract decimals; that is, simply align decimal points and perform the operation as with whole numbers. Of course, answers are obtainable using this rote technique, but understanding can also be achieved if the child uses such devices as an abacus or a pocket chart to explore solutions and to note patterns in decimal placement as he works. In addition to manipulative devices, he may be encouraged to use techniques such as the following one which utilizes the idea of extending place value.

$$.36 + .45 = \square$$

Ones	Tenths	Hundredths
	1	
	3	6
	4	5
	8	1

In this problem, the child incorporates regrouping and place value when he totals 6 hundredths and 5 hundredths and gets 11 hundredths, which may be represented as 1 tenth and 1 hundredth. Hence, the sum becomes 8 tenths and 1 hundredth, or .81. In the abstract form, then, the sum may be represented as: .36 + .45 = .81 or

$$\begin{array}{r} .36 \\ + .45 \\ \hline .81 \end{array}$$

Some teachers prefer to use the form 0.36 and 0.45, but this is more of a personal preference than a mathematical necessity.

If the child is experiencing difficulty with the decimal form of a number, he may benefit from experiences which show the fraction form of the decimal. In the preceding example, .36 + .45 might have been represented as $\frac{36}{100} + \frac{45}{100}$ and, then, following the algorithms for whole numbers and fractions,

$$\frac{36}{100} + \frac{45}{100} = \frac{36 + 45}{100} = \frac{81}{100}.$$

In another way, .36 could be represented as $\frac{3}{10} + \frac{6}{100}$, and .45 as $\frac{4}{10} + \frac{5}{100}$ The sum might then be written as

$$\left(\frac{3}{10} + \frac{6}{100}\right) + \left(\frac{4}{10} + \frac{5}{100}\right).$$

Using associativity and commutativity, the child can obtain

$$\left(\frac{3}{10} + \frac{4}{10}\right) + \left(\frac{6}{100} + \frac{5}{100}\right)$$

or $\frac{7}{10} + \frac{11}{100}$. But $\frac{11}{100} = \frac{1}{10} + \frac{1}{100}$, so that now

$$\left(\frac{7}{10} + \frac{1}{10}\right) + \frac{1}{100} \text{ gives } \frac{8}{10} + \frac{1}{100} \text{ or } .81.$$

This latter method emphasizes both regrouping and place value of whole numbers and emphasizes an understanding of the process through the step-by-step analysis of what is happening.

As the child works problems using various aids he should be encouraged to record each problem and his solution, and he should try to find emerging patterns which will enable him to solve decimal problems without aids. Of course, aligning decimal points may be a generalization arrived at, but aligning like units may also be a workable technique which is found. The latter generalization may reveal the emergence of a core of understanding.

Finally, the child should have an opportunity to verify that all of the properties associated with addition and subtraction of whole numbers and fractions also apply to decimals. Continual restatement of these properties helps the child to see how the number system is being developed into a basic structure which features related facts and concepts.

Multiplication of Decimals.   Learning how to multiply decimals should involve if not the discovery of the rule regarding decimal placement, then at least the verification of the rule. You should help the child to see that the process of multiplying decimals is similar to the process of multiplying whole numbers, except that the decimal must be accounted for. There are several ways to approach the problem, some of which are described throughout the remainder of this section.

Visual and manipulative aids may be used in the solution of a problem such as .2 × .3 = □. Identifying the unit region as with fractions is the first step.

This is followed by marking off units on each side to correspond to the factors.

The product, as with fractions, is represented by 6 units of the 100 units in the unit region (see the shaded figure), which may also be represented as .06.

Relating the decimal placement in a problem such as .2 × .3 to the equivalent fraction form is also helpful. From the preceding example,

$$.2 \times .3 = \frac{2}{10} \times \frac{3}{10} = \frac{2 \times 3}{100} = .06.$$

Hence, the product of .2 × .3 is the same as the product of 2 and 3 in the numerator divided by 100 in the denominator, both operations which were discussed in the previous chapter. The final placement of the decimal point relates back to multiplication and division of whole numbers by powers of 10. In the example just completed, dividing by 100 moves the decimal point two places to the left. So we have 6 ÷ 100 or .06. This latter statement is one which all children should understand prior to successfully functioning with the multiplication algorithm for decimals.

Estimation also should be of value in determining decimal placement, that is, too often decimal points are placed in a problem with little or no attention as to whether the answer makes sense. A child who is encouraged to approximate results consistently, regardless of the type of problem, will not only have more confidence in his answer but will find that estimation is a ready tool in real life mathematical situations. Regarding specifically the multiplication of decimals, the child should be encouraged to think:

> In the problem .5 × 9.1 = □, I can begin by multiplying to get the numeral sequence, but where should the decimal be placed? Which product would be most reasonable: 455, 4.55, or 45.5? Because I am looking for a number *about* half of nine, the most reasonable answer would be 4.55.

or

> *Approximately* what should my answer be, given the problem 2.3 × 4.9 = △? Rounding off the two factors yields 2 × 5, giving a product of 10. Therefore, my result should approximate 10. Multiplying the original factors gives a numeral sequence of 1127, and my approximation tells me that the decimal placement should be after the 11, or 11.27.

A child who has a thorough understanding of the multiplication of whole numbers and fractions should encounter little difficulty in mastering multiplication of decimals. Although the greatest obstacle for a child will probably involve the placement of the decimal point, several techniques can be used to make the procedure sensible.

Division of Decimals

Perhaps the most difficult of the algorithms associated with decimals is the one pertaining to division of decimals. To master this algorithm, a child must be able to perform adequately with the formal division algorithm of whole numbers and to understand the concept of division.

A child's early experiences with division of decimals, assuming the prerequisites just mentioned, should involve a decimal divided by a whole number. For example, consider a problem such as .6 ÷ 3. This problem, when related to its multiplicative counterpart, could be pictured as follows using the unit rectangle.

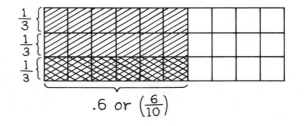

Of the 30 small rectangles in the unit rectangle created by the subdivisions, 6 relate to the problem .6 ÷ 3. The 6 shaded rectangles represent $\frac{6}{30}$ or $\frac{2}{10}$ of the rectangle. Hence, .6 ÷ 3 = .2. Relating to fractions, the problem can be represented as

$$\frac{6}{10} \div 3 = \frac{6}{10} \div \frac{3}{1} = \frac{6}{10} \times \frac{1}{3} = \frac{6 \times 1}{10 \times 3} = \frac{6}{30} \text{ or } \frac{2}{10} \text{ or } .2.$$

All of these activities are leading to the familiar form

$$3\overline{)\,.6}$$

which the child should have an opportunity to explore. He should be helped to see that because the divisor is a whole number he may simply place the decimal point immediately above the decimal point in the dividend and then continue with the solution of the problem. The child must completely understand this important fact in order to successfully apply the algorithm to more complicated examples. He should also see that once the decimal point is placed in the quotient, the operation of division proceeds exactly as it does with whole numbers. Hence, the preceding problem now appears as

$$3\overline{)\overset{\displaystyle .}{\,.6}}$$

and he is ready to proceed with

$$3\overline{)\overset{\displaystyle .2}{\,.6}}$$

Initially, the child should verify his solution by multiplying the quotient by the divisor. In this case, he can see that .2 × 3 = .6 and the solution is correct.

The child is now ready to consider the division problem in which the divisor is a decimal and to see what alterations must be made in the form of the problem to make it solvable. Consider the example of 4 ÷ .2. It will be helpful to the child to realize the fact that 4 ÷ .2 has the same quotient as 40 ÷ 2. It is easily verified that the quotients are the same, but the child may be unable to see the relevance of this sameness.

Referring back to the fraction form is sometimes helpful.

$$4 \div .2 = \frac{4}{1} \div \frac{2}{10} = \frac{4}{1} \times \frac{10}{2} = \frac{40}{2}$$

Alternatively,

$$\frac{4}{.2} = \frac{4}{\frac{2}{10}} = \frac{4 \times 10}{\frac{2}{10} \times 10} = \frac{40}{2}.$$

The latter alternative shows the changing of the problem form to one with the same solution but whose divisor is a whole number. This latter fact leads to the traditional use of the "karat."

$$.2\overline{)4} \text{ or } .2\overline{)4.0}$$
$$\times 10 \quad\times 10$$

At all times the child should see that the "karat" loop reflects multiplication by a power of 10 and that the number of loops necessary is determined by the power of 10 which must be used as a multiplier in order to create a whole-number divisor. The child should also experience the difficulty of trying to solve a division problem correctly where no provision has been made to make the divisor a whole number.

At this point the child is ready to inspect problems of the form

$$.16\overline{).032}$$

By multiplying both the dividend and divisor by 100, the problem may be rewritten as

$$\frac{32}{1000} \div \frac{16}{100} = \left(\frac{32}{1000} \times 100\right) \div \left(\frac{16}{100} \times 100\right)$$

$$= \frac{32}{10} \div \frac{16}{1}$$

$$= \frac{32}{10} \times \frac{1}{16}$$

$$= \frac{2}{10} \text{ or } .2$$

$$\text{or} \quad .16\overline{).03.2}$$

Zeros in the partial quotient will again be a problem as they were in the division of whole numbers. For example, a problem in whole numbers like

$$6\overline{)606}$$

will often result in an answer of 11 rather than 101. A similar problem will exist for some children when they encounter

$$6\overline{)6.06}$$

and obtain a solution of 1.1 instead of 1.01. Activities on place value seem a logical place to start to correct this difficulty.

To summarize, the algorithms related to operations on decimals, illustrated through examples, relate closely to the respective algorithms for whole numbers and fractions. This relationship is one which you must strongly emphasize as the structure of mathematics is built for your pupils. Let us look now at an extension of the ideas already advanced in the previous two sections of this chapter as we discuss percents.

PERCENT

Introducing Percent

An important application and extension of the ideas discussed earlier with respect to fractions and decimals is found in the study of percent. A thorough understanding of the notion is especially important for children because percents are mentioned almost daily by most people. For example, in a single day a person might hear "there is a 20% chance of rain tomorrow;" "you will receive a 5% raise next year;" and "clothing is reduced 25% during our midsummer sale."

Children should have experiences that relate percent to both fractions and decimals. This can be accomplished when percent is established as meaning a certain number of hundredths; indeed, percent derives from the term *per centum,* meaning per hundred.

Initial experiences, then, should involve work with graph paper using a 10 by 10 square as in the following diagram:

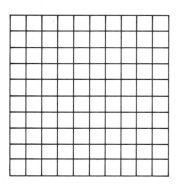

The notion that each small square represents 1% and that the entire square represents 100%, or the unit square, should be strongly emphasized. Practice activities using this figure should be plentiful as the child names the percent number to be assigned to shaded areas such as the following:

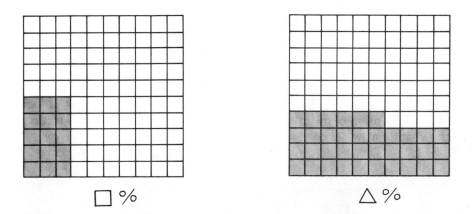

In the figures, of course, □ = 15 and △ = 36 so that the shaded areas of the grids represent 15% and 36% respectively.

Once the child has indicated a basic understanding of percent by being able to write a percent number represented by a given shaded figure and to shade a grid to represent a given percent, he is ready to relate percent to fraction and decimal equivalents. For this purpose, he should practice the conversion of percent to fractions and decimals and vice versa. For example, "write 25% as a fraction and as a decimal"

$$25\% = \frac{25}{100} \text{ or } \frac{1}{4} = .25$$

or "write .36 as a percent and as a fraction."

$$.36 = 36\% = \frac{36}{100}$$

It is probable that many children will need extra practice converting fractions and decimals with more or less than two decimal places into percents. Mastery of the conversion process is a prerequisite to the successful solution of problems involving the use of percents.

Once the child has mastered the ability to work with percents from 1 to 100, he is ready to study percents between 0 and 1 and percents greater than 100. Again the square grid may be helpful in illustrating the meanings of these numbers. For example, $\frac{1}{2}\%$ and 150% may be represented as follows:

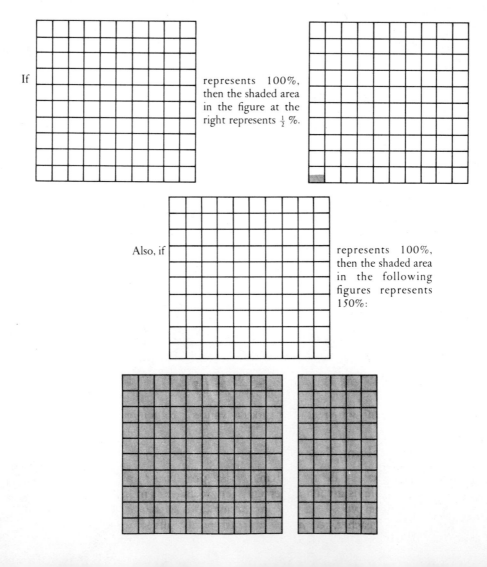

If represents 100%, then the shaded area in the figure at the right represents $\frac{1}{2}\%$.

Also, if represents 100%, then the shaded area in the following figures represents 150%:

In fraction and decimal form, $\frac{1}{2}$% may appear as

$$\frac{1}{2}\% = \frac{\frac{1}{2}}{100} = \frac{1}{200} = .005$$

and 150% as

$$150\% = \frac{150}{100} = 1.5.$$

Children should now be ready for more advanced problems involving percent.

Problems Involving Percent

Most children have difficulty solving verbal problems at all levels of mathematics, and problems involving percent seem to cause as much or more difficulty than any other type. It is very important (as discussed in detail in Chapter 15) for you, as teacher, to emphasize mastery of skills which may be used to solve these problems.

Problems involving percent can be placed into basically the following three categories:

Example A: What number is 50% of 16?

Example B: Twelve is what percent of 20?

Example C: Ten is 20% of what number?

In all three cases, the child should be encouraged to "talk through" the problem and to discuss verbally what should be done to solve the problem. This procedure should be used before any paper-and-pencil work is required to solve the problem. Some children may wish to "think on paper," and they should be encouraged to do so if it is beneficial for them.

In the case of Example A, the child may intuitively think of the problem as asking for a number that is $\frac{1}{2}$ of 16 (50% $= \frac{1}{2}$). He can also be encouraged to write a mathematical sentence which can be used to solve the problem such as

$$\square = 50\% \text{ of } 16$$

which may be solved as

$$\square = 50\% \text{ of } 16$$
$$= \frac{1}{2} \text{ of } 16$$
$$= \frac{1}{2} \times 16$$
$$= 8.$$

The child may solve this problem in other ways, but do not become concerned at this point. Teachers often place too much emphasis on one process to solve the problem. The result is that the child often memorizes the process and fails to comprehend the problem situation.

Example B shows a different type of situation. This time, the request is to find a percent that expresses the relationship of 12 to 20. Relating this question to fractions may be helpful so that 12 is $\frac{3}{5}$ of 20. Now, $\frac{3}{5}$ can be converted to a percent by

$$\frac{3}{5} = \frac{\square}{100}$$

where $\square = 60$, and 12 is 60% of 20. Again a mathematicaal sentence can prove very helpful.

$$12 = \triangle \% \text{ of } 20$$

which may be solved as

$$12 = \triangle\% \text{ of } 20$$
$$12 = \frac{\triangle}{100} \times 20$$
$$\frac{12}{20} = \frac{\triangle}{100}$$

when $\triangle = 60$ so that 12 is 60% of 20.

In Example C, a third type of question is posed. The problem now is to find a number such that 20% of it is 10. A child may think 20% is $\frac{1}{5}$ and if 10 is $\frac{1}{5}$, then $\frac{5}{5}$ can be found by 5×10 or 50. A more formal solution may be obtained by using the sentence

$$10 = 20\% \text{ of } \square$$

which may be solved as

$$10 = 20\% \text{ of } \square$$
$$10 = \frac{1}{5} \times \square$$
$$5 \times 10 = \square$$
$$50 = \square$$

and 10 is 20% of 50.

Two points should be noted about all three examples. First, the child should always verbalize in some form what he has found by solving the problem. This provides closure to the problem-solving process, and a quick thought can be given to the "sensibility" of the answer. Second, children should at least initially solve these problems intuitively. This procedure helps the child get familiar with the problem and its solution and avoids the additional obstacle of the formal mathematical solution. If the teacher stresses the formal solution procedure before the child understands the problem, the result is a poor performance in both areas.

CHAPTER KEY POINTS

1. Rational numbers may be expressed as fractions or decimals.

2. After the child has an understanding of fractions as part of a whole, the three other meanings of the fraction symbol (the part of a collection or set of objects, the quotient of two whole numbers, and a ratio or comparison) should be introduced.

3. The idea of renaming fractions is prerequisite to the understanding of the computational algorithms and properties associated with fractions.

4. The development of computational algorithms for fractions should include many activities on each of the three levels of learning: concrete, semi-concrete, and abstract, emphasizing not the mechanical steps but understanding the process.

5. Decimals can be related to their fraction equivalents; they can be dealt with as an extension of the base ten place value notation; and decimals should be related to real life applications and situations.

6. Percent should be established as meaning a certain number of hundredths and related to both fractions and decimals.

Laboratory 10

Operations and Properties Associated with Rational Numbers

The study of rational numbers is a difficult task for elementary school children, partly because many classroom teachers do not understand how to help children learn the operations and properties associated with rational numbers. The following laboratory experiences have been designed to acquaint you with some activities which may be adapted for use by children and to help you increase your own understanding of rational numbers.

  I. *Objectives:* Upon completion of these laboratory exercises, you should be able to do the following:

    A. Identify activities which may be used to introduce rational numbers to children. (Chapter Competencies 10–A and 10–B)

    B. Demonstrate how paper folding and colored rods may be used to help children learn the operations and properties associated with rational numbers. (Chapter Competency 10–C)

 II. *Materials:* Waxed paper; scissors; ruler; 3 × 5 index cards; magic marker; Cuisenaire rods (available from Cuisenaire Company of America, 12 Church St., New Rochelle, New York 10805)

III. *Procedure:*

    A. Read Chapter 10 of *Helping Children Learn Mathematics*. Consult your instructor if you have any questions.

    B. Paper folding is an excellent way to introduce equivalent fractions to children. Try this activity for yourself. Take a piece of waxed paper, approximately 3″ by 3″. Fold it in half. Now fold it into fourths. Open up the paper and examine it. How many fourths are there in one of the halves? _____ Fold the square into eighths. How many eighths are there in one of the halves? _____ In one of the fourths? _____ Write some mathematical sentences to express what you have found.

    Take another square of waxed paper and fold it into thirds. Now fold it along an adjacent side so that there are six parts. What equivalent fractions do you see?

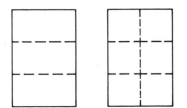

C. "Fracto" is a card game which also helps with the notion of equivalent fractions. Using the index cards and a magic marker, make cards similar to the ones below and containing the following fractions. Put one fraction on each card.

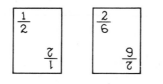

$$\frac{1}{2}, \frac{1}{3}, \frac{1}{4}, \frac{1}{6}, \frac{1}{8}, \frac{2}{4}, \frac{3}{9}, \frac{3}{12}, \frac{2}{12}, \frac{2}{16}, \frac{3}{6}, \frac{4}{12}, \frac{4}{16}, \frac{3}{18}, \frac{3}{24}, \frac{4}{8},$$

$$\frac{2}{6}, \frac{2}{8}, \frac{4}{24}, \frac{4}{32}, \frac{5}{10}, \frac{5}{15}, \text{ and } \frac{5}{20}$$

(You may add other fractions if you wish.)

Also make four cards which have FRACTO written on them; these cards will serve as "wild" cards.

The game may be played by two or three players. The cards are mixed and five are dealt to each player. The remaining cards are placed, face-down, in a pile in the middle of the playing area. The top card is then turned face-up and placed beside the pile. The first player must play a card from his hand which is equivalent to the fraction on the upturned card or which has the same denominator. He may also play a FRACTO card and change the denominator to any one that he wishes. If he can play neither, he draws a card from the pile until he finds one that he can play. The second player then tries to match the card discarded by the first player. Play continues until one player has played all his cards and has none left in his hand; he is declared the winner.

D. Colored rods may be used to illustrate various facts and operations with fractions. Let's work through some exercises which will illustrate how they might be used. (You may wish to review Laboratory 8 for the description of the rods.)

1. Suppose that the P rod is used as the unit rod. What number would each of the other rods represent?

W	___	Y	___	BR	___
R	___	DG	___	BL	___
LG	___	BK	___	OR	___

2. Now let the DG rod represent the unit rod. What number does each of the other rods represent?

    W ____   P ____   BR ____

    R ____   Y ____   BL ____

    LG ____   BK ____   OR ____

3. Suppose that you are asked to find $\frac{1}{2} + \frac{1}{3}$, using the rods.
   a. If R is taken as 1, then W is $\frac{1}{2}$. What rod represents $\frac{1}{3}$?
   b. Could the LG rod be used as 1 to solve the preceding problem? Explain.
   c. What rod could be used as 1 to solve the problem?
   d. Draw the train that represents $\frac{1}{2} + \frac{1}{3}$.
   e. What single rod represents the sum of $\frac{1}{2} + \frac{1}{3}$?
   f. What is the number value of this rod? Is this the correct solution to the probem?

4. Now try $\frac{1}{4} + \frac{3}{8}$. Draw a diagram to show your work.

5. Try $\frac{5}{6} + \frac{2}{3}$. Draw a diagram to show your work.

6. Consider the sentence $12 \div 6 = \square$. You are being asked how many groups of 6 there are in 12. Consider $\frac{1}{2} \div \frac{1}{4} = \triangle$. How many $\frac{1}{4}$'s are there in $\frac{1}{2}$?
   a. What rod could be used as the unit rod?
   b. Show how you would use the rods to show that there are two $\frac{1}{4}$'s in $\frac{1}{2}$.

7. Now consider $\frac{1}{2} \div \frac{1}{3}$. How many $\frac{1}{3}$'s are in $\frac{1}{2}$? That's right. There is one $\frac{1}{3}$ but not two $\frac{1}{3}$'s. So our answer should be between 1 and 2. Let's show our answer with the rods.
   a. What rod could be the unit rod?
   b. Now place the rods in front of you on the table. The LG rod represents $\frac{1}{2}$ and the R rod represents $\frac{1}{3}$.

   c. How does the length of the LG rod compare to the length of the R rod? How does this result compare with the quotient of $\frac{1}{2} \div \frac{1}{3}$?
   d. Now use the rods to show $\frac{7}{8} \div \frac{1}{4}$ and $\frac{1}{8} \div \frac{1}{2}$.

E. How would you introduce a child to the concept of fraction?

F. How would you introduce a child to the concept of decimal?

G. How would you introduce a child to the concepts of ratio and proportion?

H. What would you do if one of your sixth grade pupils:

1. consistently adds fractions this way?

$$\frac{1}{2} + \frac{1}{3} = \frac{2}{5}$$

$$\frac{3}{4} + \frac{2}{4} = \frac{5}{8}$$

2. asks you to explain WHY

$$\frac{2}{3} \div \frac{1}{4} = \frac{2}{3} \times \frac{4}{1}$$

3. explains that he prefers to use a common denominator in multiplying fractions as well as in adding fractions.

4. asks WHY the rule for decimal placement in a product works.

11
Number Theory

Teacher Competencies

After studying Chapter 11 and completing Laboratory 11, you should be able to achieve each of the following:

A. Given a selected concept or skill in the area of number theory, design foundational activities which may be used in the acquisition of that concept or skill. (Part Competency III-A)

B. Given a selected concept or skill in the area of number theory, identify activities which may be used to develop proficiency in the use of that concept or skill. (Part Competency III-B)

C. Given a selected concept or skill in the area of number theory, identify and/or demonstrate the use of selected instructional aids which might be used to help a child learn that concept or skill. (Part Competency III-C)

Numbers behave in special ways; that is, when numbers are examined according to any particular characteristic, patterns often emerge. At the elementary level, studying various properties or characteristics which numbers possess constitutes the study of number theory. Unlike some branches of mathematics, number theory is an area which has appeal for both the professional mathematician and the new learner. The mathematician may approach number theory as a gigantic intellectual puzzle in which he or she tries to prove what, why, and how numbers behave as they do. The beginner, on the other hand, may approach the subject casually as a sometimes awesome, but usually interesting, study of number characteristics. Even children may study figurate numbers, odd and even numbers, prime and composite numbers, perfect numbers, or any of numerous other number types.

Unfortunately, although certain aspects of number theory are readily understood and most often enjoyed by young children, the subject has historically been considered "off limits" for elementary school mathematics programs. In fact, such study was reserved entirely for higher level undergraduate and graduate mathematics students. Of course, the proofs associated with how numbers behave should be postponed until the student can cope readily with the process involved.

However, it is now considered advantageous to let primary-age children discover and examine characteristics of numbers since they are working with these numbers every day. Why not seize the opportunity for such study as it arises and as it fits naturally into the mathematics program? Even the more skeptical educators, who believe that elementary school mathematics should revolve around the fundamental operations of arithmetic, find that number theory utilizes these operations to such a great extent that children will experience firsthand a need to master such skills in order to do number theory work. In this way operations mastery becomes a means to an end rather than an end in itself.

CONFIGURATIONS OF NUMBERS

Long ago the Pythagoreans used symmetric arrays of dots to represent specific numbers. Study of these diagrams, or arrays, led to the derivation of properties of various series of numbers. Children today enjoy studying numbers which can be associated with shapes; these are called *figurate* numbers.

Consider triangular numbers, for example.

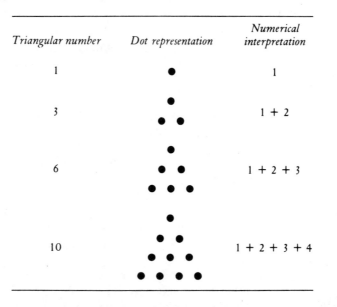

Triangular number	Dot representation	Numerical interpretation
1		1
3		1 + 2
6		1 + 2 + 3
10		1 + 2 + 3 + 4

Do you see why 1, 3, 6, 10, . . . are called triangular numbers? What is the next triangular number after 10? How did you find it? Can you find a general rule for determining triangular numbers?

What would square numbers look like? Can you determine some by their configurations? by their numerical interpretations? How about these?

Square number	Dot representation	Numerical interpretation
1	●	1
4		1 + 3
9		1 + 3 + 5
16		1 + 3 + 5 + 7

What patterns do you see? Square numbers are often written in a special way. What is it?

Using another dimension, we can speak of cubic numbers. How would they be formed? What are some? Could there be rectangular or oblong numbers?

Questions such as the preceding ones spark the imagination and energies of most children. These questions are a challenge, but in the form of a puzzle and not as a frustrating experience. The problems are sufficiently open-ended to allow latitude for different abilities. Some children may move immediately to manipulative aids in the form of blocks or checkers to line up or stack. Other children may wish to visualize their problems. Either way, they will arrive at a better understanding of some relationships existing between numbers and shapes.

Odd and even numbers have shapes, too. Children will soon see a pattern developing as they study arrays of dots representing numbers.

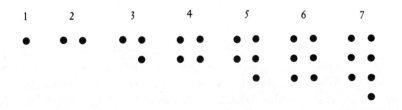

They see, for example, that some arrays have an "extra" dot while others fit conveniently into a "pairs-of-dots" pattern. The arrays with an "extra" dot, of course, represent odd numbers while the others represent even numbers.

Euclid, a famous Greek mathematician, was fascinated with odd and even numbers and made some discoveries about them. He found that the sum of an even number of odd numbers is even, the sum of any number of evens is even, the difference of two odds is even, and so forth. But to memorize these findings is to deny the adventure. Children need to explore for themselves what happens when odds and evens are added, subtracted, multiplied, and divided. Initially, for example, when adding they might use shapes designed to represent various odd and even numbers. As they join various shapes, they begin to see a pattern. To illustrate, using shapes related to the dots just given and joining various odd and even combinations, they find the following:

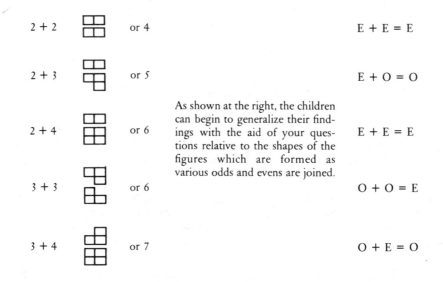

2 + 2	or 4	E + E = E
2 + 3	or 5	E + O = O
2 + 4	or 6	E + E = E
3 + 3	or 6	O + O = E
3 + 4	or 7	O + E = O

As shown at the right, the children can begin to generalize their findings with the aid of your questions relative to the shapes of the figures which are formed as various odds and evens are joined.

Soon they may want to summarize their work. A table might be in order.

+	O	E
O	E	O
E	O	E

They may extend their work, as Euclid did, to include more than two addends. Also, they may investigate odd and even patterns within other operations. As before, the problems posed may be open-ended enough to allow great flexibility of activity within any classroom.

Certainly, the discussion to this point has only served to introduce number pattern possibilities. You will note additional uses of diagrams to represent numbers in the following section. Many others can be found, too—many of them by your students. You create the investigative environment; be ready for your students' discoveries, and then take advantage of them as springboards for further study.

Let us turn now to an exploration of numbers which may be characterized by their factors.

NUMBERS AND THEIR FACTORS

If $a \times b = c$, then a and b are each called a *factor* of c, while c is called a *multiple* of a and of b. For example, since $3 \times 4 = 12$, then 3 and 4 are factors of 12, and 12 is a multiple of 3 and of 4. A number may have several factors. The number 12, for example, has 1, 2, 3, 4, 6, and 12 as its factors.

Primes, Composites, and One

The factors of a number can reveal a great deal about that number, and children should have ample opportunity to explore ideas relative to this area. Subsequent to their determining sets of factors associated with various counting numbers, for example, they should be encouraged to note similarities and differences existing among the factor groups. What patterns do you yourself note?

2	*3*	*4*	*5*	*6*	*7*	*8*	*9*	*10*	*11*	*12*	*13*
1	1	1	1	1	1	1	1	1	1	1	1
2	3	2	5	2	7	2	3	2	11	2	13
		4		3		4	9	5		3	
				6		8		10		4	
										6	
										12	

Of course, one of the first patterns noted by children is the existence of the number 1 as a factor of each of the numbers. Also, 2 is a factor of each of the even numbers. They see that 12 has many factors. As the sequence develops, mention should be made (by you or the children) regarding the fact that some numbers have only themselves and 1 as factors while others have more factors than the two just mentioned. This observation can lead you and the students into a discussion of *prime* numbers (numbers having exactly two distinct factors) and *composite* numbers (numbers greater than 1 which are not prime).

Note that children who study factors may make all kinds of observations other than the one relative to primes and composites—the one which you probably consider to be most important at this time. Accept and discuss all of their observations during the "brainstorming" sessions; in fact, you might make a few observations yourself as a member of the investigative team. To dismiss valid observations by students because you are anxious for a specific observation to be made serves only to diminish the number of contributions that will be volunteered during the next discovery session. In short, do not conduct an extensive "guess-what-the-teacher-is-thinking" session unless a game is the intent.

Once the existence of prime numbers and composite numbers has been discovered, investigations may turn to the finding of prime numbers. Although no one has discovered a convenient way to determine prime numbers, there are still some techniques which do work. Of course, dividing a number by all numbers less then that number will ultimately produce its factors, but this can be a cumbersome problem. Following a systematic procedure helps.

Centuries ago, Eratosthenes developed a technique to determine prime numbers. It is called the sieve method, probably because originally it involved punching holes in parchment, producing a sievelike effect. The method is well adapted to today's elementary school manipulative aids. Instead of punching holes in parchment, however, the children can use a *hundred board*. A hundred board, you remember, can take many forms, but basically it consists of the numerals 1 through 100, spaced evenly in a 10 by 10 array. Those boards in which individual numerals may be hidden in some way are especially useful. To determine primes, the child merely proceeds through the series, obliterating those numerals which he knows not to be prime. One, by definition, is not prime because it does not have exactly two distinct factors; therefore, it may be crossed out or hidden from view in some fashion. (Of further interest, the number 1 has a classification of its own, being neither prime nor composite.) Two is prime because it satisfies the definition of prime numbers, but any subsequent multiple of 2 will not be prime because by its nature it will have 2 as a factor in addition to itself and 1. All multiples of 2, therefore, may be obliterated at this point. Three is prime but multiples of 3 will not be prime and so must be hidden. Four has already been shown to be composite. What about 5? its multiples? Why does one only have to try numbers through 10 in order to determine all primes less than 100? Can the method be extended for numbers greater than 100?

Using the sieve method and a hundred board to determine primes produces a chart similar to the following one:

To summarize briefly, the counting numbers may be classified according to their factors as prime, composite, or the number 1. The study of prime and composite numbers and factors of numbers in general leads to the determination of some properties which numbers possess, and it thus becomes an integral part of number theory. Let's examine some of these properties and characteristics as they apply to the study of number in the elementary school.

One important property is stated in the *fundamental theorem of arithmetic,* which says that any composite number can be expressed as a product of primes in one and only one way. The order of the factors is not important and so is disregarded. To illustrate, 12 can be expressed as a product in different ways, 3 × 4 or 2 × 6 or 1 × 12, but it can be expressed as a product of primes in one and only one way, 2 × 2 × 3, disregarding the order of the factors. No other number can be written using the same factors the same number of times.

To factor a composite number until all of its factors are prime is called the *prime factorization* of that number. For example, 6 × 9 = 54 is a way to factor 54, but it does not represent the prime factorization of 54 because 6 and 9 are not prime numbers. A factor tree helps to systematically show the prime factorization. Although you may begin with any pair of factors of a number, the factoring always ultimately arrives at the same set of primes as illustrated in these factor trees:

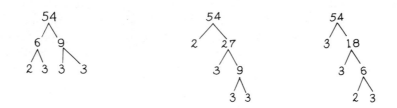

Students begin to see the usefulness of prime factorization when they are confronted with finding least common multiples and greatest common factors relative to their work with fractions. A great deal of unnecessary calculation and uncertain technique is eliminated if prime factorization is used to compute the least common multiple and the greatest common factor. Let's see how this might be done.

Suppose we wanted to calculate the least common multiple of 4 and 6. Showing both as the product of prime factors, we have

If we now consider the factors of 4 in one set and the factors of 6 in another set, we can take the union of the two sets as follows: (Note: The factors are being treated as numerals and not as numbers; thus they are repeated within the set.)

$$A = \{2,2\} \qquad B = \{2,3\}$$

Now, A ∪ B = {2,2,3} since one factor of 2 appears in both sets, leaving another factor of 2 in A and a factor of 3 in B. Taking the product of the elements of A ∪ B, we see that the least common mulitple of 4 and 6 is 2 × 2 × 3 = 12. You should verify this procedure for 8 and 12.

The greatest common factor of 4 and 6 can also be computed using set operations. What factor did A and B have in common; in other words, what is A ∩ B? Of course it is 2, and 2 is the greatest common factor of 4 and 6. Again, you should verify that 4 is the greatest common factor of 8 and 12.

The preceding examples show children how the notion of prime numbers and prime factors may be used to find the least common multiple and greatest common factor. They should have an opportunity to explore the reasons why the process works as it does; such study can provide excellent coordinating experiences by referring back to operations on fractions. We'll turn now to another special kind of number called a *perfect number*.

Properties associated with perfect numbers also offer possibilities of pursuit for interested students. A perfect number is one whose factors other than the number itself total the number when added. Six is a perfect number because its factors (other than 6 itself) total 6 when added; that is, $1 + 2 + 3 = 6$. Twelve, on the other hand, is not a perfect number because its factors total more than 12, or $1 + 2 + 3 + 4 + 6 > 12$. Ten is not a perfect number because its factors total less than 10. What are some other perfect numbers besides 6?

Divisibility Rules

Because numbers possess certain characteristics, it is often possible to determine whether they contain a specified factor simply by inspection; that is, it is possible to examine a number such as 3,147,228 and state whether such numbers as 2, 3, 4, 5, or 9 will divide into it evenly.

How you and your students approach the learning of divisibility rules depends largely upon your preferences. You may wish to begin by having the children search for patterns which exist among numbers that they have found to be divisible by a given number, thereby discovering divisibility rules for themselves. Or you may wish to supply a divisibility rule and have them try to determine why the rule works. Since we have already described several pattern searches, let's examine some possible activities relative to the second option.

Divisibility rules for 2, 4, 8 and for 5 and 10 are based upon particular characteristics of our system of numeration. The rules are as follow:

To be divisible by 2, the last digit of the number must be divisible by 2.

To be divisible by 4, the last two digits of the number must be divisible by 4.

To be divisible by 8, the last three digits of the number must be divisible by 8.

To be divisible by 5, the number must end in 5 or 0.

To be divisible by 10, the number must end in 0.

Why do these rules work as they do? Consider an example, 2436, and write it in expanded form as shown here:

$$2436 = (2 \times 1000) + (4 \times 100) + (3 \times 10) + (6 \times 1)$$

Note that positional values automatically make any digit in the ten's position or greater an even value regardless of the face value of the digit. To clarify, the 3 in 2436 really represents 3 tens, or 30, a number divisible by 2 because its positional value automatically renders it even. The same can be said of any greater positional values. The digit in the one's position is determinant, however, because if it is not even then the number cannot be even (via the distributive principle as it applies to the expanded form of the number). The example then is divisible by 2 because the digit occupying the one's position is divisible by 2.

Similar arguments can be established for divisibility tests for 4 and 8. In the case of divisibility by 4, any multiple of 100 will be divisible by 4; therefore, the number represented by the last two digits is the only part which must be tested for divisibility by 4. We find that the example 2436 is indeed divisibile by 4 because the number represented by the last two digits is divisible by 4, or

$$2436 = \underbrace{(24 \times 100)}_{\text{(divisible by 4)}} + \underbrace{36.}_{\text{(to be tested)}}$$

The number is not divisible by 8 because, even though 2000 is divisible by 8, 436 is not.

Just as all multiples of 10 are divisible by 2, so also are they divisible by 5; therefore, it is again necessary only to examine the final digit of a number to see it if is divisible by 5, or more simply, to see if it ends in 5 or 0. Divisibility by 10, perhaps the most simple test of all, is based upon the same principles as divisibility by 5 and requires only a check to see if the number ends in 0.

Actually, divisibility rules for 3 and for 9 are based on very similar reasoning to that just given, with the aid of some additional renaming. The rules, however, are quite different.

For a number to be divisible by 3, the sum of the digits must be divisible by 3.

For a number to be divisible by 9, the sum of the digits must be divisible by 9.

To illustrate why such rules have basis, consider the divisibility of 2436 by 9. Again express the number in expanded form.

$$2436 = (2 \times 1000) + (4 \times 100) + (3 \times 10) + (6 \times 1)$$

Of course, positional values in their current form will not insure divisibility by 9. As we have indicated previously, however, numbers have many names; by renaming the positional values of 10 and powers of 10, we may at least insure that some part of the number be divisible by 9. Transferring these ideas to our example we have the following:

$$2436 = (2 \times 1000) + (4 \times 100) + (3 \times 10) + (6 \times 1)$$
$$= [2 \times (999 + 1)] + [4 \times (99 + 1)] + [3 \times (9 \times 1)] + (6 \times 1)$$

Using the distributive principle, we arrive at

$$2436 = [(2 \times 999) + (2 \times 1)] + [(4 \times 99) + (4 \times 1)]$$
$$+ [(3 \times 9) + (3 \times 1)] + (6 \times 1)$$

With the aid of the commutative and associative principles we have

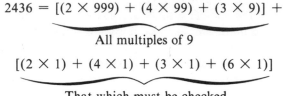

$$2436 = [(2 \times 999) + (4 \times 99) + (3 \times 9)] +$$

All multiples of 9

$$[(2 \times 1) + (4 \times 1) + (3 \times 1) + (6 \times 1)]$$

That which must be checked
for divisibility by 9

Multiplications within the second set of groupings yield $2 + 4 + 3 + 6$. This constitutes a simple addition of the digits of the original problem.

Generalizing, we see that isolating those parts of the number which will automatically be divisible by 9 from those which must be tested each time results in the procedure described in the divisibility test; namely, for a number to be divisible by 9, the sum of the digits must be divisible by 9. In this case we find the sum to be 15, a number not divisible by 9. The original number, 2436, then, is not divisible by 9.

The technique just outlined will work equally well to illustrate divisibility procedures for 3 because any multiple of 9 is also a multiple of 3 and so will be divisible by 3. Performing the test, we total the digits as before and, finding the sum divisible by 3, conclude that 2436 is divisible by 3.

Other divisibility rules exist. Divisibility of a number by 6, for example, depends upon divisibility by both 2 and 3. It remains only to apply both rules. What tests would you apply to determine divisibility by 12? Can you think of other numbers which might have divisibility rules assigned to them?

To conclude, we have approached the study of divisibility rules by their justification through various number properties. Now we will consider briefly how children may approach the learning.

Upper level elementary school children who have had optimal preliminary experiences with basic number properties can comprehend the reasoning used in the illustrations already provided. Note that these were not formal proofs; instead, specific numbers were used, with basic properties used to justify the steps.

Some children, however, might benefit better by only initial experiences with divisibility rules, the justification of the rules being postponed until later. Perhaps they would benefit best by a series of discovery sessions of a "guess-my-rule" type. Enthusiastic responses can follow an initial activity in which you, the teacher, list several numbers horizontally across the board (such as 2, 3, 4, 5, 6, 8, 9, and 10) and you say to the class that you can do an "amazing thing," namely, if one of the pupils calls out one of those numbers on the board and then writes another multidigit number on the board beneath that first number, you can tell him immediately if the multidigit number is divisible by the first. (You should practice prior to this exhibition because your students will soon begin a real challenge of your talents.) After the class curiosities are sufficiently whetted, you may explain that you are not actually dividing each time and that each of the numbers you placed on the board has its own divisibility rule. Then challenge the students to look for patterns. You might expect 2, 5, and 10 to yield more promising results initially, and some directive questions might be needed depending upon your group. Generally, the discovery of divisibility rules is best done over a prolonged period of time. If possible, leave the chart which you have begun on the board so that the pattern search can continue during free moments of the day. Before too long you might expect to find children in your classroom who also can do "amazing things." Some will be able to tell immediately if a number is divisible by 2 or 3 or 5 and so on. Of course, after a period of time, a few children will experience more frustration than you feel desirable for them; a hint by you or by one of their peers is acceptable. For example, as the list of numbers divisible by 4 increases and you have some who cannot grasp the rule, why not underline the last two digits of each number and then begin a pattern search with these numbers as they relate to 4? The activity can continue for as many days as your students are interested and may still occupy only a few minutes of direction each day.

CHAPTER KEY POINTS

1. Number theory, the study of properties and characteristics of numbers, finds many uses at the elementary school level.

2. Numbers can be studied according to the shapes which may be associated with them.

3. Children can learn to classify numbers as primes, composites, or one. Eratosthenes sieve is a useful means of classifying.

4. Children can learn to factor numbers and to apply divisibility rules as part of their number theory work. Finding greatest common factors and least common multiples is an associated activity.

Laboratory 11

Number Theory

Every child should have an opportunity to explore the "world of number magic." The study of number theory can provide the opportunity for such exploration as well as help a child understand the structure of mathematics. These exercises, then, are designed so that you can have an opportunity to explore some number theoretic ideas and to consider how ideas in number theory may be introduced to children.

I. *Objective:* Upon completion of these laboratory exercises, you should be able to do the following:

A. Identify activities related to number theory which may be used with children. (Chapter Competencies 10-A and 10-B)

II. *Materials:* None

III. *Procedure:*

A. Read Chapter 11 of *Helping Children Learn Mathematics.* If you have questions, consult your instructor.

B. The sieve method, as discussed in your reading, may be used to identify prime numbers. Use the following diagram to try the method for yourself. Start by crossing out 1 and then proceed to cross out the multiples of 2, 3, etc. Check the numbers that remain; these numbers should be the set of prime numbers between 1 and 100. Does your set match the set found in your reading?

1	2	3	4	5	6	7	8	9	10
11	12	13	14	15	16	17	18	19	20
21	22	23	24	25	26	27	28	29	30
31	32	33	34	35	36	37	38	39	40
41	42	43	44	45	46	47	48	49	50
51	52	53	54	55	56	57	58	59	60
61	62	63	64	65	66	67	68	69	70
71	72	73	74	75	76	77	78	79	80
81	82	83	84	85	86	87	88	89	90
91	92	93	94	95	96	97	98	99	100

Now, using the sieve method, find the set of prime numbers between 100 and 200. (The divisibility tests may be helpful.) Are there as many primes between 100 and 200 as there are between 1 and 100? Do you see any similarities between these two sets of prime numbers?

C. You remember that numbers have many names. For example, there are triangular numbers and square numbers, so named because they can be made into arrays which form geometric shapes. Pentagonal numbers might look like this:

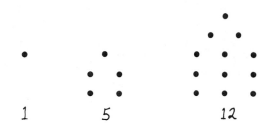

$$1 \qquad 5 \qquad 12$$

What are the first six pentagonal numbers? Do you see a pattern so that you could name the tenth pentagonal number? The nth pentagonal number? (You might also try to find a pattern for triangular and square numbers to help in your thinking.)

D. Here is a problem which will fascinate many children and will, at the same time, encourage some careful thinking. Take the name of a year, such as 1827, and see how many of the counting numbers you can write using only the four digits, either singly or in combination, and the four basic operations. For example,

$$1 = (7 + 2) - (8 \times 1)$$
$$2 = (8 + 2) - (7 + 1)$$
$$3 = (8 + 7) - 12$$
$$4 = (8 + 2) - (7 - 1)$$
$$5 = \frac{8 + 7}{1 + 2}$$

All four digits must be used and may be used only as often as they appear in the number. Now, try to write 6 through 10 as above, using 1827. Using 1986, rename the first six counting numbers.

E. Of what value to a child is the study of number theoretic ideas? Why do you feel as you do? Is this study appropriate for *all* children? Why or why not?

12
Informal Geometry

Teacher Competencies

After studying Chapter 12 and completing Laboratory 12, you should be able to achieve each of the following:

    A. Given a selected concept or skill in the area of geometry, design foundational activities which may be used in the acquisition of that concept or skill. (Part Competency III-A)

    B. Given a selected concept or skill in the area of geometry, identify activities which may be used to develop proficiency in the use of that concept or skill. (Part Competency III-B)

    C. Given a selected concept or skill in the area of geometry, identify and/or demonstrate the use of selected instructional aids which might be used to help a child learn that concept or skill. (Part Competency III-C)

The study of geometry is relatively new to the elementary mathematics curriculum. Inspection of elementary mathematics textbooks published during the early to mid-fifties shows that very little, if any, geometry was included in the program of study. Study of the subject was reserved for the high school years, usually the sophomore year, during which the student studied Euclidean geometry. This study usually consisted of the memorization of axioms, postulates, and theorems and the reproduction of proofs. The result was that many students approached the study of geometry with hesitancy and trepidation.

The recent revolution in the mathematics curriculum has resulted in a gradual increase in the amount of geometry studied by the elementary pupil. However, even with this increase, geometry is still viewed by many classroom teachers as an "extra." The result is that geometry has been ignored in favor of other mathematical topics, to be studied "if there is time at the end of the year because there are more important concepts and skills for children to learn." Perhaps teachers have adopted this attitude because of their own unpleasant experiences with the study of geometry. Most teachers, however, are beginning to realize the value of their elementary students studying geometry on an informal basis.

There are several reasons why geometry should be included as an integral part of the elementary mathematics curriculum.

1. The study of geometry helps children understand the physical world about them. Geometry is everywhere; it is everyday life.
2. There is an esthetic value to the study of geometry for children as they look at both man-made and natural creations.
3. Geometric models help children understand many arithmetic concepts and principles.
4. The study of geometry assists children in understanding concepts of measurement.

The study of geometry in the elementary school should be conducted on an informal basis. It is not necessary for a child to learn many formal definitions of terms nor to be able to produce rigorous proofs and explanations. Rather, geometry should appeal to a child's intuition and senses because this is the way he will most likely encounter geometry throughout the rest of his life. Also, the study of geometry should be activity-oriented for the child. It should emphasize the use of physical models and drawings, and not be text-oriented. The child should become actively involved with these models and not simply read about the model or idea in the text or observe the teacher's demonstration.

This chapter discusses the child's early experiences with geometry, his movement toward formal geometric abstractions, and the inclusion of enrichment topics in geometry in the elementary mathematics curriculum. The discussion of enrichment topics and activities includes selected areas of topology and symmetry.

EARLY EXPERIENCES IN GEOMETRY

Readiness

A child must be ready to study geometry. Geometric readiness involves two areas: *mathematical* readiness and *psychological* readiness. Mathematical readiness can be gained by the child through the handling of objects. From this activity, he learns of square corners, straight and curved sides, and curved surfaces. He can also cut out geometric figures and arrange them in patterns of his own choosing. Handling blocks and making tinkertoy constructions will also help develop a child's mathematical readiness for geometry.

These activities also help develop a child's psychological readiness to study geometry by offering ample opportunity for success; nothing makes a child more willing to learn a new concept or skill than to realize that he can be successful at it.

Topological Concepts

As the child demonstrates readiness to study geometry, you, as teacher, should begin instruction with ideas of a topological nature, such as "inside," "outside," boundary and region, and others.

These topological concepts are familiar to children on an intuitive basis, and they help relate the study of geometry to everyday life, an important factor in developing a child's desire to study geometry.

The importance of relating geometry to everyday life cannot be overemphasized. It is much more desirable for you to develop a child's understanding of meaningful relationships than to require him to work with abstractions from memory alone. For example, having children look for geometric shapes in their environment can be a meaningful activity.

Returning to our discussion of the topological concepts, there are many activities which you can use to help a child understand these concepts. For example, have some children form a circle with some others inside the circle and outside the circle. Ask them questions to help them understand the relationships of "outside," "inside," boundary, and region. A hula hoop or a piece of string wih some other objects may also be used to help a child to learn these relationships.

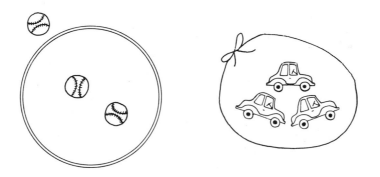

Order is also an important concept for a child to learn during early experiences with geometry. The use of a tinkertoy model may be very helpful. The child can construct his own model as in this picture:

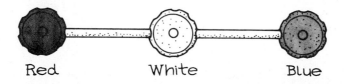

Red   White   Blue

Looking at the three knobs, he can see that the white knob is "between" the red and blue knobs. He can also see that the red knob is on the "left" of the white knob and the blue knob is on the "right" of the white knob.[1]

The child should also work with activities involving depth perception. Going outside to the playground or looking out the classroom window and examining objects to determine which is closest to him provides a good starting point. He should realize that the further away an object is

---

1. Although "left" and "right" are not topological concepts themselves, the learning situation affords an excellent opportunity to study them.

from his eye, the smaller it appears. This fact can be demonstrated by taking two identical objects and placing one close to the child and the other at some distance away. The child can decide which appears larger in size, and then by moving toward the more distant object, he can see the change in relative size even though the object's actual size remains invariant.

Figure Recognition

Figure recognition also develops early in the geometric sequence, and it should follow the development of the topological concepts mentioned earlier. The child is already familiar with different geometric shapes such as

but he has generally not learned their names. The child should handle models of these figures and compare their similarities and differences. Looking for examples in the classroom, in the schoolyard, at home, and in pictures helps the child recognize the shapes. You may assign the names and ask the child to point out examples which you have given. In this way, the child associates the name with the figure. An activity which might be used to develop figure recognition involves the use of a *geoboard* and rubber bands.[2] The child can produce requested figures on the geoboard.

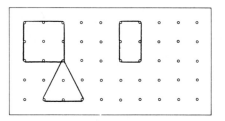

Attribute blocks may also be used. These blocks are generally available in different sizes, shapes, thicknesses, and colors. They may be used in figure recognition and also in classification activities. For example, the child may be asked to group all blue triangles, all red squares, all thin yellow circles, and so forth. These exercises require a child to be able to discriminate different characteristics of the pieces and to classify them according to directions.

2. A geoboard may be made from a piece of wood which has a rectangular array of nails (finishing nails with no heads are best) tacked into it, or from a piece of pegboard with golf tees substituting for the nails.

When children are given free time to work with geometric shapes, they may make different designs and pictures among the shapes. This type of work allows each child to be creative and to make something totally his own. The following figures might be a result of this activity:

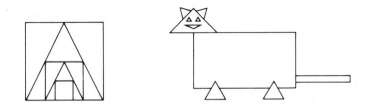

Pattern Recognition

Pattern recognition is another concept which the child should study during early experiences with geometry. There are many different types of patterns with which a child may work, but it is important that he discover the pattern involved. For example, the child may work the the completion of patterns such as the following ones:

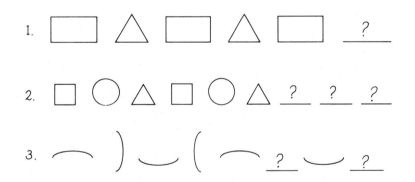

Other types of exercises can be used to help a child develop pattern recognition. He may be asked how many different ways a square can be divided into two parts which are the same size

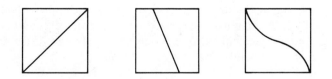

or to arrange a certain number of squares in as many different patterns as possible. For example, a set of four squares may be arranged in the following ways:

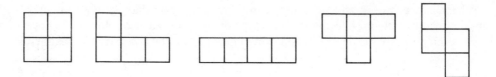

Tangrams also provide an opportunity for a child to search for patterns. These pieces may be made in many different ways and used either to create a new figure or to fill in the outline of a given figure.

After a child has mastered readiness activities, topological concepts, and figure and pattern recognition, he should proceed to more formal geometric concepts, which we will discuss next.

GEOMETRY IN THE PRIMARY GRADES

Most children are ready to consider more formal geometric concepts at approximately age seven. They have probably been able to attain reversibility, an ability which will be helpful in their study of Euclidian concepts. At this point you should use correct examples and correct vocabulary, but the child should not be expected to always use vocabulary correctly. The classroom experiences in geometry should rely heavily on the child's intuition and his manipulation of physical materials.

Point, Curves, Line Segments, and Lines

The study of Euclidean geometry begins with the *point*. A point is an undefined term, but it has many physical and pictorial representations. The child should look for many representations of points such as a pencil point, a thumbtack, or the corner of a cube. A point may also be pictured on a piece of paper and is named by a capital letter of the alphabet.

● A

The child should then place on the piece of paper another dot different from the first dot.

Placing a pencil on one of the dots and moving to the other dot without lifting the pencil from the paper forms a *curve*. This path may be drawn in many different ways, and the child should draw several examples. He could also take a piece of string or yarn and show examples of different paths between the two points.

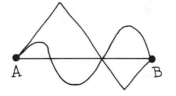

One special path between the two points may be drawn using a straight edge, which can be either a ruler or a folded sheet of paper.

This path is known as a *line segment,* and the child should practice drawing line segments between two points on his paper. If he has some difficulty with this task, the practice will be helpful to him.

During the practice of drawing segments between two points, the problem of how many segments can be drawn connecting the two points may be posed for the child. He will soon realize that, as soon as one segment is drawn, any other segment connecting the same two points must lie on top of the first segment drawn. The child has thus verified an important geometric concept.

You should emphasize to the child that a line segment contains many points. This fact can be illustrated by drawing three distinct points on a piece of paper using a straight edge and then drawing a segment connecting the two furthermost points. The segment will pass through the third point, *B,* which is between the two points *A* and *C.*

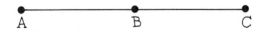

Tinkertoys may also provide a physical model of the fact that a line segment is made up of points.

The line segment is named by writing the two endpoints and drawing a bar over the top of them. In the preceding example, $\overline{AD}$ or $\overline{DA}$ may be used to name the segment connecting points *A* and *D.*

The concept of the line segment may then be extended to develop the concept of a *line.* There are no real world examples of geometric line because it has only one dimension, direction. A line differs from the line segment in that it has no endpoints, but it may be pictured and named in a similar way to the line segment.

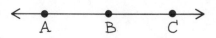

Notice the arrowheads in the picture. They indicate that the picture continues in either direction with no end. Again, tinkertoys may be used to show a physical representation of a line.

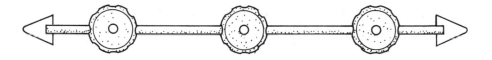

As with the line segment, the line is made up of many points and may be named by using the names of two points on the line. For example, the following figure

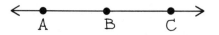

may be named as line *AB*, line *AC*, line *CB*, or any other way we choose as long as two points on the line are used. The interpretation of line *AB*, for example, is that it is the line passing through points *A* and *B*. Line *AB* may be symbolized as $\overleftrightarrow{AB}$.

Another geometric property may be examined by the child at this point. Have him place a dot on a piece of paper and ask him to draw lines which pass through that point.

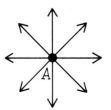

Ask him how many lines could be drawn through the point. He will probably tell you "lots of them," which means that he has discovered an important geometric property.

Let us turn now to a detailed discussion of curves and how they relate to polygons. This discussion with the child affords an opportunity to summarize what he or she has learned about geometry.

Closed Curves and Polygons

Curves which begin and end at the same point are called *closed curves*.

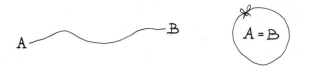

Pieces of string or yarn tied together to form a loop may be used to represent the closed curve.

The child has had previous work with these types of curves in exploration of region and boundary. Using the loop, he can make many examples of closed curves.

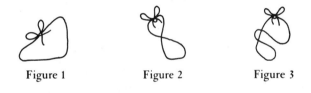

| Figure 1 | Figure 2 | Figure 3 |

A geoboard is an excellent aid to the child in exploring polygons. He should make figures on the geoboard which are examples of polgyons.

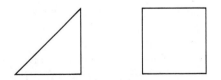

The closed curves may be classified as *simple* or *nonsimple*. The simple closed curve does not overlap its boundary while a nonsimple curve does. Looking at Figures 1, 2, and 3, which are simple and which are nonsimple?

A simple closed curve which is made up of line segments is called a *polygon*. The child has seen many examples of polygons in earlier geometric experiences with figures.

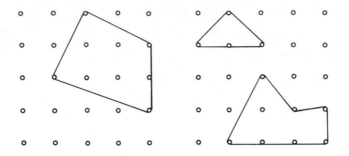

Graph paper and a straight edge may also be used to make examples of polygons.

Names may be assigned to the various polygons according to their characteristics, such as the number of line segments used to make up the figure. The child should make examples of these polygons on a geoboard or graph paper and record results in a table such as the following one. For future study, he should also record the number of corners in each figure.

Name	Number of line segments	Number of corners
Triangle	3	3
Quadrilateral	4	4
Pentagon	5	5
Hexagon	6	6
Heptagon	7	7
Octagon	8	8
Nonagon	9	9
Decagon	10	10

In studying this table, the child should realize two characteristics of polygons. First, since he is already familiar with two special kinds of quadrilaterals, squares and rectangles, he should be able to give five reasons why squares and rectangles differ from other quadrilaterals. Second, the child should explore the way in which the names of the polygons are chosen. For example, in quadrilateral, "quad" means four while "lateral" means side. So a quadrilateral has four sides. Similar activities may be used to derive the names of the other polygons; these activities provide an opportunity to integrate the curricular areas of mathematics and language arts.

As an additional activity in studying polygons, the child may wish to make physical models of the various polygons using pipe cleaners, art straws, or strips of thin cardboard fastened at the ends with paper fasteners. This activity may prove helpful to an understanding of the different polygons.

Circles

The child should now examine a *circle,* an example of a simple closed curve which is not made up of line segments. Since he is already familiar with the shape and name of this geometric figure, he should now be able to realize that the circle has a very important property which distinguishes it from other simple closed curves. The property is that every point on the boundary of the circle is the same distance from the center. The child should verify this property by examining different circles, choosing different points on the boundary, and then measuring the distance from the chosen point to the center point with a straight edge or a piece of string.

The child should also learn to draw circles using a compass or a piece of string with a pencil tied to one end and a thumbtack tied to the other. He may need considerable practice in drawing circles because this skill is not an easy one for some children to master. He should also practice drawing circles with given radii and should realize that the longer the radius, the larger will be the size of the circle. He should examine the relationship between the radius of the circle and the diameter and should verify this relationship through measurement.

To summarize, geometric concepts presented in the primary grades should be examined by the child on an intuitive basis in an activity-oriented program, thereby building a solid mathematical base upon which more advanced geometric concepts such as congruence and similarity can be developed.

GEOMETRY IN THE INTERMEDIATE GRADES

Before proceeding to a discussion of new geometric concepts, you should review with the children the concepts of point, line segment, curve, polygon, and circle. It is important that each child have a clear understanding of these concepts since they will be used as a basis for further study.

Rays and Angles

The concept of *ray* can be extended from line segment and line. The child will already have an intuitive idea of what a ray is due to familiarity with, for example, a ray of light or a ray gun from a science fiction movie. The use of a flashlight will help him realize that a geometric ray has similar properties to what he knows as a ray. He should realize that a ray has an endpoint and has direction and that rays may be named in a similar way to that of line segments and lines.

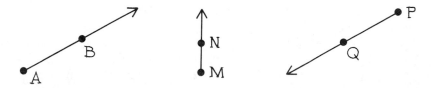

In the preceding figures, the rays *AB, MN,* and *PQ* may be symbolized by $\overrightarrow{AB}$, $\overrightarrow{MN}$, and $\overrightarrow{PQ}$. The child should realize that a ray is a part of a line. In the following picture, line *AB* has rays

AB, BA, CA, and *CB* contained within it (and others if more points are identified). He should practice naming rays just as he did line segments and lines.

Once the concept of a ray has been learned by the child, it may be used to build the concept of *angle*. Angles are formed by two rays with a common endpoint. In this example,

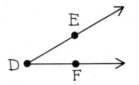

∠*EDF* is formed by the two rays *DE* and *DF* with the point *D*, called the *vertex*, in common. The child is already familiar with angles from his handling of physical objects and looking at geometric shapes. He should also realize that ∠*EDF* is the set of points on the rays *DE* and *DF*.

Measuring Angles

One way to help a child understand the measurement of angles is to relate the measurement to the division of the circle boundary into 360 equal parts. Each of the 360 parts represents one *degree*, and the measurement is made by placing the vertex of the angle at the center of the circle and determining how many degrees lie between the points of intersection of the angle's rays and the boundary of the circle as in the following figure:

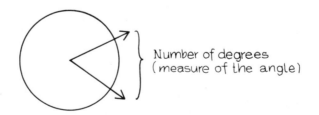

An initial experience for the child might be to take a transparent circle and mark off a quarter of it to represent 90 degrees.

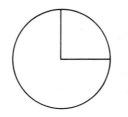

The circle can be placed over the top of different angles to determine whether the angles are greater than 90 degrees. The child can also investigate the approximation of angle size. Ask him if he can draw an angle of 45 degrees using his circle, for example.

The child can also use paper folding to form a right angle by folding a piece of paper into two parts and folding again in the opposite direction into four parts as follows:

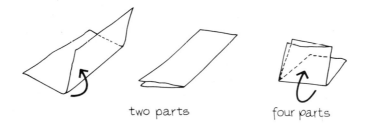

two parts   four parts

A 45-degree angle can be formed by folding this figure until the two straight edges coincide.

The child can use the right angle formed by his paper folding activity to check different angles around the classroom to determine whether they form right angles, such as the angle between the wall and floor.

After working with this type of activity, the child should learn to use a *protractor*. The protractor is used in a similar fashion to the transparent circle shown earlier. The child should practice

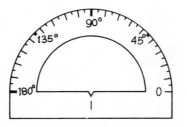

measuring angles with the protractor and also draw angles of a designated size. He should also learn that angles may be classified as right (90 degrees); acute (less than 90 degrees); obtuse (greater than 90 degrees but less than 180 degrees); or straight (180 degrees).

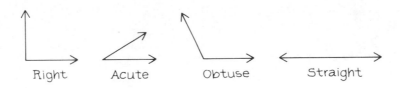

Right   Acute   Obtuse   Straight

More Advanced Properties of Polygons

Now other properties of polygons may be studied. The child has classified and studied polygons through their sides and should now consider some properties related to their angles.

A laboratory activity might include the study of quadrilaterals. How is a square different from a rhombus? What do you notice about the angles of a rectangle and a square? These and other questions might be asked of a child working by himself or in a small group. The child may wish to make models of different quadrilaterals to aid in his examinations. These models can be easily made using strips of paper or cardboard and paper fasteners.

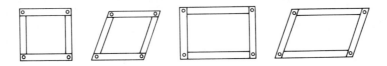

The notion of a *parallelogram* can be introduced during this study and the properties of this quadrilateral discussed. A suitable culmination for this study would be to summarize the findings in a table such as this:

Name	Distinguishing characteristics
Square	
Rhombus	
Rectangle	
Parallelogram	

Triangles may be examined in a similar way. The child can make models of scalene, isosceles, and equilateral triangles using paper strips or cardboard and paper fasteners as with the quadrilaterals.

Scalene   Equilateral   Isosceles

He can measure the angles of these triangles with his protactor to see what conclusions can be drawn about the angles of these triangles. How do the angles in an isosceles triangle differ from the angles of an equilateral triangle? Can two angles in a scalene triangle have the same measure? Are the measures of the angles in an equilateral triangle always the same? He should also realize that triangles can be classified according to the measures of their angles. What do we mean by an acute triangle? an obtuse triangle? a right triangle?

The results of the investigations about triangles might be summerized, as with quadrilaterals, in the form of a table.

Name	Distinguishing characteristics
Scalene	
Isosceles	
Equilateral	
Acute	
Obtuse	
Right	

The child might also be asked questions such as "can a scalene triangle be obtuse?" or "can a right triangle be isosceles?" Examples may be drawn or constructed to asnwer these types of questions.

An important characteristic of triangles can be verified by the child. Have him cut out a triangle and label the vertices *A*, *B*, and *C*. Tear off the corners of the triangle and place the corners so that their three vertices coincide.

The resulting figure forms a straight line segment

which means that the sum of the measures of the angles of the triangle is 180 degrees.

Geometry in Three Dimensions

Up to this point in the chapter, we have been concerned only with the study of geometric concepts in the *plane*. The child may have difficulty understanding the concept of a plane because of its abstract nature. He will be able, however, to understand physical representations of planes such as a desktop or the chalkboard. At this point in the child's experiences with geometry, it is appropriate to discuss plane on an intuitive basis but to reserve concepts such as parallel planes and the intersection of two planes until later years.

A child, however, can engage in some meaningful experiences with three-dimensional figures, which belong to the class of figures called *polyhedrons*. He should handle physical models of polyhedrons and discuss the viewed characteristics of the figures. He should also make models of some of the polyhedrons; constructions of the figures using patterns which he has made himself will enhance his understanding of their characteristics.

Prisms and *pyramids* are perhaps the most familiar types of polyhedrons to the child because he has seen pictures and models of these figures in the classroom and at home. He has probably also studied the concept of volume; study of volume and the properties of various polyhedrons in relatively close proximity to each other should increase the child's understanding of both.

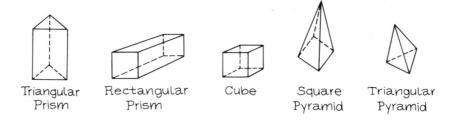

Triangular Prism   Rectangular Prism   Cube   Square Pyramid   Triangular Pyramid

Here are some questions which might be asked of the child.

1. How are prisms and pyramids alide?
2. How are prisms and pyramids different?
3. What shape are the faces of a prism?
4. What shape are the faces of a pyramid?

A child might be asked to look at cut-out figures and to determine which of the cut-outs would make a certain figure if we folded along the indicated sides. For example, which of the following figures would make a cube?

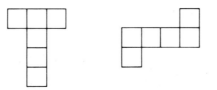

Activities such as these enable the child to apply his understanding of the figure to a problem posed for him about the figure.

Enrichment Activities in Geometry

Geometry, as much as other areas of elementary school mathematics, provides numerous opportunities for enrichment activities. The remainder of this chapter includes some activities which might be used in the classroom. These activities will probably suggest other activities or variations of the ones given.

Symmetry.   Lines of symmetry and point symmetry provide the basis for some excellent discovery activities. For example, consider the letters of the alphabet. Which letters have an axis of symmetry? Do any letters have more than one axis of symmetry? Below are two examples of letters which have an axis of symmetry.

No axis of symmetry

Axes of symmetry can also be examined with the use of mirror cards and a small pocket mirror. By placing the mirror perpendicular to the card, a mirror image of the card should appear. The Elementary Science Study project (ESS) has a set of mirror cards (available from Webster Division of the McGraw-Hill Book Company), or a set can be constructed. Use the mirror to check the axes of symmetry for the capital letters from the preceding activity.

Point symmetry can be defined as a point about which a figure can be rotated 180 degrees and have exactly the same picture. Below are some figures and their points of symmetry. What others could be included?

No point of symmetry

Topology.   An excellent enrichment activity in the area of topology is to study the behavior of a Mobius strip. This is a strip of paper which can be taped end-to-end so that it forms a loop after the strip has been twisted. Take a strip of paper and twist it once (through 180 degrees) and tape the ends together. Cut down the middle of the strip with a pair of scissors.

Mobius strip with one twist

What is the result? What will be the result if the strip is twisted through 360 degrees and then cut? Are the results the same?

Networks may also be explored. Nearly everyone has tried at one time or another to "trace the path" back to the starting point without retracing any of the lines, although a line may be crossed. Which of the following figures can be traced and which cannot?

Paper Folding.   There are many activities involved in paper folding. This art can be used to illustrate symmetry, conic sections, polygon constructions by tying paper knots, circle relationships, and various other geometric concepts. The best single source for paper-folding activities is a booklet written by Donovan Johnson entitled *Paper Folding for the Mathematics Classroom,* published by the National Council of Teachers of Mathematics.

Geoboard Activities.   Many excellent activities can be used with different types of geoboards. Most people are familiar only with the square geoboard (pegs arranged in square arrays), but geoboards may also be circular (pegs arranged at equal intervals in a circle with a peg in the middle) or isometric (pegs arranged so that alternate rows are offset by one-half space).

On the square geoboard, congruence and similarity of geometric figures may be explored. For example, you can make a figure such as a triangle or a rectangle and ask the child to make another figure on the geoboard which is the same shape and size as the figure supplied. The child might also be asked to make another figure which has the same shape but which is, for example, half as big or twice as big as the original figure.

Slides, flips, and rotations of geometric figures may also be investigated on the geoboard. Ask the child, for example, to describe the moves that must be made to make triangle A coincide with triangle B.

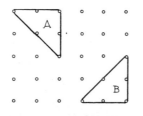

On the circular geoboard, 12 pegs could be used so that each peg is 30 degrees from the next one. Similar activities can be performed with 16, 24, or 36 pegs, however. Using 12 pegs, activities such as making different quadrilaterals can prove interesting. Which of the following can be made on the circular geoboard: square, rectangle, rhombus, parallelogram, trapezoid, or kite? Other activities include making a six-pointed star using two rubber bands, or a dodecagon using three squares with three rubber bands.

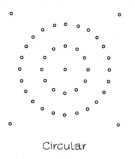

Circular

The isometric geoboard has a different array of pegs than the other two geoboards. The child should be familiar with the square geoboard before engaging in the following activities on the isometric geoboard.

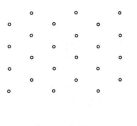

Isometric

One such activity is to change the units used to measure area. Instead of one square unit as the basis for measuring area, use one triangular unit, represented by the size of the smallest equilateral triangle which can be made on the isometric geoboard.

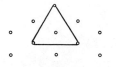

Now construct a triangle which has an area of four triangular units. Construct a regular hexagon with an area of six triangular units and another with an area of 18 triangular units. Are there any geometric figures that can be constructed on the isometric geoboard which could not be constructed on the square geoboard?

CHAPTER KEY POINTS

1. Geometry is everywhere in everyday life and provides children with models to help them understand many arithmetic concepts and principles as well as concepts of measurement.

2. Geometry in elementary school should be studied on an informal or intuitive basis.

3. Early experiences in geometry should begin with readiness activities such as handling objects.

4. The introduction of topological concepts, such as "inside," "outside," boundary and region, order, and others may begin as the child demonstrates readiness to study geometry.

5. Figure and pattern recognition are both developed early in the geometric sequence through a wide variety of concrete activities and materials.

6. Geometry in the primary grades when built on previously learned concepts should follow the developmental sequence of point, curve, line segment, line and then be extended to closed curves and basic properties of polygons and finally, circles.

7. The geometric concepts presented in the primary grades should be examined by the child on an intuitive basis in an activity-oriented program, thereby building a solid mathematical base which more advanced concepts can be developed.

8. In the intermediate grades, the child moves in the sequential development to a study of angles, learning to use a protractor to measure angles. Also the child becomes familiar with new properties of polygons.

9. A basic study of three-dimensional figures known as polyhedrons may then be studied on an informal basis by constructing physical models and examining the properties of polyhedrons.

10. Enrichment activities in geometry may include areas such as symmetry, topology, paper folding, and the use of square, circular, and isometric geoboards.

Laboratory 12

Informal Geometry

The study of geometry is relatively new to the elementary school mathematics curriculum. Even now, teachers often consider it secondary to "more useful" study of computation or other areas of the mathematics program. However, the study of geometry can provide excellent experiences for children to develop perceptual and thinking skills. These laboratory exercises are designed to acquaint you with some of the activities and materials which may be used to learn geometric concepts in the elementary classroom.

I. *Objective:* Upon completion of these laboratory exercises, you should be able to do the following:

    A. Identify activities and materials which may be used with children to develop geometric concepts on an informal basis. (Chapter Competencies 11-A, 11-B, and 11-C)

II. *Materials:* Geoboard; rubber bands

III. *Procedure:*

    A. Read Chapter 12 of *Helping Children Learn Mathematics.* If you have questions, consult your instructor.

    B. The geoboard is very useful in helping children develop visual images of geometric concepts. Try the following activities to acquaint yourself with the geoboard.

        1. Construct a square with a perimeter of 20 units and a square with an area of 9 square units.

        2. Construct a rectangle which is 4 units long and 3 units wide. What is the length of one of its diagonals? What is the perimeter and area of the figure in the following picture?

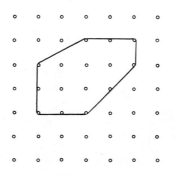

        3. Construct a scalene triangle, an obtuse triangle, and an equilateral triangle so that they all have the same area.

4. Construct a triangle and a square which have the same area. Which figure has the greater perimeter? Will your answer always be true? Why or why not?

C. There are many patterns which exist in geometric shapes. In Figure A, count the number of triangles (there are over 100). In Figure B, count the number of squares (there are over 50).

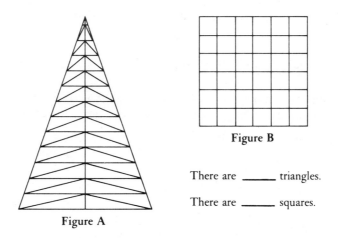

Figure B

Figure A

There are _____ triangles.

There are _____ squares.

D. Many interesting properties of geometric figures are not often explored in the classroom, but they are interesting and help develop a child's reasoning powers. Perhaps you have examined the following one. Look at the following geometric figures. Which of these can you trace with your pencil without retracing any of the lines of the figure?

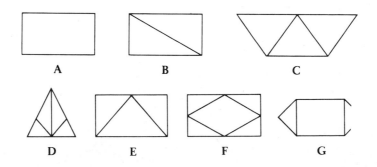

If you need some help, look at the number of odd and even vertices in each figure and complete the following table. (An odd vertex has an odd number of lines of the figure emanating from it, and an even vertex has an even number of lines of the figure emanating from it.)

Figure	No. of vertices		Can it be traced?
	odd	even	
A			
B	2	2	yes
C			
D	4	2	no
E			
F			
G			

From your table, what conclusions can you draw concerning the number of odd and even vertices and tracing the figure?

13
Applications of Mathematics

Teacher Competencies

After studying Chapter 13 and completing Laboratory 13, you should be able to achieve each of the following:

A. Given a selected concept or skill in the area of measurement, design foundational activities which may be used in the acquisition of that concept or skill. (Part Competency III-A)

B. Given a selected concept or skill in the area of measurement, identify activities which may be used to develop proficiency in the use of that concept or skill. (Part Competency III-B)

C. Given a selected concept or skill in the area of measurement, identify and/or demonstrate the use of selected instructional aids which might be used to help a child learn that concept or skill. (Part Competency III-C)

D. Given a selected concept or skill in the area of relations and graphs, design foundational activities which may be used in the acquisition of that concept or skill. (Part Competency III-A)

E. Given a selected concept or skill in the area of relations and graphs, identify activities which may be used to develop proficiency in the use of that concept or skill. (Part Competency III-B)

F. Given a selected concept or skill in the area of relations and graphs, identify and/or demonstrate the use of selected instructional aids which might be used to help a child learn that concept or skill. (Part Competency III-C)

G. Given a selected concept or skill in the area of probability and statistics, design foundational activities which may be used in the acquisition of that concept or skill. (Part Competency III-A)

H. Given a selected concept or skill in the area of probability and statistics, identify activities which may be used to develop proficiency in the use of that concept or skill. (Part Competency III-B)

I. Given a selected concept or skill in the area of probability and statistics, identify and/ or demonstrate the use of selected instructional aids which might be used to help a child learn that concept or skill. (Part Competency III-C)

To this point in the book, we have discussed the learning of mathematics from the standpoint of concepts and skills associated with number and geometric manipulation. These areas are obviously important to a child's fundamental understanding of mathematics and how it is used in everyday life.

However, there are areas in which mathematics has a direct influence and basis. Applications of mathematical concepts and skills help the child describe, in some quantitative manner, the world about him or her. In this chapter we will discuss the learning of concepts and skills in the following areas: measurement, metrics, time, money, probability, statistics, relations, and graphs.

MEASUREMENT AND THE METRIC SYSTEM

Measurement is one of the most practical studies in mathematics because it brings into use all of the fundamental operations which may occur at any time in a person's life. Complications in measurement education may arise, however, both in *what* is taught and *how* it is taught. In this chapter, we discuss important measurement concepts which should be developed at the elementary school level. Also included are both a description of selected premeasurement activities designed to determine if a child can understand basic measurement concepts and a description of selected measurement activities designed to help the child who is ready to measure develop understanding and skill in that area.

BASIC MEASUREMENT CONCEPTS

The fundamental concepts associated with measurement are so basic to us as adults that we rarely think of them. The term "measurement" usually brings to mind thoughts of standard units like pounds, inches, or centimeters. It is not surprising, therefore, that the teaching of measurement to children often becomes a study of how to measure and how to perform basic operations on denominate numbers. Certainly, measurement skills are important and should not be diminished in value; but of equal, perhaps greater, importance is the development of general measurement concepts. Equipped with an understanding of measurement, as well as with measuring skills, the child can be expected to make the appropriate selection of a measuring unit and a measuring instrument for a given situation and to utilize measuring concepts more efficiently. Let us review some fundamental concepts associated with measurement which should be developed at the elementary school level.

What Is Measurement?

Comparison is the basis of measurement. Comparing is a natural activity and is a process with which we are almost constantly involved, as indicated by the following examples:

Jane stops pouring milk in her glass when her comparison of the amount of milk to the size of the glass tells her that the glass is in danger of overflowing.

Daniel rushes home when he notices that it is growing darker outside and so must be getting late.

Mary compares two dresses and decides that the red dress is prettier than the green dress.

In each of these cases there has been a common property to compare: volume in the first instance, light intensity in the second, and prettiness in the third. Each of the comparisons in the examples is simple, general, approximate in nature, and typical of basic comparative activity with which people have been invovled for centuries.

Measurement, like comparison, also requires the identification and observation of a property to be compared. Length, area, volume, weight, temperature, time, and density are such measurable properties. In addition, however, measurement requires a *quantification* of the comparison. The degree of likeness, or difference, or change in a property is compared to an appropriate base. More precisely, measurement is a process whereby a number is assigned to a physical property for purposes of comparison to a reference unit.

No measurement is exact, regardless how well refined. *Counting,* on the other hand, is an exact procedure. While counting could be described as a measure of the numerosity of a given set, a distinction is usually made between counting and measuring. Counting involves the assignment of a number to a set of separate, discrete objects; one counts the fingers on his hand or the crayons in a box, for example, and finds that he has exactly five and twenty-four respectively. *Measuring,* however, involves the assignment of a number to quantities of a continuous nature; one measures his weight in terms of pounds, for example, and finds that he weighs about 145 pounds, an approximation. Even if he manages to find a more sensitive scale which measures to the nearest tenth of a pound, he does not know his weight to the nearest hundredth of a pound. Therefore, one distinguishing characteristic of any measurement is that it is approximate because the number assigned to the property in question has been obtained through the process of comparing against a scale associated with a base unit.

The scale for any measure may be likened to a segment of a number line. A point of origin, a direction of change, and a unit specification are needed. Consider some familiar measuring instruments and notice how the scale of each relates to a number line segment. Think first of the numerals on the bathroom scales and note that they have a point of origin (zero pounds), a different direction of movement for heavier and lighter weights, and the units are identified; the markings on the scales could easily be transformed into a number line segment. Also, the scale on a thermometer can be likened to a section of a vertical number line, just as the markings on a clock can be mentally transformed from their circular appearance to a straight line segment. The same conclusions can be drawn by studying a speedometer or any other of numerous measuring devices.

The reference, or comparison, unit upon which measures are based may vary according to feasibility or desirability. When a precise quantitative measure is not necessary, a simple, impromptu comparison of one object to another may suffice. This simple type of comparison may be qualitative in nature, as with the prettiness of one dress as compared to another in the example of Mary given earlier; or it may be quantitative in nature, as with the volume of milk as compared to the capacity of the container in the example of Jane given earlier. When a more precise quantitative measure is desirable and feasible, however, a selected standard usually is incorporated as the reference or comparison unit. Comparing an object to the scale of the standard provides a number which is the measure of the object. The measure of the object in question then can be communicated efficiently to anyone who is familiar with the standard.

Development of Standard Measuring Units

Just as concepts associated with number became more sophisticated through the ages, so too did concepts associated with measurement. Also, as with number, need dictated the development of measuring concepts and skills; that is, as man needed more precise measurements he developed more refined standards, tools, and techniques to accommodate these needs.

Crude comparisons were all that were needed initially as, for example, when early man compared the weights of two objects by placing one in each hand, or when he decided to make a spear out of one piece of wood rather than another because it was longer. As people grew more dependent upon one another and trade became more common, standardized units of measure became necessary.

Finding suitable standards was not an easy task. Certain criteria were, and still are, important in selecting a standard. A standard should remain as constant as need dictates; it should possess the same property as the object to be measured; and it should be available and familiar to all who need it. Upon meeting these criteria, though, the choice of the appropriate standard is arbitrary. This arbitrary choice, based upon need, has produced many random, unrelated measuring units possessing interesting histories. Consider, for example, various measuring units incorporated by man through the ages to measure length.

Cubit: Ancient Egyptians and Babylonians used a unit of measure called the cubit. The measure of the cubit was the length of a person's forearm from elbow to middle fingertip.

Inch: In the fourteenth century, King Edward II declared the inch to be the length of three barley corns, round and dry, taken from the center of the ear and laid end to end.

Fathom: English sailors found need to devise a unit to measure the depth of water. The simplest way to measure lengths of rope in sailing was to stretch the rope repeatedly across the length of a man's outstretched arms, or approximately six feet today.

Yard: English cloth merchants developed a measurement equal to one-half of a fathom or the distance from the middle of the chest to the fingertip of an outstretched arm. This measurement varied greatly according to the length of the arm of the individual doing the measuring. In an effort to standardize this measure, King Henry I declared the lawful yard to be the distance from the tip of his own nose to the end of his thumb. King Henry VII later ruled that the standard yard measured three feet, and he had the measure marked on a bronze yard bar.

Mile: In the days when Roman legions were marching throughout the known world, attempts were made to measure distances by means of the set pace of the soldiers. At every 1000 double paces in a march, the official counter would establish a marker. Since a pace was about 2½ feet, a double pace would measure approximately 5 feet, and 1000 double paces wold measure about 5000 feet, very close to the measure of today. By the way, note the relationship between the Roman word for 1000 (*mille*) and the term "mile."

Meter: In the eighteenth century, the French proposed a decimal system of length based upon permanent natural standards. The meter was the basic unit of length, and was to have been 1 ten-millionth of the distance from the earth's equator to either pole.

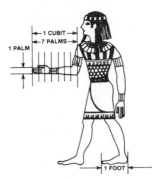

Historically, parts of the body were used as measurement standards

With the exception of the meter, people have used whatever was convenient to help them determine a crude unit of length. Then as more accuracy was needed, as in the case of the yard measure, efforts were made to establish more refined standards and tools. Measures of other properties like capacity, time, and weight have also experienced interesting, but erratic, development over the ages and deserve to be investigated by prospective teachers of measurement.

The English and Metric Systems of Measurement

In the world today two systems of measurement predominate, the English system and the metric system. The English system, with which Americans have been most familiar, is characterized by the random growth associated with historical development, as described previously, with its arbitrary choices of standards based upon availability and familiarity. The metric system, on the other hand, was developed purposely and logically and thus has gained favor in world markets. In fact, so popular has it become that the last two major countries to use the English system, the United States and Canada, are now engaged in a process of reeducation preparatory to total conversion to metric usage. (Canada is approaching total conversion more quickly than the United States.)

One of the greatest disadvantages of the English system is its lack of continuity, in that, conversion from one unit to another within the system is difficult. For example, while most people learn conversions in inches, feet, and yards, remembering how many yards in a mile or feet in a rod becomes more difficult. The size of an acre, the number of pecks in a bushel, the number of tablespoons in a cup, and the temperature at which water boils on the Fahrenheit scale pose more problems for both children and adults. Children in classrooms have spent many hours converting from one obscure English unit to another only to eventually forget the conversion units.

In the latter part of the eighteenth century, the French developed a system of measurement which, unlike other systems to that time, would be based totally on a scale of ten as was the counting system, and it would be uniform worldwide rather than varied even within a single country. The basal unit was to have an arc 1 ten-millionth of the distance from the equator to either pole. Even though certain difficulties resulted in a slight error of the measurement, a definite unit of length—the meter—was established. The meter then could be divided into thousandths (millimeters), hundredths (centimeters), or tenths (decimeters), and it could be multiplied by thousands (kilometers), hundreds (hectometers), or tens (decameters)[1] to obtain measuring units convenient to measure any given length.

To arrive at the basic unit of volume, the French made a cube 10 centimeters on a side and called it a liter. The gram, the basic unit of weight, was simply the weight of 1 milliliter of water. In addition, an offshoot of the metric system was devised. It is called the Celsius, or Centigrade, scale of temperature. Instead of water boiling at 212° and freezing at 32° on the Fahrenheit scale, it boils at 100° and freezes at 0° on the Celsius scale. Notice that it is only the scale and the basic unit of measure which changes in each case.

In practice, no difficult fraction work is necessary in metric measuring. Also, no complicated calculation with denominate numbers is needed. Converting from one unit of measure to another only involves shifting decimal points because of the base of ten for our number system and for measuring metrically.

The person who is already more familiar with the English system may note two possible problems: converting from English measures to metric and vice versa, and the necessary familiarization with metric units. Actually the first problem will be minimized when the second is overcome; that is, once Americans begin to think in terms of meters, liters, and grams, there will be no need to convert back to such units as yards, gallons, and pounds.

Then, too, problems associated with a transition to the metric system do not seem quite so overwhelming when one realizes that American mechanics have long been repairing foreign-made autos based on the metric scale. For decades scientists have used the metric system exclusively. Americans already can operate a 35-millimeter camera, watch Olympic swimmers race in a 50-meter pool, and take a 250-milligram vitamin tablet without a second thought. Cooks, seamstresses, carpenters, and automobile drivers are encountering "dual dimensioning," a process whereby both metric and English measures are expressed on tools and equipment. In a few years the metric system will seem quite natural to most adults. Certainly, children growing up in a world measured metrically will adapt to it readily and will have no need for extensive knowledge of the older English system.

Of course, standard units of measure are not limited to length, weight, temperature, and capacity. The brightness of stars and the hardness of rocks are also measured; the passage of time is a measurable property, too. In addition, measurement can be related to geometric figures in what has come to be known as *metric geometry*. Angles can be measured in terms of degrees or radians, line segments can be measured, and areas and volumes of geometric shapes can be calculated. Tools and techniques associated with metric geometry can be applied to real life situations and are important aspects of the learning of every child. In fact, a knowledge of metric geometry so compliments fundamental knowledge of certain aspects of measurement that the two are often presented to children in conjunction with one another.

---

1. Note that Roman prefixes were chosen for measures less than the meter and Greek prefixes were chosen for measures greater than the meter.

Now that basic concepts associated with measuring have been capsulized, let us proceed with a description of how these ideas, along with basic measuring skills, can be utilized to help children learn measurement.

HELPING CHILDREN LEARN TO MEASURE

To help children learn to measure, you, as teacher, must first assess premeasurement abilities to determine how and at what point to begin with each child. Then you must make decisions relative to beginning measurement work wthin the confines of the situation; subsequently you must consider suitable activities which allow each child to progress as rapidly as he or she can with understanding. Throughout the entire process you should remember the fundamental measurement concepts described earlier so that you may plan activities which will instill these ideas in your students.

Initial Considerations

Certain developmental factors should be included as initial considerations of every teacher of children who are about to begin learning concepts and skills associated with measurment. Every such teacher should be able to identify abilities which children must possess in order to measure with understanding, and he or she should know certain characteristics which children at different points in their learning typically exhibit.

A child who is to learn measurement must be able to *conserve.* Obviously, a child who thinks that the length of a stick does not remain constant through change of position cannot be asked to manipulate a ruler with understanding. Conservation does not apply only to length, but also to such properties as distance, area, and volume. Also, a child who can conserve one property may not be able to conserve another. Conservation of distance, for example, does not insure conservation of volume.

Numerous activities are available to help you determine a child's ability to conserve. Consider conservation of length. Using colored rods or perhaps lengths of stick candy, you can, after allowing the child to verify that they are the same length, place them in different positions and determine through questioning if he believes that lengths have been altered through the movement. The child should not be influenced by the wording of the questions asked him. A typical example would be to position two sticks of equal-length candy which the child likes.

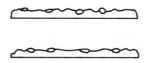

After giving the child an opportunity to verify that the candies are the same length, move one piece as shown.

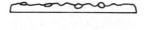

The child who does not conserve at this time may decide that he wants the candy on the bottom because it is now longer, or he may want the one on top for the same reason. Basically, he has focused on only one characteristic, the leading or trailing end of the length of candy; he does not realize that the length has remained constant. Envision what use a child who does not yet conserve length will make of a ruler as he manipulates it to arrive at different measures.

Other principles of measurement which a child should understand are those of *unit iteration* and *substitution*. He must also understand that the whole is equal to the sum of its parts. Using length again as an example, a child who is capable of unit iteration and substitution can determine the length of his teacher's desk by using a ruler repeatedly end-to-end as the basic unit of measure. He knows that the total of all these separate unit measures will be the measure of the entity, which is the desk length in this case.

Piaget and his proponents have conducted numerous studies with children which relate to measurement. Many are quite simple in form and may be used as models by the classroom teacher who is interested in determining his or her students' responses. A classic, as summarized by Flavell, follows:

> In one study the child is presented with a tower of blocks which stands on a table. His job is to build a second tower the same height, but with the following restricting conditions. His building blocks are of a size different from the model's; his tower stands on a lower table than that of the model; and a screen prevents him from actually seeing the model as he builds, although he can at any time go around it to look. Various sticks and paper strips are available as measuring tools, but child is not told how to use them. The principal developmental stages were as follows. In stage 1, the child simply makes a crude visual comparison, often failing to take account of the fact that the towers are on tables of different heights and thus estimating height from floor rather than height from table. Following this, there are various attempts to bring the two towers closer together in order (again visually) to compare them. Stage 2 is interesting because it presages genuine measurement. The child tries to use himself as a common measure, e.g., he holds his hands apart the height of the tower, uses reference points on his torso, etc. Following this comes the use of body-independent measures: a third tower or a stick. But tower or stick has to be exactly the same lengh as the tower it measures, neither longer nor shorter. In the next stage the child is able to use a stick longer than the model (i.e., by marking off the height of the tower on it), but he cannot iterate a shorter stick along the tower height. Finally, the child can do it either way; in particular, he is now able to use the shorter stick as a *unit measure*—"this tower is 2½ sticks high." With this achievement, measurement along a single dimension is constituted on an operational basis: the child is now aware that a length is composed of unit lengths of arbitrary size and can be measured by stepping one of these along the total length.[2]

Another experiment which Flavell describes is concerned with the conservation and measurement of area.

> . . . the child is confronted with two identical rectangular sheets of green cardboard and a number of identical toy houses. A toy cow is placed on each cardboard and the child grants that each cow has the "same amount of grass to eat" on each "meadow." Then one farmer builds a house

---

2. John H. Flavell, *The Developmental Psychology of Jean Piaget*, pp. 335–336. Reprinted with permission of author.

on his meadow and another farmer does the same on his. Do the two cows still have the same amount of grass to eat? Each farmer then adds a second house, then a third, etc., the test question being repeated at each new addition. However, one farmer arranges his houses in a tight cluster in one small area of the meadow while the other spreads his all over; this results in the *perceptual* impression of more free meadow—more grass to eat—for the first farmer's cow. And it is precisely this perceptual impression which the younger children succumb to and the older ones manage to resist. For the former, a typical pattern was that of asserting equality of area for addition after addition, only to have it break down when the perceptual disparity finally became too strong. In some children, however, equivalence was already abandoned with the first or second set of houses. Older children took note of the illusory impression but confidently discounted it by reasoning. As one child put it: "No, it looks as if there's more green there . . . but it isn't true because there's the same number of houses."[3]

These two examples are only a small sampling of voluminous experiments involving the conceptual development of children. They should be sufficient, however, to allow the conclusion that not all children view a measurement problem with the same backgrounds and abilities. Teachers unaware of such differences in children may begin trying to present abstract measurement concepts to a child who believes, for example, that the distance from a chair to a given table is not necessarily the same as the distance from the table back to the chair, or who believes that the distance between two objects is lessened when a screen is placed between them because some of the intervening space is used up by the screen. Most assuredly, measurement activities for such a child should be at the most basic levels possible; more advanced activities would only force him to work at the rote level.

How, then, should you begin once you have determined the child's ability to conserve various quantities and have assessed the child's understanding of such principles as substitution, unit iteration, and part-whole relationships? Some of the numerous options available are described in the next section.

Beginning Formal Study of Measurement

Having done the preliminary work necessary to determine a child's premeasurement capabilities, you will be ready to begin. Your students, the physical environment of your classroom and indeed the community itself, the quantity and quality of resource materials available, and the knowledge and ingenuity which you bring to the situation all will influence decisions relative to ways to proceed. Because the possibilities are so numerous, general suggestions must suffice at this point. You, the teacher, must make final decisions according to your particular circumstances.

Certainly, the beginning of any study should involve establishing an environment conducive to the learning of the topic under consideration. Establishing a measurement environment can and should include the introduction of contrived situations and materials; that is, you may bring into the classroom activities and materials designed to help the child learn a specific measurement concept or skill. Such activities might revolve around materials like rain gauges, tape measures, thermometers, balances and weights, volume relationship sets, clocks, or meter sticks. You and

3. Ibid., p. 338.

the students can also collect various size containers (milk cartons, cottage cheese containers, cans, etc.) which can be filled with sand, water, or sugar cubes to determine capacity relationships. Pieces of cardboard, floor tile, or linoleum cut to a given area measure can be placed over various items to determine approximate size, the result being compared to answers obtained by purely mathematical means. Children often find it interesting to compare actual relative sizes of a square inch, a square foot, and a square yard and then decide which units would provide the best measurement for various plane surfaces in the room. Metric comparisons can be made in much the same way.

Some teachers like to provide additional motivation for children through the use of films, trade books, or other written, taped, or printed materials. For example, you could bring the book *The Wonderful World of Mathematics* into the classroom. Although not directed totally to measurement, the book is colorfully illustrated, practically oriented, and it contains interesting stories about measuring which could lead your students to conduct concrete measurement experiments. Similarly, charts may be used to stimulate interest in measurement. The Ford Motor Company, for example, has made available to teachers an excellent series of "history of measurment" charts which may be used in a classroom in numerous ways. The National Council of Teachers of Mathematics also offers souce material for teachers interested in enriching the measurement backgrounds of their students.

In addition to introducing materials into the child's environment designed specifically for a measurement purpose, you should also use as much of the child's natural, everyday environment as possible in measurement activities, since measurement involves the application of mathematics to real life situations. What better way to help a child learn this fact than to provide him with the opportunity to measure in situations arising in his own life?

Some teachers like to take advantage of the application aspects of measurement to integrate its study with other subject areas. Certainly, measurement may find real use in history, geography, science, and even in building a set for the class play. However, the study of measurement should not be reduced totally to its tool dimension. It is a good idea to sometimes use other subject areas as tools in the study of measurement instead of always using mathematics as the tool.

Measurement provides what may be the most productive area in mathematics for actively learning by doing. Careful planning for active learning is still desirable, however, because the activity is not the end being sought, but is instead a means to the end. Nonproductive activity still cannot be justified. Note also that careful planning does not preclude impromptu use of various classroom items for specific measurement purposes.

Illustrating how to put the rather abstract treatment of basic concepts into a form suitable for children can only be fragmentary; an exhaustive discussion of possibilities at the elementary school level would be prohibitive. However, a brief description of a suitable sequence of beginning learning activities should help provide a frame of reference. Length, time, weight, temperature, density, or any measurable property of an object can be taught by using basic concepts and by adjusting the general sequence to the specifics of the particular property in question.

Because comparison is the basis of measurement, beginning measurement work should be based in activities of comparing. The child should be encouraged to make numerous broad comparisons. Over a period of time, for example, he should do such things as hold a book in each hand and determine which is heavier; find a classmate taller than he; jump higher than a given mark; decide which pan contains the warmest water; and determine which drum beat is faster.

After general comparative activity, arbitrary reference units may be incorporated as the basis of different measures. Again, we will use length as an example. Teams of children can measure different parts of the classroom, or the school, or the playground. Often, children enjoy using parts of their own bodies as the basic unit of measure just as man did of necessity centuries ago and still does today to some extent. They may use cubits, or "giant steps," or their own feet, or some dedicated young student may even volunteer the length of his body to measure the playground. As children continue to measure, they conclude that some units are more appropriate to measure certain lengths than are other units. For example, a thumb-length is acceptable for measuring the length of a pencil, but it certainly is not suited for measuring the length of the playground. Also, no measurement is exact. Something must be done about that little bit of length "left over" which will not accommodate another full unit measure and certainly what is done is dependent upon the use to be made of the measurement. As children continue to record and analyze their findings, they find that using parts of their bodies results in widely diverse measures. Mark's foot is not as long as David's foot, they find, and so the classroom measured a confusing 45 "Mark's feet" long and 41 "David's feet" long. A more standard unit should be used, an eraser perhaps. Even better, they conclude, would be a standard unit of measure with which every person is familiar. Now they may proceed with rulers and meter sticks, scaled appropriately for their level, of course.

Your job as teacher throughout a learning sequence such as this will be multifaceted. You should provide activities which are purposefully planned so that there will be maximum opportunity for learning basic principles, and you must organize them so that there will be minimal confusion in the process. In addition, you must be ready to lend direction when it is needed and to use learning opportunities when they arise. For example, when the students note that no measurement seems to be exact, you should readily help them extend their thinking in terms of rounding off, accuracy and precision, and perhaps relative error.

Certainly there are pitfalls in such an approach. Some children may immediately grasp concepts while a few may need more work. You must be fully aware of alternative strategies as well as the subject matter. Many factors lead to the success or failure of such an approach. Regardless, however, a child who has actually used basic measurement ideas will be less likely to do the following than a child whose total measuring experience has come from working problems in a book. The child without measurement experience may

. . . when asked the area of a room, given its dimensions, answer in linear units instead of square units.

. . . when asked approximately how many feet long a given room is, or how much a certain book weighs, have no idea.

. . . when asked what to do when a particular measurement does not come out exactly even, not know how to proceed.

The discussion so far has been directed primarily to teachers getting started with new learners of measurement, although many of the activities are suitable for children who have had previous study in measurement. Teachers beginning with older students who have had only a book-oriented, more traditional background in measurement may be confronted with special problems, however, one of which is convincing the students that there are more aspects and experiences in measurement than using a ruler or multiplying two numbers given on a page to obtain area. Since every situation is somewhat unique, no one set of suggestions can insure success. Usually helpful, though, is the supplying of problem situations and activities unlike those usually encountered and not easily solved by traditional means, but they should still be motivating in nature. An activity meeting these criteria and also making use of estimating and approximating and the basic idea of what constitutes a square unit might revolve around this question: About how many square inches of skin do you have on your body? A simple question such as this does no only elicit many elaborate schemes for solution, but it can also lead to good additional learning in measurement. (By the way, how might you approximate a solution to the above question?)

Basically, then, getting started with measurement learning involves establishing an appropriate mental and physical atmosphere and then planning purposeful learning experiences. Active learning is especially suited to the nature of measurement and so should be emphasized, both in *initiating* and in *continuing* learning in the area.

Learning Actively[4]

Active learning experiences need not be confined to initial work. Students already well based in basic measurement concepts can still make productive use of measuring devices and other suitable materials. This section provides suggestions for such materials followed by a random selection of measurement activities which could be used in the classroom.

Materials.   Appropriate materials include both refined measuring devices and commercial and self-made varieties which are intended to emphasize only facets of a particular measuring process. Numerous suggestions have been made for each of these specific types of materials. Basic guidelines which apply to all materials naturally still apply in the case of measuring. You should be aware of the following:

1. The safety factor should be considered. Note the case of the geoboard (or perimeter-area board) made of corkboard with straight pins and rubber bands for constructing the figures; a misplaced pin with a taught rubber band could become a dangerous missile.

2. Mathematical correctness is also a factor, especially at certain levels of development. Consider, for example, an enlarged foot-rule model, calibrated exactly as a ruler would be, but which is actually a yard long. While it has been designed for demonstration purposes, it can be confusing to a child trying to envision just how long a foot really is. An acceptable substitute might be to use a clear plastic ruler and merely project its image by means of an overhead projector when demonstration is necessary.

3. Most often the real object, or a model as similar to it as possible, is preferred. Approached properly, for example, helping children learn about coins and making change is best done by as-

---

4. Although "active learning" is a term often used currently, perhaps a better term would be "involved learning"; a child does not always have to be physically manipulating a mathematical device to be learning. Much highly productive learning occurs with a motivated mind, a challenging problem, and a little solitude. Perhaps the activity aspect has been emphasized to effect a balance with the overemphasis on paper-and-pencil activities in previous years.

signing each child an envelope containing real money. By impressing each child with the importance of keeping track of the coins assigned him and then by having him count his money at the close of each session, very little if any loss accrues. Play money, on the other hand, still requires a translation to real money by the child, in addition to being more likely to be misplaced and lost because of it being assigned so little value of its own. Naturally, though, some classroom situations necessitate the use of play money. Again, you, as teacher, must make the final decision.

4. If you are allowed only a small budget and must decide among several items, you can easily make some objects, and the money can then be directed to the better quality item(s). In learning about the clock, for instance, the money could be invested in several small clocks for group and individual work or in a large clock for general class work instead of in demonstration clocks which do not reveal the movement of the clock hands and their relationship to one another. Individual clock models can then be made from paper plates and paper fasteners for practice in telling time.

5. Finally, regardless of the specific materials decided upon for inclusion in the classroom, each must be suited for use. Learning results through the child's manipulation of the object, not through the storage of the object for safekeeping.

Selected Activities.   Because materials are to be used, activities should be designed which encourage exploration and practice. A random selection of such activities and associated materials follows. Included are measurement and metric geometry activities representing only a small sample of possible activities. Compare the suggested techniques with traditional approaches to the topic, and try to think of other measurement topics which could be learned actively.

1. A rectangular geoboard can readily be adapted for use in measurement activities. If one thinks of it as a grid, like graph paper, then scale figures can be made on it using rubber bands. You can describe a problem situation which incorporates the geoboard in the solution, thereby initiating activity. The following represents one such problem situation.

> John has just received a rabbit as a gift, and he wants to make a pen for it. His father has given him a piece of wire netting to be used for a fence around the pen. John wonders where to put the pen. Should he fence in the long, narrow strip of grass between the house and the garage, or should he make a pen of a different shape on the grass behind the garage?
>
> His father asks, "Have you thought about whether the shape of the pen will make any difference in the amount of ground space for the rabbit?"
>
> John wonders, "Why wouldn't the amount of grass for my rabbit be the same for any shape that I can make with my 20 feet of wire netting? If the distance around different shaped pens is the same, wouldn't the room inside the fence be the same also?"
>
> Is John correct? Why or why not?

The number and kind of suggestions which follow the offering of such a problem situation depend on the experience and maturity of the child. Some will find the problem situation itself sufficient, while others will need more direction. Possible help might reside in having the students complete a table as in the following:

Use the geoboard to make several models of pens with different dimensions but with a perimeter of 20 units. Use only rectangles at this point. What is the area of each of these pens? Record your findings in the blanks, as shown by the first example.

Dimensions	Perimeter	Area
9 units × 1 unit	20 units	9 square units
_____	20 units	_____
_____	20 units	_____
_____	20 units	_____
_____	20 units	_____

What shape is the pen with the largest area?

What generalizations can you draw from your work?

If your work had not been limited to rectangles, might you have found other shapes which would have yielded even more area for the rabbit? What might they be?

2. A study of the circle and its associated measurements provides opportunity for active learning. For example, instead of telling children that $C = 2\pi r = \pi d$, why not let them determine for themselves the relationship between the diameter and the circumference? This can be done quite readily by providing them with narrow strips of ribbon, tin cans of various sizes, and graph paper (or any other item which will help the child mark off units of equal lengths, a tape measure for instance). The children can form teams for the purpose of counting the number of units required to measure around each can and across the widest point of the circle formed by the base of each can. Each measure should be recorded on the board and a search for patterns made.

	Diameter	Circumference
Can #1	4 units	12+ units
Can #2	_____	_____
Can #3	_____	_____

Among the discoveries that can be made through this activity is that, regardless of the size of the circle involved, there is a constant relationship which exists between the diameter and the circumference, or π.

3. Area measurements of unusual shapes also lead to useful activity and may provide a springboard for later work. For example, $A = \pi r^2$ makes little sense to most children. Perhaps you could begin with an overhead projector and an irregular figure, as shown below, on a transparency, along with a supply of grids which differ only in unit size. Approach the children with this problem:

This is a scale model (a map perhaps) of a pond. How might you find its area? Among the solutions might be the suggestion to place one of the transparency grids over the shape on the overhead projector and count the number of square units required to cover the pond. Now extend the problem: What about the uneven edges? Someone may suggest that an approximation must suffice. Again the problem can be extended with such questions as: Can the maximum area be determined? How? Then how might the minimum area be determined? There are several grids here of different unit size. Which would give the most accurate answer to the question of area? Why?

Upon completion of activity necessary to prove or disprove various suggestions set forth in answer to the preceding problems, attention could be turned to a special variation of the kind of work done thus far—that of finding the area of a circular shape. The suggestion will probably be made to count square units contained in the circular region; indeed, this should be done. In moving toward a verification of the area formula for a circle, older children can be asked to complete a table showing the relationship between the radius and the total area of the figure. They could also examine relationships such as implied in the following figure, the area of the circle being approximately three times the area of a square drawn on its radius.

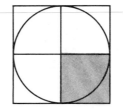

The examples just described represent only some of countless activities which may evolve from measurement study. Because they reflect only general patterns of measurement, though, and because the specific area of metric measurement is becoming increasingly important to our society, let us turn our attention particularly to the metric system in the classroom.

THE METRIC SYSTEM IN THE CLASSROOM

Discussion to this point has been balanced between metric and English systems of measurement. Perhaps such a "dual approach" would also be desirable in the classroom during the interim period in which the United States changes to the metric system. Ideal, of course, would be total immersion in metrics without the use of *any* English measures, but children growing up in the transitional period would still require some knowledge of feet, pounds, gallons, and so forth.

Perhaps the term "dual approach" should be clarified. Certainly this does not mean a constant, or even occasional, conversion from one system to the other. Converting from one system to the other does not facilitate learning in either. Instead "dual approach" as used in this context implies the learning of both systems to some degree, with emphasis on the metric system. A student who has had a variety of general fondational measuring experiences will have little difficulty learning the metric system, while still being able to communicate with his parents about the more common English measurements.

The teacher who is more comfortable with the English system, however, must exert extra effort to become familiar with the metric system at more than the paper-and-pencil level, and he or she should strive to gain confidence in measuring metrically. Certainly, a teacher who is comfortable with the metric system will be better able to create a classroom environment suited to metric investigations—the major emphasis of measurement endeavors today.

Whether you choose a dual approach or a totally metric approach, it is clear that the metric system must be learned well. Two suggestions to facilitate such learning are to *think metric* and to *do metric*.

Think Metric

The "think metric" phrase has gained popularity during the transition to the metric system. Although succinctly stated, it is the key to the most successful learning of the system. Trying to learn metrics through the English system is at best an indirect approach and has been discouraged by most mathematics educators. Instead, it is recommended that the learner actually see and feel the length of a centimeter or the mass of a kilogram, for example, and learn to think in terms of such units when measuring metrically.

The learner of the metric system should be surrounded with metrics in the form of activities and materials. Activities should deal naturally and normally with metric measurements. The teacher developing metric activities for pupils has available a wealth of resources. Current mathematics literature abounds with such activities. Those teachers with older sources at their disposal need only translate activities described in the English system to corresponding activities in the metric system. A good measurement activity is not dependent upon the system of measurement; if the activity is suitable, it can easily be made a metric problem when metric measuring is appropriate.

Do Metric

Just as the learner of the English system of measurement traditionally used aids calibrated accordingly, so also should the learner of the metric system use metric aids. In short, he or she must learn to "do metric" activities with metric tools. However, since there is not always a plentiful supply of metric aids in the classroom, today's teachers should be ready to cope with the possible scarcity.

Commercial metric teaching-learning aids are appearing in abundance on the education market. While many teachers will be able to purchase necessary quantities and varieties of such aids, most will find the expense a limiting factor, and they will have to be prudent in their selections. By following general guidelines given earlier in the chapter, satisfactory choices are possible.

Then the problem of how to supplement commercial purchases with inexpensive, self-made aids arises. The preparer of inexpensive metric teaching aids will find that he or she must make some items, but some devices used formerly for English measurement can be converted for metric use by recalibration. A cursory examination of metric aids and related activities may help the beginning teacher to see how metric measurement in the classroom might be managed on a budget.

Linear Measurement.   Varieties of materials are available for linear measurement. Both rigid and flexible models of meter measures are easily reproduced for classroom use if one has a commercially prepared meter stick from which to copy. To reproduce meter sticks, wood laths or window shade sticks can be cut to one-meter lengths and calibrated in decimeters and centimeters. A variation of the meter stick is a meter pole; it is still a meter long, but it has four faces with a square base instead of the usual two faces.

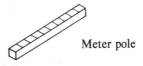

Meter pole

On one face the meter is indicated; on the second face decimeters are calibrated; on the third face are centimeters; and on the fourth are millimeters.

Metric tapes can be made from a variety of materials; buckram (a stiff material available in narrow widths), ribbon, twill tape, and adding machine paper all make satisfactory metric tapes. A length of two meters per tape is suitable. The extra length and the flexibility allow a kind of measuring different from the rigid meter stick. Calibrations can be made with a felt-tip pen.

A trundle wheel becomes a useful tool for measuring distances of some magnitude. The wheel itself can be constructed from plywood, film cans, or even pizza tins. The diameter should be about 31.9 centimeters to produce a meter circumference measure ($C = \pi d$). The wheel can be rolled by attaching a handle to the center of the wheel.

Trundle wheel

Remember to mark the edge of the wheel to enable a person to count the number of revolutions of the wheel and thus the number of meters it travels.

With the above linear measurement tools the child can determine some metric measurements for himself. After gaining some facility with the tools and the units of measure, he should try to make estimates of the measure first and then do the measuring to check the estimate. He should make as many different mesurements as possible: the length of his shoe; the circumference of a volley ball; the width of his math book; the length of the classroom; his waist; the distance around the school building. The child needs to be comfortable with metric measures of length, and to do this he needs practice.

Area Measures.   Area measures can be made using varieties of materials. Rugs, cardboard, or vinyl flooring of a square-meter measure can help the child visualize that area. Similarly, plastic or tagboard can be made a decimeter square or a centimeter square. Grid paper and transparency film grids can also be made based on metric measures.

The child can then find the answers to such questions as: How many of these square-meter sheets of linoleum will be needed to cover the floor? How many square-decimeter tiles are needed to cover your desk?

Volume/Capacity Measures.   Capacity can be measured in already available containers such as coffee cans, ice cream containers, and milk cartons by calibrating them metrically. Consider a half-gallon milk carton, for example. Fill it with a quart of water, note the level, and then measure up a distance of 8 millimeters to arrive at the level representing 1 liter. Millimeters (measurable with an eyedropper) are best contained in baby food jars, test tubes, half-pint milk cartons, Dixie cups, or Alka Seltzer bottles. Also, English liquid-measuring devices (cups, pints, quarts) may be recalibrated and used.

A volume aid which is easily made from posterboard and a little tape is a metric box. A metric box is merely a cube which measures 1 decimeter (10 cm) on an edge. A convenient pattern for making such a cube is shown here:

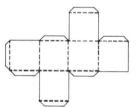

The box has a volume of 1 cubic decimeter or 1000 cubic centimeters (10 cm × 10 cm × 10 cm = 1000 cm³). If one could fill it with water, it would hold 1000 milliliters or 1 liter. In turn, the water would have a mass of 1000 grams or 1 kilogram. Notice how the meric measures relate.

With volume tools such as those just described, a child could determine the number of liters of water in his aquarium or perhaps even the number of deciliters of water a Colonel Sanders chicken bucket would hold.

Weight/Mass Measures.   Measures of mass involve a balance scale. If a balance is not available, something as simple as margarine containers may be hung from the ends of a clothes hanger or metric stick.

Weights are easily obtained. Some possible objects to be used in gram calibrations are washers painted different colors for different weights, paper clips (1 gram each), a nickel (5 grams), poker chips, or checkers. Line the metric box with a sturdy plastic bag and then fill it with water to obtain a kilogram measure.

As a final thought in the weight department, consider using an old bathroom scale. Remove the window from the scale and recalibrate the scale in 5-kilogram units by taping new units over the old. Children will then be able to determine their own weights in kilograms.

Temperature Measures.   As with the bathroom scales, recalibration is an easy solution here. The simplest thermometers to recalibrate are the wall-mounted type which have the scale on the frame. Simply cover the old Fahrenheit markings with the Celsius scale. To do this, change the 32°F mark to 0°C and the 104°F mark to 40°C, and divide the interim space into degrees Celsius at 1° or 5° intervals. A thermometer which has a 212°F reading can be converted by recording that mark as 100°C and subdividing the interval as before.

In conclusion, you may choose to help children learn both the metric system and some units of the English system, or instead you may decide to study only the metric system. Whichever approach is chosen, however, you should not make the learning of one system be dependent upon the other; that is, the child dealing with the metric system should be able to think and do activities totally within a metric framework and not have to translate through the English system. Initial learning proceeds just as before with comparative activity and moves to nonstandard and standard measures. The primary standard measures are now metric, however, and not English.

TIME

Most classroom teachers will readily admit that the learning of time concepts and skills is one of the most difficult areas for many elementary school children. There are probably many reasons for the above statement.

In this section, we will discuss the learning of time concepts and skills and why children have difficulty. We will also give some examples of activities which might be used in the classroom. For our discussion, time will involve the use of the clock, the calendar, and computation with time units.

Learning Time Concepts and Skills

Why do children seem to have so much difficulty with time concepts and skills? Among others, perhaps the major reason is that time concepts and skills are very abstract in nature. These concepts and skills are usually presented initially during a child's first year of elementary school at a time when many children have not yet reached the abstract level of working with numbers. Time involves the use of numbers and, if a child is having difficulty working with number concepts, he or she will most certainly have difficulty with time.

In addition to the abstract nature of time, most children have little or no feeling for time. When children study numbers, they can represent "seven" by counting out seven objects or drawing a loop around seven ice cream cones that are pictured on a page in a book. Time has no similar analogy.

Interestingly enough, children seem to have some intuitive understanding of time. They can show on a clock where the hands will be when their favorite TV program comes on or when it is time to go to school, but they then have difficulty bridging the gap to the formal skill of telling time.

Clock.   Traditionally, the initial time skill presented to children is telling time by looking at a clock face. The sequence from there may vary slightly but is usually presented in this order: hour, half-hour, quarter-hour, and minute. Hours are spent by children looking at clock faces and trying to recognize the time by giving the correct response, such as, "It is three o'clock" or "It is twelve minutes after seven." Some children are able to learn to tell time using the above sequence while others flounder.

Another factor complicating the traditional instructional order for telling time has been the introduction of the digital clock pictured below.

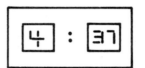

This clock is not easily used as a model for telling time except by the minute but is becoming more and more in evidence in everyday life.

Clearly, children should have as many experiences as possible at the concrete and semi-concrete levels with clocks. Each classroom should have an old or discarded clock whose hands can be moved by turning the stem on the back. This model will allow the children to move the minute hand and watch the corresponding change in the hour hand. Drawing hands on clock faces or setting the hands on a small clock-face according to a specified time are good activities to reinforce skills of recognizing and telling time.

For children who are having difficulty with the traditional instructional sequence, we suggest consideration of a teaching sequence espoused by Fredricka Reisman.[5] She suggests a sequence which is analogous to the way that number concepts are developed.

5. Fredricka K. Reisman, *A Guide To The Diagnostic Teaching of Arithmetic, second edition,* pp. 4, 32–35.

Her sequence for teaching time begins with a clock face being viewed as a circular number line 60 units long, as pictured below.[6]

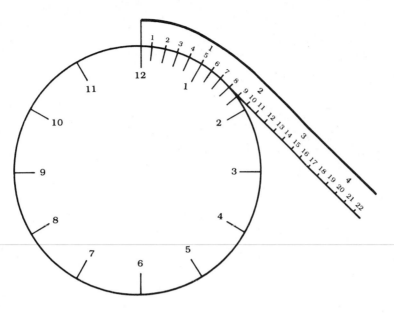

The minute hand moves along the number line and when it reaches 60, it starts over. The numbers on the clock face (1–12) are used to help tell the position on the number line (each number represents 5).

When the minute hand reaches 60, it starts over and to keep track of how many times the minute hand has started over, the hour hand is introduced.

The essential change in the traditional sequence is that the child learns to tell time by the minute before learning to tell time by the hour. This change is in line with the way a child learns to count; he or she does not start in increments of 60. Reisman's sequence then shifts to the traditional sequence and follows it in the usual order.

Calendar. Calendar concepts and skills involve the study of the four seasons, days of the week, months of the year, and the various relationships that exist among these areas. Quite often, especially in the primary grades, the calendar is used as an integral part of class exercises at the beginning of school each day.

The daily routine described above offers excellent opportunity to reinforce calendar concepts and skills. Other activities utilizing the birthdays of the children in the class and the holidays of the year also emphasize and reinforce the desired skills.

6. Ibid, p. 5.

Computation with Time Units.   Computation with time units is a skill often neglected by classroom teachers perhaps because they assume that if children can add and subtract whole numbers, they can add and subtract time units. Many children have a great deal of difficulty solving a problem such as "It is now 11:15 A.M. What time will it be 2½ hours from now?"

Ample opportunity to solve problems such as the one above should be given to children in the intermediate grades. The problems to be solved should be in the context of everyday life situations. For example:

> The cake is supposed to bake for 50 minutes.
> If I put the cake in the oven at 9:45, what
> time should I check it to see if it is done?

Selected Activities

Here are some examples of activities which could be used in the classroom to help children reinforce time concepts and skills.

1. Activities involving time and the reading of clocks vary from basic learning experiences to activities designed totally to provide practice for children. An initial experience might involve making number strips which simulate minute-markings on a clock and number strips with hourmarkings. By arranging these number strips in circular fashion and then describing how hand movements would proceed as time passes, children at least have an opportunity to observe clock faces and clock action firsthand.

To provide practice for children in telling time a game might prove appropriate. For example, the game of "Match," a variation of "Concentration," can be played. "Match" is played by two or three players and involves cards like the ones in the next illustration. The cards are placed facedown and spread out so that they do not touch each other. The first player turns over a card so that other player(s) can see it; then he picks another card to match it. If he is successful, he keeps the cards. If not, the cards are returned to their original position, face-down, and play proceeds to the next player. The game is over when all of the cards have been matched. The player with the most cards wins the game.

2. Activities using songs about time are usually very appealing to children. Two examples[7] of such songs are shown below. In both songs, underlined words may be changed to suit instructional needs.

---

7. Gregory R. Baur and Darleen Pigford, *Musical Math for the Young Child,* pp. 11, 19. Reprinted with permission from Bauford Press.

In using "Today's a Jolly Good Day," the teacher can use the song with the entire class during opening morning exercises. A variation of the song could be used at the end of the day by changing the word "is" to "was."

In using "Old MacGregor Had a Watch," the entire class can sing the song while the teacher shows the time to be used in the song on the clock face. Animation by the children could be used to act out the various activities such as rubbing their stomachs on the "to eat" verse. Variations could include other verses such as "to play" or "to help" with corresponding changes appropriate to the verb.

3. Activities using rhymes about time provide good large-group reinforcement of time concepts and skills. The examples below illustrate what we mean.

Tick Tock

Tick tock, tick tock,
    Hanging on the wall,
The clock tells the time,
    Tell it now to all.

If I Were a Clock

If I were a clock,
    And I struck one,
I'd make one bong,
    And that would be fun. Bong. (loudly)
If I were a clock,
    and I struck two,
I'd make my sounds softly,
    As I struck for you. Bong, Bong. (softly)
If I were a clock,
    And I struck three,
I'd make every bong,
    As fast as could be. Bong, Bong, Bong. (quickly)
If I were a clock,
    And I struck four,
I'd take a minute,
    Or maybe two more. Bong, Bong, Bong, Bong. (slowly)

Today's a Jolly Good Day
(Tune: For He's A Jolly Good Fellow)

Today's a jolly good day.
    Today's a jolly good day.
Today's a jolly good day
    And *Tuesday is* its name.
    And *Tuesday is* its name.
    And *Tuesday is* its name.
Today's a jolly good day.
    Today's a jolly good day.
Today's a jolly good day
    And *Tuesday is* its name.

Old MacGregor Had a Watch
(Tune: Old MacDonald Had a Farm)

Old MacGregor had a watch, e-i, e-i, o.
And on his watch there were some hands, e-i, e-i, o.
With a tick tock here and a tick tock there.
Here a tick there a tock, everwhere a tick tock.
Old MacGregor had a watch, e-i, e-i, o.

Old MacGregor wants to eat, e-i, e-i, o.
Twelve o'clock is when we eat, e-i, e-i, o.
With a *yum-yum* here and *yum-yum* there.
Here a *yum,* there a *yum,* everywhere a *yum-yum.*
Old MacGregor had a watch, e-i, e-i, o.

Old MacGregor wants to rest, e-i, e-i, o.
Two o'clock is when we rest, e-i, e-i, o.
With a *zzz-zzz* here and a *zzz-zzz* there.
Here a *zzz,* there a *zzz,* everywhere a *zzz-zzz.*
Old MacGregor had a watch, e-i, e-i, o.

4. Games can provide good reinforcement of time concepts and skills. For the game *Calendo* described below, the only materials needed are a large wall calendar (any month will do), a die, and two game markers. Directions for the game are as follows:

a. Each player rolls the die. The player with the greater value on the die goes first. Both markers are placed on the first day of the month.
b. In alternate turns, each player rolls the die and moves the marker that many spaces. The marker follows the dates in order.
c. If a player lands on a space already occupied by the other player's marker, he or she must return to 1 and start over.
d. If a player lands on his or her birthdate, an extra turn is taken.
e. The first player to reach the last day of the month is the winner.

Variations of the game might include:

a. Use 2 dice. The player moves the marker the number of spaces represented by the difference of the two dice values.
b. Make a card deck which tells the player how to move. Sample direction cards might include:

Move to the 15th

Move to the third Thursday in the month.

Go back 3 days

Move ahead 6 days

Other examples of useful games for time concepts and skills may be found in professional journals or from other teachers. A limited number of games are available commercially.

MONEY

Like time, concepts and skills associated with money are often difficult for children to learn. In this section, we will discuss the learning of money concepts and skills and present a sample of selected activities which may be used in the classroom.

Learning Money Concepts and Skills

As with time, children seem to have an intuitive understanding of money. They learn at an early age that money is useful because it can be traded for items that they believe they would like to have. They have little or no concept of where money comes from except that, in many cases, it comes from Mom and Dad.

Money is an abstract concept but, because it is fairly easily quantified, it can be presented with good success to most primary-age children. The recognition of coins and their values along with money notation (dollar and cent signs) with its corresponding manipulations is the basis for the study of money in the elementary school.

Initial learning experiences should involve the handling of actual money although many teachers are reluctant to use the activity for fairly obvious reasons. Excellent facsimiles of coins are commercially available so that teacher reluctance can be overcome. However, whenever possible, actual coins are the best medium.

The experiences that children have with money should include as many real-life applications as possible. Activities using a buying situation will help children apply money concepts to solve a problem. For example, "I have $2.00. How many pencils can I buy if each pencil costs 39¢?"

While money concepts and skills are often emphasized for their own sake in the early grades, the amount of instructional time spent on applications is often minimal, especially in the intermediate grades. For example, the skill of making change has traditionally been neglected although some emphasis on this skill has been more in evidence in recent years. It is still appalling, however, when a high school student (or graduate) is not able to give correct change to a customer in a retail store.

The point is that money concepts and skills must receive concentrated attention in the elementary school. These concepts and skills cannot be taken for granted or the current state of disarray relative to money will be perpetuated.

Selected Activities

A wide variety of activities for reinforcing money concepts and skills are available for classroom use. Here are some examples.

1. Songs about money provide good variety to the instructional program. An example of such a song is "Put Your Money in the Bank" [8] which is shown below.

As with the songs described in the previous section, underlined words may be changed to fit desired instructional needs. An appropriate activity to use with his song is to have the child named in the song activity take the amount of money (cited in the third verse) from a box of coins and give it to the teacher.

2. Rhymes about money also provide good classroom activities for the entire class and, as with songs, give good variety to the instructional program. Some examples of money rhymes are shown below.

If I Were a Coin

If I were a coin
    I'd be worth a lot.
If I were a penny
    I'd go in the pot.
If I were a nickel
    I wouldn't be tiny.
If I were a dime
    I'd really be shiny.
If I were a quarter
    I'd know who to thank.
If I were a dollar
    I'd buy me a bank.

8. Ibid, p. 21.

Put Your Money in the Bank
(Tune: She'll Be Coming Round the Mountain)

Put your money in the bank to keep it safe (clap, clap).
Put your money in the bank to keep it safe (clap, clap).
Put your money in the bank.
Put your money in the bank.
Put your money in the bank to keep it safe (clap, clap).

Mary will be the banker that we'll see (stomp, stomp).
Mary will be the banker that we'll see (stomp, stomp).
Mary will be the banker.
Mary will be the banker.
Mary will be the banker that we'll see (stomp, stomp, clap, clap).

We should save *three dimes* for today (wow-ie).
We should save *three dimes* for today (wow-ie).
We should save *three dimes*.
We should save *three dimes*.
We should save *three dimes* for today (wow-ie, stomp, stomp, clap, clap).

These Are My Coins

These are my coins,
        Look so you'll see,
Tell me their names,
        What cents will they be?

A Penny Is a Coin

A penny is a coin
        That doesn't buy much.
But five make a nickel
        I know it as such.
And ten make a dime
        As shiny as can be.
Twenty-five make a quarter;
        Do you have one like me?

3. There are many games that can be used with money. One such game is "Coin Computo" whose description is shown below.

Materials for the game (intended to provide practice in coin recognition and money computation) include a "money" die (faces printed with the words "penny," "nickel," "dime," "quarter," "half-dollar," and "dollar"—one word per face), a regular die, a marker for each player, and paper and pencil. The directions for the game are as follows:

    a. Players roll the "money" die; the player with the greatest money value is first.

    b. The first player rolls both dice and moves his or her marker the number of spaces indicated by the "number" die. He or she then adds the money value of the coin picture on the game board to the money value of the "money" die. The total is then recorded.

c. Play moves in a clockwise direction until each player has had ten turns. Scores are then totaled and the player with the greatest score is the winner.

d. If a player's marker lands on a square already occupied by another player, he or she doubles the score for that turn.

e. If a player records an incorrect sum, he or she may be challenged by another player. If the challenge is correct, the challenging player receives the challenged player's score as a bonus. The challenge must occur before another player takes a turn.

Variations might include:

a. Instead of pictures of coins on the game board and "money" die, the cent value may be used. Names of coins may also be used.

b. If the coin on the "money" die is the same as the coin in the square landed on, the player may triple his or her score.

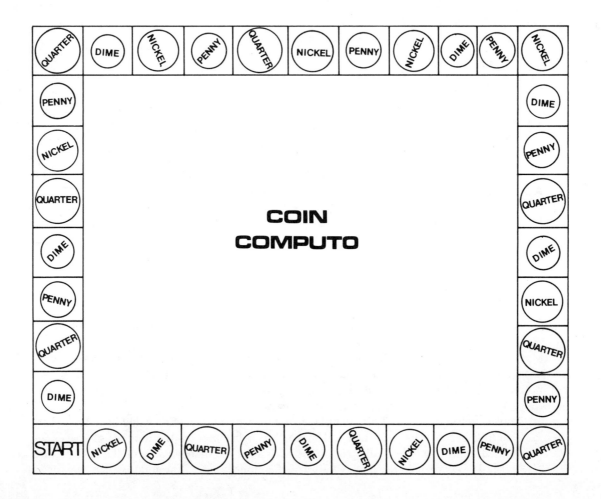

PROBABILITY AND STATISTICS

The study of the areas of applied mathematics concerned with probability and statistics is reasonably new to the elementary mathematics curriculum. In the past, children performed the exercise of constructing and reading graphs, but few other activities were considered. Because knowledge of these areas is increasingly important in society, they are receiving increasing emphasis in the elementary school curriculum.

In this section, we discuss appropriate experiences for children in both areas. Emphasis is on the collection, organization, and interpretation of data and on statements that may be made about the data.

Probability

Probability is perhaps one of the most interesting and challenging areas which a child can study. There are numerous real life applications of probability, and one is constantly exposed to probabilistic-type statements such as, "there is a 70% chance of rain today" or "the Bears are 15 to 1 to win the National Football League championship."

Initial experiences with notions of probability may begin in the kindergarten or first grade. No numbers need be assigned yet. The discussion of "more likely" and "less likely" should be involved in the first experiences. For example, hold up a paper bag with, say, five red marbles and three blue marbles in it; the number doesn't really matter. Ask the children to guess what color of marble is more likely to be drawn if they reach in and draw out one. A record can be kept of actual draws and a graph made of the results. The point should also be made that a statement based on probability does not guarantee that the event in question will *actually* occur but only that it *might* occur.

Other events should then be discussed so that children can have an opportunity to predict what will happen. Sometimes they find out immediately if their predictions were correct, as in the tossing of a coin or a die; other times they may have to wait to see what happens such as with weather predictions or guessing who will get all of their spelling words correct on Friday's test. Keeping a record of each child's predictions and checking the results can be a stimulating activity.

As the child learns to use fractions, he can begin to use them to describe the probability that an event may or may not occur. The assignment of a probability number to an event is based upon the ratio of the number of ways the event is favorable or successful to the number of ways the event can occur. It seems best, if possible, to have the child enumerate the list of all possible ways the event can occur (called the *sample space*). For example, if a coin is tossed, the possibilities are

$$H \qquad T$$

or if a die is tossed, the possibilities are

$$1 \qquad 2 \qquad 3 \qquad 4 \qquad 5 \qquad 6$$

The child is then ready to consider the probability that a certain event will happen. He can use the picture of the sample space to help decide what probability number is needed. In the case of the coin, the probability that a head will come up can be shown by

(H) T

He can then see that there is one head and two possibilities for the coin to land so that the probability of getting a head is $\frac{1}{2}$.

A similar diagram can be used for the die. The probability that a 4 will land upward on the die can be shown by

1   2   3 (4) 5   6

which is $\frac{1}{6}$. Such a diagram can be quite helpful for discussing a more complicated event such as the probability that an even number will land upward. This event can be illustrated by

1   (2) 3 (4) 5 (6)

and then the child can easily see that the required probability is $\frac{3}{6}$ or $\frac{1}{2}$.

Performing simple events such as the ones just described and recording the results gives the child practice in collecting data and organizing it. Comparing the results, for example, of tossing a die many times and comparing the results against the expected results emphasizes the fact that probability numbers tell us only what might happen, not what will happen.

Discussion of the *range* of probability numbers is an important point in the study of probability. Looking at the probability number as a ratio, the child can determine that the largest ratio is 1 (the event cannot be favorable more often than it can occur), and the smallest ratio is 0 (the event cannot be favorable). Let the child think of examples of events with probability numbers of 1 and 0; then he can discuss the meanings of such examples (the event will always happen; the event will never happen).

Along with discussion of the contrived situations, a discussion of real life applications should be encouraged. Asking questions such as, "what does it mean when the weatherman on TV says that the probability of measurable precipitation tonight is 60%?", can spark a lively and interesting as well as informative discussion.

An interesting sidelight of the notions of probability could be a discussion of the problem of how many arrangements of objects can be made from a given set, or the number of permutations that can be made. In this case, consider simple examples such as

How can we arrange four children in a row?

or

How many three-digit numbers can be made from 4, 5, 6, and 7?

Questions such as these provide excellent situations for problem-solving and discovery activities involving the writing down of all possibilities and then trying to find a pattern or formula to easily compute the number permutations. Similar activities can be used with combinations.[9]

9. If you have forgotten these terms, the laboratory exercise at the end of this chapter will be helpful to you.

As the child progresses in his probability education, more complicated situations can be posed. Questions such as

What is the probability of obtaining a sum of 6 if two dice are tossed?

or

What is the probability of obtaining two heads if two coins are tossed?

pose situations which allow the child to explore and to work on problem-solving skills.

To conclude, the study of probability in the elementary mathematics curriculum can be a rewarding and stimulating experience. Its study offers many opportunities for the child to be involved in and to see mathematics at work.

Statistics

Statistics is another area which gives children many excellent learning opportunities, especially the chance to see mathematics work for them. It is through the study of statistics that the child learns to collect, organize, and interpret data in a way that can be communicated meaningfully to others.

The child can begin statistical work by collecting data and summarizing it in the form of a table. First, he can work with simple comparisons such as how many classmates have pets and what kinds of pets they have, or by recording how many days it rained so that he had to stay in from recess. The child can be helped to collect his data and to learn how to organize it into a table.

Number of days it rained so I couldn't go out to recess					
March	1111 1	6	May	1111 1111 11	12
April	1111 1111		June	1111	4
	1111	15			

The child can be questioned about the table and the data he obtained to determine whether or not the table was meaningful to him.

After he is able to summarize the data in the form of a table, the child is ready to make a graph of the data. He should have the opportunity of making several different kinds of graphs for the same set of data and to compare his graphs to see which he feels is most appropriate. The most popular types of graphs are bar, broken-line, and pictorial. The child's graphs from the preceding table might look like this:

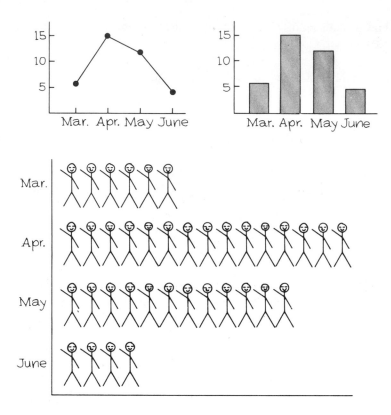

Collecting graphs of all kinds from magazines and newspapers is an excellent activity. At this time, the child can have ample practice in reading and interpreting the graphs. The same can be done wth a classmate's graph, for the real test of the effectiveness of a graph is whether or not another person can grasp the idea being conveyed.

The complete exercise of collecting, organizing, and interpreting data and conveyance of the information to others should begin at an early age, probably in kindergarten or first grade. The first examples must obviously be very simple, but skills developed at this point can be built upon later as the child begins to work with problem-solving situations.

In the upper elementary years, the child should have an opportunity to study the measures of *central tendency.* The mean, median, and mode provide much information about a set of data and are terms often used in everyday life, especially the mean or arithmetic average.

Activities such as computing the average temperature recorded at a certain time during each school day for a month or so or computing the average score on the last class mathematics test provide good practice in computing the mean. A graph of the data can also be made, and the point locating the mean can be located. At the same time, the median and mode can be determined and a discussion about the values of the three measures and their relationship to each other can be a valuable learning experience. Such activities provide an excellent basis for laboratory-type experiences.

RELATIONS AND GRAPHS

The ability to discover relations (relationships) which exist in mathematics and to communicate these relations to others through the use of graphs is important for a child to develop. It is these existing relationships which coordinate the fields of mathematics into a meaningful structure instead of a series of isolated parts. Hence, you, as teacher, must use every available skill and tool to help the child discover these relationships so that understanding can be achieved. At the same time, the child must learn to communicate these found relationships to others, often through the use of graphs. Graphs are a means of describing situations, such as the range of daily temperature or the change in a child's height during the year, and they may be an invaluable aid in the solution of problems.

In this section we discuss the development of mathematical relations by the child and the ways in which graphs, particularly the number line, may be used to report these relations.

Relations

The child's first experience with mathematical relations should begin with an examination of some familiar relations which are a part of his everyday life. For example, a familiar relation to nearly every child is the set of relations found within his family. A relation such as "is the father of" or "is the sister of" will provide an excellent beginning.

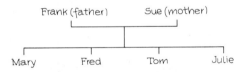

The child may draw pictures to illustrate the relations of "father" and "sister" as shown next. He has used a type of graph to describe the relations.

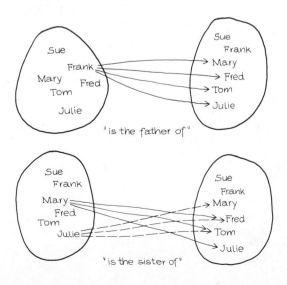

As the child begins to study these types of relations he can also begin to study some very simple mathematical relations. For example, he can work with some classification activities involving geometric shapes. Attribute blocks are well suited to the purpose. He may be asked to group all of the pieces which are related to each other because they have the same shape or color. Activities such as these form the basis for the child's later work in which he will state and illustrate requested relations. They also form the basis for the study of two very important mathematical relations—equality and inequality.

Equality.   The child should learn that equality means "the same as" or "two different names for the same thing." Initial experiences with this concept occur when the child is working with one-to-one correspondence. He has not yet learned the concept of number, but his experiences with the matching of two equivalent sets tells him that he can match each object in one set with one object in the second set and have none remaining. This matching idea leads, of course, to the development of the concept of number.

The concept of equality is basic to the powerful concept of *renaming*. The renaming concept is associated with number when the child sees that, in the statement $3 + 4 = 2 + 5$, $3 + 4$ and $2 + 5$ are two different names for 7. The child should view equality in this way because often the solution to a mathematical problem is dependent upon the renaming principle.

Inequality.   As the child studies the matching of sets, he should also be given examples of sets which cannot be put into one-to-one correspondence, as shown in sets A and B which follow. He will learn that set A has more objects in it than set B and that set B has fewer objects in it than set A.

This relationship should be related to the fact that, when sets A and B are matched on a one-to-one basis, there is an object in set A which is left over. You should give the child ample practice in working with these concepts so that he achieves thorough understanding.

As the child develops the concept of number, he begins to realize that he can compare sets by comparing their number properties. He learns that, as in the following picture, set D has a greater number of objects in it than set C and that set C has a lesser number of objects in it than set D.

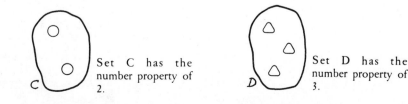

Set C has the number property of 2.

Set D has the number property of 3.

Again, you should provide practice in comparing sets using the number properties of the sets.

In his study of inequalities the child might have difficulty in remembering the proper symbol for greater than ($>$) and less than ($<$). Teachers have tried many different methods to help the child remember these symbols. One popular technique is simply to remind him that the symbol always "points" to the lesser number. It makes little difference what method is used as long as you first are certain that the child understands the concepts of greater than and less than.

Mathematical Sentences.   During his early experiences with the basic operations and the concept of renaming, the child will encounter mathematical sentences of the forms $3 + 4 = 2 + 5$ and $1 + 2 < 5$. These sentences express relationships between numbers and serve to reinforce what the child has learned about equalities and inequalities. He should have many opportunities to write such sentences and to decide whether the sentences are true or false. For example, he may be asked to write sentences which express a given relationship between expressions such as $3 + 4$ and 7 or 3×2 and 6. This activity is good reinforcement for the learning of basic facts. At a given point the child can consider other operations such as subtraction in sentences like $5 - 3 = 2$.

The study of the preceding mathematical sentences is a preview to the problem of solving open mathematical sentences such as $5 + 4 = \square$ and $2 + \triangle = 6$. At this point, as earlier, you must be certain that the child understands the meaning of the symbols with which he is working. In essence he is learning the language of mathematics; failure to understand its symbols will cause frustration for the child and for you.

The child who is having difficulty with the solution of sentences such as $5 + 4 = \square$ and $2 + \triangle = 6$ should be allowed to use concrete objects like popsicle sticks or bottle caps to aid in the solution of the problem. A piece of string or yarn may be placed on the child's desk and the concrete objects placed on either side of the string to represent the sentence under consideration. Consider $2 + \triangle = 6$. The problem might be set up as in this diagram:

The child should be asked how many objects must be placed on the left side so that there are as many objects on the left side of the string as on the right side. If the child has difficulty with this task, he should be encouraged to use one-to-one correspondence. From this activity, the child should realize that 4 is the solution to the problem.

When the child has mastered this task at the concrete level, he is ready to move to the semiconcrete level. Here, the activity will be similar to the preceding one except that he will draw pictures of the sets of objects on a piece of paper instead of manipulating physical objects.

It is important that the child work at the appropriate level when he is asked to solve mathematical sentences such as the ones mentioned earlier. A child who is working at the improper level may, after solving problems such as $2 + 3 = \boxed{5}$, give 8 as the solution to $2 + \triangle = 6$.

This mistake is probably caused by the fact that the child has memorized a process without understanding it; therefore, the change in the order of the symbols in the sentence has no special meaning for him.

Mathematical sentences in two variables such as $\square + \triangle = 6$ should pose little problem in solution for the child who has learned to solve sentences in one variable. He should have an opportunity to make up his own sentences to solve and to solve problems where he is given the solution to a sentence and asked to write the sentence. For example, the child may be given the following table

and asked to write a sentence for which the values for $\square$ and $\triangle$ form the solution, or ($\square + 3 = \triangle$). Working with exercises such as these enables the child to discover mathematical relationships and patterns.

The study of the solutions to mathematical sentences in one and two variables enables the child to discover mathematical relationships and patterns. One means of communicating mathematical relationships is *graphing*.

Graphs

Graphs are used to communicate mathematical relationships. They form a picture or diagram for the child and may be the key to the child's understanding of a given relationship. The child should engage in many activities which require him to draw graphs to illustrate what is happening. In this section we discuss a particular type of graph called the *number line* and investigate its uses, both in one and two dimensions.

The Number Line in One Dimension.   In recent years the number line has become popular with classroom teachers because of its many uses. It can help a child picture what is happening in basic operations on numbers. It can also be used to help determine the solution sets of open mathematical sentences and to discover mathematical relationships between pairs of numbers. On the other hand, since it tends to be of a more abstract nature than many other instructional aids, it will not necessarily be helpful to every child for every problem. The teacher who realizes these limitations can make effective use of the number line as a tool.

Initial experiences with the number line should not begin for a child until he has mastered the concept of number and the ordering of whole numbers. Once the child has mastered number and order, he is ready to engage in activities such as making a number line on paper, the chalkboard, or the floor. Real life examples of number lines such as thermometers and rulers should also be presented to him.

A difficulty experienced by many children in working with the number line lies in the problem of how to count on the number line. In the problem $3 + 4 = \square$, for example, they may start at 1, count 3, and land on 4. Counting 4 more, they land on 8 and cannot understand why they are incorrect. The problem, of course, is that they are counting the numbers and not the "jumps." They must begin at 0 and make 3 jumps and then 4 jumps, thereby landing on 7. Practice in making jumps on the number line to correspond with mathematical sentences can be made more fun for children by any of a number of game variations involving kangaroos, frogs, or grasshoppers. Note the following illustration:

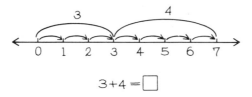

$$3+4 = \square$$

The Number Line in Two Dimensions.   As the child develops proficiency in the plotting of points on the number line, he may move to the plotting of points on a rectangular grid formed by the intersecting of two number lines perpendicularly at their origin as shown in the following figure. As the child progresses in his mathematical thinking, he will utilize sets of numbers other than the whole numbers on the rectangular grid.

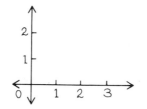

The child should have ample practice in plotting points on the rectangular grid so that he becomes proficient at this task. Activities such as the locating of cities and points of interest on a map or playing the game of "Battleship" (sometimes called "Salvo") provide this type of practice. A geoboard or pegboard to plot the vertices of various geometric figures may be used.

As the child practices the plotting of points on the number line in two dimensions, he should realize that, by common agreement, the first number in the ordered pair refers to the location on the horizontal number line while the second number in the pair refers to the location on the vertical number line. The point (3,2) for example, has a location three spaces to the right of the origin and two spaces above the origin. However, the child should also realize that it makes no difference if he moves up two spaces and then to the right three spaces or if he first moves to the right three spaces and then up two spaces.

Graphing Solution Sets.   Besides illustrating basic operations on whole numbers and fractions, the number line may also be used to help the child find or record the solution sets of open sentences. He should work with the graphs of solution sets of sentences which represent both equalities and inequalities. For example, the graph of the whole-number solution set of $\square + 3 = 5$ might look like:

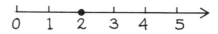

The graph of $\triangle \leq 2$ in the set of whole numbers might be represented by the following:

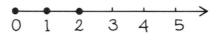

After working with graphs of solution sets of open sentences such as the preceding ones, the child should be helped to realize that changing the set of numbers from which the solution set may be chosen may change the solution set. For example, in $\triangle \leq 2$ just illustrated, changing the set of numbers which may be used in the solution set from whole numbers to real numbers will alter the solution set so that the graph of the sentence might now look like:

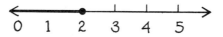

The child should experiment with different sets of numbers from which a solution set is to be chosen to see what effect, if any, the change has on the solution set.

In considering the graphs of the solution sets of sentences with two variables, the child should also have activities with both equalities and inequalities. It may be interesting for him to explore whether any type of geometric figure is formed by the solution set. A geoboard might be useful at this point. For example, the child may plot three number pairs which are in the solution set of $\square + \triangle = 10$.

$\square$	$\triangle$
6	4
3	7
0	10

Hence, (6,4), (3,7), and (0,10) are three ordered pairs of whole numbers that will satisfy the open sentence $\square + \triangle = 10$. The child may plot the points on the graph as follows and, by placing a straight edge on the graph, discover that the three points lie in a straight line. By checking other points which lie on the line, he will see that they also satisfy $\square + \triangle = 10$.

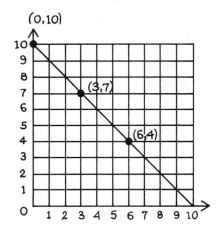

Another activity related to the location of points on the coordinate grid involves giving the child a set of points and asking him to determine the relationship between that set of pairs. For example, the points (2,4), (0,2), and (4,6) are related to each other in that the second number in the pair is two more than the first number in the pair. Children can experience a lot of fun and also meaningful activity by making up pairs and asking classmates to "guess my rule."

Graphs in the Classroom.   As the number of graphing activities increase in the elementary school classroom, there is a concomitant increase in the need to reproduce basic graph forms for individual and group work. While line graph reproduction poses only minor problems, making grids for work on the coordinate plane has proved more difficult. Possible classroom solutions to the reproduction of both types of graph forms are described in this section.

Number lines and coordinate grid forms should be reproduced on paper so that each child, seated at his desk, may plot points and determine solutions. Of course, the simplest way to provide grids is to obtain a supply of graph paper. However, if graph paper is not obtainable, or if its squares are not the appropriate size for the children, then you can trace a grid of the desired shape onto a master ditto and reproduce as many as necessary. Number line forms can be provided in the same way for general use. Also, rubber stamps can be purchased with a variety of graph forms on them so that you can stamp a grid on whatever sheet of paper you choose.

When you and a group of children want to work together on a graphing problem, however, there is need for a way to reproduce graphs which will allow accurate plotting but which will also be quickly made and easily seen by all. If your classroom has grids already painted on the chalkboard, you will have no problem; without painted grids, you must improvise. Frames made to hold five pieces of chalk and originally designed to make bars for music can be used to make grids by making two sets of line marks, one perpendicular to the other. Of course, a new graph may have to be made with each new plotting.

More advanced techniques involve the use of an overhead projector and transparencies of various types. The more familiar transparency which produces a black image when run through a thermographic machine[10] can be used to make the appropriate master graph forms. Some children can then use markers to plot points directly on the transparency while others view the work projected on the screen. Less familiar, but very useful in all graphing work, is a type of transparency film made by the 3M Company which when run through a thermographic machine produces a white image. Just as the black image in the previous example projected well on a white screen, the white image shows well on a dark chalkboard. Now the children can simply use chalk and work directly at the board plotting points on the line or coordinate graph projected there. Erasing removes their work, but the basic graph form will remain until you switch off the overhead projector light.

CHAPTER KEY POINTS

1. Measurement concepts and skills help a child describe, in some quantitative terms, the world around him or her.

2. Comparison is the basis of measurement.

3. The scale for any measure may be likened to a segment of a number line.

4. The comparison unit of measure may vary according to feasibility or desirability.

5. Finding suitable standard units of measure has historically been difficult.

6. Two systems of measurement, English and metric, predominate the world today.

7. Children's premeasurement skills must be assessed and considered before they can learn to measure.

8. A child must learn to conserve before measurement becomes meaningful.

9. The concept of a standard unit of measure is prerequisite to the development of measuring skills.

10. Children might become actively involved in learning experiences dealing with measurement.

11. The metric system should not be introduced through comparison with the English system.

12. To learn metrics, a child must think and do metrics.

13. Children have a great deal of difficulty learning time concepts and skills.

14. An alteration in the traditional sequence of learning to tell time may be helpful for some children.

15. Money concepts and skills are difficult for children to learn.

16. Wherever possible, real money should be used in the learning experiences of children.

17. The study of probability and statistics will help children understand the world about them.

18. The abilities to discover relations (relationships) and to represent them graphically will help the child communicate with others in the real world.

---

10. The term "thermographic machine" refers to any machine using infrared light to create images on acetate.

Laboratory 13

The Metric System

The United States will soon adopt the metric system as its official system of measurement. Thus, it is imperative that teachers of elementary school mathematics be prepared to implement the metric system into their programs of instruction in the classroom. These exercises are designed to help acquaint you with some of the basic concepts found in the metric system and to help you design classroom activities which may be used with children.

I. *Objectives:* Upon completion of these laboratory exercises, you should be able to do the following:

    A. Design classroom activities which may be used to help children learn the metric system. (Chapter Competencies 13-A and 13-B)

    B. Choose and use appropriate measuring units and instruments in the metric system. (Chapter Competency 13-C)

II. *Materials:*

file folders	M & M candy
scissors	coins (pennies, nickels, and dimes)
lined notebook paper	3-cubic-centimeter syringe
balance scale	small nut cups
sugar cubes	

III. *Procedure:*

    A. Read Chapter 13 of *Helping Children Learn Mathematics.* Consult your instructor if you have any questions.

    B. Linear measure

    First consider linear measurement in the metric system. To do this, you need to construct an instrument which can be used for linear measurement. Cut out 10 rectangles which have the same shape and size as this one:

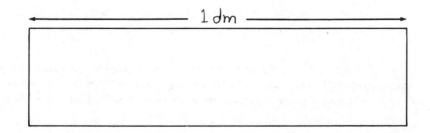

Tape the 10 pieces end-to-end. Now compare the length of the strip of 10 pieces to the length of a meter stick. What do you find? In the strip which you made, there are 10 pieces of the same length. What is the name of each piece? You are correct if you said that each piece is a *decimeter* (dm).

1. Measure the length and width of your desk or table using the meter strip. (If you are at a round table, measure its circumference.) Record your answers in decimeters or a combination of meters (m) and decimeters.

   Table length _____ Table width _____
   Table circumference (if applicable) _____

   Compare your findings with those of a classmate. Do you agree? How accurate are your measurements? Do you think that your measurements would be more accurate if your meter strip had smaller units on it? From your reading, you know that there are 10 centimeters (cm) in a decimeter. How could you divide your decimeters into centimeters? Here is a simple method. Take a piece of lined paper and place your decimeter strip at an angle until there are lines at either end of the strip and 10 spaces in between. Mark off several of your decimeter strips into centimeters.

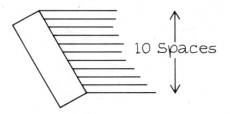

   You may wish to number your centimeter units for easier reference later. Now measure the length and width (or circumference) of your table again. How do your results compare with your first measurements?

2. Estimate the distances below and then check to see how close you were to the actual measurement. Which units are appropriate to use in each case?

   Estimate   Actual measurement

   a. Palm of your hand
   b. Span (tip of your thumb to the tip of your little finger when your hand is extended)
   c. Cubit (tip of your elbow to the tip of your second finger)
   d. Fathom (tip of second finger on left hand to tip of second finger on right hand when arms are extended)
   e. Your waist
   f. Your height

How close were you in your estimates to the actual measurements? How do your measurements compare with those of a classmate?

3. Find examples of objects in the classroom or at home which have a length or width of 1 centimeter. Do the same for 1 decimeter. Record what you have found.

C. Mass (weight)

The concept of mass in the metric system can be demonstrated through the use of a balance scale and common objects. The balance may be either homemade or commercial in construction.

1. Using the balance, complete the following exercises. Let ABW represent "almost balances with." Use only natural numbers in your answers. (1 nickel ABW 5 grams.)

_____ pennies ABW _____ sugar cubes.
_____ pennies ABW _____ M & M's.
_____ pennies ABW _____ dimes.

2. Fill the nut cup with 10 cubic centimeters (cc) of water and place on one side of the balance scale. How many of each of the following items will be needed to almost balance with the nut cup of water?

_____ nickels
_____ M & M's
_____ dimes
_____ pennies
_____ sugar cubes

3. Using your results from above, give the approximate weight in grams of each of the following. The fact that 1 cc of water weighs approximately 1 gram (g) will be helpful. You may use fractions but only in the decimal form.

1 nickel weighs _____ g.
1 M & M weighs _____ g.
1 dime weighs _____ g.
1 penny weighs _____ g.
1 sugar cube weighs _____ g.

D. Choose an elementary mathematics textbook (grades 3–6), and examine it to see how the metric system is presented. What aspects of the presentation do you like or dislike? Why? What changes would you make if you were presenting the metric system at that grade level?

E. Name some inexpensive materials which you could use as teaching aids for a child learning the metric system. Briefly describe how you would use each set of materials.

Time and Money

The topics of time and money are difficult for children in elementary school. Because of their importance to everyday life, these concepts must be learned by every child. Therefore, you, as classroom teacher, must make certain that each child has the maximum opportunity to learn to work with time and money.

 I. *Objective:* Upon completion of these laboratory exercises, you should be able to do the following:
   A. Design a procedure which could be used to help a child learn the concepts of both time and money. (Chapter Competencies 13-D and 13-E)
 II. *Materials:* Any elementary mathematics textbook series; other available sources of activities related to time and money
III. *Procedure:*
   A. Read Chapter 13 of *Helping Children Learn Mathematics*. If you have any questions consult your instructor.
   B. With some classmates, outline a procedure which could be used to help a child learn the concept of time. Do the same for money. Each procedure designed should be appropriate for the second-grade level and should include the following points:
      1. Informational objectives
      2. Prerequisite skills and knowledge
      3. List of materials
      4. Instructional strategies
   Compare your work with that of other groups of classmates. On what points do you agree or disagree?

Probability and Statistics

The study of probability and statistics is relatively new to the elementary mathematics curriculum. Because it is often a part of each child's everyday life, it should be included in instructional programs. These exercises are designed to acquaint you with some of the basic concepts of probability and statistics which may be used in the classroom.

 I. *Objectives:* Upon completion of these laboratory exercises, you should be able to do the following:
   A. Design activities which may be used in a classroom to help a child learn basic concepts of probability and statistics. (Chapter Competencies 13-H and 13-I)
   B. Utilize various mathematical materials associated with the learning of probability and statistics. (Chapter Competency 13-J)
 II. *Materials:* Two dice; two coins; two different colored pencils
III. *Procedure:*
   A. Read Chapter 13 of *Helping Children Learn Mathematics*. Consult your insructor if you have any questions.

B. In the study of probability, the listing of all possible outcomes which an event may have is called the *sample space*. For example, if a coin is tossed, it will fall in one of two ways, either heads (H) or tails (T). (The possibility of the coin landing on its edge is not being considered.) Thus, there are two elements in the sample space of the toss of a coin, H and T.

1. Give the sample space for the tossing of two coins.

2. Give the sample space for the tossing of three coins.

3. The probability that an event will occur is given by the ratio

$$\frac{\text{no. of ways an event is successful}}{\text{no. of ways the event can occur}}$$

For example, the probability of obtaining two heads if two coins are tossed is given by

$$P \text{ (two heads)} = \frac{1}{4}$$

since there is only one way of getting two heads (H,H) and there are four elements in the sample space for the tossing of two coins.

Give the following probabilities if three coins are tossed.

P (three heads) =
P (two heads and one tail) =
P (at least two heads) =
P (at most one head) =

4. How does the weatherman determine that "the probability of measurable precipitation tomorrow is 40%"? (Don't answer the question too hastily!)

5. What is the largest possible probability number? What type of event does it represent? Give an example of such an event.

6. What is the smalest possible probability number? What type of an event does it represent? Give an example of such an event.

7. Write the sample space for the tossing of a die.

8. Give the probability that each of the numbers will land upward if the die is tossed.

P (one) =   P (four) =
P (two) =   P (five) =
P (three) =   P (six) =

What do you notice about this set of probability numbers?
What can you conclude from this observation?

9. Give the sample space for the tossing of two dice. (There should be 36 elements in your sample space.)

10. Compute the following probabilities.

P (sum of 6) =
P (sum of 9) =
P (at least a sum of 10) =
P (at most a sum of 5) =

11. Toss a pair of dice 36 times and record your results in the following table.

Sum	Frequency
2	
3	
4	
5	
6	
7	
8	
9	
10	
11	
12	

Graph your results in the following space using a colored pencil to connect the dots.

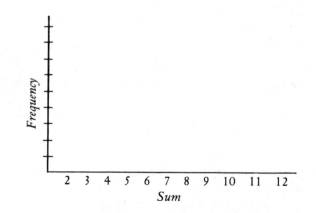

On the same graph, use a different colored pencil to show the *expected* frequency of each sum. (A sum of 4 would be expected three times in 36 tosses, a sum of 7 would be expected six times in 36 tosses, etc.) Now compare the results of your two graphs.

C. Design a classroom activity which might be used to introduce probability and statistics to children. Specify the grade level for which the activity is intended.

Relations and Graphs

It is through the study of elementary relations and graphs that the child begins to discover mathematical relationships and ways to illustrate these relationships. These discoveries aid the child in the development of mathematical understanding and rational power, two important goals of elementary school mathematics. The following exercises will acquaint you with some elementary relations and ways of illustrating these relations.

I. *Objectives:* Upon completion of these laboratory exercises, you should be able to do the following:
   A. Design activities which might be used to help a child learn the fundamentals of graphing mathematical relations. (Chapter Competencies 13-F and 14-G)
   B. Design an instructional sequence which might be used to introduce a child to the concepts of equality, greater than, and less than. (Chapter Competencies 13-F and 13-G)
   C. Describe appropriate uses of the number line. (Chapter Competencies 13-F and 13-G)

II. *Materials:* Elementary mathematics textbooks at the kindergarten and first-grade level; geoboard (at least 8″ × 8″) and rubber bands

III. *Procedure:*
   A. Read Chapter 13 of *Helping Children Learn Mathematics.* Consult your instructor if you have any questions.
   B. Practice in the plotting of points on the coordinate axes can be gained through the use of a geoboard. The vertices of various geometric figures can be given by ordered pairs, and the child can then give the name of the figure.

   Using the geoboard as pictured here, tell what geometric figures are formed by each of the following sets of ordered pairs.

   1. (1,3), (2,4), (5,7)   _____
   2. (1,1), (2,2), (3,3), (4,4)   _____
   3. (2,3), (2,6), (4,3), (4,6)   _____
   4. (2,2), (7,2), (4,6), (6,6)   _____

   Give an example of another activity which might be used to help a child develop the skill of plotting points on coordinate axes.
   C. Design an instructional sequence of activities that *you* would use to help a child learn the concepts of equality, greater than, and less than. You may wish to consult an elementary textbook series to see what it provides in this area.
   D. With some classmates, identify three situations at each level, K–3 and 4–6, in which a number line may be used to help a child learn specific concept(s). State the concept to be learned in each situation. Discuss your situations with other groups of classmates. Does each situation lend itself to the use of the number line? Why or why not?

14
Computer and Calculator Literacy

Teacher Competencies

After reading Chapter 14 and completing Laboratory 14, you should be able to achieve each of the following:

    A. Describe what is meant by the terms "computer literacy" and "calculator literacy." (Part Competency II-A)

    B. Describe various instructional uses for the microcomputer and the hand-held calculator. (Part Competency III-C)

    C. Describe the criteria for the selection of appropriate microcomputer hardware and software and the calculator. (Part Competency II-C)

The period of the past few years has seen the rapid growth of technology, especially in the areas of the microcomputer and the hand-held calculator. This growth has been so rapid because of the decreasing cost of purchasing these tools. The number of homes which own one or more microcomputers and/or calculators continues to increase daily.

The impact of microcomputers and calculators on the nation's schools has been tremendous. While many classroom teachers resisted (and still do) the use of the calculator, the microcomputer has "opened the flood gates" to the point that many (if not most) teachers now recognize that both tools are here to stay.

This chapter will deal with computer and calculator literacy. Because tools are often used inappropriately, the chapter will also discuss the appropriate classroom use of both the microcomputer and the hand-held calculator as well as criteria for the selection of each.

COMPUTER LITERACY

There is much talk today of computer literacy and the growing need for students to become computer literate in order to be adequately prepared for the future demands of society. There is not general agreement among experts in the field as to what constitutes computer literacy but all agree that it is an important goal of education at all levels.

Simply stated, computer literacy means being aware of the computer, its operation and uses, what it can do and what it cannot do. It means being aware that the computer is *not* able to think for itself, a popular myth for many people. It also means being aware that the computer is a very useful tool for some tasks but quite inappropriate for others.

There are several components of computer literacy. To be computer literate, a person must have knowledge of the basic parts of the computer, how it operates, its uses and misuses, simple programming techniques, computer occupations, and the history and development of the computer industry. These components should form the basis for a unit on computer literacy which may be used in the classroom.

It seems appropriate here to briefly discuss what topics might be included in each of the five components of computer literacy listed above. Obviously, the level of depth depends upon the children's grade level and previous exposure to computers.

Basic Parts and Operation of the Computer

As children learn about the basic parts and operation of a computer, they should recognize that the basic purpose for using a computer is to solve problems. To solve problems, the computer must be told what to do and when to do it. In order to perform the task of solving problems, the computer must receive instructions and data (input), process the input (central processing unit), and give the results (output).

Each of the three main parts of a computer is needed to solve problems. The diagram below shows the main parts of the computer. The arrows indicate direction in which information flows within the computer.

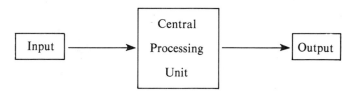

Figure 14.1.

After input is given to the computer, it is acted upon by the computer following the set of prescribed instructions called a *program* which was given to the computer through input. After the computer has processed the program and data the results are given through the output.

The central processing unit (CPU) has three parts as shown in the diagram below. *Control* decides whether the input should go to *memory* for storage or to *arithmetic/logic* for calculators. The program tells control what to do with the data and when to do it. When the instructions for processing the data have been completed, control sends the results to output.

How does the computer operate to solve a problem? Once it has been decided that the computer is the appropriate tool to solve the problem, a program must be written in a language that the computer can understand such as BASIC, COBOL or any one of many other languages. Before

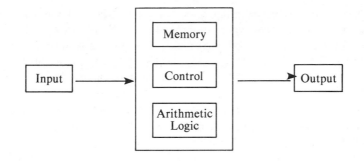

Figure 14.2.

the program is written, a *flowchart (discussed later in this section)* is often prepared. The flowchart is a map of the step-by-step procedures which will be used to solve the problem and is useful in being sure that the proper instruction occurs at the proper time in the problem-solving process.

Once the program has been written, it is sent to the CPU along with data needed to give the desired results. The CPU translates the language of the program into *machine language* (zeroes and ones) for processing. The control checks for syntactical errors which must be corrected before processing can begin. If all is correct, processing occurs and the results are given to output.

Computer Uses and Misuses

As children learn about the uses and misuses of the computer, there will be many opportunities to relate this area to everyday life. New applications are being discovered daily.

How does society use the computer? The bank keeps track of money with the computer; it also prints statements of monthly balances for savings and checking accounts. Department store billing and inventory records are done by computers, especially in larger stores. Cash registers in grocery stores tell the clerk how much change should be received and sometimes the registers actually count it out. A doctor uses the computer to help diagnose illness and it may indicate what medicine should be prescribed. Law enforcement officials make heavy use of the computer in their work. And, of course, all levels of government use the computer for their handling of data including tax returns. Machines in many industrial plants operate automatically; the automation is possible because of a computer program. Even some of the larger commercial airplanes take off and land by using a computer program rather than a pilot. There are thousands of other examples which could be included in the instructional unit.

Education is beginning to make greater use of the computer both for instructional and record-keeping purposes. Student records are kept on a computer in many school systems and in almost all colleges. Transcripts and report cards are printed by a computer program.

In the classroom, Computer-Assisted Instruction (CAI) has been introduced in recent years. CAI allows a student to sit at a terminal and interact with a computer. The computer is programmed to help the student learn something and is often able to adjust instruction according to student response. Computer-Managed Instruction (CMI) is a system for the use of the computer in management aspects of teaching. For example, daily and weekly records of student performance on quizzes and homework may be kept on the computer.

Data processing has become an integral part of most industrial operations today. The computer is able to organize and analyze vast amounts of data and return it to the user in nearly any form desired. This task often could not be physically done by people or it would take so long that its results would be of no use. Not only is the task able to be completed, but it usually saves the organization a great deal of money in terms of manpower. Without data processing and the computer, we would never have been able to make our manned space flight.

Unfortunately, there are many ways in which a computer can be misused. There is a great deal of confidential information about many things and people which is stored on computers. This information can be accessed just as easily as it can be stored and, in the hands of unscrupulous people can be very damaging. Passwords and codes are used to try to control this potential danger but there is no guarantee of security. For example, there have been cases where money in a bank has been stolen by someone who transferred funds from one account to another. Complexity of programs and the amount of data involved makes detection of crimes by computers almost impossible to detect and solve.

Many people have the fear that the computer has robbed them of their privacy. So much information about a person, especially on government computers, is on the computer that their fear of access by anyone cannot be disregarded. Information required for credit purposes is so extensive and easily available that privacy is a real problem.

Simple Programming Techniques

A third aspect of computer literacy is the study of simple programming techniques. To be computer literate, a person need not become adept at writing programs (unless he or she desires to do so), but should have some idea of how a program is written up to the point of actually writing the computer language (BASIC, etc.)

The techniques involved in writing a computer program are ones which have applications in other areas of learning. The ability to solve a problem by preparing a step-by-step procedure is a skill that all classroom teachers should strive to develop in their students.

One of the useful skills in this regard is that of *flowcharting*. A flowchart is a diagram or a map of how a particular problem is to be solved. As such, making a flowchart involves the use of some standard symbols which are shown below.

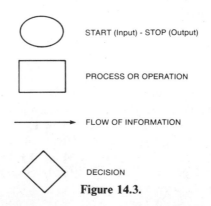

START (Input) - STOP (Output)

PROCESS OR OPERATION

FLOW OF INFORMATION

DECISION

Figure 14.3.

An illustration of the use of a flowchart to solve a problem would be helpful at this point.

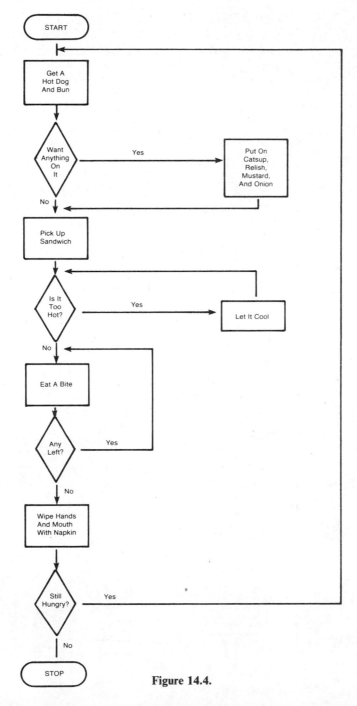

Figure 14.4.

Most people would agree that, in solving the problem of how to eat a hot dog, it would not be necessary to make a flowchart and the authors would agree also. However, this example is a good one to use with children who are trying to develop logical thinking skills.

Here is an illustration of a direct classroom use. Suppose a child is having difficulty remembering the process for addition of two two-digit whole numbers. Having the child make a flowchart and then allowing him or her to use it may give sufficient impetus for the child to commit the algorithm to memory. The flowchart might look like Figure 14.5.

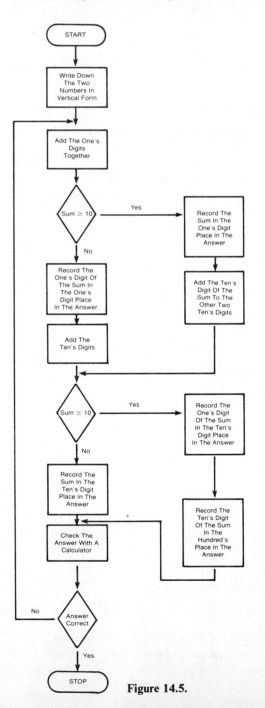

Figure 14.5.

Computer Occupations

The growth of the computer has created many new occupations for people. Some of the occupations require a great deal of training while others require very little. The occupations range from those that deal with the actual operation of the computer to those that deal with the computer as a tool. The number of job openings in the computer field will continue to increase in the next several decades.

Classroom discussions about various computer-related occupations offer an excellent choice for children to become acquainted with this area. Field trips and visits to the classroom from community personnel who work with computers also provide excellent and useful learning experiences for the children.

History and Development of the Computer

From the beginning of time, man has used computers in primitive forms. Fingers were probably the first form used and they were used for counting purposes. The early Chinese and Japanese used the abacus for their computation and, in fact, still use it today.

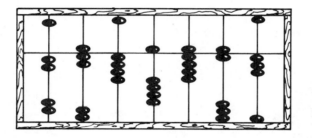

Figure 14.6.

The operations of addition, subtraction, multiplication, and division were invented long before the year 1600, but except for the abacus few computing aids were available. Finally in 1600 some people began to try to build machines that could do arithmetic quickly. These inventions are best illustrated on a time line:

1614   Napier's Bones (Figures 14.7(a)) were sticks that were used for purposes of multiplying two numbers.

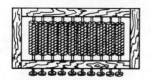

Figure 14.7(a).

Figure 14.7(b).

1620   The slide rule (Figure 14.7(b)) was developed. It used numbers represented by distances on a scale but could be used only for solving multiplication and division problems.

1642   Pascal invented a calculator (Figure 14.8(a)) which could add a column of eight numbers. However, his machine could only perform addition and subtraction.

1671   Leibniz invented a machine (Figure 14.8(b)) which could perform the operations of addition, subtraction, multiplication and division.

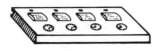

Figure 14.8(a).

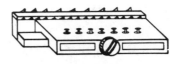

Figure 14.8(b).

1801   Jacquard's loom (Figure 14.9(a)) used punched cards to weave various patterns into fabrics.

1889   Hollerith invented a punch card machine (Figure 14.9(b)) which was a forerunner of the digital computer. The machine could sort, count, and tabulate data from punch cards.

Figure 14.9(a).

Figure 14.9(b).

1944   Aiken's Mark I was developed. It was the first large-scale automatic digital calculator.

1946   The ENIAC computer was developed by Edkart and Maachly. It was designed to develop mathematical tables for firing projectiles. ENIAC was very large in size and used the vacuum tube.

1951   The Universal Automatic Computer (UNIVAC I) was developed. It was the first commercial computer. It was capable of adding two single-digit numbers in 2 micro-seconds and could multiply two single-digit numbers in 10 micro-seconds.

1959   Computers entered their second generation. Computer size became much smaller with the invention of the transistor. The number of computers produced began to increase. FORTRAN was developed as a computer language. Mass storage (2,000,000 characters) became a reality.

1965	Computers entered their third generation. The use of miniature electronic and solid-state circuits made faster, more reliable, and less expensive computers possible. More programming languages were developed.
1970s	Computers entered the fourth generation. The development of microelectronics, manifested in the microcomputer, caused tremendous changes in the industry. Authoring languages began to appear.
1983	There are now more computers (of all types) in the world than there are people.
Future	The future of the computer is very much unknown. Robotics and artificial intelligence loom distinctively with more and more applications.

USING COMPUTERS IN THE CLASSROOM

As was stated in the previous section, one of the major goals of the instructional program should be the development of computer literacy by children. Ideally, there will be access to microcomputers for the computer literacy component, but even if not, the topic should not be ignored. However, the development of computer literacy is not the only use for computers in the classroom. This section will examine other instructional uses for the computer that can be incorporated into the instructional program. This examination, of course, assumes that microcomputers are available for use, either in the classroom or in another location in the building. These uses of the computer in the classroom also depend upon the availability of software, either commercial or teacher-made, and a computer literate teacher.

How can the computer be used in the classroom? It is a popular myth among many people that the computer can be only used with one student at a time. This is just simply not the case. The computer can be used quite well with a small group of children working together or with the entire class; simulation type activities, especially, lend themselves to the latter use. The discussion in this section will focus on the use of the computer in simulation, game and tutorial activities.

Simulations

The term "simulation" means many things to many people so that a precise definition is difficult to agree upon. For purposes of this discussion, a simulation situation is a problem solving situation which can be presented to children for their action and reaction. The situation may be scientific or social in scope and be either real-life or make-believe in nature. Simulation is useful in helping children develop problem solving skills and in giving meaning and relevance to the instructional program.

Simulation activities can be used not only in the mathematics instructional programs but also in other curricular areas. Investigating changes in profit or loss in a manufacturing situation caused by economic and other conditions is an example of a simulation activity which could be used. Looking at the mathematics involved in weather prediction or bank transactions are other examples of simulation. The point is that simulation activities can be an integral part of instruction that will be enjoyable and meaningful to children.

How does the computer help with simulation? The computer can be programmed with a simulation situation to which children can respond and get immediate feedback. Because of its capabilities, the computer can handle simulation situations which are too complex or time-consuming to do by hand. The result will be increased student learning and motivation.

More and more simulation programs on a wide variety of topics are being developed commercially every day. The chances are excellent for finding one or more simulation programs that will fit the children's instructional needs at a reasonable cost. Some teachers have decided to write their own simulation programs with varying degrees of success. Before attempting to undertake this task, be advised that there is a tremendous investment in time and effort needed to successfully write a simulation program for the computer.

Games

When the topic of computer games is mentioned, there is always mixed parent and teacher reaction as to their educational value. The authors believe that computer games, properly used, can have a very positive influence on students. The points for using computer games successfully in the classroom are essentially the same as for general games, a topic discussed in Chapter 5. The following reasons strongly support the use of computer games in the classroom:

1. Students like them.
2. Games can help develop thinking and decision-making skills.
3. Games can be used to introduce new ideas and skills.
4. Games can be played in groups which can emphasize collective group effort to solve a problem situation.
5. Games can be used to spark an interest by your students in a new area.

There are literally millions of computer games commercially available today. Choose a game carefully and the results will be positive.

Tutorial

A third use for computers in the classroom is with tutorial activities. As the term "tutorial" implies, these types of activities can be used to either help a student acquire a new skill or maintain an already-existing one through drill and practice. There have been many forms of tutorial learning programs which utilize the computer introduced over the years, including, among others, Computer-Assisted Instruction (CAI) and Computer-Assisted Learning (CAL).

The primary advantage of tutorial programs is that a one-to-one teaching situation is provided for the student that can be completed at his or her own rate. These programs usually include good audio and visual stimuli and, while not as effective as the human teacher, do provide a good alternative for many students.

As with simulation and game activities, there are many commercial tutorial programs available. Good professional judgment will be required by teachers so that appropriate choices can be made for students.

A Final Word

Ideally, the availability of microcomputers will be such that one machine will be available for every two or three children. Realistically, the ideal situation will probably not occur. Many activities related to computer literacy can still be used in the classroom even though a limited number of microcomputers (or none for that matter) is available; ideas for such activities may be found in books, journals, or conversation with classroom teachers.

SELECTING COMPUTER HARDWARE AND SOFTWARE

Selecting appropriate computer hardware and software is of paramount importance to the successful use of computers in the classroom. The selection process is time-consuming but, properly done, will pay rich dividends.

Selecting Hardware

Selecting appropriate hardware is not an easy task. In some sense, the selection task is analogous to that of selecting a new automobile. There are a great many brands and types of microcomputers available and one can literally spend as much money as desired. Remember that microcomputers sales are highly competitive so beware of sales personnel; take your time and shop wisely.

When purchasing a microcomputer, there are several steps that need to be followed:

1. Identify the objectives of the learning environment (who will be the audience—what are the skills to be learned?).
2. Identify the necessary content/presentation modes (audio/visual, motion/still, illustrative/verbal, etc.).
3. Identify constraints (economy, learner, physical facility, qualified teacher availability).
4. Identify features of the microcomputer in terms of *must* have, *should* have, and *like to* have.
5. Select the microcomputer based on the information gathered in steps 1 through 4.

These five steps will give a systematic approach to the selection of the appropriate hardware.

Some of the features alluded to in Step 4 above might include such things as the following:

1. color
2. audio
3. voice recognition
4. touch panel (light pen) input
5. printer
6. graphics output/input
7. alternative character sets
8. music
9. memory size (RAM and ROM)
10. external memory (cassette/disk drive)

Priorities relative to features must be established as *must* have, *should* have, and *like to* have.

As you are pondering the available information about the various microcomputers there are features about the microcomputer which must be considered. Information about these features can be gained from brochures and sales personnel but talking to other people who have knowledge of or have purchased the equipment may be the most beneficial. Some of the qualities to consider include:

1. durability/reliability
2. memory expandability
3. interface capability with other brands of input/output devices
4. simplicity of operation
5. memory size
6. keyboard type (touch panel or key)
7. availability of software and documentation support by the manufacturer
8. output quality of text and/or graphics
9. availability of local service

There are two common errors made by purchasers of microcomputers. One is the failure to recognize that microcomputers are machines and must therefore be routinely maintained (at additional cost). More than one school corporation has purchased microcomputers and failed to budget money for maintenance and repair. The result is that an expensive piece of equipment lies idle because there is no money for repair.

The other error occurs when random-access-memory (RAM) is too small to be useful. The latter error usually occurs because of a desire to lower the cost of purchase. While this is understandable, we recommend that RAM size be at least 48 to 64 kilobytes. A smaller RAM eliminates the opportunity of using many programs because they are too long.

Selecting the appropriate hardware is not an easy task. It is time-consuming at best. But, properly done, the shopping efforts will be greatly rewarded, both in usability and enjoyment.

Selecting Software

We have mentioned earlier about the importance of software availability relative to the selection of hardware. The usefulness of the hardware selected will only be as good as the software selected. The hardware can do nothing without software.

The selection of software involves much of the same type of consideration given to selection of a textbook or other supplementary instructional materials. The major obstacle that will be encountered is the reluctance of commercial software companies to let software be previewed before purchase. Their reluctance is understandable because of the ease of copying a preview program, a problem that does not exist with textbooks or other instructional materials.

The only ways to overcome the previewing obstacle are to seek software products that can be evaluated at a local store or to consult independent evaluation groups for their opinions. Quite frankly, there is a proliferation of "garbage" software on the market so you must be very careful before you pay good money. This money will not usually be refunded once you break the seal on the disk. Be sure to check return provisions *before* the purchase is made.

When the opportunity to preview and evaluate software programs is available before purchase, there are several criteria which should be considered. For ease of application the criteria can be divided into three classes; technical, educational, and management.[1]

The technical area deals with software as it relates to the microcomputer and its execution of the software. The following questions should be asked about the technical area.

1. Does the software utilize the microcomputer's capabilities?

A good piece of software is one that does something different, because of the microcomputer, which would not normally be done otherwise. For example, a simple drill sheet in which the child simply gives the answers is not really an appropriate exercise for microcomputer software. However, if the software gives immediate feedback and/or branches to a tutorial situation, then the software is using the unique capabilities of the microcomputer.

2. Is the software "bomb proof?"

Good software should provide for student responses other than the correct response. These responses should branch meaningfully to another part of the software program that will assist the student in "getting back on track."

3. Does the software have pleasing graphics and/or sound reproduction?

Nothing will turn children off more quickly than graphics or audio provided by the software that are not pleasant to see or hear. A flickering screen or raspy audio is sometimes found on software. Another problem commonly encountered is software time delays that do not give adequate time for the child to read a message on the screen before the software progresses on to the next phase. Similarly, software that takes too long to respond with screen feedback is equally distasteful to the child.

The educational area relates to the educational quality of the software. Of course, software that is not educationally sound will be of no benefit whatsoever. The following questions should be asked about the educational area.

1. Is the software educationally correct?

Many times software has incorrect grammar, spelling, or mathematical mistakes. Some software will develop a concept or skill in a sequence that is not appropriate. Avoid software that is not educationally correct.

2. Does the software provide assistance to the child in understanding incorrect answers?

Some software will simply tell the child that a response is incorrect with no help or explanation. Good software guides the child towards a correct response.

3. Does the software specify necessary prerequisite concepts and skills needed by the child who is using it?

It is not always obvious what prerequisites and skills are needed by the child to use the software successfully. Be sure you can determine what the prerequisites are and that the child has had those prerequisites before using the software. A lot of frustration will be avoided if this is done first.

4. Does the software have clear and appropriate objective(s)?

The software objectives should be clearly stated. Also, the objectives should be appropriate for the instructional program. If the objectives are not appropriate, the software will not be of use to the child.

---

1. From *A Survival Guide for the Junior High/Middle School Mathematics Teacher,* by Gregory R. Baur, Ed.D., and Darleen Pigford, Ph.D., pp. 247–249. © 1984 by Parker Publishing Company, Inc., West Nyack, New York.

5. Does the software encourage learning through feedback?

One of the main advantages of a microcomputer as a learning tool is that it can give immediate feedback to a child's response. But, this feedback must encourage the child to continue. Positive feedback is the kind to look for.

The management area is concerned with how easily the software can be used in a classroom situation. Software that cannot be easily managed in a teaching situation will be of no help. The following questions should be asked about the management area.

1. Does the software have directions that are easy to understand and follow?

The directions should be easy to understand and follow for *both* teacher and child. Confusion about directions causes frustration and negates any instructional benefits the software might have had.

2. Does the software assist in tracking a child's progress?

It is very helpful if the software gives a summary at the end (of its use) of how well the child performed. This summary will give beneficial feedback to the child and also assist the teacher in assessing a child's performance.

3. Is the software flexible so as to meet different learner needs?

Software that has different levels of difficulty that can be chosen by the child will be of most benefit to the instructional program.

A Final Word

Selecting appropriate hardware and software is the key to the successful use of the microcomputer in the classroom. Common sense and wise comparison techniques will help you get the most appropriate equipment for the money.

CALCULATOR LITERACY

There are many parents and teachers who do not believe that students should be allowed to use the hand-held calculator in the classroom. They believe that no mathematics will be learned and that the students will do nothing more than "learn to punch buttons." In addition, students will, they believe, become "mentally lazy" and their education will be less than adequate.

There is a distinct possibility that the above concerns are valid *IF* there is no careful effort made by the classroom teaching in planning the use of the hand-held calculator and in choosing activities for the calculator.

As with computer literacy, there is lack of widespread agreement among educators as to the meaning of calculator literacy. In a broad sense, it probably means that a person has a knowledge and understanding of the functions (keys) on the calculator as well as the use of the calculator as a tool to solve problems.

USING CALCULATORS IN THE CLASSROOM

As a teaching tool, the hand-held calculator can be invaluable. But it is like any other tool—it can be greatly misused.

One use of the calculator in the classroom that is accepted by a growing number of teachers is the checking of work done by paper-and-pencil. There are several advantages for this use:

1. Teachers need not check every answer on a student's paper.
2. Students receive immediate feedback and reinforcement.
3. Students may build self-confidence by being able to check work for accuracy before it is turned in to the teacher.

Another use of the calculator is in helping children "debug" problems in which they have a wrong answer. For example, in a multiplication or division problem, the child can use the calculator to check each of the individual steps. This use also helps reinforce the process or algorithm for solving the problem.

A third use of the calculator is with problems involving the application of a formula to solve the problem. Allowing the child to use the calculator in these types of situations does not force the use of tedious and time-consuming computation. The child is thus free to concentrate on the problem to be solved and the application of the formula. The child should, of course, demonstrate an understanding of the formula and how it works before being allowed to use the calculator in the manner described.

Some teachers have used calculators as a motivational device. Children are allowed to "mess around" with the calculator when they have earned some free time. Such spontaneous play with a calculator has a place in the very beginning but there is better use for the free time. If such play is considered important, then include *all* of the children in some carefully planned activities which utilize this play.

To effectively use calculators, there are at least four areas in which children need to develop skills. Among others, these areas include:

1. Problem Solving: Children need problem solving skills such as those listed in Chapter 16. It is very easy for children to become involved in using a calculator in a problem which they do not understand. For example, they must be able to interpret the meaning of a negative number when a greater number is subtracted from a lesser number. The calculator is of no use if children do not have a sense of the problem and the solution.
2. Estimation: Children must be able to estimate if they are to effectively use the calculator. For some reason, many children have developed a "blind faith" in the calculator; whatever answer is shown on the display must be correct because "calculators don't make mistakes." They do not realize that there may have been a mistake in entering data on the calculator. If they have good estimation skills, such mistakes will nearly always be caught. A calculator with a weak battery may give faulty answers but, with proper maintenance procedures, such a mistake should almost never occur.
3. Decimals: Children must be proficient with all phases of decimals including the reading, writing, and understanding of decimal notation. The ability to change fractions to decimals is also important because many application problems from everyday life will contain fractions. The use of rounding is also a part of a child's work with decimals. There is seldom a need to report all eight digits shown on the display and children must be able to round to whatever accuracy is required.

4. Place Value: Skill in working with place value is important in all operations at all levels of mathematics. On the calculator, a child can check the expanded form of a number by listing digits with the appropriate number of zeros after them and then performing whatever operation desired.

SELECTING A CALCULATOR

As with the microcomputer, the selection of calculators for the classroom is important. The cost of calculators has decreased dramatically in recent years to the point that one or two classroom sets is quite affordable for an elementary school.

Obviously, the type of calculator purchased is dependent upon its predetermined use. But some general pointers[2] are useful and apply to almost any need.

1. For most purposes, the four basic operations (addition, subtraction, multiplication, and division) with whole numbers are all that are needed. Other desirable functions might include memory and clear entry. Some calculators will display fractions rather than converting the number to the decimal format.

With respect to the display, it should be readable even when the classroom lights are on. It should also be clearly indicated on the display if an "overflow" situation has occurred. Also, the display should accommodate at least eight digits and should have a floating (rather than a fixed) decimal point.

Physically, the calculator should have a hard, durable case that is not likely to break easily. An automatic shut-off switch is very desirable to combat the situation in which someone accidentally leaves the calculator on for a long period of time. Long-life batteries or a recharge unit that plugs into an electrical wall socket will ensure that the calculator will be operational when needed.

The structure and make-up of the keyboard must be considered. The keys should be fairly large, raised, and well-spaced so that small hands can press them easily. The symbol designation on the key should be notched into the key surface; decal designations tend to wear off through use. It is also desirable that each key represent exactly one function so that confusion does not result.

Finally, a calculator that uses algebraic logic is preferable to one that does not. By algebraic logic, we mean that a problem such as 34 + 98 is entered into the calculator as 34, +, 98, = in order to get the sum. Some calculators enter the problem as 34, 98, + but this is contrary to the way most children think.

While most calculators have all or almost all of the qualities mentioned above, do check out all these features on the calculator before the purchase is made.

CHAPTER KEY POINTS

1. Computer literacy means being aware of the computer, its operations and uses, what it can do and what it cannot do.

2. Ibid. pp. 222–4.

2. To be computer literate, a person must have knowledge of:
   a. the basic parts and operations of the computer,
   b. its uses and misuses,
   c. simple programming techniques,
   d. computer occupations, and
   e. history and development of the computer industry.

3. Computers may be used in the classroom with one student, a small group, or the entire class.

4. Activities that may be used with a computer in the classroom include:
   a. simulation,
   b. games, and
   c. tutorial.

5. In selecting a computer:
   a. identify the objectives,
   b. identify necessary content/presentation modes,
   c. identify constraints,
   d. identify features of the computer that are in terms of *must* have, *should* have, and *like to* have; therefore,
   e. select a computer based upon the information from the first four items above.

6. Software should be evaluated for possible purchase in the technical, educational, and management areas.

7. Calculator literacy means a knowledge and understanding of the functions (keys) of the calculator and its use as a tool for problem solving.

8. Calculators may be used to:
   a. check work done by paper-and-pencil,
   b. "debug" problems, and
   c. solve problems which involve the application of formulas.

9. Using calculators involves certain prerequisite skills in the areas of:
   a. problem solving,
   b. estimation,
   c. decimals, and
   d. place value.

Laboratory 14

Microcomputers and Hand-held Calculators

The use of microcomputers and hand-held calculators in the classroom has become much greater in recent years and no doubt will continue to increase. Children need to learn at an early age how to use these tools to solve problems.

I. Objectives: Upon completion of these laboratory exercises, you should be able to do the following:

A. Describe what is meant by the terms "computer literacy" and "calculator literacy." (Chapter Competency A)

B. Describe various uses in the classroom of the microcomputer and the hand-held calculator. (Chapter Competency B)

C. Describe criteria which might be used in selecting microcomputer hardware and software and the hand-held calculator. (Chapter Competency C)

II. Materials: None

III. Procedure:

A. Read Chapter 14 of *Helping Children Learn Mathematics*. Consult your instructor if you have any questions.

B. Examine current periodical literature for articles on computer literacy programs for the elementary school. What are the components of the programs? How do these components differ (if at all) from the five components of computer literacy described in the chapter? What components of computer literacy would you include in YOUR instructional program? Why? Does your college or university require (or offer) a course in computer literacy for teachers and/or other students? If not, why not? What could you do to help implement such a course?

C. Examine periodical literature to find articles discussing the use of microcomputers and hand-held calculators in the classroom. Do you find common uses described? What are they? Inquire in local school systems (or buildings) to find out how (if at all) microcomputers and calculators are being used. Do you find uses not described in your reading and vice versa? What are they? Assume that you have microcomputers and hand-held calculators at your disposal for classroom use. What uses would YOU make of these tools?

D. Develop a rationale for the use of microcomputers and hand-held calculators in the classroom that could be presented to:

   a. parents

   b. school administrators

   c. school board

   d. fellow teachers

   Would your rationale differ from group to group? Why/Why not?

E. Do YOU believe that microcomputers and hand-held calculators are useful teaching aids? Why?/Why not?

F. Based upon the criteria presented in the chapter, investigate sources for the purchase of microcomputer hardware and software and hand-held calculators. Which criteria do you feel are most important? Why? If you were to purchase for a school (or yourself), which product(s) would you purchase? Why?

15
Problem Solving

Teacher Competencies

After studying Chapter 15 and completing Laboratory 15, you should be able to:

   A. Identify suitable problem solving situations. (Part Competency III-D)

   B. Establish a problem solving environment in the classroom. (Part Competency III-D)

   C. State the four phases of a general problem solving strategy. (Part Competency III-D)

   D. Identify specific tools and techniques which may be used in problem solving. (Part Competency III-D)

   E. Incorporate textbook word problems effectively in the classroom. (Part Competency III-D)

Problem solving must be the focus of school mathematics in the 1980s.[1]

Learning to solve problems is the principle reason for studying mathematics.[2]

Results of the Priorities in School Mathematics (PRISM) survey and recent curricular recommendations by the National Council of Teachers of Mathematics indicate that problem solving should be the focus of mathematics education in this decade.[3]

P roblem solving is a major concern of mathematics education. While problem solving has long been recognized as important, the need to teach computational ability often took precedence in the past, thereby leading to the neglect of problem solving. Some people assumed that problem

1. *An Agenda for Action: Recommendations for School Mathematics of the 1980s,* National Council of Teachers of Mathematics, 1980, p. 2.
2. "National Council of Supervisors of Mathematics Position Paper on Basic Skills," *Arithmetic Teacher,* October 1977, p. 20.
3. Carole E. Greenes and Linda Schulman, "Developing Problem-Solving Ability with Multiple-Condition Problems," *Arithmetic Teacher,* October 1982, p. 18.

solving ability would be a natural by-product of learning how to compute. Others knew that it was a learned skill, but there was no agreement as to how that skill was best taught.

According to the results of standardized tests, whatever problem solving practices were used in the past have not been as effective as they should have been. Perhaps the most convincing results are evident in the 1978 National Assessment of Educational Progress in mathematics which showed a lack of even the most basic problem solving skills by those participating. Also, a comparison of the 1972 and 1978 results revealed that while computational proficiency increased among 9- and 13-year olds, there appeared to be a decline in performance on applications and problem solving by the same age groups.

Clearly, the teaching of problem solving needs to be approached with renewed vigor. Research and practice have revealed strategies and techniques which work. It is time to get effective problem solving practices into every classroom.

First, let's clarify what is meant by the term, "problem solving." *Problem solving is the process of utilizing previously acquired knowledge in the resolution of new and unfamiliar situations.* While problem solving can be variously referred to as a skill, a process, or a goal, most educators will agree that it is the process which should be our primary focus. Note also that problem solving involves the resolving of unfamiliar situations through the application of knowledge already attained. There is uncertainty involved; an immediate answer is not obvious. The problem solver is required to search actively for an answer using various problem solving strategies which he has learned.

It may be inferred from these statements that a problem for one student may not be a problem for another. One student may never have encountered the problem situation before and so must search for a solution; for another student, however, the situation has become an exercise because he has dealt with the same problem type before.

Also, in the strictest sense, problem solving is not synonymous with application problems, even though some people use the terms interchangeably. Applications problems include all USES of mathematics, while problem solving must satisfy the requirements as stated earlier. Of course, there are applications which also satisfy the requirements for problem solving situations, and vice versa.

In this chapter we will examine problem solving in the classroom environment. We will discuss both general strategies and specific tools and techniques to help children learn how to solve problems.

PROBLEM SOLVING IN THE CLASSROOM

Several abilities have been identified as characteristic of good problem solvers. Among these characteristics are the ability to understand concepts and terms, to estimate, and to note irrelevant detail as well as to identify important elements. Other characteristics of value are the ability to utilize problem solving techniques and strategies and to be flexible in approaching problem solutions. Lastly, the problem solvers themselves should be free from anxiety, be confident in their ability to attack a problem and solve it, and feel motivated to do so. The classroom environment is critical in fostering these problem solving characteristics in children, and the teacher is primarily responsible for creating such an environment.

Establishing a problem solving classroom environment requires three points of focus: (1) the teacher as a model problem solver, (2) the teacher as a manager of problem solving activities, and (3) the teacher as a selector and presenter of problems.

1. *The teacher as a model problem solver.* Children learn by example, and working with a teacher who has become a proficient problem solver provides an excellent model of performance. Instead of children floundering negatively alone and without direction, they and the teacher work together as the process of solving problems is learned. The children see first-hand the value of learning global strategies and specific techniques. As they work with the teacher, they note that he or she actually does such things as estimate, sort out relevant data, and draw diagrams. As teacher and children work together making "educated guesses," testing results, and using what they learn to persist until they arrive at a solution, the children will gain confidence in their own ability to solve problems.

2. *The teacher as a manager of problem solving abilities.* The teacher is responsible for establishing a positive, active, nonpunitive atmosphere in the classroom. The students should feel free to explore and to make an "educated guess" with no penalty for mistakes. Usually by analyzing and testing an incorrect answer at least some further information can be gained to help in finding the correct answer. Encourage any effort which may lead to a solution.

As manager of problem solving activities the teacher must take the responsibility for actually teaching the process of problem solving. Don't just assign and check problems. Guide the children by asking information-revealing questions about the problem situation; help them to begin to ask these same questions themselves. As the students gain facility at solving problems, their involvement will increase and teacher involvement will decrease.

The teacher must also manage time in problem solving, both long range and short range. First, time pressures should not be a factor in problem solving sessions. Children should have ample time to understand, ponder, try, and reflect without worrying about rigid time constraints. Also in the time arena is a longer range concern—that of class-time allotment. Some advocate as much as a double period of problem solving each week. They contend that this extended period will remove the time pressure and will allow more concentrated effort. Others prefer that some time every day be devoted to learning problem solving techniques, thereby continuing the effort over an extended time.

3. *The teacher as a selector and presenter of problems.* The care with which problems are selected and presented is a factor in the success of problem solving in the classroom.

Motivational appeal is important in the selection of problems. Students will be more likely to persist in the solution of a problem if they feel a need or a desire to do so. They can be motivated to solve problems which represent either real-life or interesting situations to them. Real-life problems, or applications, can range from figuring change after a purchase to calculating a batting average. Interesting problems can extend beyond the practical and even into the whimsical, fun range.

Problems should be selected which best match student problem solving ability. If the problem is too easy it becomes a calculation exercise and is no longer a problem according to the definition given earlier in this chapter. On the other hand, if the problem is so difficult that there is little chance for a solution, the student learns only failure. Success, however, begets success. Students who have experienced success and who believe they can solve problems will meet a new challenge and persist until they meet that sweet success found on earlier encounters.

Problems should be selected and presented so that children can learn and practice each specific problem solving technique in a variety of situations. Moderately vary the types of solution required—not too many or too few at a time. Use regular patterns of solution as children expand their repertoire of techniques from which to draw in solving problems.

Last, problems should be presented in more than one medium. Before children can solve any problem they must understand it. By presenting a problem through various means the teacher increases each child's opportunity for understanding. Problems can be presented orally in class or they can be placed on a tape recorder for private or small group listening. The problems can be written or diagrammed on the chalkboard or the overhead projector.

Suggestions for creating a classroom environment conducive to good problem solving have been made. Several allusions to teaching general strategies and specific techniques for problem solving have also been made. The next two sections will be devoted to describing these various strategies and techniques.

A GENERAL PROBLEM SOLVING STRATEGY

Children need the security that comes with the knowledge of a general strategy for solving problems. This general strategy provides a framework for the solution of any problem. It minimizes the need for wild guesses on the part of some children, and at the same time it minimizes the chance of total inactivity that results from other children "not knowing where to begin."

George Polya has studied the process of problem solving for decades. Long considered a master teacher of problem solving, Polya teaches by example. As he works with his learners, he assumes two distinct roles: teacher and commentator. As a teacher he works with the pupils, asking leading questions and suggesting strategies. At times, however, he steps back from the work just completed and discusses it as an outside observer, a commentator. As a teacher he helps the children to solve particular problems, while as a commentator he helps the children study and reflect upon what they have done and then place that learning within the larger framework of problem solving.

Polya has developed a four-phase procedure for problem solving which has proven to be both sound and rather simple to use. The general steps to the solution of any problem are: (1) understand the problem, (2) devise a plan, (3) carry out the plan, and (4) examine the solution.[4]

Teaching children how to use the plan in the solution of problems involves more than the enumeration of steps though. Children must be provided with a thorough understanding of exactly what each phase involves. Each child must also learn to guide his or her own thinking and question asking in the search for a solution. An example of a problem and the kinds of questions and comments which a teacher/commentator might make follows.

Problem Situation: James invited 9 friends to his pizza party. He figured that each person would eat 4 pieces of pizza. If the pizzas are to be cut into sixths, how many pizzas should he order?

Steps in the Solution

1. *Understand the problem.* At this point the teacher wants to pose questions about the facts in the problem and about the questions asked. Relevant data should be sifted from irrelevant data.

4. George Polya, *How to Solve It: A New Aspect of Mathematical Method,* Princeton University Press, 1973.

Relationships and any additional information necessary to the solution of the problem should be discussed. Questions like these would be appropriate during this phase of problem solving.

    a. What kind of party is James having?
    b. How many people will be at the party? Did you remember to count James?
    c. How many pieces of pizza will each person get? Do you think everyone will eat exactly the same, or is this an approximation?
    d. How will the pizzas be divided?
    e. What do we want to find out?
    f. Now can you tell me in your own words what this problem is about?

2. *Devise a plan.* Once the problem has been interpreted a course of action must be decided upon. The problem solver must choose a plan of attack. Any one or a combination of techniques described in the next section may be used. The teacher may have to make some initial suggestions but contributions from class members should be encouraged. In the role of commentator, it is often advisable to step back and examine various procedures and label them. These questions might be asked during this phase of solution of the example.

    a. Has anyone solved a problem similar to this one before?
    b. Could we make up a problem like this one but which has easier numbers in it? For example, what if there were 4 people at the party, each person had 2 pieces, and the pizzas were cut into fourths? What could you do to find the solution?
    c. Does anyone have another idea about how to solve it? You think that drawing a picture of the cut-up pizzas and the party-goers might help, Brandon? It might. Let's try it.
    d. Is there another suggestion?
    e. Is there more than one part to this problem? Does it matter which part we solve first? What operation might we use?

3. *Carry out the plan.* Now the chosen plan is put into effect. If it leads to a dead end, then an alternative procedure must be incorporated. Otherwise, the original plan is implemented toward that plan.

4. *Examine the solution.* This phase involves looking back at the whole process and reflecting on the problem, alternative procedures, and the solution. These questions would be appropriate.

    a. Is your answer reasonable?
    b. Shannon, would you be able to order 2/3 of a pizza? What must be done with any remainders?
    c. What method did you use to solve the problem?
    d. How might we check this problem?
    e. Is there any part of the solution which doesn't "fit" with the original facts?
    f. Let's extend this problem. If each pizza cost $5.00, how much was the bill for pizzas at this party?

Now that a general strategy for problem solving has been suggested, let's turn to that part of the strategy which involves devising a plan. To devise such a plan the problem solver must know a wide variety of specific problem solving techniques.

SPECIFIC TOOLS AND TECHNIQUES FOR PROBLEM SOLVING

The general strategies for problem solving described earlier provide a framework from which to work. In addition, however, the problem solver must also know how to incorporate a variety of specific problem solving tools and techniques within this general framework. Should one tool or technique not yield results, the child should feel confident that there is another resource available. Also various tools and techniques can be used in conjunction with one another as well as separately to find a solution to any given problem. Here are several tools and techniques which have proven effective in problem solving. Sample problem situations suitable for solution by each given tool or technique are included.

1. *Manipulative aids.* Just as manipulative aids are important in the initial learning of various aspects of mathematics, so also are they valuable tools to aid in the understanding of problem situations. Manipulative aids can mean anything from bottle caps to tape measures to colored rods. Here are two problem situations which may utilize manipulatives in their solution.

> *Problem situation:* For the very young child equipped with a milk carton "train" and tongue depressor "people," a whole range of problem solving activities becomes possible. For example, a child with a two-car train and seven people can be asked to do these things: (1) Put 3 people in the front of the train and 4 people in the back of the train. How many people are in the train? Take these people for a ride in the train. (2) Now change the people around in the train. How many people do you have in the front of the train? In the back? How many people are in the train altogether? (3) Make the train a different way. (4) Find as many ways as you can to make a seven person train.

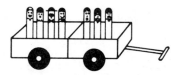

> *Problem situation:* A train engine is to be followed by five cars. How many different ways can the train be put together? (Use the colored rods to represent the different cars on the train and manipulate them to formulate an answer. By the way this problem lends itself well to solution by simplification and pattern formation also.)

2. *Diagrams and pictures.* Some children will prefer to draw diagrams or pictures to help them solve problems. Manipulatives help to illustrate movement and relationships. If these are already clear to the problem solver, then diagrams or pictures may be all that are needed to help visualize a problem such as the one below.

> Problem situation: Jeff has 6 marbles. Mary gives him 3 marbles. How many marbles does Jeff now have?

3. *Lists, charts, tables, and patterns.* Generating a table, chart, list, or pattern can be the best way to search for some solutions.

> *Problem situation:* Here are some representations of triangular numbers. What would the sixth triangular number be? (A pattern search is involved here.)

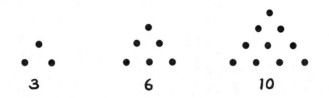

3   6   10

> *Problem situation:* David wants to make a pen for his pet dog. He has only 50 feet of fencing and four posts. What should the dimensions of his pen be if he wants to provide his pet with as much room as possible? (As David considers possible measurements he generates a table showing perimeter and area relationships.)

4. *Calculators.* The actual computation involved in problem solving can sometimes bog students down in details. Using a calculator enables the problem solver to focus on the processes involved. Its use also enables problem solvers to attack problems beyond their normal range of endeavor because of complex numbers or lengthy series of calculations. Since calculators are readily available and are used often by the general public, it would seem logical to incorporate them as a tool in solving problems such as the ones in the problem situations given below. Notice that the activities involve either complicated numbers or numerous calculations.

> *Problem situation:* You are going to carpet your living room. It measures 14.5 feet by 20.5 feet. The carpeting you want costs $15.99 a square yard. Use your calculator to find out how much it will cost to carpet your room.

> *Problem situation:* Using the second hand on the clock on the wall, take your pulse. How often does your heart beat in 15 seconds? Now use your calculator to help you find how often your heart beats in one minute, in an hour, in a day, and in a year.

5. *Math sentences.* The ability to translate a mathematical situation into a mathematical sentence often turns problems into solutions. In the past the technique was sometimes postponed until algebra was studied. Simple translations are within the reach of most children, however, and the technique can become one of the most used at an early age.

> *Problem situation:* On a math test $\frac{1}{3}$ of the class made a perfect score. If the class had 24 children in it, how many children scored perfectly? (First, restate the problem succinctly: One third of 24 children is the number who made a perfect score. Then write a number sentence for that situation: $\frac{1}{3} \times 24 = ?$)

6. *Simulation and role playing.* Sometimes a problem is best understood when it is acted out or dramatized. Sometimes, too, the actual solution can be found by letting the children role play and actually do the problem.

Problem situation: If every person at a party shakes hands with every other person, how many handshakes will there be when 6 people attend? (Using role playing, six problem solvers can be the party goers. As the handshakes progress, a counter can total the number. The teacher should encourage the search for a pattern as the hand shaking progresses.)

Problem situation: Bring sample items to class with price tags attached. With a "cash box" and play money, let the children pretend to be buyer and seller of various items.

7. *A numerically simpler problem.* One might assume that the use of calculators as a problem solving tool would obviate the need for using simpler numbers as a problem solving technique, but it doesn't. In reality, children can get so bogged down with complicated numbers that the entire problem confuses them to the point that they can't even decide upon the method of solution. Suggest that they substitute smaller, simpler numbers for the originals. Once the problem situation and procedures are clear they can return to the original numbers and do the necessary calculations with whatever tools are allowed.

Problem situation: John went to bed at 9:45 P.M. and got up at 7:20 A.M. How long did he sleep? (By substituting 9:00 and 7:00 for the original values, the problem solver can focus on the processes necessary to solve the problem.)

Problem situation: Nancy wants to buy a bicycle and has saved $118.50 toward its purchase. If the bicycle sells for $137.95 and there is a 5% sales tax, how much money does Nancy need? (Again, by substituting simpler numbers, such as $100 and $50, the problem solvers can concentrate on necessary procedures.)

Problem situation: How many squares are in this figure?

At times, as in the preceding problem situation, the simpler problem technique can be adapted to other elements in the problem besides numbers. In the situation just given the problem solver may wish to begin with one small square pattern and develop a system for solution before going on to the more complex figure.

8. *Guess-and-test (trial and error).* This problem solving technique can be valuable if used properly. Notice that the technique is NOT called "Guess." Sometimes teachers encourage children to guess. The intent is good: they want the children to try something, anything, to start the problem solving process. Unfortunately, the children often receive a different message. Too often they think that any guess—wild or random—is the basis of classroom problem solving and the object is to just keep making guesses until the teacher says it's right.

A guess is useful only insofar as it provides further information which can be incorporated in the search for a solution. A guess coupled with a test can provide such information, thereby making it a viable technique. Here are some problem situations which lend themselves well to the guess-and-test technique.

Problem situation: Pose this question to the class: "While a son was at camp, he sent his mother this message in the mail.

$SEND
+ MORE
$MONEY

How much money should she send?"

While this problem is not of the application variety, its puzzle aspect motivates almost any problem solver to action. The guess-and-test technique is a good choice here. Of course, one could begin a systematic trial and error procedure and test different numerals in the various positions. However, positions, combinations, and relative placement of letters provide clues which can narrow the initial search. By making inferences and using information given, some letters will be identified early. Then by systematic guess and test, the remaining positions can be found. (Try the procedure first. Then check your solution with that given at the end of this section.)

Problem situation: Play the game, "What's My Number?". Have a child secretly choose a number between two given parameters like 0 and 100. The rest of the class must guess the number by asking no more than twenty questions of a "Yes/No" variety. "What's My Number" lends itself well to the guess-and-test technique because every guess provides some information about the solution. With guidance and practice, children begin to realize that some questions provide more information than do others. For example, as initial questions, "Is the number greater than 50?" narrows the field more effectively than either "Is it 48?" or "Is it less than 90?".

"What's My Number?" has numerous variations and rule changes and can be adapted to any math level. "Twenty Questions," in which the guessers attempt to find the square root of a number in fewer than twenty questions, is one variation. Another variation is "Hit, Nick, or Miss," a spin-off of the "Master Mind" game in which the guessers try to identify the numerals of a three-digit sequence.

Problem situation: Show the children a book which has been opened to pages 20 and 21 and pose this problem: "This book is open to pages 20 and 21. The product of 20 and 21 is 420. To what pages would the book be opened if the product were 1260?"

Again some clues can be gained from information given. For example, the adjacent number pair is greater than (20,21). Guess another number pair and test that pair to gain further information. One child may suggest (40,41) and the subsequent test will show their product to be 1640. These two bits of information should lead to another guess closer to (40,41) than to (20,21). The guess (34,35) gives a test of 1190. A test of the guess (35,36) shows that the solution has been found.

9. *Estimation and approximation.* Estimation and approximation are used as techniques daily in real life situations, but the skills are often neglected in the classroom. Actually, three different aspects of estimation can be addressed: rounding off, reference point estimation, and estimated range of solution. Each aspect is illustrated in the following sample problem situations.

Problem situation: A farmer notes on the commodities report that corn is selling for $2.91 a bushel. If he has 1214 bushels to sell, approximately how much money will he receive for the corn? (By rounding off both numbers, the problem can be done mentally. $3 \times 1200 = $ 3600).

Problem situation: Daniel has been practicing punting his football in a fenced lot. He has observed that the ball has been traveling a distance equal to 5 fenceposts which are about 12 feet apart. About how far is he kicking the football? How might he actually find out the distance the ball is going? (In this situation Daniel is using a reference point estimation to help him arrive at an approximate distance; that is, he mentally visualizes a foot measure between the fenceposts and then uses that estimate to get the total.)

Problem situation: The square root of 59 is between what two whole numbers? (Here we are looking for parameters for an answer, or the estimated range. By mentally noting that 7^2 is 49 and 8^2 is 64, we know that the square root of 59 must be between 7 and 8. This estimation process is helpful in deciding whether or not an answer is reasonable.)

The tools and techniques just described do not exhaust all the possibilities, but they should provide problem solvers with the means to attack any problem with confidence. Now that general strategies and specific tools and techniques have been discussed, let's turn to word problems and their relationship to problem solving in the classroom of today.

(NOTE: If Mom does as her son in camp asks, she will send him $106.52.)

WORD PROBLEMS

Until now no mention has been made of textbook word problems, or story problems. You knew them as a child and if you were typical of other children, you didn't like them. Neither did your teacher. This harboring of negative attitudes toward textbook word problems has been the pattern for generations of children and teachers.

Actually, in theory, the inclusion of word problems seems reasonable. It can demonstrate the application of the mathematics to real world situations. In practice, however, something has gone awry. Not only do negative attitudes prevail, but there is some evidence which indicates that children who are assigned traditional textbook word problems do even less well on standardized test word problems than children who have been totally excused from those tasks for a year.[5] What has gone wrong between theory and practice? Can textbook word problems be a viable tool in teaching problem solving?

Certainly, many of the suggestions made earlier in this chapter have direct application here. Children who have a teacher who has developed his or her problem solving ability and who actively teaches these problem solving skills will have greater opportunity to succeed themselves. Children who have been taught both general strategies and specific techniques for problem solving will be better equipped to attack problems than will children who have been offered a few random suggestions but have generally been left to work out problems on their own. Children at all levels who have been given extensive experience with concrete materials and who understand the concepts associated with each computation will be better able to cope with problem situations, whether textbook or classroom generated.

5. Robert W. Wirtz and Emily Kahn, "Another Look at Applications in Elementary School Mathematics," *Arithmetic Teacher,* September 1982, pp. 21–25.

But other factors, specifically associated with written word problems, need to be addressed at this point. For example, a teacher needs to know how to make effective use of word problems in the classroom, how to identify useful forms of word problems, and how to help children develop reading skills particularly associated with word problems.

1. *Effective use of word problems.* In spite of numerous pitfalls, word problems do have the advantage of being readily available. They can be ONE good source for problem solving activities. They should not be the ONLY source. They should be carefully selected. Remember that in problem solving, a few problems solved slowly but well are better than many problems solved rapidly but randomly. Just as the textbook is a tool to be used by the teacher when the teacher sees fit, so also is each word problem contained in that text. Read through each word problem before assigning it. It is not a good policy to assign all odd problems (or all even ones) because quite often one problem is designed to build upon previous problems. Instead, check the problem for type, difficulty, motivational value, application value, and so on. If the problem meets your criteria for use, then use it—within YOUR framework for helping children to learn how to become problem solvers.

2. *Identifying useful forms of word problems.* Because problem solving involves more than just "getting the right answer," there should be more emphasis placed on those other processes and skills which are brought to bear in the solving of problems. For example, "John has 21 fish. Mary has 18 fish. How many more fish does John have than Mary?" is a perfectly acceptable problem. However, if we are trying to emphasize the processes and skills involved in getting to the correct answer, perhaps we should start asking more questions about the problem which are directly related to these tasks.

Here are some variations of written problems with tasks which focus more on the process of solution than on a numerical final answer.

a. Problems which contain too much information.

Problem: Alan and Fred went to a fast food restaurant. Fred bought a hamburger for 59 cents and a milkshake for 80 cents. Alan bought a sundae for 49 cents. How much did Fred pay for his lunch?

Task: Cross out all unnecessary information given in the problem.

b. Problems with too little information.

Problem: Lisa bought 6 pieces of bubblegum for 12 cents. How much change did she receive?

Task: What else do you need to know in order to find out how much change Lisa should receive?

c. Problems which require process identification.

Problem: Brad wanted to buy 3 packages of stickers. The stickers cost $1.09 a package. How much would 3 packages cost?

Task: Which operation would help you to find out how much money Brad would need?

d. Problems which require a math sentence.

Problem: Billy had 10 baseball trading cards. John gave him 15 more cards. How many cards did Billy now have?

Task: Write a mathematical sentence which could be used to help solve the problem.

e. Problems which require the creation of a word problem to fit a given math sentence.

Problem: 12 × 6 = _____ .

Task: Make up a word problem which would fit the math sentence.

f. Problems which require the child to make up questions to fit a given situation.

Problem: On a spelling test Ann spelled 16 of 20 problems correctly. Her friend Beth answered 18 of the problems correctly.

Task: Make up some questions which could be asked about this situation.

3. *Helping children develop reading skills particularly associated with word problems.*

While reading is a skill of inestimable importance, it is not a primary factor in problem solving. In "real life" problem solving, the problem confronting us is almost never presented in written form. It is primarily in school that reading becomes a factor in problem solving, and then only when written word problems are used.

As a matter of fact, recent research has indicated that the reading factor may have been given too much importance in the solution of word problems. "At the early primary level, it is obvious that reading can be a deterrent to problem solving success but, equally obvious, only when problems must be read. . . . Studies at the upper elementary level do not indicate that reading is as big a deterrent as commonly believed. . . . Perhaps factors other than reading far override the importance of the reading factor."[6]

Still, however, there are reading skills particularly associated with mathematical word problems, and these should be developed. Here are some activities which teachers can use to help students learn to read their mathematics word problems better.

a. Familiarize students with textbook features.
Children seldom look beyond the pages assigned in their mathematics textbook. They should be taught how to use the index, glossary, and any chapter vocabulary lists.
b. Discuss vocabulary and symbols.
To understand a word problem clearly the student must be able to interpret words and symbols in a mathematical context. In mathematics some words have a special meaning quite different from their counterparts in ordinary usage. For example, words like times, operation, by, and power, have specific meanings in mathematics different from ordinary prose. Students need to recognize mathematical usages special to word problems.
c. Help students adjust their reading habits to mathematical word problems.
Reading in mathematics is much slower than in almost any other area. Mathematical reading also involves varied eye movements, including some regressions. Mathematical reading is not a passive act; it involves an attitude of aggressive thoroughness.[7]

These three practices are important to reading math materials but are not usually advocated in reading ordinary prose. The teacher needs to provide his or her students with direct help in adjusting their reading habits to fit these special materials. This can be done by pointing out the

---

6. Marilyn N. Suydam, "Untangling Clues from Research on Problem Solving," in *Problem Solving in School Mathematics,* NCTM, 1980, p. 41–42.

7. N. Wesley Earp, "Procedures for Teaching Reading in Mathematics," *Arithmetic Teacher,* November 1970, pp. 575–579.

differences in reading materials and by actually practicing the reading together, silently or orally, in small groups or large.

In conclusion, word problems have been a source of confusion and negative attitudes in the past, but they can be a useful tool in the teaching of problem solving if they are chosen carefully and used effectively.

CHAPTER KEY POINTS

1. Problem solving is the process of utilizing previously acquired knowledge in the resolution of new and unfamiliar situations.

2. Establishing a problem solving environment in the classroom requires three points of focus: (1) the teacher as a model problem solver, (2) the teacher as a manager of problem solving activities, and (3) the teacher as a selector and presenter of problems.

3. Problem solving in the classroom should be characterized by an active, cooperative, nonpunitive, unpressured atmosphere.

4. Problems should be presented in more than one medium and they should be selected on the basis of their realism and/or interest to the students, their match with student ability, and their type of solution.

5. A general problem solving strategy includes this four-phase procedure: (1) understand the problem, (2) devise a plan, (3) carry out the plan, and (4) examine the solution.

6. Among the many specific tools and techniques which can be used within the general framework for problem solving are the following:
   a. Manipulative aids.
   b. Diagrams and pictures.
   c. Lists, charts, tables, and patterns.
   d. Calculators.
   e. Math sentences.
   f. Simulation and role playing.
   g. A numerically simpler problem.
   h. Guess-and-test (trial and error).
   i. Estimation and approximation.

7. Textbook word problems and traditional teaching techniques have not been as effective as they should have been in teaching problem solving.

8. Word problems can be varied to emphasize the process of solution. Variations include the following:

    a. Problems with too much information.

    b. Problems with too little information.

    c. Problems which require process identification.

    d. Problems which require a math sentence.

    e. Problems which require the creation of a word problem to fit a given math sentence.

    f. Problems which require the child to make up questions to fit a given situation.

9. Certain reading skills are associated specifically with mathematical word problems. Teachers can help students read their word problems better by familiarizing them with textbook features, by discussing mathematical vocabulary and symbols with them, and by helping them adjust their reading habits to mathematical word problems.

Laboratory 15

Problem Solving

Development of problem solving ability has been assigned as a major role of education. The teaching of problem solving is at best a difficult task requiring an understanding of alternative processes and approaches. These laboratory exercises are designed to help you extend your own problem solving awareness through textbook and professional journal examination.

I. *Objectives:* Upon completion of these laboratory exercises, you should be able to do the following:

    A. Given a selected mathematical concept or skill, identify a real or natural situation in which the child needs to use that concept or skill. (Chapter Competency 15-A)

    B. Identify both general methods and specific techniques which can be used in solving problems. (Chapter Competencies 15-C and 15-D)

    C. Vary word problems so that the process of solution is emphasized. (Chapter Competency 15-E)

    D. Examine elementary mathematics textbooks and make decisions about the relative effectiveness of the various approaches to problem solving. (Chapter Competency 15-E)

II. *Materials:* At least two elementary mathematics series (K–6), access to professional journals.

III. *Procedure:*

    A. Read Chapter 15 of *Helping Children Learn Mathematics*. Consult your instructor if you have any questions.

    B. Below is a list of mathematical concepts and skills at various levels. Briefly describe for each item in the list a real or natural problem solving situation with which the child at that age level could easily identify.

        1. Use of money (grade 1)

        2. Telling of time (grade 2)

        3. Multiplication of whole numbers (grade 3)

        4. Addition of fractions (grade 4)

        5. Division of decimals (grade 5)

        6. Use of percent (grade 6)

    C. Select ONE situation from the preceding list and describe how you would incorporate general strategies as discussed in the chapter to help children learn to solve the problem. More specifically, for each of the four general steps as described by Polya, list the kinds of questions you would pose to guide the children in their solution of the problem situation you selected.

    D. Several specific techniques to help children acquire problem solving skills were described in the chapter. Select five of these techniques and state specific ways in which each technique can help the child's ability to solve problems.

E. Written word problems can be varied so that they focus on the process of solution. Name five ways in which problems may be varied and then make up a sample problem to illustrate each.

F. Select an elementary school mathematics series to examine for its treatment of problem solving. Consider these questions as you examine the series.

   1. At what level is problem solving begun?

   2. Is problem solving treated as a separate topic or is it incorporated throughout study?

   3. What form does problem solving take; that is, do word problems comprise the totality of treatment or are specific problem solving methodologies incorporated.?

   4. Study the form and style of written word problems which are included. Are the problems relevant to the child? Is there any evidence of varied forms which require special analysis, such as problems with too much information, no numbers given, no questions asked, etc.? Compare and contrast the forms which written problems assume from primary level to intermediate level texts.

   5. Share your findings with a classmate who examined a different series. What commonalities/differences did you find?

G. Consult the literature (professional journals) and select an article dealing with problem solving. Read the article and then write a brief for it. Included in your brief should be the bibliographic data, a summary of the article, and your reaction to it.

PART IV
Evaluating Mathematical Outcomes

Teacher Competencies

After studying Part IV and completing the laboratories in Part IV, you should be able to achieve each of the following:

A. Identify a child's learning difficulties in mathematics and plan remediation activities to correct the found difficulties.

B. Develop selected evaluation skills which will help you design a program of evaluation for your classroom.

16
Diagnosis and Correction of Learning Difficulties

Teacher Competencies

After reading Chapter 16 and completing Laboratory 16, you should be able to achieve each of the following:

    A. Define diagnosis and correction.

    B. Identify error patterns in computational skills which exist in a given case study.

    C. Identify oft-found sources of errors in computation made by elementary children.

    D. List and describe various diagnostic and corrective techniques and cite advantages and disadvantages of each.

The use of diagnosis and correction as integral tools to improve learning in the elementary school mathematics classroom has received much attention from mathematics educators and teachers in recent years. Diagnostic and resulting corrective (prescriptive) techniques are viewed as a way of improving mathematics instructional programs at all levels of learning from kindergarten to adult. This chapter will examine the nature of diagnosis and correction and discuss how these techniques may be used by the classroom teacher. Some common error patterns in arithmetic which are often made by learners will also be discussed.

THE NATURE OF DIAGNOSIS AND CORRECTION

Teachers are certainly familiar with the term "diagnosis." Its use has probably been in the context of what a medical doctor does when a patient goes to the office because of illness. By using information about the patient's symptoms and possibly some tests, the doctor tries to diagnose the illness and prescribe corrective treatment which will cure the illness. If the doctor makes an accurate diagnosis and prescribes the proper treatment, the patient will be well.

In a sense, the teacher is faced with the same problem as the medical doctor. A learner may come to class with one or more "mathematical ills." To be able to help the learner cure the "mathemetical ills," the teacher must first decide the nature of the ill(s), and then plan and apply an instructional program designed to correct the diagnosed mathematical illness. The measure of a teacher's ability to diagnose and plan corrective procedures is the extent to which the learner is able to progress towards a cure of the found mathematical illness. Of course, since a teacher is only exposed to the learner for a relatively short period of time, it is not reasonable to expect the teacher to be able to cure all of the learner's mathematical illnesses. But, it is possible at least to start the learner along a path of recovery so that needed additional corrections can be performed by other teachers in the future.

Diagnosis, then, is the process which is used to determine what learners *are* and *are not* able to do mathematically. Correction is the process to help learners progress towards mathematical levels which are appropriate for their chronological and intellectual age.

Together, the two processes described above may be summarized as a series of steps in the form of questions in the following way:

1. What is the exact nature of the error?
2. What appears to be the cause or source of the error?
3. At what level (concrete, semi-concrete, or abstract) is the student capable of working?
4. Given answers to questions one through three, what is the appropriate instructional strategy which may be used to correct the error?

Application of these four steps will give a systematic way for implementing the diagnostic-corrective process.

To illustrate the above technique, suppose that the following sample of a student's work was received by the teacher.

A.	1.3	B.	1.01	C.	.71	D.	2.2	E.	2.5
	$\times 7$		$\times 3$		$\times 5$		$\times 3$		$\times 4$
	9.1		30.3		35.5		6.6		1.00

It is clear that problems B through E are incorrect. The first impulse may be to say that the student cannot multiply decimals. However problem A is correctly done. Closer inspection will show that the learner is quite capable of doing the multiplication part of the problem but is not able, for some reason, to place the decimal point correctly in the answer. (Decimal places are counted from the left in the answer rather than from the right.) Thus the exact nature of the error is the student's inability to place the decimal point correctly, his knowledge of basic multiplication facts, and/or the multiplication algorithm for whole numbers.

Possible sources of the error may be in the student's lack of understanding of the multiplication algorithm for decimals or of the concept of decimals in general. An oral interview with the student or examination of other work involving decimals may be needed to help identify the exact source of the error.

After the nature and source of the error have been identified, it follows that consideration of alternatives for correcting the errors must be considered. For example, if the student is working at the abstract level, a brief re-explanation of the procedure for placing the decimal point in the answer may be all that is needed. As a teacher's experience grows, it will be possible to draw from a variety of instructional strategies which may be used in this situation. Hopefully, the right choice of a corrective strategy will be made the first time and success (correction) will result. If not, other corrective strategies must be tried until the appropriate one is found.

IDENTIFYING COMMON ERROR PATTERNS

It is generally accepted among mathematics educators that learners tend to make errors systemically, especially in computation. In other words, errors are often consistent as they appear. To help a teacher begin to be able to identify the consistent errors, we will turn our attention to how skills are broken down into component parts and examine some common errors made by learners.

Analyzing a Skill to be Learned

Mathematics is a highly structured subject. Learning from the very beginning (concept of number, spatial relationships, etc.) is used as a basis for building additional mathematical concepts and skills. What this means is that a learner may have gaps in mathematical background, which may have occurred in the early primary grades.

To assess these gaps accurately, it is necessary to have a thorough understanding of the hierarchy of mathematical concepts and skills in the elementary school. If assistance is needed to gain a better understanding of the scope and sequence, consult an elementary textbook series, the state or school corporation curriculum guide, or some elementary teachers.

Before beginning to identify errors, a teacher needs to be able to analyze the skill to be learned. This analysis is done by breaking down the skill into its component parts (subskills or prerequisities).

To illustrate this point, consider the problem below.

$$\frac{1}{2} \times \frac{1}{3} = \frac{1}{6}$$

What are the concepts and skills that must be learned before the problem can be solved correctly?

1. Concept of fractions
2. Concept of multiplication
3. Algorithm for multiplying whole numbers
4. Knowledge of basic facts of multiplication (whole numbers)
5. Knowledge of algorithm for multiplying two fractions

If one or more of these concepts or skills has not been learned by the child, the end result will probably be an incorrect solution. If a teacher is not able to, or does not break down the overall skill (multiplying two fractions) into its component parts, he or she will have no idea where the error is being made. And, if the error is not known, how will correction occur?

What is being said here is that the classroom teacher must be able to analyze each mathematical concept or skill which is found in the curriculum. This ability to analyze the skill or concept will determine how effective a teacher is likely to be in correcting student errors, let alone presenting the concept or skill initially to a class of thirty.

Being able to analyze a concept or skill will go a long way toward determining patterns of errors, a fundamental skill in diagnosis. Since errors tend to occur consistently in patterns, accurate diagnosis will enable a teacher to correct error patterns more quickly and efficiently than if no analysis is used at all. How do we find these error patterns?

Finding Error Patterns

Now that we have discussed the importance of being able to analyze a concept or skill, let's see how this information can be used to search for error patterns. Let's look at some examples of student work to try to find a pattern.

Let's try an example. Consider the sample work from Ginny as she works with division problems.

Name <u>Ginny</u>

A. $\begin{array}{r} 22 \\ 3\overline{)66} \\ 60 \\ 6 \\ \underline{6} \end{array}$	**B.** $\begin{array}{r} 93 \\ 3\overline{)117} \\ 90 \\ 27 \\ \underline{27} \end{array}$	**C.** $\begin{array}{r} 52 \\ 3\overline{)75} \\ 60 \\ 15 \\ \underline{15} \end{array}$	**D.** $\begin{array}{r} 13 \\ 5\overline{)155} \\ 150 \\ 5 \\ \underline{5} \end{array}$

What is the pattern? Ginny proceeds correctly initially but records her first partial quotient above the last digit in the dividend. Then she multiplies her partial quotient by the divisor, the result by 10 and places the number below the dividend. After subtracting, she divides the divisor into the difference and records the answer in the quotient to the *left* of the first partial quotient. *Hence, her digits in the quotient are always in reverse order.*

Here are some other examples of error patterns. Find the patterns before reading the explanations.

Name <u>Tom</u>

A. $\begin{array}{r} 342 \\ +527 \\ \hline 869 \end{array}$	**B.** $\begin{array}{r} 87 \\ +\ 93 \\ \hline 117 \end{array}$	**C.** $\begin{array}{r} 39 \\ +\ 53 \\ \hline 812 \end{array}$	**D.** $\begin{array}{r} 272 \\ +391 \\ \hline 519 \end{array}$

Tom's error pattern is that he adds from left to right. Also, when he has a sum greater than 10, he records the tens digit and regroups the ones digit to the right. Now, what is Shelly's pattern?

Name <u>Shelly</u>

A. $\begin{array}{r} 1\ 1\ 3\ 1 \\ 2\ 4\ 6 \\ -1\ 6\ 3 \\ \hline 1\ 7\ 1\ 3 \end{array}$	**B.** $\begin{array}{r} 1\ 1\ 3\ 1 \\ 2\ 4\ 3 \\ -1\ 8\ 7 \\ \hline 5\ 6 \end{array}$	**C.** $\begin{array}{r} 7\ 1 \\ 8\ 7 \\ -4\ 4 \\ \hline 3\ 1\ 3 \end{array}$

Shelly's error involves the application of regrouping when not necessary.

It takes a little time to become proficient at finding error patterns. Further practice in finding error patterns may be found in the exercises at the end of the chapter.

Some Common Errors in Computation

To aid in the diagnostic process here is a list of some common errors that students make with whole numbers, fractions, decimals, and percent. This list of errors is obviously not exhaustive but it will give a place to start.

A. Addition of Whole Numbers

Error	Example	
1. Basic facts are incorrect.	$\begin{array}{r} 8 \\ +9 \\ \hline 16 \end{array}$	$\begin{array}{r} 47 \\ +39 \\ \hline 87 \end{array}$
2. Renaming is not performed correctly.	$\begin{array}{r} 38 \\ +19 \\ \hline 417 \end{array}$	$\begin{array}{r} 29 \\ +13 \\ \hline 312 \end{array}$
3. Addition with zeros is incorrect.	$\begin{array}{r} 40 \\ +37 \\ \hline 70 \end{array}$	$\begin{array}{r} 102 \\ +93 \\ \hline 105 \end{array}$
4. Ones digit in one addend is added to both tens and ones digits in the other addend.	$\begin{array}{r} 1 \\ 48 \\ +\ 7 \\ \hline 125 \end{array}$	$\begin{array}{r} 1 \\ 66 \\ +\ 9 \\ \hline 165 \end{array}$

B. Subtraction of Whole Numbers:

Error	Example	
1. Basic facts are incorrect.	$\begin{array}{r} 17 \\ -\ 9 \\ \hline 10 \end{array}$	$\begin{array}{r} 2 \\ 36 \\ -19 \\ \hline 16 \end{array}$
2. Subtraction with zeros is incorrect.	$\begin{array}{r} 37 \\ -20 \\ \hline 10 \end{array}$	$\begin{array}{r} 50 \\ -13 \\ \hline 43 \end{array}$
3. Lesser digit is always subtracted from greater digit.	$\begin{array}{r} 43 \\ -27 \\ \hline 24 \end{array}$	$\begin{array}{r} 234 \\ -146 \\ \hline 112 \end{array}$

C. Multiplication of Whole Numbers:

Error	Example	
1. Algorithm is performed like addition (by columns).	$\begin{array}{r} 23 \\ \times 17 \\ \hline 41 \end{array}$	$\begin{array}{r} 14 \\ \times 13 \\ \hline 22 \end{array}$

2. Digit "carried" is added before multiplying.

$$\begin{array}{r} 2 \\ 35 \\ \times 14 \\ \hline 200 \\ 35 \\ \hline 550 \end{array} \qquad \begin{array}{r} 4 \\ 26 \\ \times \ 7 \\ \hline 422 \end{array}$$

3. Multiplication is performed from left to right.

$$\begin{array}{r} 23 \\ \times \ 4 \\ \hline 812 \end{array} \qquad \begin{array}{r} 16 \\ \times \ 8 \\ \hline 848 \end{array}$$

4. Digit "carried" the first time is also used when multiplying by the tens digit.

$$\begin{array}{r} 5 \\ 98 \\ \times 26 \\ \hline 588 \\ 226 \\ \hline 2748 \end{array} \qquad \begin{array}{r} 7 \\ 19 \\ \times 78 \\ \hline 152 \\ 143 \\ \hline 1582 \end{array}$$

5. Digit "carried" is ignored.

$$\begin{array}{r} 1 \\ 14 \\ \times \ 3 \\ \hline 32 \end{array} \qquad \begin{array}{r} 5 \\ 29 \\ \times \ 6 \\ \hline 124 \end{array}$$

6. Multiplication by tens digit is not recorded correctly.

$$\begin{array}{r} 25 \\ \times 13 \\ \hline 75 \\ 25 \\ \hline 100 \end{array} \qquad \begin{array}{r} 13 \\ \times 12 \\ \hline 26 \\ 13 \\ \hline 39 \end{array}$$

7. Basic facts of addition and multiplication are incorrect.

$$\begin{array}{r} 27 \\ \times \ 9 \\ \hline 252 \end{array} \qquad \begin{array}{r} 19 \\ \times 17 \\ \hline 133 \\ 19 \\ \hline 333 \end{array}$$

D. Division of Whole Numbers:

| *Error* | *Example* |

1. When divisor is less than digit in dividend, division is performed normally with remainders dropped. When divisor is greater than digit in dividend, digit in dividend is divided into divisor.

$$\begin{array}{r} 213 \\ 3\overline{)639} \end{array} \qquad \begin{array}{r} 142 \\ 4\overline{)518} \end{array}$$

2. Division is performed in normal fashion but entire dividend is used for product of divisor and partial quotient. Quotient is recorded from right to left.

$$3\overline{)75}\begin{array}{r}52\\\end{array}$$

$$\begin{array}{r}52\\3\overline{)75}\\\underline{60}\\15\\\underline{15}\end{array}\qquad\begin{array}{r}68\\6\overline{)516}\\\underline{480}\\36\\\underline{36}\end{array}$$

3. After dividing initially, the next two numbers are used as dividend.

$$\begin{array}{r}32\ \text{r3}\\9\overline{)2721}\\[4pt]21\\\underline{18}\\3\end{array}\qquad\begin{array}{r}78\ \text{r2}\\6\overline{)4250}\\27\qquad 42\\50\\\underline{48}\\2\end{array}$$

4. Basic facts of multiplication are incorrect.

$$\begin{array}{r}66\ \text{r13}\\15\overline{)903}\\\underline{80}\\103\\\underline{90}\\13\end{array}\qquad\begin{array}{r}48\ \text{r5}\\7\overline{)348}\\\underline{28}\\68\\\underline{63}\\5\end{array}$$

5. Basic facts of subtraction and subtraction algorithm are incorrect.

$$\begin{array}{r}27\ \text{r2}\\12\overline{)336}\\\underline{24}\\86\\84\\2\end{array}\qquad\begin{array}{r}62\ \text{r7}\\8\overline{)547}\\\underline{48}\\16\\\underline{16}\\7\end{array}$$

E. Fractions:

Error	*Example*

1. Lesser number is divided into greater and quotient is used as numerator. Greater number is used as denominator.

$$\frac{4}{6}=\frac{1}{6}\qquad\frac{3}{9}=\frac{3}{9}$$

2. Numerators are added.

$$\frac{1}{3}+\frac{1}{4}=\frac{2}{7}$$

Denominators are added.

$$\frac{2}{3}+\frac{3}{5}=\frac{5}{8}$$

3. Whole numbers in problem are ignored.

$$\begin{array}{r}3\frac{1}{4}=\frac{2}{8}\\[4pt]+1\frac{1}{8}=\frac{1}{8}\\\hline\frac{3}{8}\end{array}\qquad\begin{array}{r}7\frac{1}{2}=\frac{2}{4}\\[4pt]+5\frac{3}{4}=\frac{3}{4}\\\hline\frac{5}{4}=1\frac{1}{4}\end{array}$$

4. Regrouping process involves ten rather than fraction name.

$$\overset{5}{\cancel{6}}\overset{1}{}\frac{1}{8}$$

$$-3\frac{3}{8}$$

$$2\frac{8}{8} = 1$$

$$\overset{3}{\cancel{4}}\overset{1}{}\frac{1}{4}$$

$$-1\frac{3}{4}$$

$$2\frac{8}{4} = 2$$

5. Subtraction process is applied incorrectly.

$$3$$
$$-2\frac{1}{4}$$
$$\overline{1\frac{1}{4}}$$

$$8$$
$$-2\frac{5}{6}$$
$$\overline{6\frac{5}{6}}$$

6. One of the two numbers is inverted before multiplying.

$$\frac{1}{4} \times \frac{2}{3} = \frac{1}{4} \times \frac{3}{2} = \frac{3}{8}$$

$$\frac{1}{6} \times \frac{1}{2} = \frac{1}{6} \times \frac{2}{1} = \frac{2}{6}$$

7. Whole numbers are multiplied and fractions are multiplied.

$$2\frac{1}{2} \times 3\frac{1}{5} = 6\frac{1}{10}$$

$$1\frac{1}{4} \times 2\frac{1}{2} = 2\frac{1}{8}$$

8. Fractions are changed to common denominators and then numerators are multiplied.

$$\frac{1}{2} \times \frac{3}{2} = \frac{3}{2}$$

$$\frac{1}{3} \times \frac{3}{4} = \frac{4}{12} \times \frac{9}{12} = \frac{36}{12} = 3$$

9. Dividend is inverted instead of divisor.

$$\frac{1}{4} - \frac{2}{3} = \frac{4}{1} \times \frac{2}{3} = \frac{8}{3}$$

$$\frac{2}{3} - \frac{1}{2} = \frac{3}{2} \times \frac{1}{2} = \frac{3}{4}$$

10. Numerator is divided by numerator and denominator is divided by denominator. Remainders are ignored.

$$\frac{13}{20} - \frac{5}{6} = \frac{2}{3}$$

$$\frac{3}{4} - \frac{2}{2} = \frac{1}{2}$$

F. Decimals:

Error	*Example*

1. Decimal places are marked off in answer.

$$\begin{array}{r} .3 \\ +.9 \\ \hline .12 \end{array} \qquad \begin{array}{r} .7 \\ +1.4 \\ \hline .21 \end{array}$$

2. Subtraction process is incorrectly applied.

$$\begin{array}{r} 4 \\ -2.3 \\ \hline 2.3 \end{array} \qquad \begin{array}{r} 5 \\ -1.49 \\ \hline 4.49 \end{array}$$

3. Numbers are added like whole numbers. Decimal point is placed in answer according to greater number of decimal places found in a single number in the problem.

$1.14 + .4 = 1.18$

4. Decimal points are kept in line.

$$\begin{array}{r} 3.2 \\ \times\ .3 \\ \hline 9.6 \end{array} \qquad \begin{array}{r} 1.2 \\ \times\ .3 \\ \hline 3.6 \end{array}$$

5. Decimal point in the answer is placed from the left.

$$\begin{array}{r} 1.4 \\ .12 \\ \hline 28 \\ 14 \\ \hline 168. \end{array} \qquad \begin{array}{r} 14 \\ 1.3 \\ \hline 42 \\ 14 \\ \hline 1.82 \end{array}$$

6. Decimal point in divisor is ignored.

$$.7\overline{)3.5} \quad\begin{array}{r}.5\\ \\35\end{array} \qquad 1.2\overline{)4.8} \quad\begin{array}{r}.4\\ \\48\end{array}$$

7. Problem is written so that divisor and dividend are interchanged.

For $.7 \div 1.4$, student writes $.7\overline{)1.4}$

8. Remainder is recorded using a decimal point.

$$4\overline{)155} \quad\begin{array}{r}38.3\\ \\12\\\hline 35\\32\\\hline 3\end{array} \qquad 3\overline{)109} \quad\begin{array}{r}36.1\\ \\9\\\hline 19\\18\\\hline 1\end{array}$$

G. Percent:

Error	*Example*

1. Percent sign is ignored.

14% of 60 = 84
10% of 30 = 300

2. Percents are incorrectly converted to decimals and vice versa.

$$.01\% = .01$$
$$.5\% = .5$$
$$.3 \ \ = 3\%$$

Thus far in this chapter we have defined diagnosis and correction and have identified some error patterns. We are now ready to examine some diagnostic and corrective techniques and their use.

DIAGNOSTIC AND CORRECTIVE TECHNIQUES

There are a variety of techniques which may be used to assess and correct learning difficulties in mathematics. Let's examine some of these techniques, beginning with diagnosis.

On a formal basis, diagnosis can be performed using a testing situation. These testing situations may be either standardized or teacher-made. Advantages and disadvantages of both types of situations are discussed in detail in Chapter 18.

There are also a variety of informal techniques which may be used for diagnostic purposes. These techniques can give a great deal of useful information and are easily applied.

1. *Observation.* The teacher should be a continual observer in the classroom. Watching children while they are doing seat work or working at the chalkboard may give valuable clues as to why they are having difficulty. Observation will also be of great benefit in classroom management and discipline as was pointed out in Chapter 6.
2. *Interview.* Sometimes, the very best way to gather information about what is causing a child's difficulty is to sit down on a one-to-one basis with the child so that the child's thinking process can be verbalized. This type of session is difficult to do with every child who is having difficulty because of time constraints but it will be well worth it.
3. *Homework.* A review of a child's homework may give the information needed to make an accurate diagnosis. It must be remembered, however, that homework problems which are assigned should be carefully screened before the assignment so that the work will accomplish what is intended.

Regardless of which diagnostic technique(s) is used, remember that an accurate diagnosis is the key to helping children correct their learning difficulties, not only in mathematics but in other areas as well.

When the diagnosis has been completed, the next obvious step is to correct the found difficulty. Correction, however, must be done in a systematic fashion to be effective.

Correction must begin by outlining the objectives to be achieved by the corrective process. These objectives should be stated in terms of observable behaviors (discussed in Chapter 3) which will be exhibited by the child. These objectives should be shared with the child so that the desired end result will be clear to both teacher and child.

There must be continuous evaluation and feedback to the child during the corrective process. Be sure the child is continually appraised on progress being made.

In addition to these two guidelines, use different kinds of activities to give the child ample opportunity to drill on the troublesome concept or skill. Games are often an excellent medium to help make drill more enjoyable. Guidelines for the choice and use of games are discussed in Chapter

5.

Some general remarks about the use of drill seem appropriate here. Drill is a very useful tool not only in the corrective process but also in the regular classroom instructional setting. However, the word "drill" has always had a bad reputation because it was associated with an unpleasant task such as doing 100 fraction problems. The difficulty has traditionally been that many teachers felt that "anything could be learned mathematically if it was drilled on long enough." Drill was the only way to learn mathematics.

A more reasonable view of drill is that its purpose is to reinforce a concept or skill to be learned. Not all children, therefore, need the same amount of drill to master a concept or skill, and drill activities should be assigned with this in mind. Drill will be most effective when there is understanding by the child of the concept or skill to be learned. Drill should also be enjoyable to the child so that motivation to learn will be enhanced. This does not mean that drill should be "all fun and games" but it means that drill must have a purpose which is understood by the child.

Whichever corrective techniques are used, the teacher must remember that the needs of the individual child must be addressed and provided for in the corrective process. If this is done and a well-planned corrective process is used, the end result will likely be that the child will be able to overcome the mathematical difficulty which will, in turn, bolster the child's attitude and self-concept.

CHAPTER KEY POINTS

1. Diagnosis is a process which is used to determine what children are and are not able to do mathematically.

2. Correction is what is done to help children progress towards mathematical levels which are appropriate for their chronological and mathematical ages.

3. The diagnostic-corrective process may be summarized by finding the
   a. exact nature of the error,
   b. cause of the error,
   c. student work level (concrete, semiconcrete, or abstract),
   d. appropriate instructional strategy to correct the error.

4. Accurate diagnosis requires that the teacher be able to analyze a concept or skill in terms of prerequisities or components.

5. Students tend to make errors systematically.

6. Being able to find error patterns is an important diagnostic skill.

7. Both standardized and teacher-made tests are useful formal diagnostic techniques.

8. Observation, interview, and homework inspection are useful informal diagnostic techniques.

9. Correction might be done systematically using objectives, continuous evaluation and feedback, and many different kinds of activities.

10. Drill should be used to reinforce a concept or skill and not just to keep students busy.

11. The need for drill will vary with different students.

12. Diagnosis and correction must be ongoing to be effective.

Laboratory 16

Diagnosis and Correction of Learning Difficulties

I. Upon completion of these laboratory exercises, you should be able to do the following:
   A. Define diagnosis and correction. (Chapter Competency 16-A)
   B. Identify error patterns in computational skills which exist in a given case study. (Chapter Competency 16-B)
   C. Identify oft-found sources of errors in computation made by elementary children. (Chapter Competency 16-C)
   D. List and describe various diagnostic and corrective techniques and cite advantages and disadvantages of each. (Chapter Competency 16-D)

II. *Materials:* None

III. *Procedure:*
   A. Read Chapter 16 of *Helping Children Learn Mathematics.* Consult your instructor if you have any questions.
   B. Using the definitions of diagnosis and correction from your reading, how do you view their viability to the elementary mathematics instructional program at a selected grade level?
   C. Inspect a Teacher's Guide to a current elementary textbook series. Is there reference to or discussion of various diagnostic and corrective techniques?
   D. How might you incorporate various diagnostic and corrective techniques into your teaching?
   E. Identify the error patterns for each student:

		5	2
Billy	126	68	241
	+213	+ 94	+783
	339	117	916
Judy	436	46	704
	−103	−20	−302
	103	20	402

	2 3	2 4	2 3 r3
Tony	13) 2639	7) 1428	12) 2439
	26	14	24
	39	28	39
	39	28	36
			3

Beth

$$
\begin{array}{r}
113 \\
\times 103 \\
\hline
339 \\
000 \\
113 \\
\hline
1439
\end{array}
\qquad
\begin{array}{r}
148 \\
\times 207 \\
\hline
1036 \\
000 \\
296 \\
\hline
3996
\end{array}
\qquad
\begin{array}{r}
245 \\
\times 304 \\
\hline
980 \\
000 \\
735 \\
\hline
8330
\end{array}
$$

Albert

$$
\begin{array}{r}
17 \\
\times 18 \\
\hline
156
\end{array}
\qquad
\begin{array}{r}
23 \\
\times 13 \\
\hline
29
\end{array}
\qquad
\begin{array}{r}
27 \\
\times 28 \\
\hline
456
\end{array}
$$

Alice

$$
\begin{array}{r}
1000 \ \ r8 \\
5)\overline{7231} \\
2 \\
2 \\
3 \\
1
\end{array}
\qquad
\begin{array}{r}
1221 \ \ r4 \\
3)\overline{4783} \\
1 \\
1 \\
2 \\
0
\end{array}
\qquad
\begin{array}{r}
1121 \ \ r2 \\
2)\overline{3243} \\
1 \\
0 \\
0 \\
1
\end{array}
$$

Mary

$$
^1\ \frac{3}{2} + \frac{1}{3_{\ 1}} = \frac{2}{3}
\qquad\qquad
^2\ \frac{4}{5} + \frac{4}{2_{\ 1}} = \frac{6}{6} = 1
$$

$$
\ _{2}\ \frac{7}{10}^{^1} + \frac{5}{6} = \frac{8}{8} = 1
\qquad\qquad
\frac{2}{3} + \frac{6}{7} = \frac{8}{10} = \frac{4}{5}
$$

F. You may find it desirable to ask a student to help diagnose his own problem. What can be gained by doing this even though you may be quite sure of what the error is?

G. Carelessness is often cited as a reason why children have made mistakes. Some possible causes for this carelessness might be:

    1. assignment is too long.

    2. child is in too big a hurry to get finished.

    3. child is sloppy in his work.

17
Evaluation

Teacher Competencies

After studying Chapter 17 and completing Laboratory 17, you should be able to achieve each of the following:

   A. Given a standardized test, identify the level of learning represented by the items on the test. (Part Competency IV-B)
   B. Given a set of objectives, design one or more evaluation techniques which might be used to measure the achievement of those objectives and give a rationale for your decision. (Part Competency IV-B)
   C. Given a content area, write informational objectives and corresponding test items at a specified level of learning. (Part Competency IV-B)

Recent changes in the elementary school curriculum have caused changes in the emphasis placed on mathematics instruction: development of mathematical understanding, development of positive attitudes, and development of rational power now share important roles along with the development of computational and problem-solving skills.

Unfortunately, evaluation techniques used by classroom teachers have not kept pace with these changes; many teachers still use only paper-and-pencil examinations which test only for computational accuracy and speed and for ability to solve verbal problems that emphasize one "right answer."

Throughout this book the functions of the teacher in preparing and implementing an effective program of instruction in elementary school mathematics have been stressed. Determining goals and objectives and formulating strategies with several alternatives are vital to any successful program in which children learn mathematics. The planning and implementing of ideas are of value, however, only if the teacher also continually assesses the effectiveness of various facets of the instructional program. Evaluation should provide not only closure to the sequence of learning experiences, but also it should provide for continual assessment during the sequence of learning experiences.

The purpose of this chapter is to place the act of evaluation—the making of value judgments—in the proper perspective with the other aspects of the teaching-learning act. The role of evaluation and various techniques associated with evaluation in different areas are discussed; selected comments about standardized and teacher-made tests are also included; and planning and construction of test items are considered.

THE ROLE OF EVALUATION

The traditional role of evaluation was to determine a mark for a child which could be reported to his parents. The usual method was the application of one or more formal written examinations from which an "average" was obtained. That average was usually matched against a scale based on 100 percent.

Evaluation, however, is potentially too useful a tool to be as severely limited as it has been by its traditional connotations. Its role should no longer be confined to the assignment of marks. Today, evaluation should also determine how effective the overall instructional program has been. It should be applied continually from the time the goals and objectives are formulated (are they appropriate?) to the time of final evaluation (have the desired goals and objectives been achieved?). It should consider pupil achievement, pupil attitudes, teacher effectiveness, and program effectiveness.

Evaluation is probably most often associated with *assessment of pupil achievement*. It is true that we, as teachers, want to take each child from where he is in mathematics as far as he can proceed with understanding; it is also true that we must assess his progress in this endeavor. To be of optimal value in terms of learning, however, this assessment should not be administered in a terminal sense; it should not be given only to see how well the child achieved the objectives in order to determine a grade. Finding out at the end of a unit or at the end of a grading period that different children are experiencing a variety of problems in their mathematical progress can only be frustrating. The material which was not understood will hinder further work by the individual child, by the class as a whole, and by you, as teacher.

Instead, evaluation techniques to assess pupil achievement should be incorporated periodically throughout the sequence of learning activities. In this way you can determine if a planned strategy is working or if the strategy needs modification to provide optimal learning opportunities for a given child. Recycling of certain portions of the learning sequence can be accomplished so that the child still has an opportunity to learn whatever mathematics he needs in order to progress.

The value of *positive pupil attitudes* in the mathematics classroom cannot be overestimated. Neither can positive attitudes be assumed to be present. But how can attitudes be assessed? How can you know the attitudes of your pupils toward mathematics? Formal evaluative techniques designed especially for this end can be incorporated. Informal techniques can also be used to advantage. The degree of formality of the technique, though, is subordinate to the idea that you use a workable way of assessing attitudes. If you are unaware of your pupils' feelings about a subject, your chances of success will be handicapped.

Evaluating *teacher effectiveness* and *instructional program effectiveness* completes the evaluation picture. Remember that both the teacher and the program he or she has designed are key factors in mathematical learning in the classroom; thus, evaluation here is also important. To a great extent, many teachers rely on the reflective nature of these two areas in order to evaluate the effectiveness of each; that is, if the pupils are achieving satisfactorily and if they have relatively positive attitudes, then the teachers tend to evaluate their own effectiveness and the effectiveness of their mathematics programs positively. They assume that they must be doing well, or else their failure would be reflected in the achievement and attitudes of the children. However, there are measuring instruments and techniques of a formal nature, as well as various informal means, through which more specific information can be gained in these areas.

EVALUATION TECHNIQUES ASSOCIATED WITH PUPIL ACHIEVEMENT

Because evaluation should be a continual process, it cannot be totally dependent upon formal paper-and-pencil tests. Other evaluative techniques must be incorporated, too. Let us examine some evaluation techniques associated with pupil achievement.

Observation

Observation of pupil behavior and work habits is an extremely useful technique of evaluation. It has the advantage of providing immediate feedback for the teacher who can then communicate it to the child in the form of help, thereby possibly correcting a perceived difficulty immediately. Many teachers have criticized this technique, feeling that it is too subjective and that the record-keeping associated with it is too time-consuming. They also fear the questioning of their observations by parents and administrators. However, these criticisms of observation, when examined closely, have little basis. We will now comment briefly on them.

First, the problem of subjectivity in evaluation is one which has been discussed for many years. Suffice it to say that no evaluation is without some degree of subjectivity because it is applied by a human being. Those who claim that the written objective test, for example, is unbiased should reflect for a moment on how the items for the test were chosen.

The time consumed in keeping written records of the observations is definitely a limiting factor in the application of this technique. There is simply not enough time to write a detailed daily paragraph for each child. However, the periodic addition of descriptive phrases into your records can provide additional information necessary for most purposes. Remember that you can never provide too much evidence when reports on a child are to be made.

Analysis of a Child's Written Work

Another useful technique is the analysis of a child's written work by the teacher. This technique, which may or may not be applied daily, has the advantage of not being a formal test with its accompanying pressures. It allows for relatively immediate feedback and enables the child to have an opportunity to make a mistake without the fear of a grade. This last point is especially important, for if a child is to develop powers of inquiry and discovery, he must be allowed to work in situations where he or she can experiment and try different methods. In this way, learning becomes meaningful, and the opportunity to develop creativity is enhanced. Analysis of written work is also important from the standpoint of early identification of learning difficulties, the importance of which was discussed in Chapter 16.

Testing

Testing, perhaps the most common technique of evaluation, causes most teachers some discomfort. This does not mean that testing is the most important evaluative technique, but it is one which, to be properly applied, needs more clarification than other techniques. In the following section we will discuss different aspects of testing, including various types of tests and the actual procedures involved in the testing process.

Types of Tests.   Tests which can be used in elementary school mathematics may be classified in various ways. They may, for example, be classified as *standardized* or *teacher-made*. A standardized test is one which has been written by experts and whose items have been carefully written, revised, and normed. A teacher-made test is one which is constructed by the classroom teacher to meet particular needs. Each type has distinct advantages and disadvantages.

Almost all school systems administer some form of standardized test to check the progress of their students. Because the administration of such tests is expensive, they are not generally administered annually but rather on an every two- or three-year basis for most children. Standardized tests have advantages insofar as the items are constructed by professionals and hence tend to have high *validity* (the test measures what it is supposed to measure) and *reliability* (the test measures consistently). Also, standardized tests have norms established on a national level. When misused, however, these advantages may induce such problems as will now be discussed.

Many school administrators believe that standardized tests are the ultimate means by which to measure progress of pupils. However, if the objectives of the standardized tests are not approximately the same as the objectives used by the classroom teacher, then the results cannot be considered valid. When such discrepancy occurs, it is a waste of time and money to administer such tests.

Second, a standardized test is likely to have some cultural bias, which means that current published tests may discriminate against cultural minorities. Norms and grade-equivalents (based upon national samples) are commonly used in reporting standardized test scores. As a result, children who differ in group composition from groups used to establish the norms and grade-equivalents often receive distorted results.

Misuse of test scores is another difficulty. Children who are placed in ability groups on the basis of one test score or who are consciously or unconsciously classified by teachers as "slow" or "fast" learners because of a test score are often penalized in their educational advancement. Also, considering the test scores of a class as a whole and comparing them to the test norms is a misuse, since it may give a false perspective of the class.

Although the negativism about misuse of standardized tests must be stressed, the positive aspects should be reviewed, too. As pointed out earlier, the tests are well written and, properly used with other evidence, they can help form a better evaluation of a child's ability than a "seat-of-the-pants" evaluation. The key point for proper usage is that the choice of a standardized test should be dependent upon the consistency of its goals and objectives with those of the instructional program to which the child has been exposed.

You might be tempted, now, to assume that the teacher-made test is the best one for the classroom teacher to use. It is less expensive and is more likely to be consistent with the teacher's stated goals and objectives.

Ironically, these advantages bear certain disadvantages. For example, while teacher-made tests do have the advantages just listed, poor test construction may be sufficient to outweigh them. Also, the skill of writing appropriate test items is one which many teachers have difficulty in performing. Careful study of the testing process, dealt with in the next section, may help improve this skill.

Tests may also be classified, according to their function, as either *performance* or *diagnostic* in nature.

Generally, in a performance test the child is to indicate what he or she has learned as a result of instruction. The vast majority of tests are performance in nature, and they may serve several functions or purposes: mastery, instructional, measurement, and inventory.

The mastery test is designed to measure essential skills which each child must master before instruction can proceed to the next level. Such a test might measure knowledge of basic facts of addition or recognition of geometric shapes.

The instructional test serves more as a teaching tool than as a measurement tool. "Pop quizzes" are primarily instructional in nature since they are designed to reemphasize important points brought out in a previous lesson. Because this type of test should receive little grading weight, it is often beneficial to let the student grade his own work. To do so enables the student to receive immediate feedback relative to specific weak points in his or her work. Hence, the pop quiz, judiciously used, can become an effective teaching device. Never use a pop quiz as punishment.

The measurement test is an achievement test which often is constructed using simple items at the beginning and the most difficult items at the end. This test is appropriate at the end of a unit and is designed to survey pupil achievement.

The inventory test is designed to help pinpoint difficulties. It differs from the instructional test in that it is primarily used by the teacher to determine at what level a student is performing along the continuum of learning. Such a test may also be used as a pretest to help a teacher modify planned instructional strategies.

Contrasted with performance, a test may be diagnostic in nature. The purpose of a diagnostic test is, as the name implies, to help a teacher identify specific learning difficulties which a child may encounter. The performance test will indicate only that a child is having difficulty; it will not identify the precise nature of the difficulty. For this reason, it is imperative that the performance test not be used for diagnostic purposes. For example, suppose a child shows difficulty with multi-digit addition problems involving regrouping as a result of poor performance on a test in which he was instructed to find the sums. This test indicates only that there is a difficulty; it does not reflect the precise nature of the problem. At this point, either formally or informally, the teacher may use a diagnostic test to determine whether basic facts, the regrouping process, or place value (or some combination thereof) caused the difficulty so that remediation may be planned and implemented.

In summary, tests may be classified in different ways. They may be classified according to the writer of the test as with standardized and teacher-made tests, or they may be classified according to the function of the test as with performance and diagnostic tests. It is important that you, as teacher, realize the purpose for which a test is being used and that you interpret the test results in view of that purpose. Using a test for a purpose other than that for which it was intended provides invalid information which could cause you to make an inaccurate evaluation about a child's performance or difficulty.

The Testing Process.   This stage includes the planning and construction of test and the interpretation of their results. Before we proceed further, however, a preliminary discussion of four levels of mathematical learning is necessary. Background information about these levels will facilitate subsequent discussions of test-item construction.

The four basic levels of mathematical learning may be characterized as: (1) knowledge or rote learning, (2) concept learning, (3) principle learning, and (4) problem solving.[1] These levels are all assessable by the classroom teacher.

Knowledge or *rote* learning is the lowest form of learning. It involves such areas as facts, terminology, criteria, and generalizations where the child is to reproduce the required information from memory. Little or no understanding is involved.

The majority of test questions asked by teachers are at the knowledge level. Of course, there are times when a child should learn information to be able to reproduce it, but repeated use of these types of questions by the teacher does little to stimulate or develop a child's thinking processes. The following items test knowledge or rote learning:

Example A: What is the formula for the area of a circle?

Example B: Give the name of this geometric figure.

The leve of *concept* learning is above the knowledge or rote level. Concepts may be described as mental structures that represent a class of experiences. A child forms a concept when he is able to generalize from a series of experiences that have one or more common elements. To be meaningful to children, such experiences should involve as many of the five senses as possible and, recalling our discussion in Chapter 2, they can be classified as concrete, semiconcrete, or abstract in nature. The following items might be used to test concept learning:

Example C: How many X's are there if they are counted in base eight rather than in base ten?

XXX XXX XXX XXX XXX XXX XXX XXX

  a. 25 eight   c. 26 eight
  b. 21 eight   d. 30 eight

Example D: Write a numeral which represents the number of stick people.

1. Robert M. Gagné, *The Conditions of Learning*, pp. 175–180.

A teacher who is not careful about the choice of items may confuse the two levels. From Example D, suppose that when the concept of "three" was developed in class the example of three stick people were used. If the same example were then used on a test, it would reduce the level of the item to that of knowledge since the child could simply have memorized the class example and therefore correctly answered the item on the test—not because of any understanding but because of memorization.

The third level of learning involves *principles*. A principle is a mental structure involving two or more concepts. For example, consider the relationship involved in the operation of multiplication of whole numbers. Before a child can understand and solve a number sentence such as $4 \times 5 = \Box$, he must have attained the concepts of four, five, product, and equality. Failure to attain one or more of these concepts will result in an improper solution to the sentence. If a child simply memorizes the product process, for example, a problem such as $4 \times \triangle = 20$ will probably produce a solution of 80. This latter example simply points out that you must be certain that a child has attained the necessary concepts and has not simply memorized them. The following test items might be used to assess the principle level of learning:

Example E: What property was used in the following example?

$$3 + (8 + 7) = (8 + 7) + 3$$

a. closure property
b. distributive property
c. commutative property
d. associative property

Example F: Use the numerals 3, 4, and 5 to illustrate what you mean by the associative property of multiplication.

Again you must insure that the test items are different in example from the experiences which the child has encountered during the instruction time. If not, memory will substitute for understanding in the child's response.

The fourth and highest level of learning is that of *problem solving*. This level is attained when the child is able to accommodate concepts and principles and to use them to solve a problem posed for him.

As an example of this level of learning, suppose that the child is told that he may buy bubble gum at 3 pieces for 10 cents. His teacher asks him to find the cost of 9 pieces. His reasoning might proceed as follows:

Let's see now . . . I can buy 3 pieces for 10¢ so I can find out the cost of 9 pieces if I draw the following picture. . . .

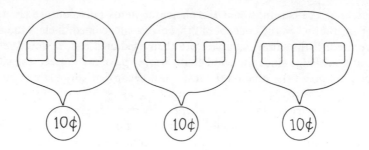

Now that's 9 pieces so that total cost would be 10¢ + 10¢ + 10¢ = 30¢. So if I have 30¢, I can buy 9 pieces of bubble gum.

In order to solve the problem, the child found it necessary to use both many-to-one and the operation of addition. He might have been able to accommodate both ideas separately, but only by combining them was he able to solve the problem.

You should use test items at all four levels of learning. In this way, it can be determined at which level a child is able to learn and where difficulties may be occurring.

Having digressed for the discussion of levels of mathematical outcomes, let us return to the matter of test construction and to its first stage—planning.

Planning the Test.   Good tests are not made by "throwing together" questions related to the goals and objectives until enough have been written to keep the children busy for a class period. A test constructed in such a haphazard way will not tell you how much your pupils have learned. Furthermore, it causes the children to be confused about exactly what they were expected to have learned. In short, good tests must be carefully planned.

Once it has been decided that the time for a test is appropriate and its function determined, you will be ready to begin. With the stated goals and objectives in mind, you must make a decision about the level at which each goal and objective is to be evaluated. To illustrate, let us follow a teacher, Ellen Smith, through a planning procedure as she prepares to construct a test for her fourth-grade class.

Ms. Smith has just completed a unit on geometry which included the study of such topics as:

Points, curves, lines, and rays
Measurement of line segments
Planes
Joining rays to form angles
Parallel lines
Closed curves
Circles
Symmetry
Area

She has decided to give a measurement of achievement test covering the unit, and she will use problems which are computation or construction in nature, thought problems using techniques previously taught, and thought problems requiring the development of new techniques. Using a two-way grid as shown in Table 1, she has decided on the number of problems in each category.

Now that Ms. Smith has completed the test outline, she must also consider the amount of time required for her pupils to complete the test. She does not want them to have to work hastily, thereby causing mistakes which would not ordinarily be made. After careful consideration, she decides that two class periods are needed, so the plan is made accordingly.

Table 1. Ways of preparing problems.

	Computation and construction	*Thought problems— previous techniques*	*Thought problems— new techniques*
Points, curves, lines, rays	3	4	4
Measuring line segments	2	1	1
Planes	2	3	1
Joining rays to'form angles	2	2	1
Parallel lines	2	2	1
Closed curves	1	3	1
Circles	3	2	1
Symmetry	3	2	1
Area	7	3	1

Writing the Test.   Once the test has been planned, it is time to start constructing it. Before construction can begin, however, the stated goals and objectives to be measured must be studied carefully again to observe the appropriate level of the test items. This level will be determined by the statement of the objective. Before Ms. Smith proceeds to the actual writing of the test items, she considers the variety of objective forms the items which she will use might take. Each type has certain advantages and disadvantages.

One type of item is the *true-false* item. These items are relatively easy to construct and to score. However, a common fault of teacher-made true-false items is that they tend to be ambiguous in their wording. There is also a relatively high (fifty-fifty) guess factor associated with the item, and these items generally measure only a rote level of learning. For these reasons, Ms. Smith decides not to use any true-false items; other types seem better suited for her purposes.

A second type is the *completion* or *short-answer* item. This type features a sentence with one or more words or symbols which are to be filled in by the student. Completion items are often used at the rote level in an example such as:

A triangle has _____ sides.

However, these items may also be used at the concept level:

A numeral which represents the number of X's in the set below is _____ .

or at the principle level such as $5 + \triangle = 7$. Since the completion item is relatively easy to construct and to score, it is fairly popular. Ms. Smith decides that some of her items will be completion items. Short-answer items generally require the child to frame some sort of multiword response and are usually used at the rote, concept, and principle levels as may be seen from Examples A, B, D, and F earlier in this section. Ms. Smith decides to use the completion or short-answer items in several areas on her test.

A third type of objective item is the *matching* item. This item is excellent for checking a child's ability to combine several related topics, and it may be used at any of the three levels: rote, concept, or principle. It is rarely used at the problem-solving level. An example of a matching item might be:

Match the number of sides with the name of the geometric figure.

1. rectangle   a. 4
2. triangle   b. 3
3. pentagon   c. 6
4. octagon   d. 7
                      e. 5
                      f. 8

Notice that the number of choices on the right is greater than the number of items on the left. This is purposely done to help reduce the guessing factor. Since the items are easy to construct and to score, Ms. Smith would like to use some if they are appropriate.

The *multiple-choice* item is perhaps the most popular objective test item today. Most standardized mathematics tests utilize this type of item because of its ease in scoring. Good multiple-choice items, however, are not easily written. The quality of a multiple-choice item is determined by the degree of homogeneity of the alternatives presented. If the homogeneity is not good, then the item is reduced to much the same status as a true-false item in which guessing the correct answer has a fairly high probability. Examples of good multiple-choice items are found in our Example C at the concept level and in our Example E at the principle level. Multiple-choice items are usually not good measures at the problem-solving level. Ms. Smith decides that she may be able to use some multiple-choice items in her test.

After considering the types of items, Ms. Smith decides that she would like to use a variety of items on the test, depending upon the objective and the level which she is seeking to measure.

Let's follow this teacher as she actually prepares her test items. One of her objectives is:

The child should be able to compute the area of a rectangle and a triangle.

The nature of this objective implies that it should be measured at the principle level of learning. So an appropriate item might be:

> Find the area of a rectangle whose length is 25 cm and whose width is 7 cm.

or

> Find the area of a triangle whose base measures 15 in. and whose height is 1 ft.

After carefully considering these items, Ms. Smith decides that both will help measure her objective and so both are included. She then turns to other objectives to follow a similar process of writing one or more items for each objective according to her plan.

As the test items are written and keyed, it is often helpful to use 3×5 index cards, placing one item and its answer on each card. The completed cards can then be arranged in order of easiest to most difficult so that they can then be transferred to duplicating masters or whatever other means is used to duplicate the test.

Whenever possible, it is best to use a separate, typed test for each child. The practice of putting a test on the chalkboard or overhead projector is often time-consuming and may prove difficult for a child with a visual difficulty to read accurately. Handwritten tests are generally more difficult to read than typed ones. It is important, therefore, to make the testing situation as comfortable and free of distraction as possible for each child so that he can devote maximum effort to completing the test.

Reflecting on the test she has just written, Ms. Smith decides that the test items appropriately measure the goals and objectives of the unit and that the test covers understandings and skills for which her children have been prepared. Therefore, she expects the best students in the class to answer all or nearly all of the items correctly and she expects even the students who were having the most difficulty to answer a majority of the questions correctly. Ms. Smith does not make the mistake of setting a standard (say, 70%) in advance for passing the test. Past experiences tell her that some of her questions might prove to be more difficult than she has anticipated. She decides to wait and to examine the entire set of test results. Then she can carefully inspect the test for particularly troublesome items before making any decisions about passing marks.

Interpreting the Test Results.   After the test has been administered under appropriate conditions as just discussed, it will be scored and returned to the children as soon as possible. Each test item should be carefully analyzed to determine whether it proved too difficult or too easy. If such items are found, they will be discarded from the test and scores adjusted accordingly.

As the test results are studied, Ms. Smith decides that it would be appropriate to analyze each test item. There are several advantages to making an item analysis.[2]

First, a test that is worth giving is worth reviewing and discussing in class. With the item analysis, you can see immediately the strong and weak points of both the class and the test, and plans can be then be formulated to help remediate identified difficulties.

---

2. N. M. Downie, *Fundamentals of Measurement: Techniques and Practices,* pp. 185–187.

A second advantage is that you can set up a pool of items which are good measures of a given objective. These items may then be used at a later time. Keeping the 3 × 5 cards with one item on each and a record of the item analysis on the same card provides readily accessible information which could prove useful in the future.

An item analysis will also provide you with a measure of the difficulty of an item. Items that prove too easy or too difficult are poor discriminators of student performance and hence should be eliminated for future use.

Finally, using an item analysis will in the end be much more likely to produce tests that have a higher reliability and validity. The net result is that you will become a better test writer and thus able to more accurately evaluate each child's performance.

Let us consider a simple item analysis technique which can be used on a small classroom group (approximately 30). This procedure may be applied either by the teacher or by a show of hands in class, integrating the analysis process with a class discussion of the test items. The following steps may be used:

1. Locate the ten papers with the highest scores and the ten papers with the lowest scores. If the tenth highest paper, for example, has the same score as the eleventh highest paper, simply pick one of the two. The reason for using ten is that it is an easy number to work with and is really rather arbitrary.

2. Count the number of correct responses to item #1 in the high group (H) and the number of correct responses found in the low group (L) as to item #1.

3. Calculate H + L for item #1 and divide by 20. (There are 10 papers in the H group and 10 papers in the L group.) The term H + L represents the number of correct responses to item #1 in the H group plus the number of correct responses to item #1 in the L group. We divide by 20 because there are 20 participants in the item analysis. If $\frac{H + L}{20} > 90\%$, then the item may be questioned as being too simple; if $\frac{H + L}{20} < 30\%$, then the item may be questioned as being too difficult. There may be valid reasons for accepting an item which falls outside the desirable range (between 30% and 90%); only the classroom teacher can make that decision. Note that the above standards, while arbitrary, are the ones usually used by professional test writers.[3]

   4. Now calculate H − L for item #1. If this difference is less than 10% of 20 (there are 20 participants in the item analysis), or 2, then the test item is not acceptable; this standard is again used by professional test writers. A word of caution is in order here. Items which appear near the end of the test may have been answered only by the high group which would tend toward an unjustifiable H − L score. Thus, don't declare an item acceptable until its location on the test is considered.[4]

   5. Continue the above procedure for each item on the test. It may be desirable to make adjustments in test scores on the basis of the item analysis.

---

3. Educational Testing Service, *Short-cut Statistics for Teacher-made Tests,* pp. 10–11.
4. Ibid., pp. 11–12.

As you can see, implementation of this procedure is not difficult and the information gained from it may be important.

It will then be time to analyze each child's paper to determine where his difficulties arose (if he had any) and to determine which of the goals and objectives were achieved and which were not. It is a good idea to discuss each child's paper individually with him to assess the possible source(s) of difficulty so that an appropriate plan of identification and remediation can be set up to help achieve the troublesome goal(s) and objective(s) using the procedure from Chapter 16.

Unfortunately, no "magic formula" exists for converting test scores to letter grades, nor is there a universally accepted way of assigning letter grades. There are almost as many methods used as there are teachers. Suffice it to say that, if letter grades are to be assigned, they should be assigned in terms of the extent to which the goals and objectives have been achieved. Even this statement is relative, however, and depends on a given situation.

Returning now to Ms. Smith, the results of the test indicate that most of the children performed satisfactorily on the test, although no one had a perfect paper. On the basis of the test, she concludes that the children achieved goals and objectives concerned with computation and construction but that some difficulty still is evident with problems concerning points, lines, curves, and rays and problems concerning planes and symmetry. Therefore, she decides to spend additional time in these areas with those children who are having difficulty and to allow the other children an opportunity to work on some selected enrichment topics.

As each item was analyzed, Ms. Smith found three items which were either too difficult or too easy and discarded the results from these items. Discussions with her pupils readily indicated some reasons for the findings, and these were noted so that the same mistakes would not occur again.

EVALUATION TECHNIQUES ASSOCIATED WITH PUPIL ATTITUDE

The importance of assessing pupil attitudes toward mathematics has been discussed earlier in this chapter. Let us now turn to the question of how pupil attitudes can be assessed.

Formal Techniques

One of the most popular techniques which may be used to assess pupil attitude toward mathematics is to give an attitude scale to each child. The scale may have been constructed by another educator or it may be constructed by the classroom teacher. Because of the economy of time, most teachers prefer to use a scale already constructed. See pp. 382–383 for an example of such an attitude scale. The teacher may read the statements to a child who cannot read them for himself.

Student Assessment Instruments—Math Attitude

Read each of the following statements and decide how you feel about each one. Then circle the corresponding letter (D) Disagree, (U) Undecided, (A) Agree.

1. Math class is really a strain for me.

   D U A

2. Math is very interesting to me.

   D U A

3. I don't like math at all.

   D U A

4. Math is fun.

   D U A

5. Math makes me feel good.

   D U A

6. I can't think very well when I'm doing math problems.

   D U A

7. Everybody else is better in math than I.

   D U A

8. Doing math problems makes me feel uncomfortable and frustrated.

   D U A

9. I feel good about math.

   D U A

10. I get very lost when I'm doing math problems.

    D U A

11. I enjoy doing math problems.

    D U A

12. I get a bad feeling when I hear the word "math."

    D U A

13. I'm afraid to do math problems because I don't think I'll be right.

    D U A

14. I really like math.

    D U A

15. I have always enjoyed taking math courses.

        D U A

16. I get nervous just thinking about math.

        D U A

17. I dread taking math classes.

        D U A

18. I am happier in math class than in any other class.

        D U A

19. I feel at ease in math class.

        D U A

20. I feel very positive about math.

        D U A

Note to Teacher: You may want to fold this part of the page under while the student is responding.

    Scoring: Positive Questions are 2, 4, 5, 9, 11, 14, 15, 18, 19, 20
             Negative Questions are 1, 3, 6, 7, 8, 10, 12, 13, 16, 17

1. If the question is of a *positive* nature, score D $= -1$, U $= 0$, A $= +1$
   If the question is of a *negative* nature, score D $= +1$, U $= 0$, A $= -1$
2. Total the number values for the items and divide by 20 (carry your answer out two decimal points).
3. This converted number should lie between -1.00 and $+1.00$, expressing a negative to positive attitude respectively. 0 indicates a neutral attitude. Record this converted score on the space provided at the top of the first page.

    For example: A raw score of -8 would be calculated as $-8 \div 20 = \underline{-0.40}$
              (converted score)
             A raw score of $+3$ would be calculated as $+3 \div 20 = \underline{+0.15}$
             (converted score)

    Another technique which may be used by the classroom teacher is the open-ended questionnaire. It may include questions as simple as the following:

1. What do you like most about mathematics?
2. What do you like least about mathematics?

Such questions provide the child with an opportunity to give an open-ended response which may be more indicative of his true feelings than responding to stated items on a scale such as the preceding one. Its limitation is that its scoring is difficult, and there is no consensus as to what constitutes a favorable or an unfavorable attitude, such as is possible with the attitude scale.

Whichever technique is used, you should strongly consider a class discussion of the results. Not only will this procedure save time for you, but it may also provide clues as to *why* certain responses were made by the children. The information gained from the assessment of pupil attitudes toward mathematics can give you additional insight into the needs of each child and help you adjust plans or make new plans for the instructional program to meet the child's needs.

Informal Techniques.   Some teachers may not wish to formally assess pupil attitudes. For them, the informal techniques of observation and listening may be used. These two techniques have the advantage of the possibility of obtaining more candid responses from the children. They can be administered at any time and for any length of time. The usefulness of the information gained, however, is dependent upon the teacher's perceptions of what he or she has heard or seen; hence, the results may be distorted.

In conclusion, the choice of formal or informal techniques of assessing attitudes is of relatively little consequence. The only important point is that you, as teacher, make continual efforts to be aware of the child's attitudes toward mathematics because attitudes do play a role in the success of any instructional program in elementary school mathematics.

EVALUATION TECHNIQUES ASSOCIATED WITH TEACHER AND PROGRAM EFFECTIVENESS

As was discussed earlier in the chapter, the areas of teacher and program effectiveness are an important part of the overall evaluation program. There are several factors to consider in assessing the effectiveness of these areas.

In the case of *teacher* effectiveness, assessment in the following areas should be considered:

1. Your own assessment of your work
2. Student achievement
3. Student attitude toward mathematics

In order to evaluate your own work, you may ask yourself such questions as:

1. Did I provide for individual differences?
2. Did I provide for each child's social development?
3. Did I provide for my own professional enrichment and advancement?

The first two questions should be considered on a periodic basis. If the responses to these questions are nonpositive, you should inquire into possible reasons so that needed changes can be made. The third question relates to more of a long-range concern. You should plan a program of professional enrichment and advancement for yourself which might include such activities as attending professional meetings and workshops, reading books and journals, and maintaining a dialogue with other teachers.

A technique which you may also use to judge your effectiveness is to analyze your class sessions through the use of audio or video tapes. This analysis may focus on such areas as questioning, class interaction, and the general management of the class session. Were these strategies appropriate? What changes should be made in teaching the lesson again?

Your effectiveness may also be judged in part on the achievement of the students in the class. An appropriate technique to use for this purpose is based upon the pretest-posttest notion. Once the goals and objectives have been determined for a particular unit of instruction or for the yearly program, a pretest should be administered to determine the position of each child with respect to these goals and objectives. At the end of the unit or year's program, a posttest should be administered. The change in achievement for each child would give an indication of your effectiveness as a teacher. The advantage of this technique over the use of the single achievement test score at the end of the year as a measure of teacher effectiveness is that it accounts for the child who has made tremendous progress but who is still not at the expected achievement level.

The same pretest-posttest technique might also be used to consider student attitude. A positive change again may indicate that you have been effective in this area.

Finally, the effectiveness of the instructional program is directly related to the effectiveness of the teacher who plans and implements it. All of the above techniques for assessing teacher effectiveness may also be used to assess program effectiveness.

CHAPTER KEY POINTS

1. Evaluation should provide not only closure to sequence of learning experiences, but also continual assessment during the sequence of learning experiences.

2. Pupil achievement may be evaluated using several techniques:
   a. Observation of pupil behavior and work habits.
   b. Analysis of written work.
   c. Testing (standardized or teacher-made) to provide diagnosis or evaluation of performances.

3. The four basic levels of mathematical learning must be considered in constructing test items. They are: (1) knowledge or rote learning, (2) concept learning, (3) principle learning, and (4) problem solving.

4. The stages of the testing process include:
   a. Planning—deciding the timing, function, the time required to complete the test, and the level at which each goal or objective is to be evaluated.
   b. Writing the test—choosing items which may take the form of true-false questions, completion or short answer items, matching items, or multiple choice depending on the level of learning to be measured for each goal or objective.
   c. Interpreting the test results—using item analysis to evaluate the strong and weak points of the class and the test.

5. Pupil, teacher, and program effectiveness may be evaluated through measures of pupil achievement, pupil attitude, and the teacher's self-evaluation.

6. Areas to consider in self-evaluation are: adequate provision for individual child needs, providing for provision for each child's social development.

Laboratory 17

Techniques of Evaluation

An important yet difficult skill for every teacher to develop is the choice and implementation of appropriate evaluation techniques. The following exercises are designed to help you evaluate different techniques which are currently available and to help you formulate techniques of your own which might be used.

  I. *Objectives:* Upon completion of these laboratory exercises, you should be able to do the following:

  A. Given a standardized test, identify the levels of learning represented by the items on the test. (Chapter Competency 17-A)

  B. Given a set of objectives, design evaluation techniques which might be used to measure the achievement of these objectives and give a rationale for your design. (Chapter Competency 17-B)

 II. *Materials:* Selected standardized elementary mathematics achievement tests

III. *Procedure:*

  A. Read Chapter 17 of *Helping Children Learn Mathematics*. Consult your instructor if you have any questions.

  B. Select a standardized elementary mathematics achievement test and examine the items on the test. What levels of learning are represented by the items? What level(s) of learning are most prominent? Give an example of a test item for each found level of learning. (Identify the test with which you are working.)

  C. For each of the following objectives, design an evaluation technique which you might use to evaluate whether a child has achieved the objective. Give a rationale for your choice.

  1. The child should be able to arrange several given fractions in order from smallest to largest.

  2. The child should be able to measure the length of a given object to the nearest centimeter.

Test Construction and Analysis of Test Results

The construction of a classroom test in mathematics and the interpretation of its results after administration are other essential yet difficult tasks for teachers. These exercises will give you an opportunity to test your skill as a test maker.

  I. *Objectives:* Upon completion of these laboratory exercises, you should be able to do the following:

  A. Given a content area, write informational objectives and corresponding test items at specified levels of learning. (Chapter Competency 17-C)

  B. Given a set of test results, analyze the items on the test in terms of the stated objectives and the criteria for judging a test item. (Chapter Competency 17-B)

 II. *Materials:* Selected readings on the metric system; index cards

III. *Procedure:*

  A. Read Chapter 17 of *Helping Children Learn Mathematics.* Consult your instructor if you have any questions.

  B. Using the elementary mathematics content area of the metric system, write six informational objectives which you believe relate to important ideas in the metric system. Write a test item for each objective which might be used to measure achievement of that objective. The test items should represent the levels of learning discussed in this chapter. At least four of the items must be at the concept level or higher. Each item should be typed on a separate 3 $\times$ 5 index card. Each card should also include the informational objective or the test item, the level of learning, and the keyed answer for the item. Your instructor will take a sample of the test items from the class and construct a test which will then be administered to the class.

  C. Using the results of the preceding test, analyze each test item in terms of the stated objective and the procedure for an item analysis. Did the items evaluate that objective?

Index